JABOTINSKY'S CHILDREN

Jabotinsky's Children

POLISH JEWS AND THE RISE
OF RIGHT-WING ZIONISM

DANIEL KUPFERT HELLER

PRINCETON UNIVERSITY PRESS
PRINCETON & OXFORD

Copyright © 2017 by Princeton University Press

Published by Princeton University Press,
41 William Street, Princeton, New Jersey 08540

In the United Kingdom: Princeton University Press,
6 Oxford Street, Woodstock, Oxfordshire OX20 1TR

press.princeton.edu

Cover images: (*Background*) Courtesy of the Jabotinsky Institute in Israel. (*Foreground*) Ze'ev Jabotinsky (1880–1940) on 100 shekel banknote from 1979. Georgios Kollidas / Alamy Stock Photo

Chapter 3 reprinted from Daniel Kupfert Heller (2015), "Obedient children and reckless rebels: Jabotinsky's youth politics and the case for authoritarian leadership," 1931–1933, *Journal of Israeli History*, 34:1, 45–68, with permission, www.tandfonline.com

All Rights Reserved

First paperback printing, 2019
Paperback ISBN 978-0-691-19712-8
Cloth ISBN 978-0-691-17475-4

Library of Congress Control Number 2017940318

British Library Cataloging-in-Publication Data is available

This book has been composed in Arno Pro

CONTENTS

List of Illustrations vii
Acknowledgments ix
Note on Terms xiii

	Introduction	1
1	Jabotinsky Encounters Polish Jewish Youth	28
2	Little Fascists?	68
3	Obedient Children, Reckless Rebels	104
4	Poland, Palestine, and the Politics of Belonging	133
5	Taming the Shtetl	167
6	Terror	201
	Epilogue	237

Notes 255
Bibliography 291
Index 313

ILLUSTRATIONS

1	Poland between the two world wars	xvi
2	Palestine under the British Mandate	xvii
3	A Betar member welcomes Vladimir Jabotinsky to Warsaw	129
4	Aharon Propes sits at his desk in Betar's headquarters in Warsaw	129
5	Attending an instructor's course, Betar members from Lublin pose with rifles	130
6	Betar members from Żabno march in the town's annual parade in honor of Poland's access to the Baltic Sea	130
7	A Polish army officer provides rifle training to Avraham Amper and Sonia Haas	131
8	The town of Suwałki's Betar orchestra poses with instruments in hand	131
9	Betar members from Warsaw at their youth movement's summer camp	132
10	Menachem Begin	132

All photos are reprinted by permission of the Jabotinsky Institute.

Figure 1 reprinted from Yisrael Gutman, Ezra Mendelsohn, Jehuda Reinharz, Chone Shmeruk, eds., *The Jews of Poland Between the Two World Wars* (Hanover: Brandeis University Press with the University Press of New England, 1989).

ACKNOWLEDGMENTS

THIS BOOK PROVIDED me with numerous opportunities to meet, work with, and learn from an incredible range of people, both within and beyond academia. They have enriched my life in innumerable ways, and I am grateful for the opportunity to acknowledge them here.

I would have never considered a career as a historian were it not for Derek Penslar. As an undergraduate student at the University of Toronto, I was privileged to take several of his classes on the history of Jews in Europe and the Middle East. His range as a historian has long inspired me and played no small role in leading me to choose a project that spanned from Warsaw to Tel Aviv. I am also thankful to Anna Shternshis and Piotr Wróbel for providing me with numerous opportunities at the University of Toronto to cultivate my interest in the history of Jews in eastern Europe.

At Stanford, Aron Rodrigue was an outstanding teacher and adviser throughout my graduate career. I am equally thankful for the sage advice of Norman Naimark. In my early years of graduate school, he generously offered his time to discuss the history of the European Right and the history of Poland. Were it not for those meetings, I would have never thought to write about the Jewish Right. In the same year I met with Norman Naimark for weekly meetings, I also had the privilege of learning with Gabriella Safran. Her graduate seminar on Russian literary theory provided a fruitful forum to think about the relationship between literature and nationalism. Years later, she enthusiastically offered to read this book manuscript in full, and offered helpful comments. I remain, as always, grateful for her encouragement.

My greatest debt of gratitude to a faculty member at Stanford is to my primary dissertation adviser, Steven Zipperstein. His extraordinary level of commitment to training historians as thinkers, teachers, and writers far surpassed anything I expected when I arrived to Stanford. He has offered superb guidance at each and every step of the way. For his wisdom, his encouragement, his generosity, and his kindness, I thank him.

My year as the Hazel D. Cole Fellow at the University of Washington in 2012 provided much-needed time to begin expanding my dissertation into a book. I remain thankful to Noam Pianko and the faculty at the UW Stroum Jewish Studies Program for their advice and encouragement. A special thank you to Devin Naar, whose friendship and intellectual comradeship has informed my work in innumerable ways.

I am grateful to have found an academic home in the Department of Jewish Studies at McGill University. I thank Liane Alitowski, David Auerbach, Eric Caplan, Carlos Fraenkel, Esther Frank, Lea Fima, Anna Gonshor, Gershon Hundert, Yael Halevi-Wise, and Barry Levy for their advice, support, and encouragement. While Ori Yehudai was a postdoctoral fellow in our department, he generously read several chapters of this book and offered deeply insightful comments. So too did James Krapfl in the Department of History and Classical Studies.

Whether at conferences, workshops, or invited lectures, I have been privileged to be in the company of outstanding scholars who have offered helpful comments on my work. My deepest thanks to Natalia Aleksiun, Karen Auerbach, Elissa Bemporad, Kathryn Ciancia, Arie Dubnov, Liora Halperin, Jolanta Mickute, Kenneth Moss, Dan Miron, Tatjana Lichtenstein, Antony Polonsky, Orit Rozin, Anita Shapira, Ellie Schainker, Jeffrey Veidlinger, and Sarah Zarrow. Laurence Weinbaum and Colin Shindler generously shared their expertise on the history of right-wing Zionism and offered critical feedback for this project. I am particularly indebted to Rona Yona and Kamil Kijek for sharing their expertise on Jewish life in Poland between the two world wars.

Numerous librarians and archivists in the United States, Israel, and Poland came to my aid as I searched for documentary evidence for this book. Zachary Baker, the Reinhard Family Curator of Judaica and Hebraica Collections at Stanford, helped bring to the university several microfilms of newspapers written in interwar Poland. Leo Greenbaum and Fruma Mohrer provided helpful guidance at the YIVO Institute for Jewish Research. When I arrived in Israel to mine the archives, I was greeted by Amira Stern, Olga Gekhman, and the wonderful staff at the Jabotinsky Institute. They warmly welcomed me into their archives and tirelessly worked on my behalf to find hundreds of files. Many thanks as well to the dedicated staff in Jerusalem at the Central Zionist Archives and the Central Archives for the History of the Jewish People. Once I arrived in Poland, Yale Reisner of the Jewish Historical Institute (Żydowski Instytut Historyczny, ŻIH) helped me determine my archival itinerary in the country. It is my pleasure to thank him, along with the staff at ŻIH, the Archive of Modern Records (Archiwum Akt Nowych), and the National Library (Biblioteka Narodowa). In Łódź, Włocławek, Lublin, Kraków, and Kielce, I was grateful for the help of the staff at the local outposts of the National Archives (Archiwum Państwowe), who directed me toward a wealth of documents about Jewish life in cities and towns throughout interwar Poland.

This book would not have been possible without the generous support of grants and scholarships provided by the YIVO Institute for Jewish Research, the Memorial Foundation for Jewish Culture, the Mellon Foundation, the Weter Dissertation Completion Fellowship, and the McGill University Start-Up Grant Program.

It has been a privilege to work with Princeton University Press. I am deeply grateful to Fred Appel for his confidence in this project, his thoughtful advice and encouragement, and his efforts to help this book see the light of day. Melanie Mallon, my outstanding copyeditor, offered immensely helpful advice for improving this manuscript.

Portions of chapter 3 were previously published in "Obedient Children and Reckless Rebels: Jabotinsky's Youth Politics and the Case for Authoritarianism," *Journal of Israeli History* 34, no. 1 (2015): 45–68. I thank Taylor and Francis, publisher, for permitting me to use this material.

A few final words of thanks, addressed to my friends and family. I am so blessed to have you in my life. My dear friends Jason Angel, Ian Patrick Beacock, Nargiza Karimbaeva, Moshe Schwartz, and Sari Siegel provided encouragement when I needed it most. A special thanks to my uncle, Dr. Frank Dimant, who has for years generously offered his insights into the world of Revisionist politics.

I could not have asked for more supportive and loving parents. My mother, Beverly Kupfert, offered me her support and wisdom at every step of the way. My father, Brian Heller, inspired me to face the challenges of academia with courage and grit. My twin brother, Joseph Heller, continues to amaze me with his insights about the world of politics and the craft of writing. I hope that when he reads this book, he will see just how profound of an impact he has had on my life. I am also grateful to his wife, Dalia, for her support and interest in my work, and to their children, Lev and Orly. My sister, Mariel Heller, her husband, Mark Steinman, and their children, Eva, Noa, and Isabelle, also provided much-needed laughter and encouragement.

Nothing I can write here will ever capture the extent of my gratitude to my husband, Alexander Taub. Not a day goes by that I am not inspired by his curiosity, wisdom, and compassion. His parents, Anne and Michael; his brothers, Steven and David; their spouses, Rina and Dvora; and their incredible children—Eytan, Dassi, Timna, Galit, Yaron, and Nadav—have made Sydney, Australia, my home away from home.

I owe my interest in Jewish life in Poland before the Holocaust to my grandmother, Eva Kupfert. Born and raised in Warsaw, she was fifteen when German forces invaded Poland. A survivor of the Warsaw ghetto, Majdanek, and Auschwitz, my grandmother emerged from the Holocaust, then twenty-one years old, as the sole survivor of her family of ten. Not long after she arrived at a displaced persons' camp in Germany, she met my grandfather, Morris Kupfert, a young man from a small town near Łódź. They were married soon after. In the picture of their wedding, eight of their friends, fellow survivors of Hitler's extermination camps, crowd around them. Legend has it that each woman in the picture borrowed the same dress when they stood under the DP camp's wedding canopy. Despite the tragedies that had befallen them, they gazed into the camera's lens with wide smiles and hopeful eyes. I place this picture at my desk whenever I write. When I look into their eyes, I am reminded of their incredible strength and resilience, as well as the power of the human spirit to triumph over even the most unspeakable of horrors. It is to them that I dedicate this study.

NOTE ON TERMS

I HAVE TRANSLITERATED Yiddish sources according to the guidelines of the YIVO Institute. For Hebrew sources, I followed Library of Congress rules. Much of this book takes place in regions with substantial ethnic, religious, and linguistic diversity. Nearly all the place names that appear in this book have multiple variants. There is no politically neutral choice for how to name these locations. I periodically provide readers with the multiple names given to one location by its diverse inhabitants (e.g., "Vilne" in Yiddish, "Wilno" in Polish, "Vilnius" in Lithuanian). In most instances, however, I have chosen to use the names given to these locations by those who wielded government power in the particular historical moment I am describing (e.g., interwar Lwów rather than [Yiddish] Lemberg or [Ukrainian] L'viv).

FIGURE 1. Poland between the two world wars.

FIGURE 2. Palestine under the British Mandate, 1923–1948.

JABOTINSKY'S CHILDREN

Introduction

I SPENT MUCH of the winter of 2010 rummaging through Warsaw's Archive of Modern Records. Among the various documents in the archive's possession are tens of thousands of reports submitted by Polish police officers in the 1920s and 1930s concerning the political activity of interwar Poland's Ukrainian, Jewish, Belarusian, German, Russian, Czech and Lithuanian minority populations, who together made up nearly one-third of the country's inhabitants.[1] Sifting through these reports, I hoped to gain a better understanding of the dynamic and turbulent political life of Polish Jewish youth on the eve of the Holocaust. One afternoon, after hours of fruitless searching, a particular police report caught my eye. It was written by a Polish officer dispatched in October 1933 to a Zionist rally in Kobryń, a market town of some nine thousand residents in eastern Poland. Perhaps to the officer's surprise, the speeches of the Zionist rally's organizers were not solely devoted to building a Jewish state in Mandate Palestine. Instead, the speakers, one after the other, insisted that it was the duty of Zionists to defend the borders of Poland. Among the speakers pledging their loyalty to Poland was a lanky nineteen-year-old with thick, round black eyeglasses and hair slicked to his side. The policeman decided to record his name. Men like Menachem Begin, he noted, left a deep impression on the town's Jews.[2]

Why was Menachem Begin, who some forty-four years later rose to power as Israel's first right-wing Zionist prime minister, offering to put his life on the line for Poland? When he described his Polish Jewish past to Israelis, Begin remembered the humiliation, harassment, and violence Jews experienced at the hands of the country's Catholic majority.[3] "The constant danger of pogroms cast its shadow of fear over us," recalled Begin some twenty-five years after his speech in Kobryń.[4] The police report told a different story.

Even more questions followed once I discovered that the officer's report was but one among hundreds that had streamed into the offices of Warsaw's Ministry of Internal Affairs in the 1930s concerning the Zionist youth movement Menachem Begin would eventually lead. Claiming over sixty-five thousand members worldwide, nearly forty thousand of whom were in Poland, the Joseph Trumpeldor League (Brit Yosef Trumpeldor), known by its Hebrew acronym, Betar, was one of the most popular Zionist youth movements in interwar Europe.[5] It was also one of the most controversial Jewish political organizations of its time. The youth movement's militaristic ethos, vehement opposition to socialism, and authoritarian leadership cult for the founder of right-wing Zionism, Vladimir (Ze'ev) Jabotinsky, led many of their opponents—and some of their supporters—to describe its members as "Jewish fascists."

Even as Betar insisted, perhaps more strenuously than any other Zionist movement, that Jewish life in Poland was doomed to fail, Polish police officers across the country described how the youth movement was placing its pledges of Polish patriotism front and center of their public activity. Some officers recounted how Betar's leaders marked Zionist celebrations by laying wreaths at Polish war memorials, imploring their followers to "act Polish."[6] Others described how local Betar units requested permission to march in parades alongside Polish scouts and soldiers during the country's national holidays.[7] During brawls with Jewish socialists, Betar's members could even be heard singing the Polish national anthem and chanting "Long live the Sanacja!," the name given to Poland's authoritarian government, which came to power in 1926.[8]

Why would a Zionist movement convinced that Jews were destined for a life of misery and persecution in Europe choose the Polish national anthem as their battle cry? What inspired them to include among their chants a call to support Poland's authoritarian regime? By 1933, officials from the Sanacja (Purification) government had tampered with elections, arrested and jailed many of their opponents, and severely limited the power of Poland's members of parliament.[9] What was it about the country's policies and practices—many of which were already the features of right-wing regimes across Europe—that could be deemed credible, logical, compelling, and even instructive to Zionists seeking to build a Jewish state in Mandate Palestine?

These questions lie at the heart of this book, which traces the history of the Betar youth movement in Poland between the two world wars. Although Betar clubs operated in more than twenty-six countries by the 1930s, the majority of the youth movement's members lived in the newly formed Polish state, established in 1918.[10] Like dozens of Zionist youth movements operating in the country at the time, Betar promised to prepare its members for a new life in the Yishuv, the Jewish community of prestate Palestine, by providing vocational training, Hebrew classes, and lessons in Jewish history. What set Betar apart was its commitment to the military training of Jewish youth, as well as its support of several prominent policies of the European Right. If the heroes of Zionism's numerous socialist youth movements were pioneers who established agricultural settlements in Mandate Palestine, Betar's ideal "new Jews" were soldiers, prepared at a moment's notice to follow the orders of their commander and carry out whatever task was required to bring about the Jewish state. They deemed rifles, not ploughs or shovels, to be the most important tools to fulfill Zionism's goals.

Betar's leader, Vladimir Jabotinsky, was described by his supporters and opponents alike as one of the Zionist movement's most spellbinding orators, brilliant writers, magnetic personalities, and provocative activists. His dark olive skin, widely set eyes, and prominent forehead reinforced the impression among Zionist activists that he was somehow more "goyish" than Jewish.[11] So too did the elegant style in which he spoke: his Odessan Russian and Germanic Yiddish lent him an almost foreign, aristocratic aura in the eyes of the eastern European Jewish audiences to whom he frequently lectured. His early life looked vastly different from the childhood of other Zionist activists from the Russian Empire, most of whom came from provincial towns and Yiddish-speaking, religiously observant homes. Born in 1880 and raised in the cosmopolitan port city of Odessa, the young Jabotinsky was immersed in Russian language and culture and well read in numerous European languages. Graduating from one of the city's finest gymnasia, he spent several months at a Swiss university, followed by three years as a student in Italy, where he simultaneously worked as a correspondent for a Russian-language newspaper back in Odessa. Although his early work as a poet, playwright, journalist, and political activist had brought him some recognition in the Zionist movement, he gained fame during the First World War for creating the Jewish Legion, which under his leadership participated in the British Army's conquest of Ottoman Palestine. He also achieved popularity among Zionists for his role in organizing the Haganah Jewish defense network during the Jerusalem riots of 1920. Soon after, Jabotinsky broke with the mainstream Zionist movement and called for a more aggressive approach to dealing with Mandate Palestine's British colonial administration and Palestinian Arab population. His Union of

Revisionist Zionists, founded in 1925, would go on to become one of the most popular Zionist organizations in the interwar period.[12]

Betar's namesake was the famed Russian army veteran and Zionist activist Joseph Trumpeldor. The same age as Jabotinsky, Trumpeldor worked closely with him in the early stages of the Jewish Legion's development. He was killed in 1920 during a gun battle defending the Jewish settlement of Tel Hai in the Upper Galilee from Arab militias. Trumpeldor's death embodied to Jabotinsky the principal message he sought to convey to Jewish youth: in a world where the use of violence was the only way to survive, they had no choice but to "learn to shoot,"[13] and become, in the words of Betar's anthem, "proud, noble and cruel."[14] Only once Jews could prove their indestructible military might, he argued, would Palestinian Arabs be willing to yield to the chief demands of Revisionist Zionists: a Jewish majority living in a Jewish-ruled state or commonwealth that stretched from the Mediterranean sea to the western borders of today's Saudi Arabia and Iraq. Fearing backlash from both Mandate Palestine's British rulers and Arab inhabitants, most mainstream Zionists of the era refused to proclaim their goal to be the creation of a state with a Jewish majority. They mocked the Revisionist movement's geographic aspirations as unrealistic, and condemned its call for the military training of Jewish youth as an unnecessary provocation that would only further aggravate relations between Jews and Palestinian Arabs. When promoting the Zionist cause, they insisted that Zionism would only use peaceful means to achieve its aims, that the demographic changes to the region proposed by the movement were far from drastic, and that Jewish immigration would ultimately benefit the region's Arab population.

Like the vast majority of Zionist activists between the two world wars, Jabotinsky sought to capture the hearts and minds of Jews living in Poland. Over three million Jews lived in the country in 1931, making up interwar Europe's largest Jewish community. Scattered throughout hundreds of provincial towns and dozens of cities across the central and eastern regions of the country, they accounted for nearly 9 percent of Poland's population.[15] Jews were second only to Ukrainians as the largest minority group in the country. The unprecedented opportunities for political activity provided to Polish Jews in the new state, coupled with the persistent discrimination they faced, inspired them to create numerous political parties to speak on their behalf. Numerous questions pitted these parties against one another. Did the Jewish future lie in Poland or elsewhere? Would Jewish political parties best be served by embracing communism, socialism, democracy, or authoritarianism? Should Jews strive to live their lives bound by strict religious observance, or should they embrace a Jewish identity defined in secular terms? Which language should Polish Jews identify as their "native tongue": Yiddish, Polish, or Hebrew? Several of these questions fueled the bitter struggle between Zionists and their chief competitors on the "Jewish street," the Orthodox political party Agudat Yisrael (Union of Israel) and the socialist General Union of Jewish Workers, known as the Bund. While Agudat Yisrael leaders condemned Zionists as heretics, the Bund's activists saw them as foolish adventurers who distracted Jews from their real salvation: the triumph of socialism and the establishment of Jewish national cultural autonomy in Poland. Questions about language, religion, and broader European political trends also served as fault lines within the Zionist movement itself, producing dozens of different parties and factions.[16] Although no one Jewish political party consistently dominated in Poland throughout the interwar period, leaders of the country's numerous Zionist factions played a critical role in the lives of Polish Jews. Some served in parliament, while others held key leadership positions in Jewish communities across the country.[17] Much like their chief political competitors among Polish Jews, Zionists founded an impressive network of organizations, from newspapers, schools, and libraries to youth movements with summer camps, orchestras, and soccer teams.

Well aware of the political power wielded by Polish Jews in the Zionist movement, leaders of various Zionist political parties in Palestine sent emissaries to Poland to mobilize support for their programs.[18] Polish Jews made up the largest number of potential voters to the Zionist Congress, which elected the movement's executive leadership. They also provided the largest number of immigrants bound for the Yishuv. Approximately 125,000 Polish Jews made up nearly half of all registered Jewish arrivals to Palestine between 1919 and 1937.[19] Poland was especially critical to Vladimir Jabotinsky's political career. Only on his arrival to the country in 1927 was he able to begin transforming his Union of Revisionist Zionists from a meek organization into a powerful mass movement. Most Revisionists in Poland were Betar members. Palestine's Betar youth movement, which claimed under two thousand members in the mid-1930s, paled in comparison to its Polish counterpart.[20]

The newly formed Polish state was more than just a reservoir of supporters for Jabotinsky. It was also an inspiration and an incubator for the development of right-wing Zionist ideology. Drawing on correspondence, autobiographies, party journals, and police reports from archives across Poland, Israel, and the United States, this book uncovers the Polish roots of right-wing Zionism. I trace how Polish Jewish youth in Betar were instrumental in shaping the attitudes of right-wing Zionists toward the roles that authoritarianism and violence could play in their quest to build a Jewish state. This book also examines how the most important developments in interwar eastern European politics—the collapse of fledgling democratic governments, the rise of authoritarian regimes, and the growth of radical ethnonationalist movements—influenced the political attitudes and behaviors of right-wing Zionists. In contrast to most historical studies of authoritarian politics in interwar Europe, in which Jews figure solely as the victims of right-wing politics, *Jabotinsky's Children* examines why many Polish Jews found much to emulate in the policies and practices of right-wing movements, even as they condemned the antisemitism advocated by many of these groups. By exploring how Polish Jews within Betar used right-wing politics to navigate the rapidly changing political landscape of Poland and Palestine in the 1920s and 1930s, this book illuminates crucial discussions that swept through Polish Jewish society. These included conversations about what it meant to be a "Polish" Jew, the role that youth could play in shaping the political destiny of Jews, the ability of democracy to defend Jewish interests, and the legitimacy of violence as a means to achieve political ends. By capturing the voices of Betar's leaders, members, sympathizers and opponents as they searched for answers to these questions, this study ultimately sheds light on the reciprocal influence that Jews living in Poland and in Mandate Palestine exerted on one another's political worldviews and actions.

Jews and the Right

At first glance, the notion that a Jewish political movement in Poland claiming tens of thousands of supporters could embrace—let alone admire—policies associated with interwar Europe's Right might seem outrageous and, at the very least, impossible. Antisemitism was a critical and often central component of radical right-wing movements throughout interwar Europe.[21] The rise of the Third Reich inspired right-wing organizations across the continent, from France's Action française to Romania's Iron Guard, to intensify their efforts to persecute their Jewish neighbors. During the Second World War, when their countries came under German occupation, many of their members eagerly helped the Nazis in rounding up and killing Jews.[22] Against this backdrop, it is unsurprising that historians have largely taken for granted that Jews living in interwar Europe viewed right-wing politics only as a threat.

This study restores a historical moment in which Polish Jews had good reason to think otherwise. The history of interwar Europe's Right does not begin with the rise of the Third Reich in 1933. In the mid-1920s, Europeans turned to Fascist Italy, not Germany, as the model for what a country could look like if right-wing politics reigned in full force. In power a full decade before the Nazi takeover of Germany, Italian Fascists for their first sixteen years in power viewed antisemitism as neither an effective mobilizing tool nor a critical component of their worldview. Despite the occasional antisemitism Mussolini exhibited in his prose at the close of the First World War, several Jewish industrialists and landowners were among his inner circle of early Fascist supporters. His Jewish mistress, Margherita Sarfatti, was the author of his first official biography.[23] Mussolini's supporters in Italy believed that his calls for discipline, unity, and sacrifice to pervade every aspect of society would help restore order in their country, reinvigorate its economy, and, above all, prevent the spread of communism. These views extended far beyond Italy: among Mussolini's many admirers were government officials in Britain, France, and the United States.[24]

Fascist Italy appeared all the more successful to onlookers when they compared the country to the new parliamentary democracies of eastern Europe established in 1918, following the collapse of the Russian, Austro-Hungarian, and German Empires. As the 1920s progressed, many observers of eastern European politics warned that the political mechanisms of the region's fledgling democracies—including universal suffrage, constitutional order, and parliamentary rule with a weak executive—were proving unable to contend with the social and economic turmoil that the First World War had left in its wake. A low vote threshold to enter parliament nourished political factionalism and polarization among a plethora of political parties established along ethnic, religious, and class lines. Rejecting negotiation and compromise, politicians spent most of their time in parliament spurning the type of coalition politics required to pass legislation that could stabilize their country's economy and rebuild its infrastructure.[25] Violence was commonplace in the corridors of parliaments across the region. Against this backdrop, many expressed relief when authoritarian governments took the reins of power in eastern Europe.[26]

Poland, too, was plagued by political corruption, factionalism, legislative gridlock, and violence. Tensions often ran high between Catholic Poles and the country's minorities. The deep divisions pitting peasants against urban dwellers, socialists against conservatives, and liberals against radical nationalists only multiplied the staggering number of political parties clamoring for power. In the first eight years of Poland's existence, fifteen governments collapsed, wreaking havoc on the young country's already miserable economy.[27] The desire for economic stability was only one reason many Polish Jews criticized the country's parliamentary system. Democratic politics were also seen as a breeding ground for antisemitism. One of the most popular political parties among Catholic Polish voters was the National Democracy movement, also known as the Endecja. Founded at the end of the nineteenth century by Roman Dmowski, the party exploited long-standing anti-Jewish attitudes to promote its vision for a Polska dla Polaków—a Poland exclusively for Catholic Poles. The Endecja accused Jewish merchants and shopkeepers of exploiting the Polish peasantry, depriving Poles of jobs in towns and cities, and accelerating the moral corruption of Polish society. In the interwar period, they added the accusation that all Jews were communists-in-disguise, secretly working to overthrow Poland and place it under Soviet rule. When an opponent of the Endecja, Gabriel Narutowicz, was chosen as Poland's first democratically elected president in 1922, they branded him a "Jewish president." As proof, they pointed to the support he received from a loose coalition of Ukrainian, Belarusian, German, and Jewish parties known as the National Minorities' Bloc. Within hours of Narutowicz's victory, bloody antisemitic riots shook Warsaw. He was assassinated less than a week later.[28]

These were among the reasons that many Polish Jews welcomed authoritarian rule following a coup d'état in May 1926.[29] At the helm of Poland's new regime was Józef Piłsudski. A longtime opponent of Roman Dmowski and a former leader of the Polish Socialist Party, Piłsudski was the famed founder of the Polish Legions during the First World War. According to his admirers, Piłsudski's leadership of the legions made him the man most responsible for Poland's independence. His relatively tolerant approach to the country's national minorities, as well as his determination to prevent public outbursts of violence, including antisemitic riots, proved a welcome respite from the previous years of democracy. Piłsudski's call for unity among all of Poland's citizens and his opposition to the Endecja resonated with many Polish Jews. So too did his government's hostility toward the Soviet Union as well as local communist and socialist movements, which were viewed with suspicion by many among Poland's largely traditional Jewish population. When the government launched a public campaign for Poland's citizens to conceive of Piłsudski as the liberator of Poland and to envision themselves as citizen-soldiers who would save the state from destruction, it proved popular among many Jews.[30] Some Jews turned to his calls for moral revolution, unity, and patriotism as a model for thinking about the Jewish future in Mandate Palestine. Piłsudski's contempt for what he perceived to be the excesses of parliamentary rule especially resonated with Revisionist Zionists, who frequently accused the elected representative bodies of the Zionist movement of fomenting factionalism and corruption.

Piłsudski's government was far from the only model of right-wing politics from which Betar's leaders drew. They often turned to Fascist Italy for inspiration as well.[31] Many of Betar's leaders and members embraced a range of convictions and values that they themselves described as fascist. Among them was the desire to create a nationalist state that rose above sectional interests; contempt for established elites; the belief that one had to relinquish individual interests if they obstructed the road to national revival and purification; the call for a total ideology, covering all aspects of human experience, to inspire personal sacrifice and instill discipline, order, and unity; faith in a near-omnipotent leader expressing the will of the masses; the exaltation of violence and war to defend the nation's interests; the privileging of deeds over words and emotion over reason; and finally, the moral necessity of suppressing opponents of the nation.[32]

No discussion of Betar's relationship to fascism can dodge the fervent debate among historians of the European Right about what constitutes fascist politics in the first place. Not one of the political beliefs and practices associated with fascism was unique to fascist movements in interwar Europe. Throughout the nineteenth century, left-wing political organizations across the continent organized paramilitary movements. Liberals and conservatives throughout Europe frequently expressed hostility toward socialism. Nearly all European political movements in the interwar period were preoccupied with the sacralization of politics through creating political myths and orchestrating mass spectacles. Despite their preference for preserving the power of traditional elites, authoritarian governments in interwar Poland, Romania, Hungary, and elsewhere in eastern Europe shared many components of Fascist Italy's ideological repertoire.[33]

The sheer diversity of movements that described themselves as fascist between the two world wars makes comparative work all the more challenging. Of the variety of Europeans who described themselves as fascist, Italian and German fascists alone managed to seize the levers of power at a national level. Despite their formal alliance in 1938, Mussolini and Hitler differed in numerous respects in how they exercised power, with Fascist Italy tending toward conservative authoritarian rule, and the Third Reich seeking the total dominance of the Nazi Party.[34] Although the remaining fascist groups—wielding little to no state power—conceived of themselves as part of a global network, their attitudes toward modernity, religion, women, and the efficacy of alliances with other groups varied greatly. It is no surprise, then, that historians, political scientists, and sociologists endlessly debate the criteria that a political movement must meet to be considered fascist.[35]

As historians such as Robert Paxton have argued, scholars searching for ideological coherence among Europe's fascists not only risk flattening the internal ambiguities and contradictions of fascist thought and behavior. They also miss a crucial point. As much as fascists across the continent issued bold, brash, and sweeping political declarations, they saw little need to present an ideologically seamless world to their followers and were constantly redefining their aims and practices.[36] The very terms "fascism" and "democracy" were in a constant state of flux in the interwar period. Political leaders on the radical right often insisted that their form of rule was more democratic than parliamentary politics because they represented the will of the masses better than any election ever could.[37] Betar's leaders, too, spent much of the interwar period not only debating the value of democracy and fascism, but also questioning the very meanings of these terms and the boundaries separating them. Rather than attempt to create a stable definition of fascism against which I can judge the politics of Betar's members, I instead explore how and why many of them continually struggled to define the term in order to make it their own. This book provides a case study of an interwar youth movement continually reshaping the meaning of fascism, while simultaneously questioning its efficacy as a worldview and behavioral code.

Deciphering Jabotinsky's relationship to the European Right proves no less challenging than mapping the perspectives on fascism expressed by his followers in Poland. Jabotinsky's attitudes toward the roles that liberalism, democracy, and authoritarianism could play in the Zionist movement have been the subject of intense debate among his biographers for decades. Early chroniclers of the Revisionist movement sought to find in his writing a clear, coherent ideological position that somehow definitively answered the question of whether Jabotinsky was an admirer of fascism or a staunch defender of liberalism and democracy.[38] More recent historical scholarship, initiated by the pioneering work of Ya'akov Shavit, has done much to complicate these narratives. Instead of seeking a "definitive" political philosophy from Jabotinsky, historians have drawn attention to the ways in which his evolving political positions were shaped largely by his increasingly futile efforts to maintain control over the Revisionist movement's various competing factions. Jabotinsky's sometimes contradictory approaches to democracy and authoritarianism, they argue, reflected his struggle to balance his commitments as democratic leader of the Revisionist movement and commander of Betar.[39] Many of these historians take pains to insist that Jabotinsky was a devout and steadfast proponent of liberalism and democracy until the end of his life. Departures from these values—whether in his political prose or behavior—are explained as the product of pressures from his young followers, who forced Jabotinsky to adopt an "authoritarian guise" and pay lip service to beliefs that were not his own.[40] In these renditions of the Revisionist movement's ideological development, Jabotinsky is often portrayed as an unwitting victim of his own political prose, a leader who, despite his best efforts to articulate a clear position, was helpless in preventing his membership from misinterpreting or deliberately distorting his ideological proclamations.[41]

This study proposes a different way to read Jabotinsky. As Michael Stanislawski has shown, the brash, idiosyncratic, and contradictory tendencies of Jabotinsky's prose as an adolescent in turn-of-the-century Russia were deliberate aesthetic choices deeply rooted in Europe's fin-de-siècle cosmopolitan culture, which eschewed rigid definitions of identity.[42] His refusal to be restricted to any particular worldview persisted throughout his career as a Zionist leader. Provocative prose was more than just a literary habit he retained from his adolescence. Rather, it was a political strategy; "an exaggeration," he explained in one of his most famously controversial articles, "can sometimes be an entirely practical means to beat into our dull, drowsy heads a little bit of truth."[43] It was the incendiary nature of Jabotinsky's weekly columns in Polish Jewish newspapers that kept the rapt attention of his allies and adversaries alike. "On the day that the newspaper was published," a Betar member from the northeastern city of Grodno recounted decades later, Jabotinsky's "supporters and opponents would read his articles, and afterwards, the arguments would begin without end, because they were like little atomic bombs."[44]

Above all, however, Jabotinsky's talent as a political writer rested in his ability to situate his bold, provocative claims within an intricate web of contradictions and conditional clauses. Despite the fervent passion with which he employed the terms and phrases that became staples of Betar's unique political vocabulary, he simultaneously offered multiple, often conflicting interpretations for what these terms actually meant. Reflecting on the constantly shifting meaning of a typical Jabotinsky slogan, a member of Betar's national leadership in Poland found himself explaining to the youth movement's membership in 1933 that "its form has yet to be frozen, it finds itself in a dynamic, developing state; changes are still likely to take place."[45] The movement's first official ideological brochure, entitled *The Betar Idea*, was similarly elusive; "the soul of Betar," Jabotinsky wrote, "is still a secret, even for its supporters . . . and its leaders, and naturally, for the writer of this brochure."[46] Even the very name of the youth movement possessed two interpretive options for its members. Should Betar, the Joseph Trumpeldor League, strive, like its namesake, to represent all Zionist youth who supported the principles of national unity and self-defense? Or should they build an elite group motivated by the ideals of revolt, guerrilla warfare, and zealotry evoked by the legend of the Jewish rebels who died at Betar, the last standing fortress in ancient Palestine during the Jewish revolt against the Romans between 132 and 136 CE?

Like the name of the youth movement, the ambiguities of Jabotinsky's prose were essential because they allowed Betar activists to interpret their leader's writings as they saw fit. The intellectual arithmetic performed on his essays by Betar's leaders in the youth movement's journals—adding and embellishing several points, subtracting or minimizing others—allowed ample space within the movement for militarist and, in turn, fascist ideas, even if its leader occasionally declared himself to be an opponent—or reluctant supporter—of both. Providing Betar members with a diverse set of images and arguments, Jabotinsky and his colleagues allowed their followers to flirt with fascism's values while dodging, if they so desired, the term itself. In this study, I highlight the ways in which Jabotinsky deliberately infused his provocative prose with numerous ambiguities and contradictions. I also put Jabotinsky's writings into conversation with the thousands of articles and pamphlets written by those in Poland who claimed allegiance to him—a source base virtually untapped by historians. In doing so, I demonstrate how Jabotinsky's followers pruned his writing to match their visions for the development of Zionism. By embracing the contradictions inherent in Jabotinsky's texts, along with those produced by his followers, I hope to help readers arrive at a better understanding of the discursive system in which the early right-wing Zionists operated, as well as the strategies that Jabotinsky adopted to maintain his hold over his ideologically diverse constituency.

Polish Jews and the Politics of Nationality

Ever ready to denounce Betar, its opponents saw in the youth movement's flirtations with fascism a full-fledged acceptance of radical right-wing politics. From the moment Betar gained supporters, its members were accused of being Jabotinsky's "little Jewish fascists," the brutal "foot soldiers" of "the

Jewish Mussolini" or "the Jewish Hitler."⁴⁷ Betar's competitors in Poland drew in equal measure from examples closer to home to discredit the youth movement. Zionist leaders who were critical of the Sanacja regime accused Betar's members of serving as Piłsudski's Jewish henchmen.⁴⁸ Other Zionist opponents of Betar accused its members of behaving like antisemitic youth affiliated with the Polish radical Right.⁴⁹

While Betar's supporters insisted that they had nothing in common with radical antisemitic nationalists, they expressed little discomfort with the claim that they were linked to the Sanacja. No other Zionist youth movement worked as strenuously to create links with the Sanacja regime. In Betar's journals and newspapers, local youth movement leaders boasted whenever local Polish military officials participated in their events.⁵⁰ During Polish national holidays, Betar was the only Zionist youth movement whose leaders routinely searched for opportunities to march in parades alongside Polish scouts and soldiers, sing Polish patriotic songs, and deliver speeches pledging to defend Poland from attack.⁵¹ The youth movement also created rituals that blurred the boundaries between Zionism and Polish patriotism. Several months after Piłsudski's death in 1935, thousands of Betar members gathered in a village near Kraków, where a monument commemorating the fallen leader's role in Poland's struggle for independence was being constructed. In the ceremony that followed, Betar leaders poured over the memorial the contents of an urn filled with soil from Tel Hai, the Jewish settlement where Joseph Trumpeldor had been killed.⁵²

No less significant was the reaction of Polish government officials to Betar's pledges of loyalty and their ceremonies blending Zionism and Polish patriotism. In dozens of market towns and cities across central and eastern Poland, they not only encouraged Betar members to participate in Polish patriotic parades, but also gave them access to their paramilitary training programs for Polish youth.⁵³ By the late 1930s, as civil war raged in Mandate Palestine, pitting Palestinian Arabs against the British colonial administration and the Jewish population, the Polish government accepted Jabotinsky's request for diplomatic and military aid. They lent public support to Revisionist petitions to the League of Nations, helped young Polish Jews immigrate illegally to Palestine, and provided military training and arms to the Revisionist organization's armed underground in Palestine, the Irgun Tsva'i Le'umi (National Military Organization).⁵⁴

How might historians make sense of Betar's relationship to Polish nationalism, the Polish state, and its officials? Most scholarly accounts of interactions between Catholic Poles and Polish Jews in interwar Poland focus on antisemitic ideology, anti-Jewish violence, and the responses of Polish Jews to these phenomena.[55] This scholarship has shed critical light on the pervasiveness of Polish antisemitism between the two world wars and its profound impact on the lives of Polish Jews. Its focus on moments of crisis, however, risks leaving the impression that Poles and Jews lived in entirely separate spheres and were destined to remain in a perpetual state of conflict. The very term "Polish-Jewish relations," used by these scholars to describe their work, implies that "Polish" and "Jewish" were fixed and static terms that clearly separated one group's ethnic, religious, and political sense of self and community from the other.

To be sure, there was much that distinguished Jews from the region's non-Jewish majority. Religious beliefs and customs marked Poland's largely traditional Jewish population as a people apart, with different eating habits, dress, educational patterns, and ritual calendars. The country's Christian population was overwhelmingly made up of countryside peasants. Most Jews lived in towns and cities, eking out a living as peddlers, small shopkeepers, and artisans. Although economic interactions between Jews and non-Jews were usually cordial, their religious and economic differences formed the basis for conflict. Jews had to contend with long-standing Christian beliefs that they bore responsibility for the crucifixion of Christ and that they economically exploited their non-Jewish customers. Traditional hostilities toward Jews were easily integrated into the modern antisemitism peddled by members of the Endecja, who insisted that Jews posed an existential threat to the Polish nation. Their claims that Jews unjustly dominated the economic life of the country, polluted its national culture, and were plotting to overthrow the state were not only condoned but promoted by clergy in interwar Poland's powerful Catholic Church.[56]

Jews had little reason to feel welcome in the new Polish state. Poland's independence and subsequent battle with Ukrainian and Soviet forces were accompanied by pogroms perpetrated by Polish soldiers and civilians. Polish government officials resented the Minority Rights Treaty imposed on them by the Allied powers in 1919. Its call to guarantee the equality and safety of the country's minority populations, and its demand that minorities receive a fair share of state funds for religious, educational, and welfare services were all but ignored. So too were the demands of Jewish parliamentary representatives to abolish discriminatory legislation left over from Russian and Habsburg rule.[57] Although state discrimination against Jews lessened somewhat under Piłsudski's Sanacja regime, following his death in 1935, his successors condoned the economic boycott of Jews, enacted anti-Jewish legislation, and poured their energies into seeking the mass emigration of Jews from Poland. Contemporary observers spoke of a mass emigration drive among Jews, fueled by their increasing sense that their prospects for a decent future in Poland were dim.[58] Between 1921 and 1938, nearly four hundred thousand Jews left Poland. In a country whose rulers embraced ethnic nationalism and often deemed Jews to be foreigners, it is perhaps unsurprising that Zionism, itself a form of ethnic nationalism, surged in popularity among interwar Polish Jewry.

The steady rise of ethnic nationalism among Catholic Poles and Jews alike, however, was accompanied by a paradoxical, seemingly contradictory trend. The interwar period saw an unprecedented acceleration of acculturation among Poland's Jews. The acquisition of Polish linguistic, cultural, and social habits had mostly been the preserve of wealthy urban Jewish elites under Habsburg and, to a lesser extent, Russian rule, but by the interwar period, acculturation had extended its reach to Jews from all walks of life. Although nearly 80 percent of Jews in Poland declared Yiddish to be their mother tongue in 1931, Polish increasingly became one of their daily vernaculars and, for some, their preferred language. No group was more affected by this linguistic revolution than Jewish youth.[59] By the late 1930s, over 80 percent of Jewish school-age children were attending a state public school, an experience unknown to most of their parents. The students spent as many as twelve hours a week learning Polish, reading Polish romantic literature, and listening to their teachers recount the history of Polish kings, noblemen, politicians, and soldiers. Many graduates of these schools not only viewed Polish as a natural language of communication; they also admired Polish culture and expressed an attachment to the Polish state.[60] As historian Kamil Kijek has observed, the increased popularity of Polish language and culture among Jewish youth meant that "feeling and thinking in more than one cultural universe was natural and unavoidable" for them.[61]

Generational differences were not the only fault lines within Poland's Jewish communities to produce diverse attitudes toward Polish language and culture, as well as conflicting attitudes toward the Polish state. Geography played a powerful role as well. "Polish Jewry" in reality comprised three "Polish Jewries," formerly under German, Habsburg, and Russian rule. The differing status and development of Jews in these empires influenced the degree to which their leaders identified with Polish language and culture, as well as the ways in which they interacted with the new Polish state.

Formerly under German rule, the bulk of Jews in the western fringes of the recently established Polish state held deep attachments to German language and culture. Over the course of the nineteenth century, most of the region's

Jewish inhabitants had migrated to German lands, leaving a negligible number of Jews living in Poland's western borderland provinces.[62] Jews in the southern region of Galicia, formerly under Habsburg rule, had similarly enjoyed full civic equality. The relationship of the region's Zionist activists to Polish language and culture, however, was far more intimate. In the fifty years preceding the collapse of the Austro-Hungarian empire, it had granted Galicia's Polish population a tremendous scope of autonomy, including control of the province's government institutions and public schools. This autonomy applied not only to the western region of the province, in which Jews were the only significant ethnic minority, but also to its eastern region, where Ukrainians made up the majority of the population. Many early Zionist activists in the province came from urban middle-class homes, attended Polish-language gymnasiums, and chose Polish as their primary spoken language.[63] Their participation in parliamentary politics under Habsburg rule had accustomed them to pursuing compromise and moderation with government officials. They brought these political habits to their interactions with the new Polish government and continued to express strong attachments to Polish language and culture.

The country's central region, formerly known as Congress Poland, was home to the largest number of Jews in the new state. Like their contemporaries in the western region of Galicia, they lived among non-Jewish neighbors who were predominantly Catholic Poles. Nonetheless, they came of age in a fundamentally different social and political context than their Galician counterparts. Under Russian rule, Jews, like others, were subjects, not citizens. After years of experience battling the Russian Empire's restrictive policies toward its non-Russian subjects, they were far less reticent than their Galician counterparts to confront the Polish government. Despite the existence of a small modernizing urban elite who spoke Polish, the majority of Zionist activists in the region tended to be raised in religiously observant homes where Yiddish was their primary spoken language. Jews living in the kresy, Poland's eastern borderlands formerly under Russian rule, had even less contact with Catholic Poles. Belarusians predominated in the north, and a sizable Ukrainian population lived in the center and south of these borderland regions. Prior to Poland's independence, the modernizing Jewish elite in the kresy opted to embrace Russian, while nearly no Jews in the region spoke Polish.[64]

Many Zionist activists viewed these regional differences, coupled with the increasing pace of acculturation among Polish Jewish youth, as major obstacles in their quest to imbue in their supporters an original and authentic Jewish national identity that transcended regional divisions. A critical component of this new national identity was its call for *shlilat ha-gola*, a rejection of the Diaspora. Many Zionist leaders urged their followers to accept the futility of Jewish life in the Diaspora, envision Europe's Jews as physically and spiritually disfigured, and view with contempt any Jews who sought to deny their distinctiveness and merge with their non-Jewish neighbors.

Paradoxically, however, these very same activists, in their quest to bring about the "normalization" of the Jewish nation, often drew inspiration from the histories, literatures and rituals of other European nationalist movements, and envisioned them as models for Jewish behavior.[65] Even Yitzhak Grinboym, one of the most outspoken critics of the Polish government during his years as a member of Polish parliament, described in his memoirs how his turn to Zionism as a youth in the Russian Empire was prompted, in part, by his love of Polish literature, which "awakened my love for the Poles, who fought for their rights."[66] Betar was far from the only Zionist movement in interwar Poland to forge connections between the Polish struggle for an independent Poland and the quest for a Jewish state in Mandate Palestine.[67] Betar's chief competitor on the "Jewish street," the socialist Zionist youth movement Ha-shomer Ha-tsa'ir, initially drew inspiration from Polish scouting movements in Habsburg Galicia dreaming of Polish independence.[68] The curriculum of interwar Poland's Tarbut school network, which sought to immerse its students in Hebrew and nourish their commitment to Zionism, instructed teachers to identify links between the Polish and Zionist national liberation narratives.[69] Even as these nationalist activists insisted that they sought to forge a distinct national identity, they constantly debated the extent to which they could draw from the beliefs and behaviors of their non-Jewish neighbors.

These debates were inextricably connected to broader discussions among Poland's Zionist activists about the national loyalties of Polish Jews. In a country where Jews were widely perceived by their Christian neighbors to be threatening foreigners, Zionists understood that their calls for Jews to express loyalty to a homeland hundreds of miles away could serve as fodder for antisemites. Well aware that Polish government censors combed Jewish newspapers in search of seditious statements, Zionist journalists writing in the country's Polish-language Jewish daily press spilled much ink to demonstrate that their loyalty to Poland and Zionism could coexist. Their insistence that Polish Jews were patriotic citizens of Poland was often coupled with demands that Jews receive full civil rights, a quest that many Zionist leaders undertook in tandem with their work to build a Jewish state.[70] Yet their efforts to publicly reconcile the commitments of Jews to Poland and Palestine were not merely pragmatic performances of loyalty to the Polish state. They also reflected a genuine attempt by some Polish Jews to make sense of their own entangled political and emotional commitments to both Poland and Palestine.[71] This was especially the case for Zionist activists from Galicia who spoke Polish as their mother tongue, as well as Zionist youth who had gained an intimate acquaintance with Polish patriotic culture in the state's public school system. While they certainly did not view their Zionism as a "ticket of admission" into Polish society, some Polish Jewish Zionists believed that Zionism was as much about gaining the respect of their non-Jewish neighbors as it was about creating a Jewish state in Mandate Palestine.[72] Even as life in Poland appeared increasingly bleak, many Zionists insisted that they had a right to live in Poland as much as they did in Palestine, that they could belong to a nation whose homeland was hundreds of miles away but still view Poland as their "local fatherland," "second fatherland," or "fatherland."[73]

Given the staggering diversity of Poland's Jewish population, as well as the ambivalent relationship of many Polish Jews to the Polish state, there was unsurprisingly little consensus among them about what it meant to be a "Polish Jew." This was true not only for Polish Jews at large, but for Betar's members and leaders as well, who reflected the geographic, linguistic, and religious diversity of the country's Jewish population. Only against this backdrop can we begin to understand Betar's relationship to Polish nationalism and the Sanacja. Historians have depicted the Revisionist movement's relationship with the Polish state and Polish nationalism as a "marriage of convenience" or, in the recent work of Timothy Snyder, a genuine expression of mutual affection and solidarity between Polish government officials and right-wing Zionists.[74] Both of these interpretations risk ignoring the diverse and frequently contradictory approaches taken by right-wing Zionists and Polish government officials to the politics of national belonging in interwar Poland.

Betar's leaders deftly drew from Polish patriotic culture to attract Jewish youth into its ranks and gain government support. Yet despite agreeing that there was something "Polish" about Revisionist Zionism, Betar's members and leaders frequently debated what it meant for a Zionist to "act Polish" or what functions these performances of "Polishness" could serve. These debates are what I seek to capture in this study. Some Betar members viewed the Polish national struggle as an inspiration but simultaneously insisted that they felt no connection to the Polish state and were foreigners en route to their distant homeland.[75] Others insisted that every Jew bore the responsibility to make sacrifices for their "two fatherlands," the Land of Israel and Poland.[76]

Still others within the movement vacillated between these two options over the course of their lives—or simply accepted the numerous inconsistencies that characterized their political affiliations. The definitions of "Polishness" presented by the youth movement's leaders also fluctuated according to their particular aims. Some described "Polishness" as a state of discipline and obedience, while others celebrated Polish acts of revolutionary violence as models to emulate.[77] Still others depicted Catholic Poles as eternal antisemites who proved the futility of Jewish life in the Diaspora.[78] Although Betar's leaders had hoped that the links they drew to the Sanacja would inspire new recruits to Zionism and consolidate their ranks, the conflicting ways in which they imagined Polish identity reveal instead how their nation-building project, much like those of other nationalist activists in central and eastern Europe, was a deeply contested process.

Polish state officials who dealt with Betar were no less conflicted in their efforts to determine the meaning and limits of Polish identity. On the one hand, Piłsudski claimed that the country's national minorities could be loyal citizens of a multiethnic state, albeit one dominated by Catholic Poles. The Sanacja's education system encouraged Jews and other minority students to treat Polish patriotic culture as their own.[79] At the same time, however, the Sanacja's political elite held a vast range of views concerning the country's minorities.[80] Their brutal "pacification campaign" against Ukrainian nationalists in the early 1930s was but one example of how the Polish state's desire to maintain a monopoly of power frequently overrode any commitments to minority rights. The policies enacted by many Sanacja officials often reflected widespread antisemitic beliefs, including that Jews were naturally predisposed to communism and were overrepresented in key sectors of the Polish economy.[81] Even as they insisted on restraining radical antisemitism, they were deeply sensitive to Polish popular opinion and anxious to avoid being labeled as allies or accomplices of Jews.

Recent scholarship on the Sanacja regime has called into question the extent to which 1926 was a beneficial turning point for the country's national minorities. Instead of presenting a portrait of a centralized political system that enforced a coherent policy, this scholarship points instead to how a variety of factors—from the competing ambitions and goals of various state institutions to the whims of local political officials—could influence how the Sanacja's mandates were interpreted and implemented.[82] Police reports concerning Betar, found in Polish state archives in towns and cities across the country, confirm these findings. Some Sanacja officials depicted Betar's performances of Polishness as admirable and saw the youth movement as a potential ally in their war against communism. Others feared that the Endecja would use these performances to paint Polish officials as pawns in the hands of Jews. Still others expressed the very same fears about Jews expressed by the Polish radical Right and sought to prevent their activities altogether.

By exploring the multiple ways in which Betar's leaders, members, and Polish government officials interpreted the youth movement's performances of Polish patriotism, this study aims to contribute to a growing body of scholarship on the fundamental contingency, fluidity, and contested nature of national loyalties in central and eastern Europe.[83] Like other instances of nationalism in the region, the case of Betar illuminates how nationalist activists continually changed the contours of national identity to correspond with their evolving social, economic, and political goals. It also highlights how the imagined constituents of nationalist activists and, at times, the nationalist leaders themselves, defied the constraints of ethnic nationalism they claimed to endorse. Instead of revealing a fixed pattern of "Polish-Jewish relations," Betar's performances of a Zionist "Polishness," as well as the government reactions to them, demonstrate how Polish Jews and Catholic Poles were constantly negotiating the social and political boundaries that defined how they imagined each other and, in turn, themselves.

Youth and the Limits of Modern Jewish Politics

Just as Betar's leaders and members continually adjusted their definitions of Polish identity, so too did they craft definitions of "youth" that were flexible enough to serve their ever-changing goals. Interwar Poland was by no means the first time or place where political activists in Europe turned their attention to mobilizing youth. Throughout the nineteenth century, imperial armies, religious authorities, school reformers, and leaders of nascent nationalist movements were preoccupied with transforming young people into emissaries and embodiments of their cause. Recreational activity was increasingly viewed as a conduit to shape the political beliefs and behaviors of young people. In manifestos, pamphlets, and newspapers, political activists across the continent frequently invoked long-standing ideas about the nature of youth—from their virility, enthusiasm, and idealism to their recklessness and impulsiveness—as a way to promote their views.[84] By the turn of the twentieth century, youth movements were emerging in western Europe as one of the most popular organizational models to mobilize young people. On the eve of the First World

War, Germany's Wandervogel movement, with its calls for youth to return to nature and shed the excesses of modern life, boasted 25,000 members. In France, youth movements run by Catholic organizations had more than 75,000 members. The British Empire's Boy Scout movement, with its emphasis on instilling patriotism through camping in the wilderness, counted more than 128,000 participants. Polish, Czech, and Slovak nationalist activists in the Austro-Hungarian Empire established scouting and gymnastics organizations of their own.[85]

Despite these precedents, the First World War radically transformed how political activists imagined the roles young people could play in the activists' quest to gain political power. The military mobilization of millions of young men across Europe proved to them just how pivotal young people could be in shaping the political destinies of the continent.[86] Drawing on ideas about the masses cultivated at the turn of the century, politicians increasingly came to believe that the only way to gain power was to appeal to the political instincts of ordinary citizens. In their view, political power would be found not in the journals, newspapers, and cafes of the educated elite but on the street, where they would stage mass public events.[87] More than ever, young people came to be seen as pivotal players in the performance and acquisition of power. Many were inspired by the spectacle of uniformed, disciplined youth in the Soviet Union's Komsomol and Fascist Italy's Balilla movement. Political leaders hoped that the elaborate public rituals of their youth movements, from parading in the streets to singing in public squares, would put on display the strength and potency of their programs and, in doing so, appeal to the emotions of potential supporters in the crowds. The very activities promoted by Europe's youth movements, from marching in unison to singing around a bonfire, aimed to be emotionally immersive experiences that would set the political allegiances of young people for the rest of their lives. As political leaders across the continent made harnessing the perceived power of youth a top priority, youth movement members were told that they had the power to shape the political destinies of their adult patron organizations. Paradoxically, political leaders hoped that their promises of youth empowerment would provide them with unprecedented opportunities to shape and control the attitudes and behaviors of young people.

The theatrics of youth movement politics were especially enticing to Polish Jewish political activists. Despite their promises to remake Jewish life, they were largely powerless to effect any significant change. As members of a beleaguered minority with little government power to speak of, Polish Jews were often at the mercy of forces far beyond their control. As the 1930s progressed, they were increasingly limited by the dire political and economic conditions in Poland. Against this backdrop, Jewish youth movements provided one of the rare avenues for political activists to exert power. Their youth movement clubs, drama societies, soccer teams, occupational training centers, and summer camps were conceived of as "republics of youth," where their visions for the Jewish political future could be realized and put on public display. With political redemption delayed, they could, at the very least, prepare young Polish Jews for the future they hoped lay ahead.

Every major Jewish political party boasted a youth movement. The Bund founded a youth movement, Tsukunft (the Future), in 1915. Socialist Zionists of a variety of ideological hues established the pioneering movements He-Halutz (est. 1917), Frayhayt (1920), and Gordonia (1925). The popular socialist scouting organization Ha-shomer Ha-tsa'ir (1916) claimed more than thirty thousand members by the mid-1930s. Even the Orthodox Agudat Yisrael Party, whose mandate was to defend traditional Jewish interests, formed its own youth movements, incorporating elements of secular youth movement culture into its program, including the establishment of choirs and drama clubs.[88] Jewish youth movement branches proliferated throughout Poland; even in small market towns with several thousand inhabitants, it would not be uncommon to find a variety of Jewish youth movements vying for the support of locals as young as ten and as old as twenty-two. Organizing dramatic productions, musical performances, and public lectures throughout the year, they played a pivotal role in the cultural life of these towns.

Despite the centrality of youth movements in interwar Polish Jewish life, we know relatively little about their emergence, cultural universe, and impact.[89] Until recently, studies of Polish Jewish politics tended to focus on the ideological proclamations of political leaders, with less attention to how politics operated on the street. This book joins a small but growing body of scholarship exploring the social history of Polish Jewish politics between the two world wars.[90] I take readers to Betar's summer camps, parades, and concerts in towns and cities throughout Poland. I also reconstruct the internal life of local Betar clubs, from their intricate rituals of dressing, reading, and speaking to the portraits, posters, and slogans that decorated their walls. Through close readings of sources designed for the members of youth movements—from pamphlets intended to make ideology comprehensible to children to curricula for Betar leaders for how to make singing, playing, dancing, and marching explicitly political acts—I reconstruct the popular political culture through which many if not most Polish Jewish youth encountered and experienced politics. To do so, I examine not only the youth movement's periodical literature, but also handwritten communal journals produced by local Betar clubs across central and eastern Poland, where most Polish Jews resided.

To reconstruct Poland's Jewish youth movement culture, I also take advantage of a treasure trove of autobiographies written by Polish Jews coming of age in interwar Poland. These autobiographies were written in 1932, 1934, and 1939 as part of a contest spearheaded by the famous Yiddish linguist Max Weinreich at the Jewish Institute for Scientific Research (Yidisher visnshaftlekher institut, YIVO), headquartered in the northeastern city known in Yiddish as Vilne, in Polish as Wilno, and in Lithuanian as Vilnius.[91] Of the 627 autobiographies collected by YIVO, just over half were lost or destroyed during the Second World War. Among the 302 autobiographies that survived, now housed at YIVO's headquarters in New York, I was able to analyze some 25 that were written by young Jews who, at one point or another, joined Betar. While sensitive to the complications that autobiographies present as historical sources, I use them to help situate the political activity of Betar's members within the broader context of their lives, including their economic struggles, religious worldviews, experiences at school, family life, and friendship networks. These documents also recover the voices of ordinary Polish Jews as they grappled with the ideologies of their day.

Paying attention to these voices has profound implications for the study of Polish Jewish history. To capture the dynamic world of Jewish politics in interwar Poland, historians frequently set their focus on urban Jewish life in cities such as Warsaw, Kraków, Wilno, and Lwów. While these studies amply document the cauldron of ideologies promoted by urban Jewish political leaders, they often pay little attention to how Jewish politics was experienced and practiced in hundreds of provincial market towns across Poland, where nearly 40 percent of interwar Poland's Jewish population resided.[92] The YIVO autobiographers, most of whom hailed from these provincial towns, provide us with unprecedented access to the politics of small-town life in interwar Poland. This book helps to bring their experiences into the study of Polish Jewish politics and examines the various political fault lines that divided Jewish small-town and urban life. The autobiographies also provide a window into the political experiences of young Jewish women, whose voices were often absent from the pages of youth movement periodicals in the country's urban centers.[93] Above all, the autobiographies provide vivid accounts of how young Jews explained their participation in Betar and, in some cases, their decision to leave the movement. These accounts alert readers to the dangers of presuming that Betar's detailed curriculum guidelines, which choreographed nearly every aspect of life, accurately represent what actually took place within the youth movement's clubs. The vast disjuncture between the party guidelines and the autobiographies reveals instead how the ideological prescriptions of interwar Poland's Jewish political leaders often did not corresponded to how their followers interpreted them.[94]

Betar's leaders in the movement's Warsaw headquarters were well aware of the vast gap between the scripts for national behavior they had devised for Jewish youth and the conditions on the ground in hundreds of their youth movement's branches across the country. Ezra Mendelsohn's observation that Polish Jewish politics oscillated between euphoria and despair certainly holds true when reading Betar's triumphant ideological texts in tandem with letters, from the very same authors, lamenting the indifference of Betar's members to the youth movement's program.[95] In this respect, Betar's activists were far from alone; across the continent, political activists struggled to convince young people to carry out their ideological guidelines, let alone understand them.[96]

At the same time, as they worried about their ability to mobilize support, some of Betar's leaders grew increasingly anxious about those who claimed to be the youth movement's most fierce supporters. Particularly worrisome for many Jewish political leaders was the tendency of their youth movements to push for more radical measures. Concerns about the zealousness and radical tendencies of youth were far from the preserve of Poland's Jews. Political leaders across Europe who poured their efforts into mobilizing youth increasingly feared that their young recruits would wrest control from them. In Italy, Mussolini spent much of the 1920s trying to reign in the violent exploits of his *squadristi*. In the first few years following the Russian Civil War, tensions ran high between Soviet officials and Komsomol youth, who accused the government of halting the revolution by allowing small private enterprises to function under the New Economic Policy. In Poland, veteran leaders of the Endecja felt increasingly threatened by their young guard.[97] Many observers of European politics agreed that a "conflict of generations" was sweeping the continent.[98]

Fears about the rise of political radicalism within Polish Jewish communities fueled constant conversations about a "conflict of generations" among Jews. "The air is full with conflict between parents and their children," wrote Max Weinreich in *The Road to Our Youth (Der veg tsu unzer yugnt)*, his study of the autobiographies YIVO had assembled in 1932 and 1934.[99] Weinreich, among other contemporary observers, spoke of a "youth with no tomorrow," pushed to radical politics as a result of deepening economic crisis and persistent discrimination.[100] This trend toward radicalization played out in various ways throughout the 1930s. The radical ideals of the Polish Communist Party became increasingly attractive to some Polish Jewish youth.[101] Members of the youth movements affiliated with Mizrahi, a religious Zionist party, defied their older leaders by calling for an alliance with the working class.[102] Many of Betar's leaders increasingly called on Jabotinsky to abandon his diplomatic ventures and embrace revolutionary violence as the only tool that could build the future Jewish state.

Throughout this book, I trace how Betar's leaders, much like their contemporaries throughout Europe, wrestled with the prospects and pitfalls of empowering youth as political actors. The book situates Jabotinsky's hesitations about youth movement politics against the backdrop of debates sweeping throughout the continent about the benefits and dangers of mass politics. I also highlight how Revisionist activists constantly drew on ideas about the nature of youth to convince the Polish Jewish public to support their movement's increasing turn to authoritarian politics and revolutionary violence. Finally, I capture the struggle of the youth movement's leaders to determine when to encourage, tolerate, or reject the young radicals within their ranks. In doing so, I hope to shed light on broader dynamics that propelled Europe's vibrant youth movement culture between the two world wars.

This book is divided into six chapters. Chapter 1 tells the story of Jabotinsky's first encounter with Polish Jewish youth, during a last-ditch effort in 1927 to gain supporters for his fledgling, feeble, and ideologically inchoate political organization, the Union of Revisionist Zionists. He initially viewed the Polish Jews flocking to greet him at train stations with a mix of pity, disdain, and suspicion. Little did he know that they would transform his very understanding of Revisionism's mission and the tools required to bring him to power. The chapter describes how members of several Jewish youth movements in Poland, some established years beforehand, helped to convince the Revisionist leader to turn the celebration of militarism and the rejection of socialism into core components of his organization's program. The chapter also traces the ways in which the movement's members drew inspiration from Polish nationalism and Poland's new authoritarian government. Culminating with the founding of Poland's Betar youth movement at the end of 1927, it reveals how Polish Jewish youth were not merely the passive recipients of ideology imposed "from above" but played an active role in shaping the political beliefs and behaviors they adopted.

The second chapter focuses on 1928–1931, the years Betar began its transformation into a mass movement in Poland. Across Europe, admirers of Fascist Italy were sifting through Mussolini's political program in search of an antidote to their own political challenges. This chapter takes the reader to the workshops of Betar's cultural architects, as they designed an array of myths and rituals linking the group to Judaism and ancient Jewish history, and explores how these projects provided fertile ground for Betar's leaders to determine the extent to which they would embrace the beliefs and behaviors they associated with fascism.

Chapter 3 focuses on how Jabotinsky deftly used his distinctive brand of "youth politics" to withstand challenges to his leadership from the Revisionist movement's moderates and radicals alike. Jabotinsky believed that he could invoke ideas sweeping across Europe about the nature of youth, their role in politics, and the challenges of "generational conflict" to convince his followers that his increasingly authoritarian behavior was the only mode of leadership available to Zionist leaders in the 1930s. The chapter demonstrates how his deliberately ambiguous and provocative writing about generational conflict, as well as the innovative ways in which he delimited "youth" from "adult" in his movement's regulations, allowed him to further embrace authoritarian measures within the movement without publicly abandoning his claim to be a firm proponent of democracy.

The fourth chapter takes up Betar's complex relationship to Polish nationalism from the diverse and often conflicting vantage points of Betar's members, leaders, and Polish government officials. It explores the dynamics and paradoxes of acculturation for young Jews coming of age in interwar Poland, as well as the complex factors at play when government officials attempted to determine the extent to which young Jews and other minorities could be integrated into the new Polish state.

As the first four chapters illuminate the elaborate ideology designed by Betar's leaders, the final chapters highlight the challenges they faced in their efforts to transform Jewish youth into a disciplined unit, ready at a moment's notice to obey Jabotinsky's commands. The fifth chapter follows the efforts of Betar's leaders in Warsaw to capture the hearts and minds of Jewish youth in provincial towns across central and eastern Poland. Armed with long-standing stereotypes about *shtetl* life, Betar leaders were certain that bringing "modernity" and "progress" to these towns would mobilize provincial youth for the Zionist cause. This chapter examines the YIVO autobiography collection, as well as correspondence between Betar's headquarters in Warsaw and its small-town outposts, to reveal the tensions that arose between these urban activists and the young Jews they sought to transform. Providing a vivid account of Jewish life in small towns across interwar Poland, the chapter exposes the vast gap between the ideological vision of Betar's leaders and the political beliefs and experiences of its members.

The final chapter turns to Betar's activities in the twilight years of the Second Polish Republic. With Hitler's rise to power, a surge in anti-Jewish riots across Poland, and the escalating conflict between Palestinian Arabs and Jews in Mandate Palestine, numerous Betar leaders were calling for Zionist youth, no matter their location, to turn to acts of revolutionary violence to defend Jews from attack. Some of them wondered aloud whether their potential targets could include their Jewish rivals. The chapter follows Betar's overlapping conversations about their use of violence in Poland and in Palestine. Ultimately, it reveals how right-wing Zionist debates about violence in Poland and elsewhere in Europe helped lay the groundwork for justifying acts of terrorism during the Arab Revolt in Mandate Palestine (1936–1939).

The chapter brings into focus an argument that can be traced throughout the book—that Poland's Zionist politics had a decisive impact on developments in Mandate Palestine. This argument runs up against the work of Zionism historians who have focused almost exclusively on Mandate Palestine's Jewish population and its leadership to explain the rise of Israeli militarism.[103] I challenge their suggestion that Israeli militarism was principally the creation of "native-born" Jews in 1930s Palestine. Instead, I draw attention to the Polish roots of Zionist attitudes toward the use of force. Although Zionist efforts in Palestine, and the reactions they provoked among the country's Palestinian Arab majority, were crucial to the development of Zionist ideology, the influence of Poland was often no less decisive.

It is thus toward Warsaw, not Tel Aviv or Jerusalem, that we now turn to begin exploring the rise of right-wing Zionism.

1

Jabotinsky Encounters Polish Jewish Youth

ON THURSDAY, FEBRUARY 17, 1927, the train carrying Vladimir Jabotinsky arrived at six o'clock in the morning to Dworzec Wiedeński, a vast, palatial train station in the heart of Warsaw. Crowds of the city's Jews had begun to fill the platform an hour and a half beforehand.[1] By the time he arrived, the entire station was packed with his admirers.[2] Over the course of five weeks, as he wound his way through central Poland and Galicia, delivering speech after speech in Włocławek, Sowiniec, Łódź, Kraków, and Lwów, Jabotinsky reported the same scenario to his wife, Anya: "The trip is continuing as it began—the masses await at the train stations, the halls are full, and it seems to me like there is success."[3] He took special notice of the throngs of young Jews following his every move.[4] In the industrial city of Białystok, which lay on the edge of an immense forest, he recounted, "on the streets, there are thousands of youth screaming, 'Long Live Jabotinsky!'" In a city nearly two hundred miles northeast, known in Yiddish as Vilne and famed for its vibrant Jewish religious, political and cultural life, he recalled how "over the course of a long hour, the crowds paraded me through the streets. Masses of youth shouted, 'Hooray!'"[5]

The excitement Jabotinsky expressed to friends and family about young Polish Jews would have been a welcome break from his frequently tortured letters concerning the Union of Revisionist Zionists' financial woes and inability to recruit members since its founding two years beforehand. If the letters' recipients were indeed relieved, they would have been all the more surprised by Jabotinsky's enthusiasm for Polish Jewish youth. Despite Poland being home to Europe's largest Jewish population, the Revisionist movement's protocols rarely made reference to the country prior to Jabotinsky's trip.[6] Youth were similarly on the fringes of the Revisionist movement's political map. Until Jabotinsky's arrival in Poland in the winter of 1927, neither he nor any members of the Revisionist Executive in Paris had undertaken any serious initiatives to develop youth movements. Yet by the year's end, Jabotinsky considered Poland a Revisionist heartland, its Jewish youth his most important disciples.

This was more than just a shift in geographic orientation. One week into his trip, he confided to Anya that he was encountering not only scores of new supporters but a mode of political behavior that differed dramatically from his own:

> There is something unpleasant—I've felt it for some time now, and now I'm beginning to be frightened by it... they are beginning to transform me into a myth: "that man who"... My chubby body and my bald spot leave no impression.... Worst of all, this myth is beginning to transform into a legend about a "leader" [Duce]... I fear, more and more, that precisely this will bring us to "power" (God help us!), not a way of thought, and not a program, but rather panic about the lack of success in Palestine, and the stupid legend about the new rebbe [a rabbi of a Hasidic dynasty] who performs miracles. Even ruling through accepted ways is repulsive enough.... And already, there is nothing to be done.... And on the other hand, perhaps all this will increase our longevity?[7]

Jabotinsky's confession was, in part, an acknowledgment of his failed attempts to achieve substantial support by other means. At the founding of his movement, he insisted that Revisionism's appeal lay in its rational, logical critique of the Zionist Organization and its leader, the brilliant chemist Chaim Weizmann. Myths and slogans could serve as the handmaidens of modern politics, but journalism and public debate would be the key to political success. It was not surprising, then, that Jabotinsky's early recruitment efforts for the Revisionist movement focused primarily on members of the Jewish intelligentsia—whether émigrés from Russia living in Berlin and Paris, university students in Vienna, or journalists and politicians in Salonika who were educated in the westernized French-language schools of the Alliance Israélite Universelle. In Jabotinsky's imagination, Polish Jews, with their appetite for myths and hero worship, were of an entirely different nature. By likening politically active Polish Jewish youth to supplicants of rebbes, the spiritual wonder workers and leaders of the Hasidic movement, the devoutly secular Jabotinsky branded them as proponents of a traditional, "backwards" past.

At the same time, however, Jabotinsky's brief reference to being perceived as a Duce linked Polish Jewish youth to a new mode of politics gaining popularity across Europe. Politicians increasingly believed the political choices of ordinary people were guided by emotion rather than reason, a preference for aesthetics over ideas, and a desire for a strong leader. Politics had to be no longer intellectually sound but emotionally appealing. The politics of emotion had been a crucial component of nineteenth-century romantic nationalism and the mass electoral politics that emerged in western and central Europe at the turn of the twentieth century. The recent years of war and revolution made political elites in the 1920s all the more alert to the power of mass politics. Far from the preserve of fascists or communists, mobilizing the passions, rather than the intellects, of their intended recruits was given pride of place by politicians across the political spectrum. Torch-lit processions, tumultuous rallies, sporting events, and other public spectacles were designed to project an image of unity and strength, and to awaken the passionate loyalty of participants and spectators alike.[8] Youth movements became a critical means for political activists to cultivate these political practices. With hundreds of young Polish Jews awaiting his arrival at train stations across the country, proclaiming him their leader, Jabotinsky came face to face with this new mode of politics.

The young Jews who greeted Jabotinsky not only enticed him to consider recasting his style of political leadership. They also revealed to him that Poland's political scene, and Polish nationalism in particular, was exerting a profound influence on their self-image as Zionists, as well as on their expectations of the Revisionist movement. Their attitudes toward socialism, militarism, and authoritarian leadership were inspired in part by Józef Piłsudski's recently established Sanacja regime. Over the course of his trip to Poland, Jabotinsky became convinced that there was much to be gained by aligning the Revisionist movement's political platform with these attitudes.

Uncovering the story of Betar's establishment in Poland, this chapter explores how Jabotinsky's encounters with Polish Jewish youth not only changed the geographic orientation of his political activism, but also transformed how he conceived of his role as a leader and the political platform that would bring him to power. The story told here reveals how the young Polish Jewish adherents of Revisionism, many of whom drew inspiration from elements of Polish nationalism, did not simply accept a political vision imposed from above but played an active role in shaping it as well.

The Swamp: Jabotinsky on Youth and Polish Jews

Jabotinsky's initial ambivalence toward young Polish Jews can only be understood when set against the backdrop of his experiences as a Zionist activist in the preceding decade. During the First World War and its immediate aftermath, Jewish youth were at the heart of Jabotinsky's political activity. As soon as the war began, nationalist political activists of stateless nations across Europe formed military legions to fight in the service of the Triple Entente or Allied forces. They hoped that their service would be rewarded at the war's end with a state of their own. In November 1914, Jabotinsky set out to organize a Jewish Legion to fight under the command of the British Army, whom he predicted would conquer Ottoman Palestine. He insisted that Jews would only be able to stake their claim to the territory if they participated in its conquest. After spending several months in Alexandria with Joseph Trumpeldor, who commanded several hundred Jewish volunteers to transport munitions and goods for British forces in Gallipoli, Jabotinsky traveled to London to make his case to British government officials. With the exception of Chaim Weizmann, who was similarly courting the support of British statesmen, most Zionist leaders accused Jabotinsky of endangering the movement's official policy of neutrality. The most vehement opposition came from Britain's thirty to forty thousand draft-age Russian Jewish youth, whom Jabotinsky had insisted would join Jewish battalions in droves. Their opposition was not without cause. While Jabotinsky was conducting his campaign, the British government was threatening to force young Russian Jewish immigrants to choose between joining the British Army or being deported back to Russia. They were equally repulsed by Jabotinsky's suggestion that they serve in an army allied with tsarist Russia, from which they had fled.[9]

British government officials eventually acquiesced to Jabotinsky. Largely thanks to Chaim Weizmann's diplomatic efforts, they were increasingly (and mistakenly) convinced that Jews wielded tremendous political power, and that Zionists could convince Jews worldwide to support the British war effort.[10] Raised as a devout Protestant, and enchanted by legends from the Bible, Britain's prime minister from December 1916, David Lloyd George, was also enthralled by the prospect of his government helping Jews return to their ancient homeland. Religious sentiments easily fused with colonial ambitions. British officials believed that control of Palestine could provide them with access to the Suez Canal and help them create an overland route to India. Many British officials hoped that their declared support for Zionism could free them from the commitment to France they had made the same year, that Palestine would be under international rule.

In July 1917, the Jewish Legion came into being. Some five thousand volunteers from Palestine, the United States, and eastern Europe were divided into three separate battalions. Three months later, British foreign secretary Arthur

James Balfour declared British support for the establishment of a "national home for the Jewish people" in Palestine. Yet Jabotinsky's sense of victory was short lived. By the time the first Jewish Legion's battalion, with Jabotinsky at its helm, set off toward Egypt in February 1918, British forces had already conquered Jerusalem. When all the legion's battalions finally reached Palestine, they experienced little action on the front. They were instead commanded to conduct spadework for upcoming offensives and to patrol hills north of Jerusalem and in the Jordan Valley. Worse still for Jabotinsky was the fate of the legion after the war drew to a close. Despite his fervent efforts through 1919, he was unable to convince the Jewish soldiers with whom he had served that their longing for demobilization was tantamount to national betrayal.

When attacks on Jerusalem's Jewish population broke out during the Muslim religious festival of Nebi Musa one year later, Jabotinsky briefly experienced a surge in Zionist support for the reestablishment of the Jewish Legion. Several weeks beforehand, he had helped to establish a volunteer group of several hundred armed Jewish men known as the Haganah (the Defense). In the wake of the riots, Palestine's new British rulers arrested Jabotinsky and nineteen Haganah members who had attempted to defend Jewish neighborhoods in Jerusalem's Old City. They were sentenced to three years of hard labor. Their internment quickly became a cause célèbre for Jews in Palestine: visitors flocked to Jabotinsky's prison cell in Akko. By the time Jabotinsky and the Haganah members were granted amnesty three months later, he was complaining that Zionist leaders and the Jewish public at large had abandoned him and his fellow prisoners.[11] On his return to Europe in September 1920, he accepted Weizmann's offer to serve as the chief fundraiser for the Jewish National Fund. Soon after, he joined the executive leadership of the Zionist Organization. Under Weizmann's leadership, the organization controlled the principal charities of the Zionist movement, oversaw much of the administrative affairs of Jews in Mandate Palestine, and was seen by British officials as the representative body of the Zionist movement. In the months that followed, the executive's members grew increasingly irritated by Jabotinsky's demands for the British government to establish a Jewish defense force, permit the mass immigration of Jews, and dismiss any officials who were unsympathetic to the Zionist project. Jabotinsky increasingly accused the Zionist Organization's leadership of being incompetent and too timid in their interactions with British officials. On two occasions, Jabotinsky offered his resignation to Weizmann in protest, only to retract his decision soon after.

Tensions between Jabotinsky and the Zionist Organization's leaders reached their zenith in December 1921. News surfaced that Jabotinsky had secretly met that summer with Maxim Slavinsky, a member of the Ukrainian Democratic Republic's government-in-exile, to propose forming Jewish gendarmes under Ukrainian command. Between 1918 and 1920, as many as 150,000 Jews had been murdered during pogroms led by soldiers in the Ukrainian army. The sole purpose of the agreement, Jabotinsky would later explain, was to provide protection to Jewish inhabitants of towns and cities that the Ukrainian Democratic Republic's army hoped to reclaim from Soviet rule. Although the government-in-exile collapsed soon after the summer, rendering the agreement impossible to fulfill, Jabotinsky's actions were nonetheless widely condemned by most Zionist leaders. Many accused Jabotinsky of tarnishing Zionism's reputation by allying with antisemites. Others feared that the agreement endangered Zionist activists in the Soviet Union, already deemed suspect by the Red Army. In January 1923, the day after leaders from the Zionist Organization voted to open an official investigation into his pact with the Ukrainian government-in-exile, Jabotinsky resigned from the Zionist Executive. He claimed he was doing so to protest their handling of the Zionist project in Mandate Palestine. Indignant and unrepentant, he accepted an offer to serve as editor of *Rassvet*, a Russian-language Zionist newspaper staffed by a group of impoverished intellectuals, many of whom had been Jabotinsky's colleagues in Russia. In June, with wife and son in tow, Jabotinsky joined *Rassvet*'s staff in Berlin, where as many as 360,000 émigrés from Russia had fled.

Jabotinsky's early articles in *Rassvet* gave vent to his frustration with the Zionist movement. In a short column published on October 28, 1923, he lashed out at the Jewish public. He began by claiming that the paralyzing passivity of the Jewish "masses" was destroying any opportunity for Zionist national ideals to be carried out. Equally culpable were Zionist leaders. Instead of determining the correct path for the "masses . . . standing with one foot in the ghetto,"[12] they had adopted and succumbed to the Jewish public's mentality and demands. The task of a Jewish politician, Jabotinsky continued, was to relentlessly criticize the public, not to coddle its members. Should their leaders fail to live up to this task, the Jewish masses would remain trapped in their destructive patterns of thinking and behaving, which Jabotinsky dubbed "the swamp."[13] If describing the Jewish masses in this fashion was not provocative enough, the final lines of Jabotinsky's essay were even more harsh. Summing up the sorry state of affairs among Zionists, he castigated young Jewish men and women for refusing to undertake self-defense training. Their failure, he declared, meant only one thing: "the Jewish nation has no youth."[14]

Though Jabotinsky was undoubtedly aiming for dramatic effect—he had, after all, spent most of the war trying to mobilize young Jewish men—his critiques of youth and the Zionist Organization's pandering to the masses likely influenced the writing agenda he set for himself in *Rassvet*. If the wartime Jabotinsky was obsessed with the political mobilization of youth, the Jabotinsky of *Rassvet* expressed a diminished interest in engaging young Jews. In the three years following his resignation from the Zionist Executive, Jabotinsky wrote one hundred articles. Only six were devoted to the topic of Jewish youth.[15] Jabotinsky instead used *Rassvet* to cultivate political credibility as a statesman in the making. Along with other Russian Zionist activists writing for *Rassvet*, Jabotinsky wrote searing critiques of the Zionist Organization, supplementing them with detailed recommendations for agrarian and economic reform in Mandate Palestine, as well as prescriptions for the Zionist movement's diplomatic relations with Britain.[16]

Jabotinsky's ambivalence toward mobilizing youth was reflected in his interactions with young Jews in the Latvian seaside capital of Riga at the end of November 1923. The encounter would subsequently be mythologized and misunderstood by his acolytes for decades to come. In a last-ditch effort to keep both *Rassvet* and his life in Berlin afloat, Jabotinsky traveled to Latvia, Lithuania, and Estonia on a lecture tour. Only several weeks had passed since the publication of his seminal essay "On the Iron Wall," in which he insisted that the Zionist project could not succeed without Jewish armed units to deter attacks from Palestinian Arabs.[17] Riga's Jewish community represented Jabotinsky's ideal audience. Despite the influx of Jewish war refugees into the city in the preceding years, it boasted a substantial number of economically prosperous, acculturated Jews, many of whom spoke German and Russian with ease. In addition to delivering a public lecture entitled "Jews and Militarism," Jabotinsky spoke to students at the city's branch of the Hebrew-language secular Tarbut school network. Among them was the nineteen-year-old Aharon Zvi Propes. The eldest of five children, Propes had graduated from the school and was training to become a teacher for one of the school network's outposts. Propes managed to convince Jabotinsky to spend an evening with Hashmona'i (the Hasmoneans), the Zionist student corporation to which he belonged.[18]

Three years passed before Jabotinsky published an article recounting the evening. His account would become the founding myth for the Betar youth movement. Reimagining the encounter, Jabotinsky recalled how rowdy

Hashmona'i members, bellowing songs in German, Hebrew, and Russian, proceeded to scold him. "You have no right," they allegedly insisted, "to preach such views and to stir up young people if you don't intend to call them to action. You either keep quiet, or organize a party."[19] It was, Jabotinsky would later recollect, his call to arms, the turning point that would launch his political career as leader of the future Union of Revisionist Zionists.

Fragments of Jabotinsky's account match up with the historical record. One month after his visit, thirteen members of Hashmona'i, joined by several Jews from other student clubs and scouting groups, founded Histadrut Ha-Noar ha-Tsioni Ha-Aktivisti al shem Yosef Trumpeldor—the Joseph Trumpeldor Zionist Activist Youth Organization. The movement's members described themselves as Jabotinsky's disciples.[20] In the week following his visit to Riga, Jabotinsky did indeed experience a surge of enthusiasm for his political activity. Two days after his return to Paris, he sent a letter to Paul Diamant, a thirty-six-year-old Viennese Jewish academic and future head of the Revisionist movement in Austria. Jabotinsky enthusiastically reported: "My impressions [of the trip] surpassed all expectations. There truly is a new youth there, who are longing for discipline and strong leadership, something that did not exist in my generation and also not in the war generation. This impression has sealed my fate, so I have decided to turn from mere writing to deeds, in order to take the necessary steps to establish a movement that will include all the activists scattered throughout the world."[21] Betar veterans and historians of the Revisionist movement would later return to this passage as proof that Jabotinsky's encounter with Riga's Jewish youth constituted a major turning point in his political career.

A different portrait, however, emerges of Jabotinsky's attitudes toward youth and his trajectory as a political activist when one reads the entire letter from which this now famous passage is excerpted. Immediately following his account of Riga's Jewish youth, Jabotinsky added that he, along with the *Rassvet* editorial board, had already prepared a detailed plan for political mobilization before his trip. In other words, while several young Jews in Riga may have demanded the formation of a party, they were not the impetus for Jabotinsky and his *Rassvet* colleagues to form a political organization. No less telling was the letter's discussion of Jewish university students in Berlin, whom Jabotinsky had met one month prior to his trip to Riga. These young men, most of whom were Russian Jewish émigrés, had pledged to help Jabotinsky form a political party. They had already begun to send out letters to Zionist activists across Europe to gauge whether there would be any support for establishing a political party under Jabotinsky's leadership. Jabotinsky himself seemed far from convinced that their efforts were worthy of support. He cautioned Diamant, "Do not let their naïveté repel you—the boys deserve a sympathetic, albeit non-committal response."[22]

The sentiments expressed by Jabotinsky in his letter to Diamant may help to explain why he made no effort to stay in contact with the Riga youth organization in the months that followed. The only mention of Riga's youth in his later correspondence came in September 1924, when he wrote to a Zionist activist from the city that "everything we'll build will likely crumble" and that "only extraordinary circumstances will force me to fulfill my promises to them [Riga's Jewish youth]."[23] By that point, *Rassvet*'s Berlin office had folded. When Abraham Recanati, a Zionist activist in Salonika, wrote, "Is it your genuine intention to do something, or is this all nothing but fine words?" Jabotinsky replied that he was exhausted, and that he was "after all, nothing but a refugee." He would continue to try to revive *Rassvet* and organize a movement. He added, however, that if a year passed with no political success, he would send a circular "stating plainly and bluntly that life has beaten me, that I am renouncing all Jewish political activity."[24]

The youth organization in Riga was faring no better. The weekly meeting minutes of the organization between 1925 and 1927 provide a rather bleak portrait of the movement's members, leadership, and activity. Despite the group's pledge to forge a new path, little distinguished this small group of some seventy members from the myriad other Zionist youth movements operating in Latvia. They too were preoccupied with teaching their members Hebrew and providing them with agricultural training. Efforts to provide military instruction, and thus distinguish themselves from the pack of other youth movements, consistently met with failure. The closest they came to such training was under the command of a Russian army veteran. Frequently drunk, he urged the youth group's members to practice shooting by using fake rifles made out of wood.[25] The movement's leaders lamented that every time they tried to impose discipline, their group's paltry membership threatened to leave the organization. Leaders, too, continually threatened to abandon ship. The group was far from the political powerhouse promised to Jabotinsky during his first visit, and its members were far from the disciplined "new youth" he had described to Paul Diamant.[26]

Not that he or any members of the Revisionist leadership were taking notice. When leaders of the fledgling Revisionist movement contacted the Riga youth group, it was to insist that they peddle *Rassvet* editions and send the money back to Paris, where a second attempt to form a political bureau and newspaper was underway—this time, in Jabotinsky's attic. A second lecture tour to the Baltic states in 1925, in which Jabotinsky visited the youth movement's agricultural farm outside Riga, did not manage to convince him to pay more attention to its members. Far from an avant-garde of the Zionist movement, they were, at best, seen as a last resort for gathering money to sustain *Rassvet*, whose adult readership Jabotinsky considered to be his most important political constituency.

Jabotinsky's marginal interest in mobilizing youth as political activists continued with the formal establishment of the Revisionist movement. When he cobbled together a group of sympathizers at the Taverne du Panthéon on Paris's Left Bank in April 1925 for the movement's inaugural conference, not one session was devoted to Jewish youth.[27] While the movement's first publication did include a resolution to build a youth movement, it was buried toward the end of the document. In comparison to the multiple pages allotted to other resolutions, the two sentences devoted to the topic of youth seemed of little importance. One month following the conference, the youth movement's leaders in Riga lamented that the new Revisionist Executive in Paris had made no effort to be in touch.[28] Although the Riga group's leader, Aharon Propes, was invited to the second Revisionist conference, held in the fall of 1926, and was among the delegates to place a call in the conference's final resolutions for establishing a worldwide youth movement named Brit Ha-shomer, the Revisionist Executive did little to follow through with the proposal.

In the wake of the first Revisionist conference, both supporters and opponents of the movement observed that its resolutions were, above all, uneven. On the one hand, they offered a clear, decisive departure from several policies of the Zionist Organization and echoed Jabotinsky's calls in *Rassvet* for a more aggressive Zionism. Claiming that the Zionist Organization's leaders were excessively subservient to the British government, the resolutions urged Zionist leaders and supporters worldwide to reject British immigration restrictions to Palestine. They called for Zionists to openly call for a self-governing Jewish commonwealth in Mandate Palestine with a Jewish majority. The resolutions also urged Zionist officials to demand that British officials draw up a "colonization scheme" for mass Jewish immigration. In further contrast to the Zionist Organization's demands, the Revisionists insisted that the future Jewish homeland include a vast area east of the Jordan River known as the Transjordan. In 1921, the British decided to transform the region into a semi-independent protectorate ruled by members of Hashemite dynasty. Revisionists insisted that this decision constituted a betrayal of the original conditions of the Balfour Declaration and League of Nations Mandate, which included the region as part of Palestine. The resolutions also condemned Chaim Weizmann's efforts to bring non-Zionist philanthropists into the decision-making bodies of the movement.

When it came to presenting a proposal for the social and economic development of Palestine, however, the Revisionist movement was deliberately vague. Although the resolutions called for British financial support as well as a shift in the Zionist Organization's fiscal and agrarian policies, Revisionists offered little in the way of a blueprint for the social and economic development of Jewish life in Palestine.[29] This was not due to a shortage of ideas circulating among Revisionist activists. Conceiving of themselves as an all-encompassing opposition party that could rally diverse factions of Zionists against Weizmann's policies, Revisionist activists initially aimed to tread carefully, lest their statements on the socioeconomic composition of Palestine alienate potential supporters.

Many Revisionist activists had socialist Zionists in mind. The Zionist Organization's leadership had long viewed socialist Zionists as the vanguard of Jewish settlement in Palestine and offered them significant financial support for their endeavors in the Yishuv. By the mid-1920s, socialist Zionists were at the helm of creating new social welfare and employment programs for recently arrived immigrants. As a student in Rome, and as a young writer for St. Petersburg's Russian-language Zionist newspaper, *Evreiskaia zhizn'*, Jabotinsky occasionally expressed sympathy for socialism and praised socialists as the avant-garde of the Zionist movement. That said, the ideological constellation from which he drew was vast. Like many of his friends who identified with the Left, during his student days in Rome, he challenged the deterministic elements of Marxism and increasingly sought to synthesize nationalism with a bewildering number of intellectual trends, from social democracy and anarchism to revolutionary syndicalism and individualism.[30] Whatever affection he may have had for socialist principles dramatically receded with the rise of the Soviet Union. The upheavals of the Bolshevik Revolution had turned his wife, sister, and mother into refugees, as well as leaving Jabotinsky's colleagues in the Zionist movement who had remained in Russia vulnerable to persecution at the hands of Soviet officials.

Nonetheless, Jabotinsky sought for the Revisionist movement to appeal to as broad a range of supporters as possible. Although Jabotinsky objected to the Zionist Organization's preferential treatment of socialist Zionists, he rebuffed the efforts of some of his colleagues to portray the Revisionist movement as a champion of middle-class interests.[31] Writing to a political ally several months after the movement's founding, he insisted that he "would be prepared to swallow" socialism "like any other faith" so long as socialists abandoned their support of the Zionist Organization.[32] The Revisionist movement's first pamphlet—*What Do the Revisionists Want?*—presented the party as a nonpartisan group united in its opposition to the Zionist Organization's leadership. The pamphlet insisted that the party "would be moved neither Right nor Left"[33] on the question of class conflict and that it welcomed the creation of both socialist and middle-class factions within the movement. In a 1926 lecture in Tel Aviv devoted to Revisionism's political and economic vision, Jabotinsky similarly declared that the movement had an "aristocratic indifference"[34] to class conflict. He was far more concerned, he explained, with ensuring that Jewish businessmen and factory owners hired Jewish workers, rather than Palestinian Arabs.

The movement's position on recreating the Jewish Legion in Palestine was also conditioned by efforts to appeal to a broad spectrum of potential supporters. At the founding conference of the Revisionist Party, several delegates opposed the inclusion of a resolution in the party platform that would urge Jews to demand that the British government reestablish the Jewish Legion. One delegate reportedly quipped that such a call would amount to no more than "playing with tin soldiers."[35] Like the movement's resolution to create a youth movement, the Revisionist call for Jewish self-defense units to be established in Mandate Palestine was buried toward the end of the party platform, amid dozens of other policy points.[36] Much to the chagrin of several Revisionist activists, Jabotinsky refused to give up his belief that the military training of Jews in Palestine was a vital feature of the Revisionist program. In 1926, he felt compelled to remind his longtime political colleague, journalist and cofounder of the *Jewish Telegraphic Agency* Meir Grossman, that he would refuse to forge any coalitions with other Zionist factions if they rejected the importance of the legion.[37] He also recognized that his command of the legion was one of the most powerful publicity tools available to the movement; in the fall of 1926, he began to publish a serialized account of the legion's activities in Yiddish daily newspapers in Warsaw and New York.

Attempts by Revisionist activists to create alliances and swiftly rise to power were largely a failure. Much of the Jewish press dismissed Revisionism. Polish Jewish newspapers, for example, offered neither extensive coverage of the movement's inaugural conference nor commentary in its aftermath.

In Mandate Palestine, the news of the movement's founding in the Hebrew-language daily *Doar Hayom* was allotted four sentences and was buried in the bottom of a column toward the back of the newspaper.[38] Even during the inaugural Revisionist conference, delegates admitted that their conviction that Zionism was in a state of crisis would be a tough sell. The preceding year had seen an unprecedented wave of mass emigration of Jews from eastern Europe to Palestine. While Jewish-Arab relations remained tense, no major outbreak of violence had taken place for more than four years.

Jabotinsky's speeches at the Zionist Congress in 1925 and 1927 were rare moments of publicity for the movement. The remainder of Jabotinsky's time was devoted to writing articles for *Rassvet* and *Morgn Zhurnal*, a Yiddish daily in New York. A lecture tour of the United States in the spring of 1926 was a financial failure.[39] The existence of several dozen Revisionist committees in cities across Europe did little to help give the movement political momentum. The first glimmers of success came in the fall, when Jabotinsky traveled to Palestine. Although thousands of recently arrived Jewish immigrants from eastern Europe attended his lectures in Tel Aviv and Jerusalem, the rousing rhetoric of his talks—including his call to Palestine's Jewish youth to serve as the spark that would ignite change in the Yishuv—was nowhere to be found in his personal correspondence describing his trip.[40] In letters to Anya, Jabotinsky's initial enthusiasm for the reception he received in Palestine quickly gave way to frustration. Reflecting on the crowds of Jews attending his lectures, he wrote, "I'm living here in a wild tumult," and quickly added, "it appears to me that there isn't any advantage in this for either the party or myself."[41] Toward the end of his trip to Palestine, he predicted to a supporter in Romania that the Revisionist movement would likely find greater success among German Jews, who would certainly not cause the ruckus (*gevald*) that the eastern European Jewish audiences in Palestine had demonstrated.[42]

Indeed, much of the Revisionist movement's political activity in its first two years was guided by Jabotinsky's discomfort with "raucous" audiences. It was no accident that Jabotinsky envisioned the antidote to the "wild tumult" of Mandate Palestine's Jewish population to be German Jews, alternatively celebrated and mocked by their Jewish contemporaries for their refined and restrained manners, cultural sophistication, and other markers of respectable bourgeois behavior. Like German Jewish political leaders, Jabotinsky believed that if Polish Jews in the interwar period were to enter the political sphere, they would do so primarily as the recipients of charity or the potential beneficiaries of immigration reform, rather than as the vanguard of political change.[43] In the meeting minutes of the Revisionist Executive in Paris between 1925 and 1927, Poland was mentioned only once.[44] Although the Revisionist movement's president, the veteran Russian Zionist activist Vladimir Tiomkin, paid a visit to Poland in the spring of 1925 to observe local Revisionist branches, the executive concentrated their efforts on Germany, England, and the United States.

Jabotinsky was not entirely oblivious to Poland's potential as a wellspring of Revisionist support. In a note inviting an Odessa-born Zionist activist to serve as the Revisionist movement's general secretary, Jabotinsky boasted in September 1925 that there was a "great ferment among the youth and adults alike, especially in Poland."[45] Much like his approach to youth, however, Jabotinsky was far from convinced that the "great ferment" of Polish Jews was worthy of his sustained attention. One month later, he informed his wife that he had been denied a visa to enter Poland—the result, he believed, of his public condemnation, nearly fifteen years beforehand, of Polish nationalist politicians in the Russian Empire for promoting antisemitic policies to mobilize support. In a series of articles condemning the animosity of Polish nationalists toward Jews and Ukrainians, Jabotinsky had argued that any nationalism that relied on the demonization and persecution of a minority did not deserve a future nation-state.[46] Rather than express disappointment about the denial of his visa, he confided to Anya, "I'm not sorry about this."[47] He would wait a full year to try to obtain a visa once again. In his intervening correspondence, Jabotinsky expressed little concern to friends or colleagues about creating a political campaign in Poland.

Yet it was precisely in Poland that the Revisionist movement would not only find its greatest success, but also clarify its ideological course. While Jabotinsky grasped for support among small circles of admirers in Tel Aviv, Salonika, Vienna, and elsewhere, and as Riga's Betar group struggled to stay above water, three Polish Jewish youth movements in the cities of Warsaw, Kraków, and Stanisławów were developing a political culture that would profoundly influence the course of the Revisionist movement and its ideological development. To the leaders of these groups, which played a pivotal role in the formation of Betar in Poland, we know turn.

Stansławów, Eastern Galicia

On a Friday morning in November 1923, a Polish police unit set out from its headquarters in the center of Stanisławów, a city in southeastern Poland, nestled between two rivers at the foothills of the Carpathian Mountains. Nearly

50 percent of the city's seventy thousand residents were Jewish, and nearly 40 percent of its inhabitants were Catholic Poles. Southern Galicia's Ukrainian majority had a small presence in the city but dominated the surrounding villages. The policemen, on their way toward Ulica Lipowa, one of fifteen streets extending like spokes from the city square, would have passed the city's Ukrainian seminary, two Polish schools, and several Jewish *shtiblekh*, small houses of prayer. When they reached the doorstep of the Auster family's household, they announced that the Auster's son, Maks, was under investigation. The police had received a frantic report, likely from a member of the city's Polish population, that Maks, along with several other Jewish teenagers in the city, were secretly conducting military drills in nearby Romaszkana Park. A Polish newspaper in the city of Lwów, some eighty miles north, had recently claimed that Jewish youth throughout Galicia were being recruited into an underground Jewish army whose aim was to overthrow the Polish state. By questioning Maks, the policemen hoped to determine whether this was indeed the case.

According to the police report, Maks's testimony confirmed that Jewish youth were gathering at the park to conduct military exercises. They belonged to a scouting group founded a year beforehand named Żydowski Skaut (the Jewish Scout). The scouts met twice a week, in groups of no more than ten. Over the course of ninety minutes, their instructor would test their ability to decipher maps and arrange themselves in military formations. These activities, Auster explained, were all under the auspices of Żydowski Skaut's leader, twenty-one-year-old law student Adalbert Bibring. Living only one street to the west of the Austers, Bibring was informed soon after that his scouting group was no longer permitted to operate.[48]

The police investigation, along with the numerous letters Bibring submitted to Polish government officials to reinstate his movement, are among the few documents available to historians describing the activities of Żydowski Skaut.[49] Like many local scouting groups, Bibring's organization felt little need to publish ideological tracts to attract its members. One of the only other extant sources describing Bibring's work is found in Jabotinsky's correspondence from March 1927, when he named the leader of Żydowski Skaut as the first head commander of Poland's Betar.[50] Although the police reports cannot offer a comprehensive portrait of the movement's activities and ideological character, they shed light on the social and political dynamics that gave rise to the movement, shaped its program, and ultimately commanded Jabotinsky's attention.

The concerns of the Polish police, as well as the initial decision of government officials to shut down Żydowski Skaut, are best explained against the backdrop of ethnic tensions and violence that had recently ravaged the city. During the First World War, Russian and Austrian forces had fought several battles in the city, known by its Habsburg administrators as Stanislaus. In October 1918, when the Habsburg Empire collapsed, Ukrainian nationalists declared that the city was no longer Stanislaus, but Stanislaviv—the new capital to the short-lived Western Ukrainian People's Republic. Polish forces took over within six months. During the Polish-Soviet War in 1920, Red Army forces briefly took hold of the city. In the wake of these conflicts, Polish government officials remained deeply concerned that local Communists and Ukrainian nationalists within their midst were plotting to renew their struggle against Polish rule. Jews were considered particularly subversive because they could, according to many Polish officials, collaborate with both groups. Polish officials interpreted the neutral position adopted by the region's Jewish leaders during the Polish-Ukrainian conflict as proof of their sympathy for the Ukrainian national cause.[51] The fact that the commander of the Red Army, Leon Trotsky, was Jewish only stoked fears that all Jews were potential Bolsheviks-in-disguise. Far outnumbered by Ukrainians in the countryside, and living in a city where Jews predominated, Stanisławów's Catholic Poles felt themselves to be an embattled minority. Government officials saw it as their duty to Polonize the region and quell any stirrings of minority nationalism. Hence the warning from the local police to Warsaw's Ministry of Internal Affairs that permitting Bibring's group to operate would not only undermine Polish school authorities, but also promote "Jewish solidarity and separatism."[52] Even if Zionism strove to establish a Jewish homeland thousands of miles away, the movement was still deemed suspect.

Stanisławów's Polish population would have also had good reason to view a scouting movement as the foundation for an army. They needed only to look at their own scouting organizations. On the eve of the First World War, Stanisławów was one of several cities and towns throughout eastern Galicia in which the Polish Scouting Association (Związek Harcerstwa Polskiego) had taken root. The links between scouting and Polish nationalism in the region ran deep. The association was founded in Lwów, in the city's Polish-language gymnasium, which had been a stronghold for cultivating Polish culture and national identity under Habsburg rule.[53] The Polish Scouting Association's founders drew inspiration from the British scouting movement, led by Sir Robert Baden-Powell, a general in the British Army. Published in 1908, his manual *Scouting for Boys* provided a template for creating what he envisioned to be the ideal citizen-soldier. Through camping games conducted in small groups of uniformed youth, the scouts would accustom their members to patrolling, pathfinding, and signaling—skills they could later use as they matured into patriotic, courageous, and disciplined soldiers.[54] The text was translated into Polish only two years later by Andrzej Małkowski, who was a member of several Polish nationalist student groups, among them the popular Sokół gymnastics organization. *Scouting for Boys* was especially compelling for Polish nationalist activists in Habsburg Galicia because of the careful, if somewhat tenuous, distinction it drew between cultivating military preparedness and promoting militant nationalism. If they were to operate legally, Polish scouting groups would have to make a case that they did not pose a threat to the Austro-Hungarian Empire. Using language that would be echoed by Betar nearly two decades later, Małkowski's 1910 translation insisted, "It would be false... to believe those who claim that scouting develops militaristic tendencies. The opposite is the case.... The scouting of Baden-Powell is not for times of war, but for times of peace. But when the fatherland calls upon its own sons for help, they will be well prepared for battle."[55]

When the First World War broke out, many *harcerstwo* (scouts) joined in the struggle for Polish independence by enlisting in the Polish Legions. Initially under the command of Austrian forces, the legions were led by Józef Piłsudski. One of the legion's commanders, Józef Haller, had previously served as the president of the Polish Scouting Association. The legions' battles against Russian forces during the first two years of the war, and Haller's later exploits leading thousands of Polish volunteers in battle alongside the Allied powers in France, helped create the legend of Piłsudski as the liberator of the Polish nation and of the scouts as Poland's most prized soldiers.[56] In part thanks to this myth, the Polish Scouting Association became one of the most popular Polish youth movements in interwar Poland, attracting hundreds of thousands of members.[57] Almost immediately following the establishment of Poland, the Polish army forged a close relationship with the Polish scouting movement, providing substantial financial and organizational support, including the use of their weapons.[58]

Within eastern Galicia's gymnasia, Jewish students such as Bibring first encountered the harcerstwo and were inspired to form their own scouting movements. In 1867 and 1871, Emperor Franz Joseph II, as part of a broader effort to retain his hold on his multiethnic empire, granted Galicia's Polish population virtual autonomy, including control of the state apparatus and public schools. The children of Galicia's acculturated Jewish intelligentsia were increasingly sent to Polish rather than German-language schools. Many of Galicia's early Zionist activists arrived at Jewish nationalism as a result of their encounters with antisemitism in Polish-language gymnasia and universities.[59] On the eve of the First World War, Jewish students in Lwów who felt simultaneously inspired and excluded by Polish nationalist organizations such as the harcerstwo decided to form a scouting movement of their own. They named the group Ha-shomer (the Guardsman), paying tribute to a Jewish defense organization in Palestine founded in 1909. In 1916, the movement's members, now wartime refugees in Vienna, merged with a student Zionist organization to form Ha-shomer Ha-tsa'ir (the Young Guard), which would later become one of interwar Poland's most popular Zionist youth movements. During their years in Vienna, the movement's members accumulated numerous ideological influences, from anarchism, Nietzscheanism, and psychoanalysis to the romantic youth movement culture of the German Wandervogel. Nonetheless, in the group's early years, the primary frame of reference for the youth movement's members remained the Polish scouting organizations that had excluded them.[60] In 1918, a report from Ha-shomer Ha-tsa'ir's executive council explained that the Jewish scouting movement that had first formed in Galicia was "the Jewish translation of a Polish military organization."[61]

Like the prewar Ha-shomer, Adalbert Bibring's Żydowski Skaut was conceived as a protomilitary organization and was composed of middle-class gymnasium students with an attachment to Polish language and culture. Of the three people listed on one the group's many requests for legalization in 1923, two were studying in Polish-language universities, one training to be a dentist, and the other, a lawyer. The very name of the scouting movement's founder, Adalbert, along with the names of the other signatories on the legalization request, similarly marked them as acculturated Jews.[62] They likely considered it natural to articulate their Zionism using the language of Polish youth movements. Jan Bader, a contemporary of Bibring who would later become the editor of the Revisionist movement's Polish-language weekly in Kraków, reflected on his early childhood experiences within this generation of young Zionist leaders in Galicia: "Even though I was loyal to Herzl's vision, I was Polish, and didn't see any contradiction in this."[63] When Bibring appealed to the Polish government to reinstate Żydowski Skaut, describing the organization as taking on the "heavy burden in the postwar era to educate Jewish youth in the thinking of Baden Powell, the founder of scouting,"[64] he knew that this reference would encourage his readers to draw a link to Żydowski Skaut and the values espoused by Polish scouting organizations.

Given the inextricable link in the imagination of Catholic Poles at the time between the harcerstwo, the creation of the Polish Legions, and the liberation of Poland from Russian, Austrian, and German rule, it is unsurprising that Bibring's Żydowski Skaut would frame its goals bearing this narrative of national liberation in mind. In Bibring's view, Jabotinsky's Jewish Legion fit the bill perfectly as the Zionist rendition of the Polish Legion. In a memorial book devoted to Stanisławów's interwar Jewish population, one of the city's prominent Zionist activists recalled that at some point in the early 1920s, Bibring became a devotee of Jabotinsky after hearing the Revisionist leader deliver a lecture in Vienna.[65] Żydowski Skaut's regulations reflect this change; somewhere between 1924 and 1925, the movement changed its name to Menorah, paying homage to the insignia used by Jabotinsky's Jewish Legion. The movement now asked of its members to pledge to join the future Jewish Legion and fight for the liberation of the Land of Israel. By the end of 1925, the Polish government reported that the group had gained more than one hundred members and was conducting some of its activities in Hebrew.[66] In the same year, the Ministry of Internal Affairs approved the group and gave it the privilege of becoming the first Jewish youth movement in Stanisławów to receive official permission to recruit in the city's Polish-language gymnasia.[67] Although this permission was soon revoked, reflecting the still-tenuous relationship between the Polish government and the inhabitants of eastern Galicia, the government's initial decision to permit the group to operate in the gymnasia was possibly the result of the proximity of Menorah's program and aims to those of the Polish scouting movement.

The deep imprint of Polish nationalism and Polish scouting culture on Bibring's worldview remained apparent two years later, when Jabotinsky appointed him as Betar's leader in Poland. In August 1927, Bibring penned the Polish branch of the youth movement's first set of regulations and circulated them among nearly eighty scouting organizations across the country. In several crucial respects, his statutes differed from those produced four months beforehand by Riga's Betar leadership, who had changed their movement's name to the Joseph Trumpeldor Hebrew Youth League. Although the Riga protocols called for Betar's members to reject the negative influences of urban life and to engage in sporting activities, it never once mentioned scouting as an inspiration or an organizational model.[68] In contrast, Bibring's statute for his organization, the Joseph Trumpeldor Scouting Organization, stated from the outset that it would draw on "Zionist scouting" alongside "pioneering training" to prepare its members to fulfill their national responsibility to build the Jewish state. Even more significant was the code of conduct outlined in Bibring's statutes. Of the ten "Scouting Laws" he instructed Betar members to fulfill, eight were taken from the Polish Scouting Association's code from 1911. Its members were required to wear green shirts—the same color worn by the harcerstwo. For detailed instructions for how to conduct their scouting activities, Bibring referred Betar's newly minted members to textbooks from Polish scouting groups. Finally, in contrast to the Riga protocols, which did not give pride of place to the Jewish Legion, Bibring crafted a "Betar oath" asking its members to pledge that they would "always be ready to perform the obligations of the ideals of the State and Jewish Legion in the Land of Israel." The centrality of the legion was reflected in Bibring's organizational structure, which used the Hebrew terms for "company" (*pluga*) and "battalion" (*gdud*) to divide its members. The military inspiration for Bibring's Betar was also made clear in its description of the organization's leadership chain. In contrast to the Riga protocols, which had little to say about the appointment process of the youth movement's leaders, Bibring stated that Jabotinsky alone could nominate the head commander of Betar, adding that Betar's members were subject to Jabotinsky's commands.[69] Although Bibring's statute asked its members to give deference to Riga's Betar, its emphatic emphasis on scouting education and, with it, the paramilitary training of Jewish youth would ultimately serve as Jabotinsky's model for Betar, which he began to develop in earnest following his trip to Poland in 1927.

Kraków, Western Galicia

Although Adalbert Bibring furnished Poland's Betar with its first set of statutes in the summer of 1927, an illness led him to abdicate his role as head commander several months later. In his place stood the charismatic, brilliant, and tempestuous twenty-seven-year-old Reuven Feldschuh.[70] Already the leader of a Zionist youth movement founded in Kraków known as Ha-shomer Ha-tahor/Ha-le'umi (the Pure/National Guard) in Poland, Feldschuh would serve as Betar's chief local polemicist and ideological architect for nearly three years. If Bibring provided Betar with its ideological ties to the Polish scouting movement, it was Feldschuh who infused into the youth movement a ferocious opposition to socialism. Largely thanks to him, Poland's Betar declared a war against the Jewish Left and placed this battle at the center of its program.

Born in 1900 into an acculturated middle-class family in the eastern Galician town of Buczacz, Feldschuh fled with his parents during the First World

War to Vienna, joining tens of thousands of Galician Jewish refugees pouring into the imperial capital. He enrolled in a German-language gymnasium, where he became a prominent member of the city's recently founded Ha-shomer Ha-tsa'ir. Enthralled by the utopian youth communities that the group promised to cultivate, he arrived in Palestine in 1919 and was one of the founding members of Bitanya, the youth movement's ascetic commune on the Sea of Galilee. Like many other Zionist youth movement activists journeying to Palestine, he invented a Hebrew surname, Ben-Shem, to signify the personal transformation that he expected would accompany his arrival. His time in Palestine was short lived; when he received word that his father had been murdered in a pogrom in the war-torn eastern borderlands of Poland, he decided to return to Europe, settling in Vienna. During the four years he spent in the city, he mustered a vast and staggering intellectual pedigree, spending a year or two as a student of Sigmund Freud, completing a doctorate on international relations, and receiving rabbinical ordination from Vienna's chief rabbi, Zwi Perez Chajes. His mentor's commitment to biblical scholarship and Zionist activism left an imprint on Feldschuh's elegant Hebrew writing style; biblical allusions determined the rhythms of the dense and florid prose he employed in his work as a youth movement leader. He was no less talented as a writer in Polish. The newly minted doctor of philosophy and rabbi set his sights on Kraków, where he contributed literary criticism and short stories to the Polish-language Zionist daily *Nowy Dziennik* and quickly established himself as a well-known activist in the city's Zionist scene.[71]

Whether Feldschuh remained an active member of Ha-shomer Ha-tsa'ir during these intervening years is unclear, but developments within the youth movement during this period would play a decisive role in his subsequent political career. In wartime Vienna, the founders of Ha-shomer Ha-tsa'ir pledged to forge a counterculture that was fiercely antipolitical: standing at the foot of Theodor Herzl's grave, its members swore to one another that they would avoid party politics.[72] Against the backdrop of the October Revolution and the rise of the Soviet Union, their initially amorphous ideological orientation steadily gave way to a clear socialist program. In the latter half of the 1920s, when the movement grew to more than twelve thousand members, it underwent a radical shift to the Left. Despite knowledge of the violence and repression that had accompanied the early years of Soviet rule, many socialist Zionists were mesmerized by the romance of the Communist revolution, with its promise to promote social justice, abolish unearned privilege, and fight antisemitism.[73] Ha-shomer Ha-tsa'ir branches in industrial cities such as Warsaw, Białystok, and Łódź were the first to radicalize. By the fall of 1925, the youth movement's leadership in central Poland, and soon after in Galicia, were drawing battle lines at their conferences between those who endorsed communism and called for class warfare and revolutionary struggle, and those who defended the youth movement's original commitment to transcending party politics. The latter were soon outflanked by leaders who adopted a pro-Soviet stance.[74]

The radicalization of Ha-shomer Ha-tsa'ir prompted several of its activists to defect and form new youth movements. Feldschuh was among them. He described himself as a "guardsman" (*shomer*) whose task was to convince young Jews to abandon Ha-shomer Ha-tsa'ir, which was no more than a "gateway to Moscow."[75] Founded in 1926, his youth movement was aptly named Ha-shomer Ha-tahor (the Pure Guard)—that is, pure from socialism. After establishing several branches of the youth movement in Kraków and nearby towns, Feldschuh brought the movement to eastern Poland, where he briefly held a position in the small town of Kowel as a teacher of Latin and philosophy at a Hebrew-language high school. By the end of 1927, he had joined forces with Aharon Kaplan, a former Ha-shomer Ha-tsa'ir leader who had founded his own alternative youth movement in Warsaw, known as Ha-shomer Ha-le'umi (the National Guard). The newly merged youth movements brought the number of scouting branches under Feldschuh's influence to fifty.[76]

With an eye toward expanding the movement further, and with the hopes of overtaking Ha-shomer Ha-tsa'ir in its popularity among young Jews, Kaplan and Feldschuh began to publish a periodical for their movement. The periodical provides a fascinating window into the ideological worldview Feldschuh sought to construct. His programmatic essay in the periodical's first volume underscores the extent to which he envisioned his followers as Zionist soldiers commanded to fight in a life-or-death battle against socialists. Written in a florid style teeming with biblical allusions, Feldschuh's article "Zealots" began by condensing a millennia of Jewish history into three dense paragraphs. He proposed that Jewish history had been shaped, above all, by a long chain of wars. These battles, he continued, were not between Jews and those of "foreign blood" but were conflicts pitting Jews against one another. During each internal war, he explained, what saved the Jewish nation were acts of violent radicalism. As proof, he claimed that the Talmud called on Jews to murder members of their community who defied rabbinic law. Arriving in his polemic to the twentieth century, Feldschuh warned that the new enemy within were members of Ha-shomer Ha-tsa'ir, who were trying to poison Jewish youth with their calls for a proletarian revolution. Communism, Feldschuh explained, was an invention of Jews who were determined to destroy their own nation. The primary task of Ha-shomer Ha-tahor/Ha-le'umi, he concluded, was to conduct a war against the Communist infiltration of the Zionist movement, "devouring the soul of our youth," by teaching young Jews how to be "zealots of the nation."[77] Only if Jewish youth rejected class war and fought in unison to liberate the Land of Israel, he concluded, would they be equal among the nations of the world.

While Feldschuh's repeated calls for a war against the Left and his use of violent imagery echoed some of the language used by right-wing movements across Europe, the language employed by Aharon Kaplan and other leaders in Ha-shomer Ha-tahor/Ha-le'umi sought to steer the movement away from the ideological orbit of the European Right. Their articles never encouraged Jewish youth to subordinate their interests to the will of a leader, and they insisted that Jewish immigrants to Palestine should have the freedom to choose their occupation. They also sought to distance themselves from the Revisionist movement. The youth movement's statutes contained no mention of the Jewish Legion, nor did it call on Jewish youth to conduct military training or to criticize the Zionist Organization's current leadership.[78]

If Feldschuh's political activity is any indication, however, the boundaries separating the two movements were far from set. Despite becoming a member of Poland's Revisionist Executive in Warsaw in 1927 and, one year later, the head commander of Betar, Feldschuh still retained his position in the leadership of Ha-shomer Ha-tahor/Ha-le'umi, traveling throughout Poland to continue to found the youth movement's branches. Soon after, Feldschuh began to import his fiery calls for a war against the Jewish Left into Betar's program. When he replaced Bibring as head of Betar in the fall of 1928 and began to pen some of the movement's core ideological texts, he continued to describe the development of Zionism as a battle between left-wing and "pure" nationalist forces, reproducing the same militant and antisocialist language that had characterized his earlier columns.[79] His calls for a fierce struggle against socialism in Poland and in Palestine predated and even anticipated the language that Jabotinsky and the Revisionist movement as a whole would deploy against Jewish socialists.

Warsaw, Central Poland

Although Jabotinsky initially chose Stanisławów as the headquarters for Poland's Betar in 1927 and later appointed Feldschuh, living at the time in Kraków, to serve as the youth movement's head commander, in Warsaw he encountered the largest group of youth movement members to claim him as their leader. For nearly five years, Jakub Perelman, a student at Warsaw University, had poured his energy into leading a scouting organization bearing Jabotinsky's name. It boasted hundreds of members in Warsaw, Radom, and Lublin, as well as branches in large towns and cities in the country's eastern borderlands, such as Grodno, Suwałki, and Wilno. Like Bibring's Żydowski Skaut, the history of Perelman's Ha-shachar (the Dawn) reveals the deep imprint Polish scouting culture would infuse into Betar. What set Perelman's movement apart, however, was its emphasis on authoritarian and militaristic models of leadership, which would soon find their way into Betar's ideological orbit.

If the archival sources from Stanisławów allude to the influence of Polish nationalism on Bibring's group, there is no mistaking its decisive role in leading Perelman to found a Jewish youth movement bearing Jabotinsky's name. Perelman was born in 1902 to a family among the city's growing circles of acculturated Jewish traders, financiers, and industrialists. His parents would have likely counted themselves among the thirty thousand Jews who listed Polish as their primary spoken language in the 1897 census conducted by tsarist officials.[80] In contrast to most of the city's Jews, who were Yiddish speaking, Orthodox, and barely subsisting as petty merchants and peddlers, Jakub's parents could afford to send their four children to private Polish-language schools. Jakub was a student when Warsaw, along with the entire region of Congress Poland, fell under German occupation in the summer of 1915. In an effort to secure the loyalty of the region's inhabitants, the German military administration lifted many of the restrictions on political activity previously imposed by Russian officials. Jewish political activists seized the opportunity to transform the city's political landscape.[81] In addition to new newspapers and schools created by Zionist, Bundist, and Orthodox political groups, several scouting organizations emerged, inspired by the Polish scouting movement. Joining one such scouting group, Perelman was introduced to Zionism. Despite his growing affinity for their promise to serve as the nucleus for a future army to liberate the Land of Israel, he had no doubt, as he would later recount in his memoirs, that he was "Pole of the Mosaic Faith"—a term first made fashionable decades beforehand by liberal Polish nationalists and members of the acculturated Jewish elite in cities with a Polish-speaking majority.[82] Three years later, at the war's end, the sixteen-year-old Jakub greeted the establishment of independent Poland as a dream come true. Returning to his beloved Warsaw after spending the final years of the war in Włocławek with his mother and sisters, Perelman pledged to defend the city and country at any cost.[83]

His chance arrived in the summer of 1920. The Red Army was conducting a fierce counteroffensive against Polish forces and was steadily advancing toward Warsaw. Perelman joined the 201st Regiment of the Polish army's voluntary infantry. In the unit's barracks, rumors circulated that they would soon be sent to the front lines to defend their city. On the final day of July, the troops were awoken by an alarm, calling them to the foot of Poniatowski Bridge, which stretched across the Vistula River. Connecting the neighborhood of Praga on the eastern bank of the river to the city center, the bridge was one of the most important locations in Warsaw for soldiers to be dispatched.

Perelman's moment to defend Poland never materialized. Once the soldiers assembled at the bridge, a captain of the Polish army instructed the group's Jewish soldiers to report immediately to the army headquarters, where they would return their uniforms. Once Jewish soldiers did so, they were then escorted by Polish soldiers onto a freight train and sent to an internment camp in Jabłonna, some twenty-five kilometers outside Warsaw. In the city's hour of need, Polish military officials deemed Jewish soldiers potential traitors. In the ensuing months, the Polish army managed to defend Warsaw and push back the Red Army. When an armistice was signed in October, the interned Jewish soldiers were released, given back their uniforms, and sent to different Polish army units to continue their service. But the damage had been done. Perelman's dream to establish a Jewish army to liberate the Land of Israel was not forged bearing Jabotinsky's Jewish Legion in mind, but was instead the product of his experiences in the internment camp.[84]

Once Perelman returned to Warsaw to begin his university studies, he decided to throw himself into the burgeoning Zionist activity of the city. He eventually founded a scouting movement in 1922 with his childhood friend Józef Rappel, who had similarly served in the Polish army. They sought the name of a famous war hero to accompany their group. The Vladimir Jabotinsky Jewish Scouting Organization, numbering fifty members, was born. Perelman boasted that the scouting group's membership reached five hundred within three years, with branches emerging throughout the country.[85] By 1925, *Haynt* and *Der Moment*, Poland's most widely circulated daily Yiddish newspapers, were taking note of its activities.[86] The newspapers also noted that the youth movement had received the backing of two stalwarts of Warsaw's acculturated Polish Jewish community: the well-known historian Majer Bałaban and Mojżesz Schorr, the rabbi at Warsaw's palatial synagogue on Tłomackie Street. A pictorial supplement in the Yiddish daily *Der Moment* included pictures of seventy Ha-shachar scouts, some marching in unison, others standing solemnly at attention, wearing leather boots, military khakis and jackets, a scouting kerchief, and caps bearing the Star of David.[87]

While Perelman's scouting group clearly chose Jabotinsky as their role model, the youth movement's ideological configuration is more difficult to discern. Writing fourteen years after the founding of the movement, Perelman would recollect that he saw one of two options for the movement's ideological orientation—socialist or "militaristic nationalist" (*militarystyczno-nacjonalistyczny*). Despite an interest in Marxism, he explained, he ultimately considered socialism "not suitable for practical life."[88] Documents from the early 1920s, however, bear little trace of these decisions. We know that the movement chose to change its name to Ha-shachar (the Dawn) in part to pay tribute to Jabotinsky's involvement in the newspaper that bore the same name in Russian, *Rassvet*. Beyond these references, however, Perelman and Ha-shachar's leadership in Warsaw felt little need to commit to prose a fully fledged vision for their youth movement's political orientation. Not until the fall of 1926, on the eve of Ha-shachar's first national conference, did Perelman pen a brochure outlining the group's program. It declared, in no uncertain terms, their loyalty to the Revisionist movement. Had Jabotinsky flipped through its pages, he would have noticed the brochure's reports about Revisionist clubs throughout Europe. He would have also recognized Perelman's calls for Jewish students and workers alike to put an end to the political infighting that plagued the Zionist movement.[89]

Ha-shachar's brochure, however, departed from the script of early Revisionist pamphlets in two crucial respects. In contrast to the Revisionist movement's official publications, which mentioned but did not emphasize the necessity of a Jewish Legion, Ha-shachar's brochure gave the military training of Jewish youth pride of place in its depiction of the Revisionist program. In addition to amplifying the movement's military components, the brochure also departed from official Revisionist publications in its depiction of Jabotinsky. Taking up the largest space in the brochure, Perelman's biography of Jabotinsky cast the Revisionist leader in mythic terms. He enthused that Jabotinsky was a "supernatural man," a "tireless fighter," who refused to "surrender to the rules of nature."[90] After chronicling his career as a brilliant writer, a fiery polemicist, and commander of the Jewish Legion—at one point, recalling an admirer who noted that it was as if God had spoken through Jabotinsky's lips—Perelman praised the Revisionist leader as the embodiment of discipline and action, and insisted that Jewish youth embrace and uphold these same values.

Jabotinsky would have likely tolerated Perelman's effusive account of his exploits in the Jewish Legion, even if they bordered on leader worship. These legends, after all, provided a good deal of political capital for his new movement. Jabotinsky was far more reticent, however, to embrace how his Warsaw acolyte blurred the lines between the Revisionist leader's roles as a military commander and as a political leader. The disjuncture between Perelman's vision of Jabotinsky as a military commander and Jabotinsky's self-image as a statesman was made particularly clear when the two men exchanged letters with one another. In the fall of 1923, Perelman had received a letter from supporters of Jabotinsky gauging whether they could muster sufficient support to establish a political party. In December of that year, Perelman responded directly to Jabotinsky, depicting him in authoritarian terms. Addressing Jabotinsky as "dear leader" throughout the letter, Perelman pledged, "I solemnly swear to submit to you, dear leader, in all matters for which you ask us to support your authority." Describing Ha-shachar's chief task to be "to [provide] moral and physical education to Jewish youth in the spirit of the military," he ended his letter by describing himself as Jabotinsky's "faithful soldier."[91] Tellingly, Jabotinsky's response bore no traces of the language of military obedience that had permeated Perelman's letter. Addressing Perelman as "monsieur," Jabotinsky thanked him for the letter and cautioned him to refrain from "meddling in the struggles of local [Zionist] groups."[92] Perelman would have likely noticed that Jabotinsky described these instructions as "advice" rather than as a command. This was the last time Jabotinsky wrote to Perelman.

If Jabotinsky's lack of interest in Perelman wounded the youth movement leader's ego, it was the first of many such slights. Over the course of 1925, a small group expressing sympathy for the Revisionist cause began to form among Warsaw's Jewish intelligentsia. At the helm of this group was the well-known Hebrew poet, novelist, and playwright Ya'akov Cahan. Nearly twenty years Perelman's senior, Cahan had risen to fame in the Zionist literary scene for a poem he had written in the wake of the 1903 Kishinev pogrom. Its chorus, proclaiming "in blood and fire Judah fell and in blood and fire Judah will rise," became a popular slogan for Zionist scouting groups in Poland and elsewhere in eastern Europe. Far more inclined to trust a man of letters to represent his cause, Jabotinsky all but forgot Perelman and his youth movement when he learned of Cahan's interest in the Revisionist movement. Of the scant letters Jabotinsky posted to Poland, nearly all of them were addressed to Cahan.[93] In the meantime, Ya'akov Cahan sought to subordinate Ha-shachar's leaders and members to his leadership. He called on Perelman to stop claiming that he was a representative of the Revisionist movement. Rather than meddle in the political work of the Revisionist leadership, he insisted, Ha-shachar's members should concern themselves exclusively with the scouting education of youth.[94]

What followed was a battle over the scope of political authority exerted by Ha-shachar's leaders and members. Perelman insisted that his youth movement had every right to participate in the emerging Revisionist movement. His attempts to preserve Ha-shachar's self-proclaimed role as the chief representative of Jabotinsky's new movement was not simply a contest for power. The conflict had an ideological component as well. By the time Cahan convened Poland's first Revisionist conference in December 1926, a local movement committee in Warsaw had drafted a series of resolutions to be published in *Haynt*. Not one resolution mentioned the Jewish Legion, so crucial to Perelman's political program.[95] Stripped of the militarism that pervaded Perelman's vision for Ha-shachar, Cahan's vision of the Revisionist movement appeared, in Perelman's eyes, to be a betrayal of Jabotinsky's ideals. His protests were to no avail. According to Perelman's account of the conference, Cahan's Revisionist committee forbade Ha-shachar members from entering the deliberation room and denied Perelman the right to serve as a delegate. Forced to pay the price of guest admission, Perelman was kicked out of the room when he tried to make his case for the movement's ideological direction and its inclusion of youth. Infuriated, he gathered Ha-shachar members in the hallway, lined them up, and ordered them to storm the room. Only with the help of Warsaw's Polish police force was a brawl broken up.[96] It was the first of many instances in the Revisionist movement's history when tensions between young militants and older moderates would take center stage at their conferences.

"The Jewish Sanacja"

When Jabotinsky arrived in Poland in the winter of 1927, he benefited from the ideological and organizational work performed by Bibring, Feldschuh, and Perelman well in advance of his arrival. But he also had much to gain from the political culture promoted by the country's new regime. In the spring of 1926, Józef Piłsudski, at the time fifty-nine years old, led three hundred mutinous regiments toward Warsaw. Only three years beforehand, he had retired from his position as chief of staff of the Polish army, convinced that Poland's parliament was corrupt and being hijacked by right-wing forces in Polish society. The ensuing years saw a series of short-lived governments, persistent economic crisis, and the continued paralysis of executive authority at the hands of the legislature. Infuriated by these developments, Piłsudski sprung into action in May 1926, when Premier Wincenty Witos formed his third Right-Center coalition, and rumors spread that a right-wing coup was imminent. The three-day civil war that ensued left at least three hundred people dead, one thousand injured, and Piłsudski holding the reins of power. By the end of the year, with Piłsudski in the role of commander of state, Poland's executive branch of government had been substantially strengthened.[97] Piłsudski would rule Poland for the remaining nine years of his life.

Piłsudski and his supporters justified the coup as an attempt to restore civic virtue and patriotism to a country on the verge of destruction. His new regime called for a *sanacja*, or "purification," of Poland's political life and the "moral cleansing" of its citizens. Several claims underpinned the Sanacja government's sweeping program of national unity. The first was that the Polish nation was at war with the country's radical Left and Right. Both groups were accused of creating a culture of political corruption and violence that had tarnished the democratic institutions of Poland. The Sanacja government also argued that they had to curtail parliamentary democracy to ultimately save it. Piłsudski insisted that the new government's reduction of the Polish parliament's powers were designed to prevent the state from being hijacked by political parties with designs to destroy parliamentarism altogether. As a gesture to prove his commitment to democracy, Piłsudski retained the country's parliament, gave the role of president to the brilliant chemist Ignacy Mościcki, and left much of the everyday operation of the government to Kazimierz Bartel, who held the post of prime minister for much of the coming four years. Piłsudski also initially permitted large spheres of public life, such as trade unions, opposition movements, and sociocultural organizations, to remain outside the government's direct control. At the same time, however, he expelled his opponents from their positions in the army and civil service and was not above bending Poland's recently modified constitution to ensure that the government complied to his demands. He repeatedly reminded Poland's politicians that he would not hesitate to make use of the Polish army, now under his control, to ensure that the government would run smoothly.[98]

The final claim of the Sanacja campaign was that semiauthoritarian rule in Poland would allow the citizens of Poland to transcend their differences and work toward the creation of a stable state. Whether landowners or peasants, industrialists or peddlers, Catholic Poles or Ukrainians, Germans, Belarusians, Lithuanians, or Jews, Poland's inhabitants were encouraged to envision themselves as citizen-soldiers, each playing a decisive role in the quest to bring peace and prosperity to Poland. To consolidate Piłsudski's power and provide a unifying symbol toward which Poland's diverse population could rally, Sanacja officials constructed an elaborate leadership cult for Piłsudski, portraying him as both a *marszałek* (marshal) commanding his troops and a *dziadek*, the grandfather doting on his beloved family.[99] Just as Piłsudski's command of the Polish Legions had brought about the independent Polish state, so too, they promised, would his command of the nation's family of citizen-soldiers return the country to its former glory.

Jews had good reason to welcome Piłsudski's regime. The widespread success enjoyed by the virulently anti-Semitic National Democrats (Endecja) in the parliamentary elections of the early 1920s, along with the violent behavior they provoked in their quest for political power, led many Jews in Poland to believe that the democratic process, with its promise to heed the voices of the "masses," did not necessarily bode well for them.[100] Nor were Polish Jews especially adept practitioners of democratic politics. Polish Jewish critics of Jewish political activity, whether within the internal governing bodies of Jewish communities throughout the country (*kehilot*) or in the Polish parliament, often spoke of the same clientism, corruption, and factionalism that made parliamentary politics in the country so infamous.[101] Many traditional Jews would have likely also been sympathetic to Piłsudski's promise to prevent socialism from overtaking the country. By the mid-1920s, Jews in Poland were well aware of the Soviet Union's vigorous and at times violent campaigns to eliminate all noncommunist political parties, suppress traditional Jewish life, and transform its two-and-a-half million Jewish inhabitants into secular communists.[102] Leaders of Jewish political parties in Poland who aimed to promote and preserve Jewish living bound by ritual observance were not the only ones to speak of a communist threat. In the latter half of the 1920s, the increasing influence of radical Marxist politics on mainstream Zionist youth movements was cause for concern among many prominent Zionist leaders in Poland, socialist and otherwise.[103] Finally, many Jews were encouraged by the Sanacja's declaration, soon after coming into power, that it intended to "follow a sincere and open policy" toward the country's national minorities. They hoped that this promise would translate into the abrogation of discriminatory laws, the support of Jewish educational institutions, and the promotion of Jewish trade interests. Most Zionist political leaders in Poland endorsed the Sanacja's "purification" campaign.[104]

The largely positive reactions of Polish Jews to the Sanacja's program help explain what made Poland particularly fertile ground for the Revisionist movement. Revisionism's call to transcend internal conflicts dividing Zionists, as well as its description of the Zionist Congress as corrupt and ineffective, mirrored the Sanacja regime's call for unity as well as its criticism of the Polish parliamentary system. Furthermore, the terms used to construct a leadership cult for Piłsudski had already been attributed to Jabotinsky by his adherents. Both men were described as charismatic military leaders, driven by an all-encompassing ambition for statehood and national unity. Revisionist leaders in Poland quickly adopted the Sanacja's rhetoric to mobilize members and secure government support. Some five months after Piłsudski's coup, a Polish government official attended one of the first meetings of Ya'akov Cahan's Revisionist organization in Warsaw. He reported that the movement's leaders had declared that "Revisionist Zionists will play the same role in Jewish society that the 'Piłsudskiites' will play in Polish society." Further echoing the language of the Sanacja, the Revisionist lecturer insisted that "a moral revolution must shake the Jewish community" to prevent "the permeation of corruption in the Jewish community [that] is destroying any remaining prestige that Jews enjoy."[105] Not to be outdone by Ya'akov Cahan's group, Jakub Perelman included an article in his pamphlet for Ha-shachar describing Piłsudski as the "living personification of the ideal of Poland."[106] By linking their program with the Sanacja, which enjoyed popular support among Polish Jewry, Jabotinsky's Polish Jewish interlocutors helped pave the way for his success in the country.

Encountering the Masses: Jabotinsky in Poland

By the time Jabotinsky arrived in the southeastern city of Lwów in the winter of 1927, nearly twenty-five days had passed since his arrival in Poland. Over the course of those three weeks, his letters home to his wife exuded a sense of surprise, confidence, and exhilaration about the political possibilities the country could offer. Taking in Lwów's cobblestone streets, baroque palaces, universities, and opera house, he gushed to Anya, "My soul is alive here; the atmosphere of Poland is, in spite of itself, cultural."[107] In Paris, Jabotinsky saw himself as an isolated journalist of a fledgling political party; in Poland, he reported to Anya, he was seen as a force to be reckoned with in the Zionist movement. Writing from Warsaw in February, he enthused that over half of the Jewish members of Poland's parliament had attended his first lecture in the city.[108] Moving westward to the industrial city of Łódź, and reporting the addition of a second lecture due to popular demand, he informed Anya that it appeared as if his trip to Poland would yield "profit... both financially and politically."[109] Even his encounters with opponents seemed to confirm his sense of power. Traveling south to Kraków, he reported a meeting with Ozjasz Thon, a member of the Polish parliament and the most prominent Zionist leader in western Galicia. "I have the impression," he mused to a Revisionist activist, "that this 'intrusion' into his private court irritates his nerves to the point of suppressed hysteria."[110]

Simultaneously, however, Jabotinsky expressed reservations about his Polish Jewish devotees throughout his trip. Jabotinsky wrote that Polish Jews had a propensity to push and shout at his public appearances. To his friend and political supporter Shlomo Jacobi he divulged his conflicting sense of concern and excitement about his allegedly simple-minded Polish Jewish devotees; "in Poland alone," he eagerly reported, "our numbers reach twenty thousand." Still, he added, "they don't know a thing about Revisionism, and in general—they know very little." Unlike the well-read and acculturated Jews he had imagined as his ideal constituency, Polish Jews only craved "pretty expressions," repeated over and over again. The only way he could reach them, he lamented, was by "chasing after effects, and in a sloppy fashion."[111]

Jabotinsky's return to Paris, and the ensuing months he spent holed up in his attic office, served as a stark contrast to the attention that had been lavished on him in Poland. Donations from Revisionist political committees across Europe were scant; talk began, once again, of shutting down *Rassvet*. He complained to several close political supporters that both the newspaper and the Union of Revisionist Zionists were on the brink of collapse.[112] The financial situation of the movement had become so desperate that Jabotinsky was forced to beg for money from Hashmona'i, the student corporation in Riga that had helped to form Brit Trumpeldor.[113] The Revisionist leadership in Warsaw was of no help; Ya'akov Cahan spent much of this period writing to Jabotinsky about how his literary ventures had left him saddled with debts.[114] Jabotinsky was bitterly disappointed by the election results of the Fifteenth Zionist Congress in the summer of 1927, when a meager 8,446 votes had been cast worldwide for the Revisionist movement, out of a total of 123,729 votes.[115] Just as youth movements and mass politics had demonstrated their potential in Poland, the prospect of success with the world of journalism and congressional elections seemed all the more dismal. Faced with a faltering political program of action, and with the experience of Poland fresh on his mind, Jabotinsky undertook a subtle but significant shift in tactics. This gradual transformation, which began during the spring and fall of 1927, clearly bore the imprint of his experiences in Poland. It was a shift in both geographic orientation and political practice. Redirecting his organizational efforts to Poland, he began to cast himself as a leader of Polish Jewry, and of Polish Jewish youth in particular. He simultaneously recast the aims and content of the Revisionist program to reflect the political attitudes and behaviors circulating among his young followers in Poland.

The first major change Jabotinsky undertook was to declare himself a champion of Polish Jewish economic interests. In doing so, he seized on the anxiety and desperation expressed by many of Poland's Zionists after a boom-and-bust mass immigration to Palestine between 1924 and 1926. In the wake of the Polish government's decision to substantially increase taxes, some forty thousand Polish Jewish merchants, traders, artisans, and shopkeepers had immigrated to Palestine. By 1925, however, the wave of immigration had dramatically receded. In the year that followed, nearly twenty-three thousand Jews poured out of Palestine following the collapse of the region's economy. Zionist leaders feared that the return of thousands of Polish Jews from Palestine would be seen as proof that Zionism could not provide an antidote to the economic and political crises faced by Jews in the Diaspora. Many prominent Zionist leaders in Poland accused the returnees of lacking the ideological commitment to reinvent themselves as farming pioneers, an ideal particularly popular among socialist Zionists. Among the most outspoken of these critics was the forty-eight-year-old Sejm deputy Yitzhak Grinboym, widely perceived at the time to be Poland's most powerful Zionist leader. Instrumental in establishing the Zionist movement in the Russian Empire, and later in interwar Poland, Grinboym's Zionist faction, Al-Hamishmar (On Guard), viewed agricultural settlement rather than capitalist development to be the key to building a Jewish state. In the wake of the failed immigration of Polish Jews to Mandate Palestine, he warned that "the world outlook of Nalewki and Kazimierz [two commercial hubs of Warsaw and Kraków, largely populated by Jews], the vulgar spirit of shopkeepers, traders and luftmentshen"[116] would destroy the Zionist project. The returnees themselves, joined by several of Grinboym's political opponents, placed much of the blame on the Zionist Organization for ignoring the needs of middle- and lower-middle-class immigrants, favoring socialist Zionist organizations instead.[117]

It was precisely the Jews of Nalewki and Kazimierz—the Polish Jewish "masses" who had rejected the ideological programs of Zionists who advocated agricultural settlement—for whom Jabotinsky now claimed to speak. In an essay entitled "We, the Bourgeoisie," published in *Rassvet* three weeks after his return to Paris, Jabotinsky rejected the notion promoted by

Grinboym, among others, that the interests of merchants, shopkeepers, and artisans would destroy the Zionist project. Jabotinsky claimed instead that the "bourgeoisie"—in his rendition, a loosely defined term for anyone self-employed—were the flag bearers of freedom, enlightenment, and responsible government.[118] In a clear effort to appeal beyond the Revisionist readership of *Rassvet* and reach Polish Jews as a whole, Jabotinsky brought this message to *Haynt*, Poland's most widely circulated Yiddish daily. Hired to write weekly articles for the Warsaw-based newspaper from February 1927, Jabotinsky devoted a series to the Polish Jewish bourgeoisie. He declared that Jews were a nation of merchants, and that merchants were responsible for all major innovations in Jewish culture and religious practice.[119] Simultaneously, Jabotinsky used the articles to attack socialism with a ferocity that marked a significant departure from his previous journalistic output. He argued that socialist and communist ideals perpetuated hunger, poverty, violence, and other social ills. These ideals, not those espoused by Polish Jewish merchants, were to blame for the crisis of Zionism. Although these articles would later be read as a manifesto of the Revisionist movement's economic program, at the time of their publication, they raised the eyebrows of some of Jabotinsky's closest allies, who had cautioned against aligning with one particular economic sector.[120]

As Jabotinsky increasingly criticized socialism in his articles, he began to court the support of organizations that clearly evinced an antisocialist stance. In October 1927, he commended Revisionist activists in Palestine for their efforts to recruit members of Brit Ha-amlanim, a faction that had broken off from the Labor Zionist Hapoel Hatzair. Its leading members, including Moshe Lurie, Baruch Weinstein, and Arieh Altman, had only recently arrived in Palestine from the Soviet Union. Most had experienced some form of persecution by Soviet officials, and some of had served time for their Zionist activity. Appalled by the pro-Soviet sympathies expressed by their fellow Labor Zionists, they called for the establishment of politically neutral labor exchanges and the creation of a national arbitration system, which would prevent the necessity of strikes. Jabotinsky's initial meeting with the group during his visit to Mandate Palestine in 1926 had left a positive impression. One year later, after having billed himself as a champion of "bourgeois" economic interests and an opponent of socialism, the time seemed opportune to ensure the integration of Brit Ha-amlanim into the Revisionist movement. Some of their most prominent members would go on to serve as Revisionist leaders in Palestine and would contribute to the movement's ideological development.[121]

Jabotinsky also began to embrace the links made by his Polish Jewish supporters between the Revisionist movement and the Sanacja regime. No sooner had he arrived in Poland than Jabotinsky began to cast himself as an admirer of Polish nationalism. During a press conference held at Warsaw's Hotel Rzymski several hours after his arrival, Jabotinsky declared his admiration for Poland and Polish nationalism: "I don't like to loudly express my delight," he began, but "all of you understand what the nationalists of independent Poland mean to me."[122] After describing the reemergence of Poland as a miraculous event, Jabotinsky hinted at the commonalities between Revisionists and Polish supporters of the Sanacja. "I am also very happy," he added, "that the most patriotic press and journalists [in Poland] become colleagues today with my [Revisionist] journalists."[123] This was a far cry from his prewar articles claiming that Polish nationalism had no right to exist because of its promotion of antisemitic and anti-Ukrainian sentiment.[124] No stranger to forging alliances with potentially problematic counterparts, Jabotinsky even welcomed his reception by the Endecja. Only two days into his trip to Warsaw, he eagerly reported to his wife that *Gazeta Warszawska Poranna*, a Catholic Polish newspaper known among Jews for its antisemitic diatribes, had lavished praise on him. Jabotinsky expressed no concern to his wife that the paper had dubbed him a "hardliner integral nationalist" and "Jewish Endek"—a reference to the right-wing, antisemitic Polish political party, the National Democrats (Endecja). Nor did he mention that the article had lauded him as a hero to Poles because of his alleged promise to liberate the country of Jews, described as "millions of destructive microbes."[125] Instead, he proudly noted that the article's author had confessed that if he were a Jew, he would have followed Jabotinsky.[126]

He also turned his attention, for the first time in nearly a decade, to creating a political organization whose goal was to mobilize Jewish youth. Already during his tour, he reported to Ya'akov Cahan that he had met with Feldschuh in an attempt to entice him to take on Betar's leadership in Poland, an offer Feldschuh initially declined.[127] Immediately on his departure from Poland, he wrote to Aharon Propes, the leader of Riga's Brit Yosef Trumpeldor movement. Although Jabotinsky had interacted with Propes at Revisionist conferences, the young student was far from Jabotinsky's inner circle of supporters. The only other letter Jabotinsky had sent to Propes was a note expressing his thanks for the warm reception he had received from Revisionist youth during a visit to Riga in 1925.[128] This time, he appealed for Propes's help to mobilize young Polish Jews. Jabotinsky informed the young man that various Zionist youth movements in Poland were uniting under the aegis of Betar, and that Stanisławów's Adalbert Bibring would serve as its head commander. Noting that thousands of Polish Jewish youth stood behind him, Jabotinsky offered Propes his most enthusiastic forecast yet, writing that Poland would "provide us with tremendous power." Still, he added, "chaos" reigned among the Revisionist youth. Stressing the importance of harnessing the energy of thousands of young Polish Jews to serve the goals of the Revisionist leadership, Jabotinsky insisted that Propes contact Bibring immediately and provide the Galician leader with as much information as he could about how to "maintain discipline" among youth.[129]

In tandem with Jabotinsky's turn to youth movements, he increasingly praised the value of sports and spectacle as tools of mass politics. When a Polish Jewish journalist asked him to describe contemporary Palestine, he answered that the country "still lacks a director who could, in this mighty theatrical spectacle, show how to build a country, and to responsibly give out the [performance] roles." Jabotinsky's new strategy to blur the lines between theater, recreation, and politics emerged once again when a sports journalist ambushed him during a train journey from Warsaw to Łódź. When asked whether young Jews could fulfill the political goals of the Revisionist movement by joining sports organizations, Jabotinsky answered, "yes, of course." Watching ten thousand gymnasts perform the same movements at the same time, he explained, "simply leaves me in a state of awe." Jabotinsky offered the journalist criteria that would make recreational activity an effective political tool. Of all athletic activity, "brutal sports" such as boxing, fencing, and rugby would "create the type of full man that I imagine the fighter [*bojownik*] to be." When asked by the journalist what his favorite game was, he responded, "when one must preserve calm despite the danger of death, listening to the commands of the captain amid whizzing bullets."[130]

Jabotinsky's Russian-speaking supporters would have likely been able to draw connections between this interview and the Revisionist leaders' work as a novelist. Between January 1926 and July 1927, he published a serialized novel in *Rassvet* reimagining the heroic military exploits of the biblical figure of Samson. At the heart of Jabotinsky's novel is a tale of political redemption. An Israelite estranged from his nation, Samson ultimately returns to lead them in battle against the powerful Philistines, the very people among whom he dwelled. In Jabotinsky's rendition, Samson's political genius is the direct result of his ability to learn from the military prowess and discipline of Philistines. In one of the most famous passages from the novel, Jabotinsky describes Samson observing the Philistines engaging in a political spectacle:

> When the music began the vast concourse stood immobile. The beardless priest turned pale and seemed to submerge his eyes in those of the dancers, which were fixed responsively on him ... all the repressed fervor of the crowd seemed to concentrate within his breast till it threatened to choke him. Suddenly, with a rapid, almost inconspicuous movement, the priest raised his baton, and all the white figures in the square sank down on the left knee and threw the right arm towards heaven —a single movement, a single, abrupt, murmurous harmony. Samson left the place profoundly thoughtful. He could not have given words to his thought, but he had a feeling that here, in this spectacle of thousands obeying a single will, he had caught a glimpse of the great secret of politically minded peoples.[131]

Jabotinsky was infuriated when critics of the novel drew parallels between its plot and his political activism. Most historians and literary critics find it difficult to ignore these connections.[132] As literary scholar Svetlana Natkovich has observed, *Samson*, a story about the political education of a leader, was written at the same time Jabotinsky was undergoing such an education. The character of Samson challenges a "fossilized" communal leadership; implores Jewish youth to take up arms in self-defense; and calls for his nation to mobilize as a disciplined unit.

Jabotinsky's interview on the train to Łódź offers a window into his emerging vision for the role that Betar's youth culture would play in helping to bring *Samson*'s lessons to life. Rituals of recreation within Betar deliberately blurred the lines between playing sports and performing military drills, between the fantasy of playing soldiers and the reality of preparing for armed combat. In Jabotinsky's imagination, the "game" of youth movements also cultivated the soldierly obedience and discipline he deemed crucial to fulfilling Zionism's goals, on and off the battlefield. Calling on Jewish youth to embody these qualities, he penned a letter addressed to young Jews in the Polish town of Włocławek, in which he declared that "every young Hebrew, whether boy or girl, is a soldier of the nation."[133]

Six months following his letter to the youth of Włocławek, the opportunity arrived for Jabotinsky to take concrete steps to mobilize and militarize Polish Jewish youth. After much planning by Adalbert Bibring and Reuven Feldschuh, Poland's Betar branches were to hold their first national conference in December 1927. On Jabotinsky's return to Warsaw in the final weeks of December for yet another publicity campaign, he placed the cultivation of militarized Jewish youth at the forefront of his activity. On the eve of his arrival, he chose to publish an article in *Haynt* on the need for young Jews to take up self-defense training.[134] The newspaper also published, in full, his speech at the Second Conference of Zionist Revisionists in Poland, held that very month. At the conference, he insisted that military culture was still a central component of the Revisionist program, even though "people have recently begun to believe that we have given up on the legionary idea." His comment betrayed what would have been obvious to most of the delegates; until that point, the Revisionist movement had not prioritized military culture or youth. Jabotinsky assured the audience not only that "we hold the [legion] question to be no less important than before," but that it was "the first article of faith" for the Revisionist movement. Combining this declaration with a sharp critique of Jewish sports organizations in Poland, he urged the delegates to "wage a holy struggle" on any sports organization that did not teach Jewish youth to "make barricades or shoot."[135]

Over the course of a two-day conference in Warsaw, more than seventy-five delegates from the various Jewish youth movements pledging allegiance to Jabotinsky gathered for Betar's first conference in Poland. The declarations made by Betar's newly minted activists, both during and following Jabotinsky's visit, reveal the extent to which their leader's new approach to mass politics and youth movement culture resonated with them. These were, after all, ideas that had been cultivated in Poland years before Jabotinsky's arrival in Warsaw. Żydowski Skaut's Bibring, now Betar's head commander, told the audience that Jewish youth were calling out of the depths for adult leaders to change their ways and "prepare every youth to be a fighter for the state," adding that "we have too many leaders and too few soldiers."[136] Betar's new leaders also echoed Jabotinsky's praise of youth as vital political actors. Following the conference, Moshe Lejzerowicz, a Revisionist activist and member of *Haynt*'s editorial board, hailed the delegates as "soldiers of the Revisionist army," each one firm in their conviction that "the revolt in the psychology of the Zionist masses is coming, *and first and foremost among the youth,* who are always the first to break barriers [*ban-brekherin*]."[137] The influence that Jewish youth could have on the Jewish masses, he continued, would ultimately lead "for the first time in the history of Jewish parties [to] the call for a dictatorship of one person, to whom one can give limitless power in its entirety. Only a conference of Revisionists could oppose the banal form of organizational power [known as] an 'Executive' . . . [and favor] subordinating the will of the individual, to sacrifice personal ambition on the altar of the nation."[138]

To what extent did Jabotinsky promote these political beliefs and behaviors during the conference? Elements of Jabotinsky's self-presentation certainly lent themselves to Lejzerowicz's vision for his leadership style. Entering the hall once the conference had already begun, Jabotinsky took to the podium and informed the audience that he had arrived to examine them, to see if they were indeed the youth that the Revisionists in Paris and Berlin had been waiting for. The entire conference proceedings were to be a test, with Jabotinsky's vision of youth serving as the criterion of excellence. In his closing speech, he presented to his audience, for the first time, his vision for Betar. The ideal young Zionist, he explained, subordinated the needs of the individual to the demands of the nation; he "does not have any face and has no will, he is the expression of a sacrifice which one brings to the nation."[139] In the second section of his speech, Jabotinsky proposed a solution to his fears that a mass Jewish youth movement could grow into a rabble beyond his control. Drawing on the culture of student corporations, the only youth he had ventured to court in the preceding years, he explained that Betar would create soldiers who were "aristocratic, knightly and spiritually rich."[140] He would later associate the Hebrew term *hadar*, meaning "majesty" or "splendor," with these qualities. Their chivalrous behavior was to be matched by their tremendous restraint. Once they were trained as soldiers, their mission in Mandate Palestine was "not to fight, to instead be prepared, to sit and wait." They were nonetheless serving the Zionist cause as soldiers, Jabotinsky added, because "the impression of . . . power will ensure calm."[141]

Poland's nascent Betar leadership encouraged Jabotinsky's performance as an authoritarian leader and a military commander. They also endeavored to convince him that the youth movement's headquarters would be best placed in Poland. To make their case, they emphasized that the ideological orientation of Jews in Poland offered far better prospects for the movement's success than elsewhere. Requesting more funds to be allotted to Revisionist activity in Poland, Lejzerowicz ended a letter to the Revisionist Executive in London with a bold and frank declaration: "[L]et's not kid ourselves. The future [of Revisionism] does not lie in America or even in the Baltic countries . . . because they lack the constructive-romantic element. Thus Poland, with its streams of masses, remains."[142] In the meantime, Betar leaders in Riga, many of whom had expressed sympathy for socialism, were sending distressed letters to Jabotinsky about rumors of growing "right-wing" tendencies within Betar groups beyond their country. They also complained about the executive's failure to keep in contact with them.[143] By the end of 1928, they admitted that their city could not serve as the center of the world movement because, as one leader put it, they did not "have the Jewish masses."[144] Soon after, Betar's "temporary headquarters" in Riga put its activities on hold. Aharon Propes, now twenty-five years old, was instructed by Jabotinsky to move to Warsaw, where he would lead the effort to transform the thousands of Polish Jewish youth who claimed to be admirers of Jabotinsky into a coherent movement. In the winter of 1929, Propes boarded a train to Warsaw, where he was joined by Jabotinsky and various Betar leaders from Europe and Palestine for the First World Conference of Betar.

A daunting task loomed over Betar's leaders in Poland: to connect with scores of branches that were emerging throughout the country, and to provide them with a uniform culture and a clear political program. This was no small feat. In Warsaw alone, there were as many as ten Revisionist youth groups operating simultaneously, each catering to a different social and religious subgroup within the city's Jewish population.[145] Among the most pressing questions the conference delegates faced in their deliberations was how to market Betar to this diverse group of Polish Jews. Did the sum of the various ideological and behavioral patterns emerging within the youth movement add up to a coherent worldview that would be familiar and attractive to their potential recruits?

Much like other Zionist organizations, Betar sought to present their movement as both the embodiment of values from an ancient Jewish past and the vanguard of the most dynamic political ideas circulating in contemporary Europe. The youth movement had already begun to draw connections between Revisionist Zionism and the Sanacja regime. Could other comparisons to the European Right prove useful? If so, how could these comparisons be reconciled with Betar's desire to present their Zionism as the most authentic embodiment of values from an idealized ancient Jewish past in biblical Israel? The coming chapter explores how the youth movement's leaders wrestled with these questions.

2

Little Fascists?

ON NEW YEAR'S Day, 1929, hundreds of uniformed Betar members from towns and cities across Poland stood at attention near the corner of Marszałkowska and Jerozolimska, Warsaw's main thoroughfares, which lay on the edge of the city's Jewish district. They awaited the signal of the Maccabi orchestra to begin their march toward the Great Synagogue for the opening ceremony of Betar's first international conference. At around ten o'clock in the morning, the band's trumpets and drums sounded. Betar's members began their parade up the streets of Twarda and Graniczna, passing by Jewish schools, charities, and the headquarters of several political parties. Once they turned onto Tłomackie Street, they approached the synagogue. Marching up its wide steps and through its corridor, flanked by four classical columns, they ascended to the synagogue's balcony, where they draped the flags of their local youth movement branches over the banisters. Below them sat journalists from every major Jewish newspaper in the country, as well as the youth movement's leaders from Poland, Latvia, Romania, Lithuania, Germany, France, and Palestine. By half past ten, the opening ceremony for the conference commenced. Rather than choose a Betar leader to open the conference, the ceremony's organizers asked the synagogue's cantor to lead the youth movement's members in prayer. He was followed by the synagogue's rabbi, who delivered a lecture in Hebrew and Polish about the benefits the Betar youth movement would bring to Poland's Jews.[1]

As soon as the day's ceremonies ended, the journalists in attendance raced back to their newspapers' offices—each one within several blocks of the synagogue—to weigh in on Betar's debut. Most of them produced detailed and favorable reconstructions of the cantor's performance and the rabbi's speech. Journalists affiliated with the socialist and anti-Zionist Bund, however, had something else in store for their readers. Their flagship paper, whose editorial office was around the corner from the Great Synagogue, offered no description of the synagogue's clergy in their report. The story began, instead: "Astonished, Jewish Warsaw watched the parade of Zionist fascists across the city."[2] In an oblique reference to the ceremony's religious content, they warned readers not to be fooled by the youth movement. They may have been marching "with a menorah in hand," but their parade in the Jewish district was "their March on Rome," their leader a "Jewish Mussolini," and its participants "our homegrown fascists."[3] These claims extended far beyond the offices of the Bund's newspaper. Just north, on Dzika Street, the journalists of Warsaw's socialist Zionist newspaper, *The Worker's Voice of Liberation*, had begun describing Revisionists as fascists the previous year.[4] As Betar's membership grew, socialist Zionist youth movements across the country increasingly warned of the "Jewish fascism" that Betar threatened to usher into Poland and, ultimately, Palestine.[5] These fears were not only the preserve of socialists. Not long after Betar's arrival in Poland, Chaim Weizmann allegedly alluded to the youth movement's connection to Italian fascism by describing its members as "youth with a Roman face."[6]

Betar's leaders hoped that the Great Synagogue ceremony would prove that their youth movement was not, as one Zionist paper put it, "wild and foreign."[7] They reasoned that if the synagogue's famed cantor and rabbi publicly praised the movement, there would be no doubt that Betar promoted Jewish values. What makes the synagogue ceremony so intriguing, however, is not the message its creators sought to convey to the Jewish public, but rather the one that they never attempted to refute. When facing the torrent of charges in 1929 that their movement's members were *fashistlekh* (little fascists), Betar leaders in Poland never once deemed it necessary to publicly insist otherwise.[8] Over the previous year, many of them had, in fact, wondered aloud whether the term "fascist" best described the aims of their movement. They were far from alone. As the 1920s progressed, political activists across Europe's fledgling parliamentary democracies increasingly turned to Fascist Italy for inspiration to restore order, reinvigorate their economies, prevent the spread of communism, and create a mobilized community of loyal followers. Like others on the European Right, Betar's leaders searched Mussolini's political program for solutions to the challenges they sought to overcome.

Their conversations about fascism took on an added urgency once they began to prepare the programming guidelines for Betar. Seeking to convince Polish Jewish youth and their parents that their movement offered the purest expression of "authentic" Zionist and Jewish values, Betar's leaders designed an array of myths and rituals linking the group to Judaism, ancient Jewish history, and the Zionist movement's founders. Although these projects provided an opportunity for Betar's leaders to articulate their attitudes toward Jewish history and tradition, they provided no less fertile ground for them to explore the extent to which they would embrace the beliefs and behaviors associated with the European radical Right, from the celebration of militarism and glorification of violence to the suppression of political dissent.

Betar's struggle to position itself on interwar Europe's political spectrum was far from unique. Most who flirted with fascism, and many of those who claimed to be its most steadfast proponents, were unsure about what it actually meant to be fascist. Was it a style of political behavior, a set of slogans, or a systematic worldview? What distinguished Fascist Italy from the authoritarian regimes cropping up across east-central Europe? What was more important: the proclamations of Italy's Fascists said or how they behaved? Contemporary observers were keen to point out the many contradictions that characterized fascist movements across the continent. Writing in 1927, Spanish liberal philosopher José Ortega y Gasset observed, "Fascism has an enigmatic countenance because in it appears the most counterpoised contents. It asserts authoritarianism and organises rebellion.... Whichever way we approach fascism we find that it is simultaneously one thing and the contrary, it is A and not A."[9] To make matters even more complicated, Italian Fascists repurposed Europe's political vocabulary to serve their interests. As a result, conversations throughout the continent about the meaning and value of fascism provoked questions about the meaning of political terms such as citizenship and democracy.

A staggering number of scholarly studies have been devoted to defining fascism. Yet, as Robert Paxton has observed, the search for the perfect definition runs the risk of creating "a static picture of something that is better perceived in movement."[10] Rather than compare a frozen image of fascism with a rigid characterization of Betar's ideology in this period, this chapter instead seeks to capture the youth group's cultural architects in movement—constantly accepting, rejecting, and reinventing interwar Europe's political vocabulary in ways that could appeal to young Polish Jews. Jabotinsky once described the ways in which socialists stretched the meaning of the term "militarism" as "playing with Latin words."[11] This chapter focuses on Betar's own attempt to play with words such as fascism, militarism, obedience, freedom, and race at precisely the moment they sought to make their definitions for these words sound like "authentic" expressions of Judaism and Zionism.

Betar's Leaders and the Quest to Define Fascism

"It has to be said fiercely and thus succinctly: we are fascists, Jewish fascists."[12] With these words, D. Stabiecki, a Revisionist living in Rome, appealed to Polish Jews reading the movement's new journal, *Der Emes* (The Truth), to adopt the politics of Mussolini's Italy. It was November 1928; six years had passed since the March on Rome and Mussolini's appointment as Italy's prime minister. Nearly two years had passed since the country had become a one-party dictatorship. In six weeks, Jabotinsky was set to arrive in Warsaw for the ceremony at the city's Great Synagogue. Stabiecki knew that Betar representatives scattered in over ninety locations across Poland would be hard at work preparing an ideological platform to serve as the blueprint for the youth movement's activity. Taking inspiration from his surroundings, he sought to convince Betar's architects that the present-day condition of Jews worldwide provided sufficient proof that Zionists had to embrace the new way of life emerging in Italy.

It was not enough, he argued, for Revisionists to glorify Jabotinsky. Nor would it suffice for the movement to strive toward creating suitable living conditions for Jews in their "national home" and in the Diaspora. The chief mission of the Revisionist movement, he argued, was to give birth to the fascist Jew. This new Jew would "glorify physical strength" and strive toward "the will to power"—the notion that, as Nietzsche put it, "life itself is essentially a process of appropriating, injuring, overpowering the alien and the weaker . . . and at least, the very least, exploiting."[13] The fascist Jew's code of ethics would follow a simple formula: "[E]verything that serves the building of the Jewish state is good. Everything that damages the construction of the Jewish state is bad." In keeping with this code, he argued, the new fascist Jew would wage war against socialists and communists on the "Jewish street" and be "prepared to use all means to stop them, not excluding physical force." He would proudly declare that the "democratic-liberal idea is not holy to us. If the realization of democratic thinking can lead to destroying the ideal of the Jewish state, we can also be anti-democratic."[14] To maintain the purity of their ideals and reach their full national potential, Betar members should refuse to compromise with any other Zionist group. This new fascist Jew could only emerge through the ranks of a militarized youth movement that exalted physical might. This, Stabiecki insisted, was Betar's ultimate goal and would determine its organizational structure and activities.

Stabiecki's article presented a repertoire of social, political, and economic convictions that Italian Fascists consistently drew on to craft their aims and practices. The aim of the Italian Fascist regime was to build a nationalist, authoritarian state. To bring about this transformation, Italy's Fascists strove to ensure that a martial ethos of discipline, obedience, order, unity, and sacrifice pervaded the public and private lives of Italians. Italy's Fascists also believed that exalting deeds over words and emotion over reason would be the key to mobilizing the masses and encouraging them to subordinate their private interests to the imperatives of the nation. They constantly proclaimed their readiness for violent action against those they deemed as traitors, chief among them socialists, communists, and parliamentary democrats. One of the only major components of fascist ideology missing from Stabiecki's article was a demand for Zionists to venerate their leader as an infallible commander.[15] Not only were Betar members well aware of this repertoire; it was the standard they and their contemporaries used when talking about and comparing themselves to fascist movements.

Stabiecki's article also anticipated the ways in which many of Betar's leaders would come to rely on the rhetorical strategies used by Italian Fascists to justify their approach to building a Jewish state. As much as Italy's Fascist leaders issued bold, brash, and sweeping statements—Mussolini once declared that the slogan of his blackshirts, *me ne frego*, "I don't give a damn," would be the guiding motto of fascist life—they saw little need to present an ideologically seamless and coherent world to their followers and were constantly redefining their aims and practices.[16] When Italian fascists did attempt to formulate a definitive doctrine, their efforts were patchy at best and never amounted to a systematic framework for Italian Fascist political practice.[17] As a result, fascist ideology in Italy was replete with contradictions and in a state of perpetual flux. Fascist leaders often used this ideological ambiguity to their advantage.

One cannot understand Betar's flirtations with Italian fascism without appreciating how central the art of blurring the lines between liberty and subordination, democracy and dictatorship, and submission and empowerment was to the rhetorical practices of Italian Fascists. If citizenship in a liberal state meant the enjoyment of constitutional rights and duties, under fascism, it meant the subordination of one's will for the nation and publicly affirming loyalty to the regime in mass ceremonies. Mussolini frequently claimed that his system of government offered the purest form of democracy, because he best represented the people's will. By understanding and meeting their needs far better than anyone else, he claimed, he would offer an "authoritarian democracy" that empowered Italians far more than slipping a vote into a ballot box ever could.[18] Taking his cue from Mussolini, Stabiecki too made his rejection of democracy conditional on its definition and outcome.

Stabiecki's ideas, and the strategies he deployed to promote them, found ample support among Betar leaders scattered across the youth movement's ninety branches in Poland in the lead-up to January's international conference. The ground had already been prepared by the movement's Polish Jewish forerunners; some of Ha-shachar's members, who made up the bulk of Betar's new membership, had already described their movement as fascist.[19] How Betar's leaders chose to define fascism, however, depended on just how much of Fascist Italy's ideological repertoire they were willing to unreservedly and publicly embrace. Given that the Italian regime itself had avoided any definitive definition of fascism, Betar's leaders felt free to determine its scope. Some adopted the brash, defiant tone of Stabiecki's article and saw little need to mince words. One such leader was Ze'ev Lorberbojm. Using the name Ze'ev Shem Tov for his Zionist activity, he led a group of Jewish students between the ages of sixteen and nineteen in a Betar branch founded two years beforehand in Stryj, a small city in southeastern Galicia. In a September 1928 issue of *Igrot Livne Betar* (Letters to Betar Members), a magazine designed to help clarify Betar's program, Lorberbojm scolded Riga's Betar branch for its timid stance toward socialism and urged his peers to declare, in no uncertain terms, "[W]e are fascists." He succinctly defined fascism as a worldview that "does not tolerate any other idea and enslaves all the powers of its adherents to its cult."[20] To make their movement fascist, Betar leaders would have to "educate youth to exhibit . . . ceaseless discipline," so they would turn away from the "philosophizing" of left-wing Jews, embrace the cult of "the deed," and be willing to sacrifice their lives in the name of the state. This included, Lorberbojm added, a willingness to engage in physical combat with socialists. Amplifying Stabiecki's distrust of democracy, Lorberbojm insisted that above and beyond all else, Betar's structure had to leave "no suspicion of democracy"; all orders had to come from above, and under no circumstances would members "waste their days and nights in general meetings."[21]

Lorberbojm's characterization of the movement and his demands for its development clearly struck a chord with the men at the helm of Poland's Revisionist movement. Soon after the article was published, they asked him to join them in Warsaw and take over the leadership of the youth movement's branches in the city.[22] Among those to welcome Lorberbojm to the movement's new office in the Zionist Organization's seven-story building on the bustling Nalewki Street was the well-known Yiddish-language journalist

Moshe Lejzerowicz. As the coeditor of *Der Emes* alongside Reuven Feldschuh, Moshe Lejzerowicz helped determine the ideological messages distributed to nascent Revisionist branches across the country. One month following the publication of Lorberbojm's article, Lejzerowicz decided to present his own endorsement of fascism.

In contrast to Stabiecki and Lorberbojm, who reveled in the provocative nature of their calls for the subordination of the individual to the state and a brutal war against the Left, Lejzerowicz sought to dampen the violent rhetoric of Italian Fascism. He shaped his definition of fascism accordingly. Revisionists, he noted, would "agree to such a worldview" so long as "fascism is the symbol of concentrated and determined power that works not for the good of classes but for the good of the entire nation." Lejzerowicz's elusive definition alluded to authoritarian rule and opposition to socialism without describing the use of violence to suppress political dissent. No less telling was the warning he offered to his colleagues immediately after defining fascism: "Let no one talk of fascism. It will be carried out without words and without discussion; on a beautiful morning, the revolution will be complete, the strongest and most energetic will stand at the helm. . . . So friends, don't speak about it, and it will be much easier."[23]

Why would Lejzerowicz feel compelled to insist that fascism would triumph in the Zionist movement only if Revisionists avoided using the term altogether? His statement may have simply betrayed a frustration with the movement's ongoing attempts to untangle the definition of fascism. What would Italian Fascists, who repeatedly claimed that democrats and socialists were paralyzed by their obsession with words, make of the Revisionist discussions about what "fascism" meant? Lejzerowicz's article presents an even more daunting question with which historians must grapple: should one presume that many Betar leaders heeded Lejzerowicz's advice and strategically refrained from publicly declaring their views to be fascist in order for these views to be realized? When Lorberbojm, for example, coauthored a proposal for Betar's statutes in 1929, he embedded within them all the demands he had articulated the year before but dropped his explicit praise of fascism.[24] Should historians rely on Lorberbojm's previous declarations in favor of fascism as a blueprint for his statutes? And should they interpret the decision of Betar's leaders in Warsaw to place him in charge of the youth movement in the capital as an endorsement of his fascist declarations?

The case of Reuven Feldschuh, who was serving as the head commander of Betar in the fall of 1928, casts into sharp relief the challenges of using

Lejzerowicz's command as a key to understanding how Betar's early leaders envisioned their mission. Feldschuh, the hot-tempered novelist, journalist, and teacher who had crusaded against the Jewish Left in his former youth movement, Ha-shomer Ha-tahor/Ha-le'umi (The Pure/National Guard), was charged with the task of proposing an organizational structure for the Revisionist movement. In December 1927, he presented his proposal to the delegates of the second national Revisionist conference. He began by urging Revisionist leaders to turn to religious and military organizations for inspiration. Religious organizations, Feldschuh explained, skillfully mobilized and manipulated emotions, while military organizations successfully instilled discipline. Both types of organizations owed their strength to the fact that "they dictate the content [of one's life] from morning till bedtime" and "embraced the entire human being."[25] Feldschuh promoted three principles frequently associated with fascism: the dissolution of the boundaries between public and private, the necessity to dictate all the beliefs and behaviors of followers, and the requirement to mobilize the emotions of the masses. The meeting minutes indicate that his speech prompted debate among two delegates about whether their movement was fascist. Feldschuh, however, never once invoked the term during his speech. When he sent a seventeen-page instruction guide to Betar branches across the country several months later, he was similarly ambivalent in its commitment to the attitudes and behaviors promoted by Fascist Italy. On the one hand, Feldschuh embedded key features of Fascist Italy's ideological repertoire within his instructions. The ideal Betar member, he wrote, was a "master of national discipline unconditionally obeying their commander."[26] The proposed structure of the organization, which divided its young members into battalions with commanders, clearly sought to enforce the military culture of discipline within the movement. He repeatedly reminded Betar members of their obligation to celebrate physical strength, reject the class conflict promoted by socialists and communists, and offer their lives to the nation.

Yet Feldschuh's guidelines for the cultural education of the youth movement's members defy easy ideological categorization. Toward the end of his handbook for Betar members, he threw together a haphazard list of books spanning across centuries and continents. His wide-ranging reading guide for the history of Jews and the Zionist movement drew from a common stock of texts used by all Zionist youth movements in Poland. Among Suskin and Holitscher's geography guides to "Jewish" Palestine, as well as Bialik and Ravnitzky's collection of Jewish "folk legends" culled from rabbinic literature, the reader could even find publications by the socialist Ha-shomer Ha-tsa'ir.

Feldschuh's reading list of European social theory, including Darwin, Freud, and Krafft-Ebbing, seems far more concerned with providing an expansive overview of "Western thought" than a rigid ideological template for viewing the world. To help prepare Betar leaders to teach their followers, Feldschuh suggested the works of Ellen Key, Janusz Korczak, and other luminaries of the progressive education movement. These thinkers rejected obedience and discipline as the foundation of effective teaching and encouraged teachers to cultivate a sense of autonomy among their young disciples. To prepare Betar's instructors to teach scouting and paramilitary training, Feldschuh suggested Polish scouting textbooks as well as the English Boy Scouts' textbook in Polish translation. No less important were the references missing from this bibliography: he made no mention of the Opera Nazionale Balilla, Italy's official Fascist youth movement, established in 1926.

What of war and violence? Across Europe, when opponents and supporters of Fascist Italy watched the rise of Mussolini to power, they set their focus on his squadristi's violent activities, from the burning of the headquarters of socialist and Catholic organizations to the intimidation, beating, and murder of their opponents. Even after these outbreaks of violence subsided, once Mussolini declared one-party rule in the fall of 1926, contemporary observers still focused on instances in which the regime's propagandists celebrated violence against the nation's enemies as a cleansing, cathartic, and even pleasurable experience. In addition to reporting instances of state-sanctioned violence in Fascist Italy, the Polish Jewish press also painstakingly documented the increasing frequency with which anti-Semitic nationalists in Poland, Romania, and Hungary claimed they were fascists.[27] This trend had become so popular that Mussolini himself felt compelled to respond. At a press conference in November 1927, the Duce quipped that "fascism is not for export," branded anti-Semites as the vestiges of a barbaric past, and insisted that fascism's call for the unity of citizens was "the antithesis of antisemitism."[28] Many of Betar's leaders understood that any public declaration from the Revisionists in favor of fascism would provide fodder for their opponents to link them to antisemitic nationalists across Europe. If they were to flirt with fascism, they would have to dwell at length on how their movement would imagine the role of violence in bringing about their goals.

If anything, Feldschuh's handbook reveals the tremendous caution with which the Betar leader approached the question of violence. The booklet made clear that the primary task of the youth movement's members was to prepare for armed conflict. Once Betar members reached the age of sixteen and advanced to the highest level of the youth movement, they were expected to spend at least three months receiving intensive military training, including the use of firearms. Feldschuh constantly reiterated Betar's mission to fight for the Jewish nation. The handbook, however, discreetly avoided mentioning toward whom Betar's members would be aiming their rifles. If there was any enemy that materialized in the booklet, it was the Jewish Left. When Feldschuh called for a war against socialists and communists, the battles he described were ideological, not physical.

If the Left barely made an appearance in Feldschuh's descriptions of conflict, Palestinian Arabs were altogether absent. Despite the claim of Revisionists that they were the only Zionists to confront the Arab-Jewish conflict in Palestine head on, early Betar leaders in Poland, like others at the helm of Zionist movements of every variety, were often silent when it came to describing what physical confrontation between Jews and Palestine's Arab population would actually look like. Much like other Zionists in Poland and elsewhere, the Revisionist writers for *Der Emes* promised that their intentions were neither to displace Arabs from their homes nor to expel them from the country. Were it not for Arab opposition to a Jewish state, they argued, the Zionist project would proceed peacefully and provide tremendous benefit to the local Muslim and Christian population.[29] As if to drive this point home, Feldschuh assured Betar's members in the introduction to his handbook that the youth movement's program of paramilitary training was "far from the concept of [the] militarism of negative and wild types."[30] From that point forward in his book, the term "militarism" is nowhere to be found. In its place, Feldschuh used the term "legionism," a reference to Jabotinsky's famed Jewish Legion of the First World War. By encouraging Betar's members to associate the movement's military training exclusively with the Zionist project, Feldschuh hoped to divert attention away from the parallels between their paramilitary training program and those of anti-Semitic movements across Europe.

Jabotinsky and Fascism

Feldschuh's handbook captures the rugged terrain of the ideological landscape navigated by Betar's leaders in their quest to define their relationship to fascism. This terrain awaited Jabotinsky on his arrival to Warsaw on New Year's Day, 1929. Prior to this point, he had been entirely absent from the conversations about fascism taking place among Betar leaders in Poland and Latvia. In the year that had passed since his previous visit to Warsaw, he had decided to move to Palestine to shore up support for the Revisionist movement, arriving to Jerusalem in the fall of 1928. Although he had confessed to a Revisionist activist in Berlin that he felt more in exile in Jerusalem than in Paris, his return to Europe for the Warsaw gathering brought him little relief. With his train from Vienna delayed, he missed the spectacle of thousands of Betar members parading through the streets of Warsaw. Once he finally arrived, most of his trip was spent holed up with about twenty Betar leaders in the office of the Revisionist movement. He was bitterly disappointed by what unfolded. Despite all the ink poured by Betar's leaders in their journals to prepare for the conference, those who had gathered had failed to forge a comprehensive agreement about the movement's ideology and structure. All Jabotinsky could report to a member of the Revisionist Executive in London the following week was that the "organization of the conference in Warsaw was terrible; we sat in dirt and in the cold... but it [the conference] passed peacefully."[31] Jabotinsky had expected conflict for good reason. The meeting was the first time profascist Betar leaders in Poland, such as Lorberbojm, met with Riga's Betar leaders, some of whom had expressed alarm concerning the movement's increasingly right-wing profile. Unable to find common ideological ground, the only decision they could reach was that each national branch of Betar would continue its own distinctive "cultural-ideological" work.[32]

Although we have no record of Jabotinsky's interventions during the meeting, his public lecture at the Kamińska Theater on Warsaw's Obożna Street, on which he would base two articles published at the end of the month in *Haynt*, made clear that he too was preoccupied with how best to define the youth movement's relationship to the European Right. Rather than elaborate on an ideological program for Betar, he felt his most urgent task was to defend Betar's members from accusations that their embrace of militarism meant that they were importing the very beliefs and practices that fueled anti-Semitic violence in Europe. In contrast to Feldschuh's attempt to purge "militarism" from the youth movement's lexicon, Jabotinsky argued that Jews should embrace the term. Shifting the focus of the public from armed conflict to military training, he argued that militarism instilled good manners, discipline, and national pride among young Jews.[33] He also addressed concerns emanating from those within the Revisionist movement's adult membership who feared that Betar's growth threatened Revisionism's democratic character. Writing in *Rassvet*, Jabotinsky urged them to exercise restraint and patience when confronted with beliefs and behaviors within the youth movement that radically challenged their own political worldviews. As if to reassert his own persona as a champion of democracy, he told them that their loyalty to Betar youth was not the "hackneyed loyalty" demanded by Chaim Weizmann's "Fascist Zionism," whose acolytes blindly followed the Zionist Organization's leader no matter the consequence.[34] Two years beforehand, Jabotinsky had likened Weizmann's leadership style to Mussolini's and critiqued Mussolini's cult of leadership. "Buffaloes," he quipped, "follow a leader. Real men have no 'leaders.'"[35]

Jabotinsky may have been able to temporarily allay the concerns of his *Rassvet* readers. Yet, his brief public relations campaign for Betar, including his critique of fascism's cult of leadership, belied a more complicated relationship to Fascist politics. Ironically, none other than Chaim Weizmann first witnessed Jabotinsky's ambivalence toward fascism. Prior to Jabotinsky's split with the Zionist Organization, he told Weizmann during a trip to Italy in 1922 that Zionists would be able to find a "common language" with several Italian Fascist leaders.[36] Perhaps bearing in mind his comments to Weizmann, he wrote to Mussolini that very same day and explained Zionist behavior in the following way: "If you want to understand our level of vitality, please study your own fascists and add only some tragedy, some tenacity—perhaps more experience."[37]

Even if Jabotinsky's comments were designed to impress Mussolini, rather than accurately describe the Zionist movement, many of his acolytes took seriously the claim that fascism and Zionism had much in common. Since 1927, Revisionist activists in Italy and Palestine had insisted to Jabotinsky that Fascist Italy had much to teach the Zionist movement, from its relationship to religious authorities to its construction of a leadership cult for Mussolini.[38] Among them was Abba Achimeir. Born and raised in Dolgi, a village near the city of Bobruisk, he had spent three years in Ottoman Palestine attending high school but returned to Russia following the outbreak of World War One. In contrast to his brother, who died fighting in the Red Army, Abba opposed communism and the Bolshevik Revolution. His doctoral dissertation, completed at the University of Vienna in 1924, examined the reactions of the Russian intelligentsia to Oswald Spengler's *The Decline of the West*, a text made famous for its scathing critique of democracy and its prediction that an age of dictatorship was imminent. Upon arriving in Mandate Palestine, he played an active role in the Labor Zionist movement, publishing articles regularly in party newspapers. His increasing critiques of Labor Zionism ultimately led to his defection in 1928 to the Revisionist movement, where he injected a fiery brand of revolutionary rhetoric into its publications and quickly became popular among Revisionist youth. In his first letter to Jabotinsky, Achimeir pleaded,

"Sir, why do you consult with us so excessively? Command us more. We are obliged to obey you." The crucial task of the Revisionist movement, he wrote, was to conquer youth by following the examples set by regimes such as Mussolini's Italy, Ataturk's Turkey, and Piłsudski's Poland.[39] Upon moving to Jerusalem in October 1928, Jabotinsky joined the editorial board of the Hebrew daily *Doar Hayom*, which published Achimeir's column, "From the Notebook of a Fascist." One month later, in a letter to Meir Grossman, who spearheaded the Revisionist movement's executive leadership in London, Jabotinsky remarked that Achimeir was "talented but too much a fascist."[40]

If Achimeir was "too much" a fascist, what degree of fascism would be acceptable to Jabotinsky? He had balked at Achimeir's reference to Mussolini's cult of leadership; but what of the young Revisionist's references to Ataturk and Piłsudski? Although most scholars would not describe either Ataturk or Piłsudski as fascist, many political observers of the era did not fuss over distinguishing between authoritarianism and fascism. When addressing Betar members in Poland, the youth movement's leaders mentioned Mussolini and Piłsudski in the same breath.[41] Jabotinsky had already begun to voice support of some of the key political attitudes and behaviors associated with Piłsudski's Sanacja, including its opposition to socialism, its call for citizens to submit their individual interests to the needs of the nation, and its demand for a military ethos of discipline and unity to pervade national life. If the boundaries separating Piłsudski's policies from those of Mussolini were unclear to Revisionist activists like Achimeir, where would Jabotinsky draw the line?

The elusive nature of fascist ideology gave ample room for Jabotinsky to maneuver as he began to publicly express ambivalence about the value of fascism. In a 1929 interview in Lwów, for example, he confirmed his commitment to democratic values but likened democracy to a sinking ship. When asked to elaborate on the nature of fascism, he dodged the question of whether it provided the most effective form of government. Further pressed to describe the ideology, he limited his critique of fascism to the leadership cult of Mussolini; fascism's crucial flaw, he explained, was that the death of a brilliant political leader could leave the nation in the hands of a blundering successor.[42] The statement was hardly a comprehensive critique of Mussolini's Italy and may have elliptically suggested that there was much to admire in the Italian dictator's leadership. In the year that followed, cracks began to appear in Jabotinsky's previously stern conviction that Fascist Italy could not provide models of leadership. To an admirer in the summer of 1930, he tempered his declaration that "the cult of the Duce awakens disgust in me" by noting, "Fascism has many good ideas." On further reflection, he continued, there were several points in the development of the Revisionist movement at which he should have exerted greater power over his colleagues.[43]

Jabotinsky increasingly paid heed to his younger followers when they presented him with fascism's "good ideas." Among these followers was Haim Vardi, a Polish Jew studying at the University of Rome. Jabotinsky claimed that Vardi, an admirer of Italian fascism, taught him the value of describing Jews as a race in order to mobilize support.[44] Like the term "fascism," the meaning and usage of the term "race" were ambiguous. From the mid-nineteenth century, many ethnic nationalists across Europe had used racial language to argue that members of their nation shared biologically determined characteristics and abilities that rendered them physically, psychologically, and morally superior to their adversaries, who were branded racial degenerates. The foremost proponents of modern antisemitism readily drew on the language of "racial science" to denigrate Jews by attributing to them negative characteristics deemed biologically determined and immutable. Despite the links between racial politics and antisemitic nationalism, many Jewish thinkers and political activists of the era readily adopted the language of racial science to refute antisemitism and to promote their visions for Jewish life.[45] For a more inclusive definition of race, Jews in interwar Europe could look to Italian Fascists, where "racial thinking" was far from systematic. While some Italian Fascist thinkers imagined the "Italian race" in biological terms, others described it as an immutable spiritual identity based on shared history and traditions.[46]

Drawing inspiration from these ideas, Jabotinsky used *Doar Hayom* as a platform to argue that Zionists constituted a special type of "spiritual race," in whose veins ran a thirst for adventure, an inclination for change, and the ability to turn words into deeds. Aware that his readers might bristle at the notion that a community's psychological traits ran like blood through their veins—an idea more often invoked by ethno-nationalist movements than by Italian Fascists—Jabotinsky immediately added, "I know that this is an exaggeration: a deliberate one, in order to emphasize the idea; but the core of the exaggeration is true."[47] His caveat was in some ways a confession concerning his decision to use the term "race"; it was precisely its ability to provoke his audience that attracted him to the term in the first place. Not long after the article's publication in the spring of 1929, his calls for a new "Hebrew race" became a core component of Betar's slogans.

As Jabotinsky watched the rising success of right-wing politics in Italy with curiosity and some admiration, he anxiously noted the growing fortunes of the Left in Palestine. During his months in Jerusalem, he learned firsthand of the vast power socialist Zionists were gathering among Mandate Palestine's Jews. Labor Zionists boasted a membership of tens of thousands in Palestine as well as a powerful institutional infrastructure. Founded in 1920, the General Federation of Laborers in the Land of Israel (Histadrut Ha-klalit shel Ha-ovdim Be'eretz Yisra'el) provided Jewish newcomers to Palestine with an array of social services, including access to employment, medical help, cultural centers, schools, and soup kitchens. By 1927, the Histadrut counted twenty-five thousand members, representing roughly three-quarters of Palestine's Jewish workforce. It had become the largest and strongest institution for absorbing Jewish immigrants in Palestine. At its helm was the forty-two-year-old David Ben-Gurion, whose skill as a shrewd political organizer and coalition builder had made him the Yishuv's most powerful Labor Zionist.[48] As Jabotinsky bemoaned the paltry number of Revisionist supporters in Mandate Palestine, he realized that the hegemony of Labor Zionists within the Zionist movement appeared to many if not most Zionists to be a fait accompli.

It was against this backdrop that Jabotinsky drew even closer to the Far Right by envisioning a war against the Jewish Left as a key feature of his movement. Between April and August 1929, he exchanged a series of letters with some of his closest political collaborators in which he argued that confrontation with Labor Zionists was inevitable. By that point, skirmishes between Revisionist and Labor Zionist workers competing for the same jobs had broken out in Palestine. In one such letter to Joseph Schechtman, a founding member of the Revisionist movement and an editor of *Rassvet*, Jabotinsky insisted that the Zionist Left had initiated the physical confrontations between Revisionist and socialist workers: "I don't understand why you are suppressing from your consciousness the fact that they are our enemies. They hate everything that is ours . . . among them, the question is clear: the youth will either be ours or theirs. The ideological gap between us is very deep. There is also an ethical gap, and this incenses them above all else. This hostility is organic and is not dependent upon our will—there is nothing to do."[49] Jabotinsky also proposed launching a worldwide publicity campaign against communism. One of the chief aims of the Revisionist movement, he explained, would be to expose "the red flag with its true symbol: gallows and a noose."[50]

At the same time as Jabotinsky began to allude to the inevitability and necessity of conflict with the Zionist Left, he also began to describe armed battle with Palestine's Arab population in similar terms. Here, too, his time in Mandate Palestine proved decisive in prompting a shift in tactics. As the editor of *Doar Hayom*, Jabotinsky took special interest in reporting the growing conflict between Jerusalem's Muslims and Jews over the Western Wall, which stood at the base of the city's Temple Mount, known by Muslims as Haram esh-Sharif, the Noble Sanctuary. In an effort to mobilize popular support against Zionism, the city's Muslim religious authorities claimed that Jews sought to take over and desecrate the Haram esh-Sharif and its shrines, the Dome of the Rock and the al-Aqsa Mosque. Incensed by repeated efforts of Muslims to disrupt Jewish prayer at the Western Wall, Jabotinsky urged the Yishuv's Jews to take action. In mid-August 1929, hundreds of Jews, among them Betar members, staged a demonstration at the Western Wall. During the protest, some of its participants symbolically laid claim to the prayer site by raising the Zionist flag in full view of both British and Muslim onlookers. Several days later, crowds of Muslims, armed with sticks, knives, and guns, descended on Jewish neighborhoods, destroying property and killing Jewish civilians. Riots spread throughout Mandate Palestine. The massacres of Jewish men, women, and children in Hebron and Safed horrified the Yishuv's Jewish community. As the British government would later admit, the inadequacy of British defense forces, who struggled for days to gain control of the situation, played no small role in the escalating violence.[51] By the time the riots subsided, 133 Jews had been killed by Muslim rioters. Muslim casualties, totaling 116, were mostly attributed to their confrontations with British military personnel. Several of the Palestinian Arab casualties were lynched by Jews; some Jews targeted in the riots were saved by their Muslim neighbors.[52]

Jabotinsky was in Europe for the World Zionist Congress when the riots broke out. Even before they had subsided, he appealed to his political colleagues to use the riots to mobilize more support for the Revisionist movement. In one such letter, he assured one Revisionist, "[w]ith the exception of the massacre of yeshiva students in Hebron, the number of sacrifices is small, despite the complete absence of the [British] army. The [notion of] 'settlements burning' is also nonsense—one needs thousands of tins of kerosene in order to burn settlements, in which even the floors are built of stone. All of this will be useful to us from a political point of view, so relax; but to the outside, we need to show shock."[53] Now that his forecast of violent clashes between Palestine's Jewish and Arab population appeared to have been realized, the political tides, he reasoned, would turn in their favor. In the coming weeks, he spearheaded a vigorous publicity campaign. Writing article after article for Jewish newspapers worldwide, as well as letters to the editor in British newspapers, he demanded that the Western Wall and its environs become the exclusive prayer site of Jews, and that the British government dismiss any officials in Palestine who opposed mass Jewish immigration.[54] Although Jabotinsky was well aware that these demands would never be met, he knew that they made for superb political theater. One demand, however, did seem possible to realize: the creation of Jewish armed units to protect the Yishuv. He urged members of the Revisionist Executive to pour their efforts into drafting a proposal to this end.[55] He hoped to make his case to the British Commission of Inquiry, which arrived in Palestine in late October to determine the cause of the riots.

Although Jabotinsky returned to Palestine in early December with the intention of making his case to the commission, he was prevented from doing so by the Zionist Executive and the commission's officials. For weeks, voices from within the Arab and Labor Zionist press blamed Jabotinsky's *Doar Hayom* for inciting young Jews to protest at the Western Wall. Both the Zionist Executive and British officials feared that Jabotinsky's presence at the inquiry would only make matters worse. Two days before his departure to Europe, an infuriated Jabotinsky decided to plead his case concerning the future of Arab-Jewish relations before six thousand Jews at a rally in Tel Aviv.

Jabotinsky's speech marked a decisive departure from "On the Iron Wall," his most famous declaration on Arab-Jewish relations, published in November 1923. In the article, Jabotinsky had forcefully argued that the creation of a Jewish state would be impossible without the presence of a military force to protect Jews from the attacks of Palestine's Arab inhabitants. Although the "iron wall" was swiftly condemned by his former colleagues in the Zionist Organization as the harangue of a belligerent militarist, the article noticeably displayed caution and restraint in its depiction of Arab-Jewish confrontation. Although he insisted on the *presence* of a military force protecting Zionist interests, he had carefully avoided describing military *engagement* with Arabs as inevitable. Instead, he had insisted that the mere presence of Jewish military units would act as a deterrence force, preventing, rather than fomenting, violence. The very power of the iron wall metaphor rested in its ability to depict a strong but static force, whose mere presence would provide protection. The article had even gone so far as to suggest that this iron wall would inspire the rise of Arab moderates, who would "honestly bargain" with Zionists about "practical issues." Zionists, Jabotinsky predicted, would guarantee equal rights to Arabs, and "the two peoples" would "live side by side peacefully and in an orderly fashion."[56]

If *Doar Hayom*'s account of Jabotinsky's speech in 1929 is any indication, he disposed of these predictions while standing before his audience of six thousand in Tel Aviv. He catalogued an extensive list of Zionist efforts to reach an agreement with Palestine's Arab population, declaring each and every one of them doomed to failure. Integration, let alone meaningful social interaction between Jews and Arabs, was impossible, because they were from "two different worlds, two different eras." Jabotinsky saw only one way out. Calling for "harsh and aggressive cures," he insisted that "there is no small and temporary cure for [the cause of] Zionism, since there is no shortcut or magic wand, *there is only the path of war* for Zionism to the fullest extent."[57] He offered no promises to uphold the principle of equal rights for Arabs, nor did he affirm, as he had in "On the Iron Wall," that the Zionist movement would never attempt "driving out or oppressing [them]."[58] Instead, Jabotinsky reminded his readers that toward the end of the First World War, Britain's assistant secretary of state for foreign affairs Robert Cecil had proclaimed, "Armenia—for the Armenians, Arabia—for the Arabs and the Land of Israel—for the Jews."[59]

Jabotinsky's speech had grave implications for his political career. British officials interpreted his reference to Cecil's speech as proof that he had called for Palestine to be entirely Jewish—a claim Jabotinsky later vehemently denied.[60] Several months following Jabotinsky's departure from Palestine, the British government banned his return, citing his speech as proof of the danger he posed to Mandate Palestine. For the rest of his political career, Jabotinsky would have to fend off claims that he could not serve as a Zionist figurehead because of his inability to understand the political reality on the ground in Palestine.

The summer riots of 1929 also proved pivotal for Betar. Heeding Jabotinsky's advice, the youth movement's leaders launched a recruitment campaign, stressing that Betar was the only Zionist youth movement that had done all it could to prepare its members for the violence of 1929. In the months that followed, thousands of Jewish youth across Poland poured into the movement. By the following summer, Revisionist internal reports estimated that Betar's membership in Poland had nearly tripled, reaching three hundred branches and twelve thousand members.[61] The riots were also envisioned by some of Betar's leaders as a *deux ex machina* that could rescue them from the ideological morass they had waded into when wrestling with whether to adopt fascist values. Having arrived to Warsaw in January 1929 to spearhead Betar's growth in Poland, Aharon Propes noted in a youth movement publication that one of the consequences of the riots was that "today we can speak openly, without being afraid of being condemned as militarists and fascists."[62]

Propes understood, however, that the riots of 1929 could only go so far to mobilize the support of the Polish Jewish public. Traveling across the country in the winter, he had not only taken note of Poland's vastly diverse Jewish communities, but had also observed firsthand the strength of traditional Jewish life. To gain the support of Jewish communities across Poland, Betar would have to convince its recruits and their parents that the elements of the youth movement's platform that echoed the values of Europe's radical Right were not simply temporary responses to the crisis in Palestine but were timeless and instinctive convictions held by every Jew, past and present, who longed for the creation of a Jewish state. In other words, the movement's culture would have to accomplish two tasks: it would have to make Betar's ideals look and sound Zionist, and it would have to prove that these ideals were embedded in the Jewish religious tradition. To do so, Propes called on Betar's cultural architects to turn to the legacy of their youth movement's namesake, Joseph Trumpeldor, to forge a youth movement culture that would embody Jewish, Zionist, and radical right-wing values at one and the same time.

Making Radical Right-Wing Values Zionist? The Legend of Joseph Trumpeldor and *Tel Hai*

At the end of February 1929, Aharon Propes mailed out his first command to Betar branches across the country. Their task, he wrote, was to stage a public commemoration of Joseph Trumpeldor's death.[63] For one złoty, they could purchase Propes's very own biography of the famed Jewish soldier, tailored specifically for Poland's Betar members, and perform its content at memorial services in Trumpeldor's honor. Ten months later, Betar members throughout Poland received the first copy of Betar's national journal. Its name, *Tel Hai*, paid homage to the Jewish settlement in the northern frontier of Galilee where Trumpeldor, along with seven others, was killed in 1920 in clashes with roaming Arab militias. *Tel Hai*'s editor explained the significance of the site of Trumpeldor's death for Betar's publicity campaigns: "Tel Hai is a symbol that creates the very content of the movement's identity.... [It] provides a satisfactory answer to the claim that 'there is no meaning in their death just as there is no meaning in their lives.'"[64] The staging of Trumpeldor memorial events, in other words, was meant to provide the Jewish public in cities and market towns scattered across central and eastern Poland with a clear performance of the aims of the Betar movement, as well as its value for the Jewish public. Betar's members were not only expected to pay homage to Trumpeldor at public events. Within the movement's ranks, Betar members were also expected to greet and bid farewell to one another with the phrase "Tel Hai," and to hang Trumpeldor's supposed last words, "It is good to die for one's country," on the walls of their clubs.[65] His death was meant to provide the framework for any conversation or activity that would ensue within the movement.

What was it about Trumpeldor that led Betar leaders to tell their followers to use his life and death as a compass for their own attitudes and behaviors? He was a natural choice for a Zionist movement seeking to expand its social base. By the time Betar arrived on the scene in Poland, Trumpeldor had long been celebrated by Zionist youth movements across the political spectrum. He had gained fame in the Zionist world for his military exploits: first in Russia, where he had lost his right arm during the Russo-Japanese War (1904–1905), and later as a founding member of the Jewish Legion. It was Trumpeldor's death while defending Tel Hai, however, that made him a cult figure for Zionist youth movements. By the mid-1920s, Zionist youth groups across Palestine joined together in pilgrimage to his gravesite. Before his death, Trumpeldor himself had sought to unify competing Zionist factions. As one of the founders of the He-Halutz movement, he aspired to create an organization independent of Zionist political parties that could serve all Jewish youth seeking agricultural training to prepare them for immigration to Palestine.

Betar's leaders hoped that Trumpeldor's widespread popularity among Jewish youth would entice them to take an immediate interest in Revisionist Zionism. Already considered an advocate of coalition politics, he could prove useful to Betar as a symbol of their oft-repeated calls for national unity. Trumpeldor also gave the movement an unmistakable Zionist imprimatur; his name alone would help ward off claims that Betar was a foreign intruder on the "Jewish street." Trumpeldor's popularity among Polish Jewish youth would prove especially useful to Jabotinsky. Having worked closely with Trumpeldor to create the Jewish Legion, Jabotinsky could claim that the man so beloved by Zionist youth movements across the political spectrum would undoubtedly have approved of his call to provide military training to Jewish youth.

Betar's use of Trumpeldor as its hero, however, was not without its complications. In 1920, the British had ceded the northern Galilee to the French, whose forces were already stretched thin trying to suppress a revolt in northern Syria. Taking stock of the situation, Jabotinsky believed that the northern Galilee's Jewish settlements would be unable to resist attacks by Arab militias. He called for Jews living in the scattered settlements of the region, including in Tel Hai, to immediately evacuate the area. Trumpeldor rejected Jabotinsky's advice. Labor Zionist leaders would later recall this incident to prove that Jabotinsky and Trumpeldor were adversaries, and that Jabotinsky was a hypocrite who displayed cowardice instead of courage when the need for self-defense arose.

Most problematic to Betar was that Trumpeldor had been a socialist from the beginning of his Zionist activity until his death. Although he had called for his organization He-Halutz to value Zionists who were not members of the working class, he called for Jewish society in Palestine to be modeled on socialist principles.[66] In 1928, He-Halutz came under the direct control of the Labor Zionist organization Ha-Kibbutz Ha-me'uhad (the United Kibbutz) in Palestine. Two years later, He-Halutz took the socialist Zionist youth groups Ha-shomer Ha-tsa'ir and Gordonia under its wing. By that point, many considered the concept of the *halutz*, the pioneer, to be the exclusive domain of the Zionist Left, for whom the term denoted a type of Jew as well as a formula for the success of the Zionist project. The ideal of the halutz embodied the Labor Zionist belief that the Zionist project would succeed only if Jews engaged in manual and agricultural labor to create a socialist society in Palestine. Trumpeldor more than once insisted that the Jewish homeland would be built first and foremost by Jewish workers.[67] His program for He-Halutz also explicitly stated that Jewish self-defense units would have to be made up of socialists to prevent a "militarist" ethos from spreading among Zionists.[68]

How could Revisionist youth movement leaders, who envisioned wars against socialists and against Palestine's Arab population as crucial features of their program, use Trumpeldor as their hero and claim to be the pioneers he had called for? To make Trumpeldor the ideal figure of the Zionist Right, Betar's leaders would need to recast his life, his death, and his vision of the ideal pioneer. In Yael Zerubavel's study of collective memory and the formation of Israeli national identity, she has shown how Tel Hai became a contested site of memory, used by Revisionists and Labor Zionists alike to highlight their ideological differences concerning the role of armed conflict in the Zionist project.[69] For Betar's cultural architects, the lessons of Tel Hai extended far beyond these debates. Talking about Trumpeldor and Tel Hai also became a way for Betar's leaders to determine their relationship to Europe's radical Right. As they set out to reinvent Trumpeldor, they sought to determine which right-wing values the movement's leaders could immediately and unequivocally declare to be features of their movement and which ones needed to be accompanied by qualifications.

The first major task Betar's leaders undertook in reinventing Trumpeldor was to map their youth movement's attitudes toward the militarized, authoritarian society promoted by Fascist Italy and its admirers. Jabotinsky frequently insisted that individual liberty be a cornerstone of the future Jewish state, and he often criticized governments that strove to stifle individual creativity and self-expression. Simultaneously, however, he demanded that Betar's members relinquish their personal needs and desires to lead lives of obedience, discipline, and sacrifice in the name of the nation. Jabotinsky's depiction of Trumpeldor played a critical role in trying to reconcile these two potentially contradictory ideals. Rather than cite Trumpeldor's He-Halutz writings, which included several potentially useful passages describing the need for the new pioneer to obey the commands of the organization, Jabotinsky chose instead to reconstruct—and perhaps invent—a conversation they had in 1916. In his 1928 book-length account of the Jewish Legion, Jabotinsky recalled how Trumpeldor had envisioned the ideal pioneer to be "a piece of iron without a crystallized form. Iron, from which everything which the national machine requires should be made." According to Jabotinsky, Trumpeldor imagined the ideal Zionist pioneer declaring, "I have no feelings, no psychology, no name of my own. I am a servant of Zion."[70] Jabotinsky elaborated on the meaning of his exchange with Trumpeldor in an afterword to the He-Halutz program, which had been reprinted by Betar that same year. "A pioneer," Jabotinsky explained, "is no more than the full, pure realization of the concept of service and national sacrifice, of the abnegation [*hitbatlut*] of the individual on society's altar—don't forget this."[71] While this explanation echoed Jabotinsky's depiction of his conversation with Trumpeldor in 1916, it also neutralized passages from Trumpeldor's "He-Halutz" program that had appeared several pages earlier. In these passages, Trumpeldor dismissed the concept of "iron discipline" and warned that the desire to entirely relinquish one's free will and suffer for the nation was the stuff of elitist romantics rather than socialist workers.[72] Not surprisingly, most of Betar's leaders avoided these passages and others penned by their iconic hero, choosing instead to invoke Jabotinsky's account of Trumpeldor's vision for the pioneer.

Jabotinsky's retelling served several functions. First, by claiming that Trumpeldor described the pioneer as "iron without a crystallized form," Jabotinsky created a rhetorical bridge between Trumpeldor's concept of pioneering and his own calls for Zionists to build an "iron wall" of military force. Revisionist leaders could thus instruct potential youth movement recruits that Betar's program for a militarized society was not merely a program of self-defense to be implemented in times of war but a guide to be followed for everyday life in Mandate Palestine. Second, by placing on Trumpeldor's lips the oft-repeated calls of Europe's Right for obedience, discipline, and self-abnegation, Jabotinsky implied that the Revisionist movement's vision of a mobilized, militarized society was an expression of Trumpeldor's core values and, by extension, the values of Jewish youth who revered him. No less significant was Jabotinsky's suggestion that Trumpeldor imagined Jewish youth joining He-Halutz of their own free will, embracing their role as obedient servants to the Zionist project. Jabotinsky would later repeat this point in an article entitled "On Militarism," in which he insisted that Betar did not compel Jewish youth to lead militarized lives and would never use intimidation or force to coerce its young recruits to follow orders.[73] Perhaps most important was the fact that Jabotinsky inserted himself into the narrative of He-Halutz's ideological formation. In the scene staged by Jabotinsky, he was both Trumpeldor's confidant and successor. With Trumpeldor's death, Jabotinsky was entrusted to preserve the vision of his fallen comrade and duty-bound to mold Jewish youth in his friend's image.

Betar leaders in Poland elaborated on and embellished Jabotinsky's reimagining of the halutz as a soldier and Mandate Palestine's Jewish community as a militarized society. Hen-Melekh Merchavia, a twenty-nine-year-old Betar leader from the northern industrial city of Białystok, published a ninety-page booklet in 1930 that used the image of the halutz to provide a Revisionist roadmap for the Yishuv's construction. Here, the halutz was cast as a soldier in a militarized, mobilized society in which every act, from buying food to working the land, was an act of war. The pioneer needed to behave "like a soldier on the front, working zealously, always under the command of the ... state [and] its leadership, always a master of complete and full discipline."[74] In the ideal pioneer society, Merchavia continued, "everything will be a front, there will be no private or public space, every place will be a place to conquer, a frontline, every citizen a defender, a builder, a settler."[75] In this perpetual state of crisis, the citizen would have not rights but obligations. By insisting that Zionism's success depended on envisioning the daily construction of Palestine as an act of war, and by painting the Yishuv's mobilized society as one built on discipline, obedience, and zealousness, Merchavia's visions of the pioneer were in line with the thinking of many Italian Fascist ideologues. "The whole country," he wrote in the first issue of Betar's journal, "is Tel Hai: every day in the land is ... a day of war."[76]

The values articulated by Merchavia found expression in Propes's twenty-five-page guide to running a Betar branch, distributed in the winter of 1929. Much like the guidebooks of other Zionist youth movements, Propes's offered an itinerary for lessons in Hebrew, Jewish history, and the geography of Palestine. The format for these interactions, however, was decidedly different from that of other Zionist youth movements in Poland. Although Propes encouraged Betar members to view their club as a second home, he insisted that military discipline inform each and every interaction, whether among the youngest group of Betar members, aged ten to fourteen, or among the oldest group, aged eighteen and above. Betar's leaders would be known as "commanding officers" (*mefakdim*); their followers were to obey their every order and view their commands as holy. The lion's share of the guide provided detailed instructions for how to deliver commands and maintain strict discipline. General meetings would consist of the officer reading out his commands; members could only intervene with permission and had to do so while standing at attention. Blurring the lines between obedience and freedom, Propes justified the intricate authoritarian choreography of his guide by noting, "The truly free society can only exist when its members are educated to be disciplined."[77] Instructing Betar members to open and close every interaction with the words "Tel Hai," Propes reminded them that their obedience and discipline honored the memory of Joseph Trumpeldor.

In addition to proving that Trumpeldor called for a militarized Jewish society, Betar's ideologues set out to convince their followers that he was a fierce opponent of socialism. To make Trumpeldor an adversary of the Left, Betar leaders had to not only expunge Trumpeldor's socialist identity from the historical record but also prove that had he lived, he would have been a stark opponent of Labor Zionism. Betar leaders adopted several strategies to transform Trumpeldor's politics. First, they produced biographical accounts of his life that erased any mention of his commitment to socialism. Published in 1930, the closest Propes's biography came to describing Trumpeldor's leftist leanings was that he had briefly flirted with "Tolstoyan ideas" in his youth.[78] Similarly, a Warsaw-based Betar journal avoided the term "socialism," describing instead Trumpeldor's desire to create a movement with a "progressive social character."[79] The article then continued, as nearly all accounts of Trumpeldor's life did, by adding that postwar socialists had betrayed him by abandoning his most important demand: the creation of a Jewish army. Betar leaders insisted that the demands and beliefs of the Zionist Left in the late 1920s would have repulsed Trumpeldor. Echoing fascist calls for action over talk, Betar guidebooks repeatedly stressed that Trumpeldor was a man of few words who saw value only in deeds; as such, he was a natural enemy of socialists, who indulged in endless debates.[80]

Jabotinsky also sought to make it appear as if Trumpeldor opposed socialist beliefs. To do so, he invoked his own rendition of Trumpeldor's ideal pioneer when critiquing socialist Zionism. After arguing in a speech to Betar members in Warsaw that the combination of socialism and Zionism could only lead to young Jews abandoning Zionism altogether, Jabotinsky immediately invoked Trumpeldor's purported call for the "iron" pioneer to serve exclusively Zionist goals.[81] By doing so, Jabotinsky had Trumpeldor posthumously endorse his claim that serving socialist ideals was beyond the pale of acceptable Zionist activity. Local Betar journals in Poland obliterated the distinction between Jabotinsky's words and those of Trumpeldor. An article in a Lwów Betar journal from 1931, entitled "The Pioneer in Trumpeldor's Thought," typified this approach when it explained, "The pioneer fights neither for himself nor for one social class, but rather for the good of the nation. You cannot serve two Gods at the same time. Trumpeldor was the first to bring this ideal of the pioneer to fruition."[82] While the first sentence vaguely resembled comments Trumpeldor had made regarding the pioneer's duties—the term "social class" was not part of Trumpeldor's formulation—the second sentence was drawn exclusively from Jabotinsky's writings on the sacrilegious mixing of socialism and Zionism.[83]

Just as Betar leaders sought to transform Trumpeldor's biography into a script for how to live in a militarized society that waged war against socialists, they were equally concerned with teaching young Jews how to fight and die for their nation. Although, as Hen Melekh Merchavia explained, Zionist youth were commanded to perform acts of "daily halutziut [pioneering]," their most important mission was to prepare to die for the nation, which was the moment of "ultimate halutziut."[84] Merchavia wrote elsewhere that young Jews in Palestine were fulfilling Trumpeldor's vision of the pioneer "not just in work but also in offering blood, real blood."[85] Like Merchavia, other Betar leaders frequently used Trumpeldor's death as the framing device for their glorifications of blood, battle, and sacrifice. Betar leaders were on far sturdier ground when it came to deploying Trumpeldor as a model for how to die. They could pair Trumpeldor's wartime diary, which at one point asked, "[I]s it not a joy to sacrifice your life for the nation and for the Land of Israel?" with his alleged final words, "It is good to die for our country."[86] Nor did much ideological labor have to be performed to make Trumpeldor a model for self-defense against armed Arab attacks. Even though Labor Zionists preferred to focus on Trumpeldor's commitment to tilling the soil of Tel Hai, they nonetheless revered his decision to defend the settlement. It was another matter altogether, however, to integrate Trumpeldor's death into a militarist worldview that aligned with right-wing attitudes toward war and violence. To do so, Betar leaders had to associate their hero with several ideas about human nature and military conflict that he had never publicly articulated.

Jabotinsky undertook this task in a foreword to Propes's biography of Trumpeldor. Originally written in 1928 on the anniversary of Trumpeldor's death, the essay would become one of the most frequently republished articles within Betar journals.[87] According to Jabotinsky, Trumpeldor was the first Jew to clearly see what Jews had denied for centuries: that human nature and social interactions were the products of "appetite and ability." Driven by an insatiable hunger for land and goods, humans constantly sought to exploit those who could not, or refused to, defend themselves. The only way to prevent one nation from plundering, persecuting, and murdering another was for the community under attack to respond in kind. Presenting Trumpeldor as both soldier and social scientist, Jabotinsky described how his friend closely followed the "experiment" of the Diaspora, "precisely and smoothly carried out according to the best scientific criteria, in all eras and all climates" to reach "the conclusion—you have to strike a blow [$m'shlogt$]." Not one corner of the "cultured world" believed in forfeiting their right to retaliate. "That's why," Jabotinsky continued, "youth love Trumpeldor *the soldier*: not his hammer, not his shovel, not his plow but his sword."[88] The message, a staple of the ethnonationalist movements across Europe, was clear: combat was not one choice among many but rather was the only option available for all. With Trumpeldor as the Jewish interlocutor for this worldview, the message was equally obvious: only military retaliation was an effective deterrent force against the persecution of Jews, who would have to hit, fight, and even kill to survive.

In Jabotinsky's retelling of Trumpeldor's life, killing one's enemy was not simply a necessity but an act of great national worth. "Trumpeldor's value," Jabotinsky explained, "lies not in the fact that Arabs killed him, but that he defended a Jewish settlement and managed to kill a number of the murderers before they killed him. This, and only this, is the meaning of the Tel-Hai cult among the masses and among the youth."[89] By killing Arab assailants, Jabotinsky continued, Trumpeldor fulfilled the fantasy of the "simple Jew of the masses" to fight back against the perpetrators of antisemitic violence.[90] Jabotinsky's retelling of Trumpeldor's death radically departed from the rendition favored by Labor Zionists. Although they depicted Trumpeldor wielding a plow by day and gun by night, they tended to leave to the reader's imagination whether the bullets from the gun he fired at Tel Hai hit their target. Jabotinsky broke the cardinal rule of Labor Zionist mythography in the 1920s: he actually described Trumpeldor killing armed Arabs, and he celebrated this act as a deed of great national worth, if not a national imperative.

No doubt aware of the potential implications of his new rendition of Trumpeldor's death, Jabotinsky assured his readers throughout most of his essay that his descriptions of armed confrontation were only within the context of Jewish self-defense. His essay's introduction, however, presented another interpretive option. Rather than open with Trumpeldor, Jabotinsky began by describing how Russian liberals on the eve of the First World War had distorted the legacy of Giuseppe Garibaldi. A guerilla commander who fought through much of the nineteenth century to unify the states of the Italian Peninsula and wrest control from the Habsburg Empire over the region, Garibaldi was deeply admired by Jabotinsky. How, Jabotinsky asked, could Russian liberals celebrate the life of "the embodiment of chauvinism," a man who had sought to create a new state through military force and insisted that his fellow Italians "drive out German foreigners"? Jabotinsky added that this model for seeking national independence was shared by "Poles, Czechs, the same Italians in Austria, and Zionists." Just as Russian liberals were unworthy of commemorating Garibaldi, so too were socialist Zionists unfit to praise Trumpeldor; "among those who sing his praises can be found the most bitter opponents of all that is connected to sword, rifle and pistol."[91]

What is most striking about this passage is how it sits uneasily with the remainder of Jabotinsky's essay. If Trumpeldor was the emblem of Jewish self-defense, as the remainder of the essay claimed, why associate him with irredentist nationalists who *initiated* military conflict to expel those they deemed foreigners from their land? Why open the article by likening Trumpeldor to a leader who saw military conflict as the key to national liberation? If Garibaldi was like Trumpeldor, was the Zionist hero's plow—and in turn, the tools of construction used by all Jewish settlers—of little importance in Betar's vision for how to bring about a Jewish state? Was Trumpeldor's rifle the ultimate instrument of creation?

The tensions in this text capture a central feature of Jabotinsky's political writing. As a journalist, Jabotinsky's talent rested above all in his ability to strike a brash, provocative, and decisive tone while simultaneously riddling his prose with contradictions. This was a skill perfected in his early days of writing in Italy and Russia. His mastery of the feuilleton writer's craft served him well when he entered the world of politics. His strategy for crafting his prose mirrored his strategy for crafting Betar's approach to the values associated with the European radical Right: the very dynamism of the youth movement and its ability to attract a mass following would rest not in its articulation of a clear stance, but rather in its ability to create youth who would provocatively walk the line between defenders and aggressors, between those who attempted to prevent violent confrontation with Arabs and those who sought it out.

Jabotinsky's elusive prose allowed ample room for Betar's leaders to amplify or diminish the various messages they deciphered in his writing. His vast repertoire of articles also provided numerous options for them to pick and choose which of Jabotinsky's opinions on a particular topic they sought to promote. In 1929, for example, the editors of the monthly journal *Tel Hai* set out to determine which Jabotinsky article would best introduce his worldview to their readers. They settled on an article he had written in 1912, praising none other than Garibaldi. His genius, Jabotinsky claimed, lay in the fact that he "ignited the hatred of the masses towards foreigners," convinced them to abandon class conflict, and "forced an entire generation" to reject the "democratization" of the region and instead "surrender their power" for national unification.[92] Through the mediation of Betar's editors, the readers of the youth movement journal encountered their leader articulating a repertoire of ideas promoted by ethno-nationalist movements of interwar Europe's Right—rejecting democracy, demanding the suppression of class conflict, and calling on the nation to hate the "foreigners" within their midst. Trumpeldor received a similar treatment in the pages of *Tel Hai*. Echoing Jabotinsky's rendition of the Zionist hero's death, Moshe Lejzerowicz mused that Trumpeldor was the ideal national martyr because he had asked, "Where is it written that in order to carry out my ideal I have to die; perhaps the opposite is true: in order to carry out my ideal, you have to die." Dying in defense of the nation was not enough; only the martyr who killed his or her enemy could "carry out national goals . . . that have use not only for the individual, but for the entire collective."[93] It would no longer suffice to defend and die; the value of young Zionists, as Lejzerowicz put it, rested in whether they could "freely shed their blood *as well as the blood of foreigners*."[94]

Making the Radical Right Jewish?

Just as Betar's leaders hoped that their reconfiguration of Trumpeldor's biography would convince Jewish youth that many of the values venerated by the European radical Right were quintessentially Zionist, they also sought to convince the Jewish public that the adoption of these values was a religious imperative. Betar's leaders were far from alone in their quest to seek religious sanctification for their political programs. For decades, the architects of modern Jewish politics had poured their efforts into reinterpreting Jewish religious traditions as the blueprints for political action. From its inception, the Zionist movement envisioned the Bible as both a guidebook to Palestine's landscape and historical proof that Jews had a right to claim the land as their own. The brochures of Zionist youth movements in Poland were replete with biblical legends of Jewish sovereignty, as well as medieval Jewish liturgy that spoke of a yearning to return to Zion.[95] Betar leaders reimagined traditional Judaism to convince their young recruits, as well as the recruits' parents, that the youth movement's hostility toward the Left, demands for obedience, and calls for violence were, at their heart, fundamentally Jewish.

Like the leaders of other youth movements in interwar Poland, Betar viewed local synagogues as arenas in which they could forge durable connections between traditional Judaism and their political goals. Synagogues had long served communities in eastern Europe as a platform for political activists to peddle their programs. One of the more popular ways in which they did so was by staging traditional memorial services in honor of political leaders. Throughout the country, Jews sympathetic to Zionism would gather in synagogues for special services in honor of Theodor Herzl and other well-known Zionist leaders.[96] Betar's leaders believed that this particular religious ceremony would provide the most compelling religious ritual to justify their attitudes toward the role of armed conflict in building the Jewish state.

The choreography of Betar's memorial services for Joseph Trumpeldor illuminates how the movement tried to blend political and religious rituals. Towns and cities across the Poland reported the same sequence of events: uniformed Betar members would file into the synagogue in uniform, carrying their local battalion flags; a rabbi or Betar leader would offer a presentation about Trumpeldor's life and the value of the Betar movement; and a prayer leader or cantor would sing "El Maleh Rachamim," a medieval prayer asking God to watch over the soul of the departed.[97] This ritual sequence performed two crucial tasks for Betar in its quest to win public approval. First, the ceremony brought the political iconography, costuming, and choreography of Betar into the synagogue, making it a central part of the ceremony's religious ritual. Second, by integrating "El Maleh Rachamim" into their service, a prayer that asked God to place the soul of the deceased in the Garden of Eden and offer it eternal protection, Betar members provided their audience with a religious approbation of Trumpeldor's life and death, as well as the political program of their movement. One Betar member from Warkowicze, a small village in the eastern borderland province of Wołyń, recounted that their movement's service at the local house of prayer had left such a favorable impression on the town's inhabitants that they had begun to describe Trumpeldor as the new "rebbe" of youth.[98]

In addition to staging these ceremonies, Betar leaders reinterpreted ancient Jewish texts to provide religious sanctification for their political beliefs. These efforts were frequently connected to their battle with socialist Zionists. In some respects, Betar was at an advantage when its activists claimed that they were far more "Jewish" than the Zionist Left. While Labor Zionist activists may have employed religious motifs in their rituals and rhetoric, they never claimed to enforce, let alone uphold, traditional Jewish religious practices.[99] Before Jabotinsky's arrival in Poland, Zionist opponents of Labor Zionism were already describing socialism as the "red assimilation," a political creed that would lead to the abandonment of Judaism and the disappearance of the Jewish people.[100] Jabotinsky invoked this claim in his campaign against the Jewish Left. In a series of speeches addressed to Betar and articles addressed to the Polish Jewish public, he claimed that his campaign against socialism was a battle to preserve the essence of Judaism. At the heart of the religion, he argued, lay the belief in only one God. Precisely because "two ideals means two Gods and two Gods is no God," Zionists were forbidden to pair their work for a Jewish state with a socialist ethos. They could only adhere to one goal—the creation of a Jewish state in the Land of Israel on both sides of the Jordan River. Drawing on biblical imagery once again, Jabotinsky promised that Betar's leaders would send Jewish youth "to the Holy Temple where there is one and not two altars."[101] Jabotinsky coined the Hebrew term *had ness*—"one banner"—as a slogan for Betar's members to associate with this ideal. Jabotinsky and other Betar leaders used the slogan interchangeably with the Greek term "monism," which denoted the belief in a single principle. As further proof that the pairing of socialism and Zionism was against God's will, Jabotinsky cited the biblical prohibition against wearing a fabric made of both wool and linen, known in biblical Hebrew as *shatnez*.[102] He explained that the biblical prohibition had been instituted because wool-wearing cattle breeders and linen-wearing farm laborers, described as "eternal enemies," needed a clear way to identify one another from afar.[103] "Shatnez" became one of the most frequently recurring terms used by Betar's leaders in their campaign against the Left.

As part of his polemic against socialism, Jabotinsky turned again to the bible to present an economic program for the future Jewish state. Writing in

Haynt, he refuted the claim of some Labor Zionists that the bible possessed a socialist blueprint for economic justice. He insisted instead that its vision for economic development was diametrically opposed to socialism. Socialists, he wrote, sought a single revolution to overthrow the social order. To ensure that the revolution remained permanent, they would stringently regulate each and every economic interaction. The result, Jabotinsky warned, was not only the stifling of individual creativity and will, but also the curtailment of political and civil liberties. In contrast to this economic vision, the Bible, in Jabotinsky's view, valued private enterprise and free competition in the marketplace. Citing a law from the book of Leviticus regulating land and property rights, he argued that the Bible called for "periodic social revolutions" as correctives to any economic injustices committed in the intervening years. These revolutions would be regulated by a parliament, a plebiscite, or a council of economic corporations. Designed in part to refute accusations that Revisionism was a reactionary force seeking to suppress workers, Jabotinsky's reading of the Bible presented the movement as a guardian of workers' rights, willing to pursue revolutionary ends while preserving individual freedom.[104] The text, both vague and utopic, was never translated into a more detailed economic program. When Betar members proposed models of economic relations for the future Jewish state, they were more likely to turn to Fascist Italy's corporatist policies.[105]

Betar's leaders also drew on Jewish holidays to reinforce their vision of the role of military leadership and conflict in building the future Jewish state. Commemorating the liberation of Israelites from their enslavement in Egypt, Passover was among the most popular religious holidays for Zionists to reappropriate for nationalist ends. Zionist organizations across the political spectrum reinterpreted the Passover narrative as a parable for national liberation. For centuries, Jews had recounted the narrative of Passover by reciting a text known as the Haggadah at festive dinners held during the first two evenings of the holiday. The Haggadah focuses on the role of God in rescuing the Israelites from enslavement. Seeking to augment the role of the Israelites in their liberation, Zionist retellings of the narrative gave greater emphasis to the role of Moses, who in the biblical narrative of the Exodus served as God's intermediary when interacting with the Israelites and Egypt's ruler.

That Jabotinsky was cast by his followers as a modern-day Moses is hardly surprising; other Zionist leaders had similarly been described as Moses by their admirers. What was unique to Betar, however, was the way in which its members imagined their ideal leader through the character of Moses. Betar periodicals did not reproduce the Bible's depiction of Moses as a soft-spoken intermediary of God. Instead, they depicted Moses as a strong-willed, passionate, and charismatic military commander. "Moses understood," one instruction manual explained, "that a half-annihilated people could not take over a land that was already settled by organized nations." His greatest gift to the Israelites was that he "organized, divided into groups and educated the future army that would later take over the land, where they could settle and live a normal and quiet life."[106] In addition to describing Moses as a commander preparing his troops for conquest, another article described his "strong will and firm patience" as key to "countering and conquering" the "ignorance of the masses." Before shifting to a description of Jabotinsky, the article's author noted, "[I]t was Moses that gave the nation a country!"[107]

Of all the Jewish holidays that Betar leaders used to sanctify their politics, the winter holiday of Hannukah was given pride of place. The eight-day Jewish holiday, commemorating the activities of a Jewish rebel army between 167 and 160 BCE that wrested control of Judea from the Seleucid Empire, provided the best model to justify their assessment of Arab-Jewish relations in Mandate Palestine. According to Jewish tradition, the Maccabee revolt erupted as a protest against the Seleucid ruler's decision to outlaw Judaism. Like other Zionists, who described the Hannukah revolt as a Zionist act *avant la lettre*, Betar's leaders turned to the holiday to prove that the Zionist struggle for national liberation in Palestine was also a struggle to preserve and protect Judaism and Jewish life. Zionist movements disagreed, however, on the essence of the Judaism for which the Maccabees had fought. Socialist Zionist youth movements, much like members of the Bund, dimmed the holiday's martial themes and instead depicted the Maccabees as protosocialists seeking justice and equality.[108] Betar's leaders believed that the Maccabees offered an altogether different model of Jewish behavior, one that recapitulated the same values as their Trumpeldor legends. An educational manual for Betar published in 1932 described the ideal Polish Jewish youth, longing to follow the example of the Maccabees "and prepare themselves for later, when they will grow up, to sacrifice their blood for the fatherland."[109] Aharon Propes's articles on the holiday focused less on national sacrifice and far more on how the Maccabees could serve as a model for the type of warriors Betar members should become. Filled with hatred of their enemies, Propes wrote, the Maccabees had no remorse and offered no compromises in their battle to restore Judaism.[110]

Propes's retelling of the war's final moments best captured the movement's increasing tendency to write, as Italian Fascists did, about violence as a redemptive, cleansing experience. According to a Talmudic legend, which became the standard interpretation of the holiday for centuries, the ultimate value of Hannukah rested not in the Maccabees' victory over the Seleucids but in God's performance of a miracle. Legend had it that when the Maccabees restored the Jewish temple, they had only enough oil to light the temple's menorah, a ritual candelabrum, for one day; God saw to it that the oil would burn for eight days, giving the Maccabees enough time to replenish their supply of oil and restore the temple to its former glory. The traditional legend, which did not appear in the original account of the Maccabean revolt, sought to write God into a narrative in which military action, rather than divine intervention, had restored Judaism and Jewish sovereignty.[111] In this rendition, Hanukkah's miracle occurred in the sacred space of the temple, the center for Jewish worship and the reputed dwelling place of God, rather than on the battlefield. Propes, unsurprisingly, took a different approach. Here is Propes retelling the tale of the *menorah*'s lighting:

> And then the battle ended, when all the nation could freely breathe, and the Temple was cleaned, they LIT THE MENORAH WITH THEIR IRON SPEARS. IRON SPEARS, PURIFIED BY BLOOD [*blut gereynikte shpeyzn*]; ONLY ONCE THEY HAD EXPELLED THE ENEMY WITH THESE SPEARS, AND BATTLED FOR FREEDOM, COULD THEY LIGHT THE MENORAH IN THE HOLY TEMPLE.[112]

By making the lighting of the menorah—and with it, the restoration of the most sacred site for worshipping God—contingent on the act of banishing their enemies and murdering those who refused to leave, Propes offered the ultimate sanctification of violence. The blood of the enemy, not oil, was the purifying element that restored the temple. Like other Zionist accounts of ancient Jewish legends, Propes was sure to end the story by collapsing past and present, placing ancient heroes alongside modern ones. To ensure that his readers understood that the Hannukah story was meant to serve as a model for their own behavior, he insisted that they light their own menorahs in commemoration of Joseph Trumpeldor, adding, "[T]hese lights, lit with iron spears will ... show the way to the Jewish state."[113]

Where does Propes's retelling of the Hannukah story, along with the reinventions of Jewish tradition and Zionist lore we have surveyed thus far, leave us in our quest to understand Betar's approach to fascism and Europe's radical Right? On the one hand, the stories and rituals performed by the youth movement's members make clear Betar's unapologetic, unflinching support for several crucial features of Fascist Italy's ideological repertoire. First, the movement insisted that only a society mobilized along military lines could bring about nationalist goals. This entailed a desire to subordinate oneself to the nation's demands and, in the context of activity within Betar, to obey one's commander. The halutz ideal, once it had been reconfigured by the movement, made every citizen a soldier and every choice they made an act of war. The myths and rituals developed in this period presented a vision of Jewish society in which the cult of believing, obeying, and fighting was the key to social progress. Furthermore, like others on Europe's radical Right, Betar leaders ensured that their culture made clear the necessity of waging war on socialists, communists, and any other enemies of the emerging nation-state. Between 1929 and 1932—the same years the movement was developing rituals to frame their program as Jewish and Zionist—Betar's leaders drew even closer to the radical Right's ideological world in their depictions of what these "wars" would actually look like. Adding to a culture that already sanctified the violent deaths of young Zionists defending the construction of the Jewish state, Lejzerowicz and Propes, who were among the most important leaders of Betar in Poland, envisioned the murder of Zionism's enemies as a national imperative.

In short, Betar's leaders had good reason to describe themselves as fascist, as many of them did in 1928. That is not to say, however, that Betar in the late 1920s was no more than an Italian Fascist organization in Zionist costuming. While many Betar leaders admired the fascist calls for discipline, obedience, and military might, and occasionally idealized their economic system, they never celebrated institutions of the fascist state designed to suppress political dissent, whether through censorship, the secret police, or squadristi. Leaders of Betar's parent organization, the Revisionist movement, were especially reticent to identify with a movement that infringed on basic freedoms of association and sought to dictate the attitudes and behaviors of its citizens. As members of a party that elected conference delegates, engaged in a free exchange of ideas, and participated in the democratic elections and proceedings of the Zionist Organization, Revisionist leaders felt, on occasion, the need to insist that their youth movement's authoritarian leanings not infringe on their party's democratic nature.[114] Hitler's rise to power in 1933 forced even more Betar leaders to scale back their claims that they shared common ideals and goals with fascists. Yet paradoxically, as they wove their way through various qualifications to frame their program as Jewish, Zionist, and, in later years, "purely" democratic, they were performing many of the same steps of intricate ideological choreography as Italian Fascists, who relished in blurring the boundaries between the meanings of democracy and authoritarianism, subservience and free will, and defense and attack. Some of Betar's leaders in Poland would continue to publish articles in praise of Italian fascism through the late 1930s.[115]

As the movement continued to expand in Poland, reaching more than 350 branches by the spring of 1931, Betar members across the country increasingly adopted the cultural templates provided to them by the youth movement's leadership. Handwritten journals produced by Betar clubs in Tarczyn, Wołożyn, and Wilno also suggest that many of Betar's members picked up on the range of rhetorical strategies employed by their leaders to describe their relationship with Europe's radical Right. Much like the official publications from the movement's Warsaw office, local Betar journals employed a range of approaches when describing authoritarian and militarist ideas. Certain values required no caveats: the glorification of military life, self-defense, and "ultimate sacrifice," for example, abounded in local journals.[116] Articles linked the "Arab threat" with the Jewish Left and urged members to prepare for a ruthless, imminent, and inevitable war against both opponents. In the communal diary of a Betar branch in Wilno, for example, one member warned his fellow activists in May 1930 that they needed to "fight and annihilate" Labor Zionist workers' organizations. "We are currently standing," he wrote, "between two fires, [the fire] of enemies from within and [the fire of] enemies from without. On one side is the Arab, and on the second side is the pioneer, the Jewish national worker with a red flag in one hand, and in the other hand a spade, or even better, a knife, and is ready ... to slaughter us."[117] Furthermore, when they deemed it necessary, Betar members readily employed the deliberately ambiguous rhetorical style of their leaders. Particularly instructive was the reaction of a local Betar branch in the northeastern town of Słonim to Stabiecki's call for Revisionists to proclaim, "We are fascists, Jewish fascists." After a debate that lasted into the early morning, the branch concluded, "We entirely disagree with Dr. Stabiecki," and then immediately added, "yet, when it comes to building a Jewish state, all means are kosher to achieve that goal."[118] This ambiguity proved critical to Jabotinsky, who was eager to draw as many Polish Jewish youth as possible into his ranks, including those who sought for Zionism to espouse fascist ideals.

Not all of the Revisionist movement's followers, however, were willing to tolerate this rhetorical ambiguity. By the early 1930s, several prominent leaders of the youth movement in Poland and in Palestine began to demand that the movement unabashedly declare itself fascist. Simultaneously, many of the veteran Russian Zionist activists who had participated in the founding of the Revisionist movement called for the movement to reject fascism in no uncertain terms and firmly anchor itself in democratic values. We now turn to Jabotinsky's quest to navigate between these two demands.

3

Obedient Children, Reckless Rebels

ON A WINTER evening in 1932, Adolf Gourevitch, a young man from Kiev studying at the Sorbonne, joined Vladimir Jabotinsky and his son, Eri, at a café in Paris. As he sat down at the table, Jabotinsky announced that he would devote the evening to composing a new anthem for Betar. Jabotinsky had good reason to create a new hymn for his youth movement. By this point, Betar had more than forty thousand members worldwide and was quickly emerging as one of the most popular Jewish youth movements in Poland, where some thirty-three thousand Jews had joined its ranks. The youth movement was also becoming one of the most controversial in the country—its rivals' accusations that the group's members were "Jewish fascists" who aspired to the same values as antisemites on the European Right only intensified with Betar's growth. Writing an anthem provided Jabotinsky with an opportunity to offer a clear declaration of his movement's goals and to finally put these claims to rest. He even promised Gourevitch that the poem would follow a mathematical logic.[1] Jabotinsky wrote the following lines to open his first verse: "Betar / from a pit of decay and dust / in blood and sweat / a new race will emerge / proud, noble and cruel."[2]

What did it mean for a young Zionist to be noble and cruel at one and the same time? Why did Jabotinsky present a vision of youth that called on them to simultaneously perform these seemingly contradictory character traits? Gourevitch explains:

> Jabotinsky wanted to express three main ideas: that of *Betar* and of course that of *hadar* [honor], and something else besides—less gentlemanly,

more challenging and rebellious. "Something mischievous, troublesome, scandalous.... Wait, I have it: *Betar-hadar-scandar*!"

Here Eri looked up in wonderment: "There isn't any such a thing in any vocabulary! What do you mean by *scandar*?"

"You don't get it?" replied Jabotinsky. "*Skandal* in Russian, in English, scandal, or if you wish—Colonel Patterson's favorite toast: 'here's to trouble!'"[3]

Although Gourevitch's retrospective account aimed to showcase Jabotinsky's craftsmanship as a Hebrew poet, it reveals far more about the Revisionist leader as an architect of political ideology. For Jabotinsky, the very dynamism of his youth movement's ideology rested not in its articulation of a clear vision of who youth were and how they were expected to behave, but rather in its ability to create youth who would provocatively walk the line between democratic and authoritarian, obedient and rebellious. Jabotinsky's conviction that scandal was an essential element of his youth movement's program also reveals his own assumptions about the political behavior and appetites of the Jewish masses whom he sought to mobilize. In his view, the rank-and-file of mass political movements cared little about the ideological coherence of political programs and craved, above all else, something provocative, daring, and dramatic. Much of the value of having young people on the political stage lay, for Jabotinsky, in their ability to make a scene.

He was not alone. In the 1920s and 1930s, European political activists of every stripe saw tremendous power in invoking long-standing ideas about the nature of youth—from their virility, enthusiasm, and idealism to their recklessness and impulsiveness—as a way to capture the attention and support of the public. Youth is not merely a biological fact—it is a cultural category, a concept as powerful as it is malleable.[4] Whether political movements in Europe chose to argue that youth were obedient children or reckless rebels would depend on the specific situation they faced and the political capital they believed could be gained. Jabotinsky, too, understood that presenting Betar's members as rebels had as many benefits as presenting them as obedient. Like the youth movement's performances of control, discipline, and order, demonstrations of their ability to be reckless, rebellious, and even threatening could provoke the political changes he sought to bring about.

Jabotinsky's provocative, elusive, and contradictory constructions of youth were put to the test when factions within his movement demanded that he choose between democracy and authoritarian politics. Touring Poland in the early 1930s, Revisionist leaders from Palestine were telling their Polish Jewish audiences that only a wholehearted embrace of authoritarianism and revolutionary violence could bring about a Jewish state. Members of the Revisionist movement's executive council, based in London, were also demanding that Jabotinsky dispose of his ambiguous political style and articulate a clear program. Their calls, however, were for the movement to reject authoritarianism and embrace democracy. Jabotinsky refused to submit to these demands. Tapping into the broader conversations about youth taking place across Europe, he deftly deployed his distinctive brand of "youth politics" to respond to these challenges to his authority. Focusing on the years 1931–1933, in which the first of several battles for the Revisionist movement's soul took place, this chapter demonstrates how Jabotinsky's construction of "youth" within the movement, as well as the innovative ways in which he delimited "youth" from "adult," played a pivotal role in allowing him to further embrace authoritarian measures while retaining his democratic persona.

Little Dictators and Frail Democrats? Jabotinsky between Betar, the Revisionist Executive, and Brit Ha-Biryonim

As Jabotinsky journeyed through cities and towns across Poland in the early 1930s, he became increasingly convinced that his role as the commander of a militarized youth movement would provide him with far more power as a Zionist leader than his role as president of the democratic Union of Revisionist Zionists. The exponential growth of Betar clubs in Poland, nearing 650 by 1933, was just one way in which local youth movement leaders could boast to Jabotinsky of their growing power in the country. They also proudly reported that the youth movement's members were among the chief generators of revenue for the Jewish National Fund, the Zionist Organization's chief fundraising organ.[5] Much more compelling to Jabotinsky was the success the movement was enjoying in fulfilling its primary goal. After years of calling for the military training of Jewish youth in Europe, Jabotinsky could now boast that Betar leaders were training thousands of Betar youth in the art of combat.

It was no less significant to Jabotinsky that the Jewish public was taking notice. Whether Jewish journalists praised or condemned Betar's activity, local and national newspapers frequently mentioned Betar's performances of power—in parades, at conferences, or in the street. To reinforce positive assessments of the youth movement circulating in the Polish Jewish press, Jabotinsky could sing the praises of Betar youth in his biweekly column in *Haynt*, Poland's leading Yiddish newspaper.[6] No less important to Jabotinsky's perception of power through youth politics were the messages of success being conveyed back to him. Whether in handwritten journals from provincial towns or in nationally circulated periodicals, Betar members fed Jabotinsky a steady diet of articles praising him as an omnipotent leader who had transformed their lives and would determine their destiny, along with the fate of Jews worldwide. The narrative arc of these articles was nearly always the same. As Propes put it in an essay written on Jabotinsky's birthday, Jews had been destined for misery, "but when he came along ... he ignited a fire within us, he gave our lives meaning." Addressing Jabotinsky directly, he insisted, "Our only desire is to be led by you for years and years to come."[7] These pledges of obedience were repeated, time and again, in telegrams sent to Jabotinsky during the numerous regional and national conferences that took place throughout the year.[8] Although Jabotinsky may have publicly evinced discomfort with the authoritarian tone of the platitudes showered on him, the youth movement was providing him compelling evidence that they were the key to his political success.

Against the backdrop of Betar's meteoric ascent, the Revisionist movement's democratic political clubs were all the more disappointing to Jabotinsky. In the early 1930s, he no longer complained about the growth rate of the Revisionist movement, but he continued to bemoan his group's financial woes and, above all, the incessant arguments that paralyzed activity within the movement's executive council.[9] At the heart of the conflict between Jabotinsky, now based in Paris, and the Revisionist Executive, based in London, was the issue of the movement's relationship to the Zionist Organization, which aspired from its establishment in 1897 to serve as the umbrella organization of the Zionist movement's various factions. From the founding of the Union of Revisionist Zionists in 1925, Jabotinsky had pleaded to the movement to consider withdrawing from the Zionist Organization.[10] Having resigned from the Zionist Organization Executive two years beforehand, Jabotinsky preferred to see Revisionism develop into an independent movement, unrestrained by what he perceived to be Weizmann's corrupt and ineffective leadership. In contrast, London Executive members argued that it was crucial for the Revisionist Union to continue to participate in the Zionist Organization. With Jabotinsky barred from Palestine in the wake of the August 1929 riots, their participation in the organization, they reasoned, had become their primary means to preserve their ability to influence British policy as well as the social and economic development of Jewish life in Mandate Palestine. Meir Grossman, the leading force in the London Executive, increasingly emphasized in the Revisionist press that participating in the elections to the biannual Zionist Congress, which functioned as the Zionist Organization's parliamentary body, would also enable the Revisionist movement to maintain its democratic character.[11] In an effort to ensure that their voices, rather than Jabotinsky's alone, would reach Revisionists, the London Executive issued circulars to Revisionist branches worldwide, contradicting Jabotinsky's position on the Zionist Organization. By the spring of 1931, an infuriated Jabotinsky was accusing the executive's members of trying to make him an outcast within his own movement.[12]

If Betar's pledges of obedience seemed to Jabotinsky an enticing antidote to the London Executive's behavior, the Seventeenth Zionist Congress, held in Basel in the summer of 1931, further highlighted for him the pitfalls of participation in the Zionist Organization. At first, it seemed as though the Revisionist delegates might have a lasting influence on the Congress: they arrived in Basel with close to fifty-six thousand supporters—nearly a quarter of all votes cast—and three times more delegates than they had representing them at the previous Congress.[13] Newspapers covering the two-week proceedings reported that the Revisionist Party might emerge as the leading force of the Zionist movement.[14] Midway through the conference, Chaim Weizmann, who had come under fire for what were perceived to be timid interactions with British officials, announced that he would not resubmit his candidacy for the presidency of the organization. As if to signal that Jabotinsky would be an appropriate successor, he added that the Revisionist leader was "a man of ability and quality" and that there were "many others in the congress who lean towards the Revisionist's views but who do not have the courage openly to confess Revisionism."[15] Emboldened by Weizmann's announcement, the London Revisionist Executive insisted that Jabotinsky could easily sweep to power by forging a bloc with several other Zionist factions who sought to prevent Mapai, the Labor Zionists' new political party, from gaining power. Despite the inevitable compromises to Revisionist doctrine that would have to take place, a coalition would allow Jabotinsky to take hold of the organization's presidency. To the shock of many, Jabotinsky refused to do so. Buoyed by the publicity that anticipated his victory at the congress, Jabotinsky may have believed that the Revisionists could sweep into power alone. But it is equally plausible that his conviction that the Zionist Organization was useless led him to deliberately sabotage his chance to rise to power within it. No matter the motive, his decision proved fatal to the Revisionist movement's success at the congress. The new executive elected by congress delegates consisted largely of people who had previously supported Weizmann's policies. Particularly humiliating for the party was the crushing defeat of Jabotinsky's proposal to define the ultimate aim of the Zionist movement to be the establishment of a Jewish state with a Jewish majority. Its opponents feared that such a declaration would incite Palestinian Arabs to further violence. Infuriated by the failure of his proposal, Jabotinsky rose up from his seat and declared, "This is no longer a Zionist Congress." He then tore up his membership card to the Zionist Organization and stormed out of the hall.[16] Equally significant was his reaction to his own executive. Almost immediately after storming out of the hall, he announced that he was taking a six-month hiatus from leading the Revisionist movement, because of the Revisionist Executive's insistence that the movement remain within the Zionist Organization.[17]

The hiatus was short lived. Several weeks later, in the French seaport town of Calais, the Revisionist Executive, including Jabotinsky, decided that their movement was in principle no longer obligated to follow the instructions of the Zionist Organization.[18] In a bid to both placate the Revisionist Executive and present himself as a leader capable of compromise, Jabotinsky accepted that individual members of the Revisionist movement could simultaneously hold membership to the Zionist Organization. The process of reaching the agreement infuriated Jabotinsky; privately, he confessed to a Revisionist leader in Palestine that he was "sick of this tradition of patience and compromise.... I feel as if our masses as well, without even knowing, long in the depths of their souls for some sort of explosion, a spark of a storm."[19] Whatever form this storm would take, it was clear to Jabotinsky that neither the democratic Revisionist clubs under the watch of the London Executive nor the parliamentary politics they pursued through the Zionist Organization would bring it about.

It was far from a coincidence that Jabotinsky chose to both vent his frustrations about the Revisionist Executive and indulge in revolutionary rhetoric with a member of Palestine's Revisionist Party. By 1931, Revisionist leaders in Palestine were sending letters to the London Executive and to Jabotinsky, urging them to adopt a more radical approach to political action.[20] Spearheading the campaign to further radicalize the Revisionist movement were Abba Achimeir, Uri Zvi Grinberg, and Yehoshua H. Yeivin. Known for the violent and revolutionary rhetoric that had previously typified their poetry and articles in Labor Zionist journals before they became Revisionists, these men founded a Revisionist faction called the Brit Ha-Biryonim—the Alliance of Hooligans—in the fall of 1930. The term *biryonim* had been used in the Talmud to portray a group of Jews who had led a failed revolt against

Roman rule, which culminated with the destruction of the Second Temple in 70 CE. The Talmud condemned the biryonim for their militarism, zealotry, and cruel behavior towards Jews they deemed as traitors. Promoting their views in Palestine's Revisionist journal *Hazit Ha'am* (the Nation's Frontline), the Biryonim's slogan was "to invigorate the movement in spirit and blood; to replace the *oppositionary* means by *revolutionary* means, action instead of talk."[21] With Abba Achimeir at their helm, the Biryonim, also known as the Maximalists, insisted that fascist rule and acts of violent radicalism against the British were the only tools with which the Jewish state could be established. Though their message was forged in Palestine, they, like Jabotinsky, believed that courting the support of young Jews in Poland would be crucial to their success. From the moment Propes launched the first journal of Betar in Poland, Abba Achimeir and Uri Zvi Grinberg appeared within the pages of Betar's press.[22] A lecture tour in 1932 throughout Poland by Abba Achimeir, in which he extolled the virtues of revolutionary violence, brought increased visibility to the group.[23] By 1933, Uri Zvi Grinberg, already a celebrated Hebrew poet in both Poland and Palestine, moved to Warsaw to take over the editorial board of the Revisionist Party's weekly Yiddish journal, *Di Velt*. Although calls for violence, revolution, and national interest over universal moral principles previously appeared in texts published by Betar's press in Poland, the fact that the Biryonim had lived or were living in Palestine gave their calls a credibility and a popularity that surpassed Polish Jewish activists with similar worldviews.

The Biryonim's increasing popularity within Jabotinsky's youth movement both exhilarated and alarmed him. In letters addressed to several Revisionist leaders, he argued that the Biryonim's radical calls not only drew scores of Diaspora youth into the Revisionist movement but also served as "accelerators" for the movement's aims in Palestine.[24] He was, however, deeply uneasy about the messages they were promoting. Despite Jabotinsky's fierce criticism of Britain's policies in Palestine, he nonetheless cautioned the Revisionist leadership to refrain from calls for revolt.[25] He was equally troubled by the crude nature of the Biryonim's calls for dictatorship and violence. As early as 1929, he had confided to a colleague that he was horrified by Achimeir's lack of literary skill.[26] One could hear echoes of this assessment in Jabotinsky's appraisal of the Biryonim's political tactics.[27] There was something repulsive to Jabotinsky about the blunt nature of their calls for dictatorship and violence. Prior to the Maximalists' rise, Jabotinsky did not object on any ideological grounds to acts of radicalism, so long as he could decide when to amplify or dim the movement's radical tendencies. He viewed the clear message that the Maximalists were delivering—leaving little room for imagination or interpretation—as a threat to his power. Further fueling this suspicion was the Maximalist demand that the Revisionist movement establish a semiautonomous wing in Palestine that could conduct acts of terrorism. Already struggling with the Revisionist Executive's vocal opposition to him, Jabotinsky feared that the Maximalists would similarly attempt to diminish his ability to determine how his followers would behave. In a letter sent to one of the Biryonim leaders in August 1932, on the eve of the Second World Revisionist Conference, Jabotinsky insisted on the democratic nature of the Revisionist movement, adding, "your [the group's] attempts to make your views prevail . . . are nothing but attempts to drive me out."[28] By doing so, he made clear that his concerns were as much driven by his fear of being displaced as they were by his self-declared ideological affinities.

Jabotinsky was especially anxious about how the Biryonim claimed to speak in the name of his prize possession, Betar youth. Their choice of the name "hooligans" was just one way in which the Biryonim sought to convince Betar members that the new group exuded a youthful sensibility. Defending their calls for authoritarianism and violence at the Second World Revisionist Conference in Vienna in 1932, Abba Achimeir proclaimed that "the twentieth century belongs to two things: youth and dictatorship."[29] Numerous Betar leaders in Poland began to echo Achimeir's claim that the ethos of the Biryonim matched the desires of young Jews. In one such article, entitled "The Sons of Betar and the Reality in the Homeland," a Betar leader argued that youth naturally strove to "renounce words in the name of deeds." After fantasizing about Jewish youth in Palestine breaking the law, the article predicted that "imprisonment [would] become the membership card for [belonging to] the national youth."[30] Even those within Betar who were less than enthusiastic about the Biryonim linked the new group's platform to ideas about the nature of youth. When explaining the Biryonim's appeal, an article that criticized the group noted that "in every moment there are always people, *mostly youth*, who excel with their special volatile temperament and with their great source of energy . . . possessed by a strong longing for real deeds."[31] An article offering total support to the Biryonim in the same newspaper argued that because "youth possess a great energy," they could not follow in the footsteps of "salon Revisionists." Their task, instead, was to ensure that Mandate Palestine's British administration and Arab population knew that "every strike of the fist we answer with the strike of the fist, every decree we answer with deeds."[32]

While the article exposes the type of uninhibited calls for violence that troubled Jabotinsky, it also highlights what tempted the Revisionist leader to harness rather than repress the Biryonim's popularity. According to the article's author, "salon Revisionists" were not merely those who abhorred acts of violence; those who longed to remain in the Zionist Organization also fell within their ranks. By linking their call to arms against the British with Jabotinsky's critiques of the Zionist Organization and the Revisionist Executive, Biryonim sympathizers presented themselves as crucial allies to Jabotinsky. The rising frequency of Biryon-inspired articles in Betar's periodicals would have provided ample evidence to Jabotinsky that such an alliance could prove beneficial to him.

Yet as much as Jabotinsky was fed up with the Zionist Organization's parliamentary politics and the Revisionist Executive's behavior, he refused to give up on describing himself as a democratic leader who was committed to the principles of parliamentary politics. According to Svetlana Natkovich, Jabotinsky became especially committed to cultivating this persona in the 1920s, the very same period in which Betar expanded.[33] Maintaining this persona seemed increasingly urgent to Jabotinsky against the backdrop of broader political developments across the continent. Two months following the Revisionist conference in Vienna, the Nazi Party received 33 percent of the national vote in what would become Weimar Germany's last free elections. Unlike Mussolini's Italy, Jews across Europe had good reason to fear the Nazi Party's version of fascism, which made antisemitism a cornerstone of its program. With the Zionist Left increasingly drawing links between the Revisionists and the Nazis, Jabotinsky understood that it was all the more crucial to publicly reaffirm his commitment to democratic politics.[34]

How, then, could Jabotinsky harness the power of the Biryonim's popularity to weaken the Revisionist Executive, while retaining his democratic persona and ensuring that the movement did not entirely reject nonviolent political practices? The answer lay in the very tactics that both the Revisionist Executive and the Biryonim had employed in their quests for power. While the Revisionist Executive and the Biryonim presented radically different challenges to Jabotinsky, they shared one crucial feature. For both, Revisionist youth were essential. One of the chief ways in which the Revisionist Executive thought it could retain whatever power it still exerted was to diminish Betar's influence throughout Poland. Over the course of 1932 and 1933, they proposed that members of Revisionist democratic clubs supervise and regulate the activity of

Betar branches. One proposal called for Betar to abdicate its near total monopoly on Revisionist youth and divide into smaller organizations, including one that that would trade militarism for democratic politics.[35] Whenever Jabotinsky heard their demands to reduce the power of Betar, the Biryonim's calls to embrace an authoritarian cult of youth were always within earshot. Paying heed to these tactics, Jabotinsky realized that to diminish the power of both the Biryonim and the London Revisionist Executive, and all the while fend off accusations that he was embracing authoritarian politics, he would have to place his own ideas about who youth were and how they were expected to behave at the center of his political prose.

Doing so would not only allow Jabotinsky to weigh in on the debates about the future of youth being fought among his ranks; it would also provide him with an opportunity to embed his case for further authoritarian measures within the fervent debates sweeping Europe at the time about the nature of youth, their relationship to their elders, and the role they should play in politics. No matter how different their images of youth were, politicians across the political spectrum in interwar Europe agreed that talking about youth and generations was a powerful way to command public attention and shape public opinion. By the 1930s, the notion of a "conflict of generations," in which Europe's young challenged the worldview of their elders, pervaded European intellectual, political, and popular discourse.[36] Conversations about this conflict nearly always wrestled with the question of whether the mass mobilization of young men in the First World War, along with the vigorous efforts of political parties to develop youth movements in the years that followed, had led to young people exerting excessive power in the public sphere. These debates became a fixture in the Polish Jewish press, where journalists not only frequently observed the increasing political radicalization of Jewish youth but also spoke of their demand to determine the political fate of all Jews, young and old alike. Whether youth were praised or condemned for the attitudes and behaviors attributed to them depended on the social, political, and economic ends the authors of these tracts sought to achieve. The meaning of the term "generation" was similarly dynamic; the boundaries of who belonged to a generational cohort, as well the characteristics they purportedly embodied, often depended on the political program of those who were employing the term. Ever attentive to popular opinion, Jabotinsky threw his efforts into creating definitions of "youth"—both within his movement's regulations and in articles addressed to the Jewish public at large—that would help him tighten his grip on the Revisionist movement's development.

Who Are "Youth"? The Genesis and Collapse of the Gentlemen's Agreement

In the wake of his dramatic exit from the Seventeenth Zionist Congress in 1931, one of the first steps Jabotinsky took to increase his power was to dismantle key components of the Revisionist movement's regulations that sought to distinguish between the activity of Betar and the Revisionist Union. Known as the Gentlemen's Agreement, the regulations were the product of a debate between Betar and Revisionist leaders concerning the extent to which the youth movement's military ethos and semiauthoritarian structure could affect the Revisionist Union's democratic activities. Exploring the genesis and collapse of the agreement allows us to illuminate the innovative ways in which Jabotinsky used the very definitions of "youth" and "adult" to adopt authoritarian measures while retaining his democratic persona.

If census data collected by Betar branches across Europe in 1930 are any indication, the movement's definition of youth was vague from the beginning. In addition to describing the gender, education level, and occupation of thousands of the movement's members, the census pointed out that 60 percent of Betar members in Poland, the Revisionist movement's stronghold, were aged seventeen or older. Betar members in Poland who were eighteen years old represented the largest number of youth movement members surveyed.[37] Two years later, Betar leaders in eastern Galicia reported that 56 percent of its members were eighteen or older.[38] The age of Betar's members had crucial implications for the political orientation of the Revisionist movement. According to the regulations of both the Revisionist movement's democratic clubs and the Zionist Organization, both of which granted voting rights to Jews eighteen and above, most Betar members were, in fact, adults. The potential of Betar members to exert their power as voters at Revisionist conferences was not lost on the youth movement's leaders. Underscoring how the very distinction between the Revisionist movement and Betar was far from clear, Propes boasted to the youth movement's members in 1930 that they would compose an 80 percent majority at an upcoming Revisionist conference in the country.[39] Many leaders of Poland's Revisionist clubs bristled at the prospect of Betar members interfering in the democratic procedures of their movement. They warned the London Revisionist Executive that Propes was increasingly behaving like a dictator, threatening to demote Revisionist leaders if they disagreed with him.[40] In one such letter, an activist quipped, "Propes may be giving commands with Revisionist content—just not the type of Revisionism we want."⁴¹ Taking stock of the demographic weight of Betar members in Revisionist elections, they urged Grossman and his colleagues on the London Revisionist Executive to "tame and isolate" the youth movement.⁴² Against this backdrop, Grossman loyalists in Poland used the Revisionist movement's world conference in Prague in the summer of 1930 as a platform to launch a campaign to gain full control over Betar's activities. In a speech devoted entirely to the role of youth in the Revisionist movement, they warned that a "painful and demoralizing" battle between democracy and dictatorship would be waged unless the Revisionist clubs' leaders had full control over the youth movement's curriculum and membership. Young Jews, they insisted, could only enter the political sphere as objects of policy rather than actors in their own right.⁴³

In an effort to prevent the encroachment of Grossman and the London Revisionist Executive on Betar's activities, Jabotinsky's response carefully walked the line between asserting his democratic credentials while preserving his authoritarian power base. He insisted that Betar was solely an educational movement; "Betar and the Revisionist Union," he mused, "are two worlds. The Revisionist movement is a political party; Betar is a Legion and a Cadet corps. Betar has nothing to do with political struggle."⁴⁴ According to this logic, echoed by many of Betar's leaders, the military training undertaken by Betar's members was beyond the pale of politics.⁴⁵ As such, Jewish youth did not have to strictly abide by the Revisionist movement's democratic code of conduct. Jabotinsky added that any grievances about Betar voiced by Revisionist leaders were the product of their envy at the youth movement's success, rather than the expression of a genuine clash of worldviews. These statements, however, were undercut by Jabotinsky's proposal for how to legislate the relationship between the youth movement and its parent organization. He insisted that Betar members who reached the age of eighteen did not have to renounce their membership in the youth movement in order to participate in the Revisionist movement's democratic process as voting "adults." To justify his proposal, he insisted that the crossover between the two movements was the product of practical necessity alone. Alluding to the meager success of Revisionist democratic clubs, Jabotinsky asked his Revisionist readership several days following the conference, "What logic is there in uprooting a twenty-two year old from Betar, where he is obligated to engage in military training, sports development, [and] continue to learn Hebrew ... and plant him into a local branch of the Revisionist Union, which currently ... does not have this type of daily activity?"⁴⁶

The imprint of Jabotinsky's views and those of Grossman's supporters could be found in the Gentlemen's Agreement forged at the conference in Prague. At first glance, the regulations appeared to work in Grossman's favor, by clarifying the age at which a Betar "youth," guided by the martial values of obedience and discipline, would begin their transformation into a democratic Revisionist "adult." The agreement stipulated that once Betar members reached the age of eighteen, they were obligated to become members of the Revisionist movement and comply with its democratic principles. Particularly crucial was the agreement's fifth clause, which insisted that there was "no place in the framework of the Revisionist movement for the characteristics of the Betar worldview"; once Betar members reached the age of eighteen, they would have to "fulfill their Revisionist duty according to Revisionist ethics." Nonetheless, Jabotinsky ensured that the agreement preserved his right to blur the lines between the Revisionist militarized youth movement and its democratic clubs. The agreement's third clause stipulated that newly minted Revisionists who had arrived from Betar's ranks would remain in the youth movement as a "reserve." If called to do so, they were expected to obey the commands of the youth movement's leaders. Once again, no specific age was given to determine when a Betar member would have to leave the youth movement. Thus, Revisionist members, while participating in a democratic organization with Jabotinsky serving as its president, could, as Betar "youth," be subject to the commands of Betar's head commander—also Jabotinsky—at any point.[47] Although Jabotinsky urged Betar members over the age of eighteen to follow the agreement's demand for them to vote as individual "Revisionists," he added that they nonetheless had the right to vote with their fellow youth movement members as a bloc.[48]

Formally ratified at Betar's inaugural world congress in April 1931, the Gentlemen's Agreement was barely four months old when Jabotinsky tore up his Zionist Organization membership card and stormed out of the congress hall in Basel. In the wake of the conference, he quickly set out to capitalize on the Gentlemen's Agreement's tenuous definitions of "youth" and their role in politics. In a letter addressed to Betar members worldwide, Jabotinsky informed them that the time had come to mobilize the youth movement's "reserve" to vote en bloc in Revisionist elections. Insisting on the need to free the Revisionist movement from the shackles of the Zionist Organization, Jabotinsky wrote, "It is the right and obligation of the sons of Betar to demand, in one voice, this liberation."[49] The language Jabotinsky employed in the letter underscored his careful attempts to retain his democratic persona while pushing for

Betar members to obey his will. As "adult" democratic voters, Betar members had a "right" to vote as they pleased; as young members of Betar it was their "obligation" to vote in a particular fashion. Two days later, Jabotinsky sent a letter to the London Executive. Rather than perform the role of the Revisionist movement's "president," Jabotinsky used the Betar movement's letterhead to make clear that he was speaking as the youth movement's head commander. The letter informed them that the youth movement had officially annulled the fifth clause of the Gentlemen's Agreement, which forbade Betar members from expressing the youth movement's worldview when engaging in Revisionist political activity.[50] Addressing party activists through the Revisionist movement's press—this time as their president— Jabotinsky overturned the strategy he had taken at the Prague conference of 1930, where he had insisted that the movement's youth had "nothing to do with political struggle." Instead, Jabotinsky argued that Betar's program to "defend pure Zionism, without compromises or concessions," was not only deeply political but also utterly incompatible with the Zionist Organization.[51] Casting himself as a staunch defender of individual choice, Jabotinsky declared that he was unwilling to force Betar's members with voting power to abandon the political credos that had nourished them within the ranks of the youth movement.

Revisionist leaders who had insisted that their clubs retain their democratic character were horrified by Jabotinsky's annulment of the Gentlemen's Agreement. Distress letters sent to Grossman by leaders of Revisionist clubs in Poland capture their fear that the movement's descent into authoritarian politics was inevitable. Writing from Lwów, Jakób Rothman, the president of the Revisionist movement in eastern Galicia, urged Grossman to try to eliminate Betar altogether from the Revisionist scene. By permitting Betar members to vote as Revisionists, he argued, the organization had created a "youth phalanx" that would undermine the movement's democratic foundations. Alluding to similar developments elsewhere in Europe, Rothmann warned, "the 'dualism' of military-civilian organizations has never brought about any good results in any location. Commands and politics, soldierly obedience and factual reasoning, discipline and parliamentarism have never gotten along."[52] The term "youth phalanx" as well as the subtle reference to other European political movements pointed to an awareness that the Revisionist movement was mirroring a process that other right-wing movements had undergone. Polish Revisionist activists needed to look no further than Poland in the early 1930s, when the National Democrats (Endecja) welcomed young militants into their ranks only to have them challenge the movement's veteran leadership.[53] Moshe Lejzerowicz's letter of protest was far more explicit in its critique of Betar's dictatorial tendencies. In the two years that had passed since his positive assessment of fascism at a national Revisionist conference, he had become more skeptical of Jabotinsky's leadership. "It's obvious," he wrote two weeks after the annulment of the agreement, "that Betar's members would vote in a democratic organization according to Jabotinsky's wishes." "If," he continued, "the head of Betar [Jabotinsky] believes that he can propose a belief with the power of a soldier, all of the democratic institutions of the Revisionist movement are entirely unnecessary: Betar should declare itself *the* Revisionist organization and a dictatorship should be declared for the movement."[54] Lejzerowicz likely knew that if Jabotinsky had his way, the letter's prophecy would only be fulfilled in part; the leadership positions within the Revisionist councils would be overrun by Betar activists awaiting Jabotinsky's command, but the movement would continue to insist it upheld democratic values. It was only a matter of time, Lejzerowicz feared, until Jabotinsky's youth-centered strategy, with the Gentlemen's Agreement at its core, would erode the movement's democratic edifice altogether.

What Are "Youth"? Making the Public Case for Authoritarianism, 1932–1933

If Jabotinsky's strategy within the party was to blur the lines between "youth" and "adult," his newspaper articles addressed to the Polish Jewish public did precisely the opposite. To help make the case for increasing his power within the Revisionist movement, Jabotinsky deftly used images of youth and generational conflict already circulating within the Polish Jewish press. He drew on two popular images of youth: the obedient child, willing to blindly obey the demands of a commanding authority, and the reckless rebel who rejected the ethical conventions of adults. Jabotinsky realized that there was as much to be gained by presenting his youth movement's members as rebels as there was to presenting them as obedient. In articles designed to capture the attention of the British government, restrain the Biryonim, and undermine the Revisionist Executive, Jabotinsky alternated between these images of Jewish youth.

One of the first advantages Jabotinsky believed he possessed by describing youth as obedient rebels was the ability to capture the attention of the British government and public. Although Jabotinsky was concerned by the Biryonim's call for insurrectionary activity, he simultaneously entertained the possibility that these threats could persuade the British government to view the Revisionist movement as a force to be reckoned with. In January 1932, Jabotinsky wrote to the *London Times* to warn the British public of the threat Jewish youth would pose to their government should it remain deaf to the demands of the Zionist movement. The letter reproduced the following passage from a speech delivered by Jabotinsky one month beforehand at a Revisionist conference in Warsaw:

> The mandatory has become an unmitigated hindrance to any progress of Zionism. This realization threatens to drive the Jewish masses, especially our youth, along a very dangerous road. The youth of a people faced with such [a] plight as ours cannot live without some kind of faith: faith either in a great restoration or in a great destruction. England acts as though she wished to set ablaze 15 000 000 torches of despair scattered in every corner of the world.[55]

Typical of Jabotinsky's prose, the letter combined a provocative description of the threat of Jewish youth with carefully embedded caveats. In the beginning of the letter, Jabotinsky assured the editors of the *Times* that he had never met a Jew who sought to harm the British Empire, adding, "It is one of our racial weaknesses ... that with us resentment does not necessarily imply the desire for revenge." In an effort to further clarify his remarks at the Warsaw conference, he added that the greatest threat posed by current British policy in Palestine lay in the fact that it was fostering "pan-Islamic fanaticism" by granting political power to Muslim clerics. Simultaneously, however, Jabotinsky added, "[Y]our cable's epitome of my Warsaw speech was in some ways rather an understatement"; Jewish animosity toward the British "grows and spreads and deepens from day to day and already cannot be contained."[56] What made Jabotinsky's veiled threat powerful was not only his description of Jewish youth on the verge of committing violent crimes, but also his subtle insistence that they would obey his demands. This point was driven home in the final paragraphs of the letter, in which Jabotinsky documented his strenuous efforts to encourage Jews to have faith in England. "I would be happy," he insisted, "if I could advocate for this ethos in the future."[57] The message of the letter was clear: so long as the British government complied with the demands of the Revisionist movement, Jabotinsky would strive to ensure that Jewish youth in Palestine and beyond would support the British government and refrain from committing acts of insurrectionary violence.

When addressing his Jewish readership in Poland, Jabotinsky similarly depicted himself as the only capable intermediary between volatile Jewish youth and adults. This approach was best captured in his first public response to the Biryonim—an article entitled "On Adventurism." Published in the winter of 1932 in *Haynt*, the article was republished one year later in Betar's first anthology of Jabotinsky's writings.[58] He began by describing "adventurism" as an activity "which all serious people hate, that only youth dream about," and added that he was a staunch defender of youth who engaged in these acts. By describing radical activity as the preserve of youth, Jabotinsky could endorse political extremism without having to claim that he himself held these beliefs. No less important was his choice to cast as wide a net as possible to define the nature of "adventurism." While in the bulk of the article, he described nonviolent acts, such as the illegal immigration of youth to Palestine, he also labeled murdering one's opponents an "adventurist" act. The example he gave made clear that this was not merely one example among many. Jabotinsky turned to the Exodus narrative, focusing on the decisive moment in which Moses—still an Egyptian prince—decides for the first time to express solidarity with the enslaved Israelites. He did so by murdering an Egyptian who was beating an Israelite slave. Reflecting on the moment in which another slave confronts Moses about the murder, Jabotinsky wrote, "There is no doubt that that Jew [*yener yid*] who sought to criticize our teacher Moses [Moshe Rabeinu] for murdering the policeman in Egypt also said to him, "you are an adventurist!" To blur the definition of adventurism even further, he added that only the outcome of "adventurist" acts could determine whether they were reckless or reasonable. It was precisely because the definition of adventurism was so vague, Jabotinsky concluded, that he alone could determine when such acts were permissible. Addressing his readers directly, he wrote, "I must reserve the right to determine when it is appropriate to address a person with the phrase: adventurist!"[59] By casting youth as volatile, framing adventurism in ambiguous terms, and presenting himself as the only leader capable of determining the actions of young Jews, Jabotinsky was implicitly making a case to his readers that he needed to adopt an authoritarian leadership style.

"On Adventurism" was not designed merely to show the Biryonim and their supporters that political radicalism was only one of many options available to the movement. Nor was it intended simply to remind them that Jabotinsky alone would determine the movement's course. The article's arguments linking the nature of youth and authoritarian politics were also a crucial component of Jabotinsky's plan to wrest power from the London Revisionist Executive without abandoning his democratic persona. In tandem with ideas about the "obedient rebel," the notion of generational conflict became a central feature of Jabotinsky's campaign to bolster his power within the Revisionist movement. In the fall of 1932, Jabotinsky began to publish a series of articles that questioned the effectiveness of parliamentary democracy. Descriptions of generational conflict pervaded these texts. By depicting himself as the leader of a generation with fundamentally different worldviews and experiences, he could claim that while he remained a liberal to his core, his ideological preferences had little hope in the world in which his followers were coming of age.

The first of such articles appeared in *Haynt* in August 1932 in the wake of Achimeir's speech in Vienna's Renz Circus, in which he called for Jabotinsky to assume the role of a dictator. In his rebuttal, Jabotinsky had declared himself a champion of equality and liberty, insisting that he would sooner leave the Revisionist movement than adopt a dictator's persona. Within his speech, however, he included a crucial caveat to his rejection of dictatorship. Even if dictatorship could never serve as a "political worldview," he observed that it could serve as a temporary "medicine" for a society in crisis: "[W]e have seen," he noted, "that this system has created order, also where previously there were no possibilities to do so."[60] Jabotinsky repeated this caveat in his article addressing the Polish Jewish readers of *Haynt*. Rebuking Achimeir, Jabotinsky insisted to his followers, "[I]n my life I've never given any 'commands' to a person—I don't even know how someone does so." He followed, however, by cautioning them, "It is [also] true that there can be periods of exceptional situations, periods of social sickness, when one needs, at times, to use exceptional means: but one cannot... make out of exceptional cases a rule to be followed by every generation."[61] Embedded within these statements was an argument that would be repeated for months to come: though dictatorship was not a timeless ideal, it could serve as a "rule" for a generation coming of age in an era of crisis.

Jabotinsky had gestured toward this argument in an article published in the Polish Jewish press several months beforehand. The article described Jabotinsky's attempt to intervene in a conversation taking place at a café in Paris between young Jewish men who were extolling the virtues of violence and dictatorship. When Jabotinsky declared that his generation fought for democracy, one of the young men responded, "My dear sir, it truly pains us that we have to so crudely destroy the laughable concept imagined by men from your generation regarding the phenomenon of 'youth.' We belong to a world that is far older than the world in which you were raised. We have seen too many terrible things." Through the voices of these young men, Jabotinsky went on to describe how the democratic ideals of the "older" generation had only brought despair to the Jews of 1930s Europe. In one such passage, the imagined youth quipped, "The elements of *your* youth rule in every country today . . . [including] the principle of responsible government with general voting (even the women), which your generation thought would surely bring redemption. You believed that redemption rested with the masses. Well, here are your folk-masses, ruling. And they're voting for Hitler."[62] In the remaining passages of the article, Jabotinsky depicted himself furiously rebuking these youth for giving into the current zeitgeist. Significantly, however, Jabotinsky did not devote time to critiquing their depiction of parliamentarism. Nor did he offer any detailed alternatives for them. The only tangible solution he could muster was to urge them to transcend their current state as a "Generation of Realists" and strive instead to seek out truth and strive for noble ideals. This hardly constituted a thorough defense of the liberal values he claimed he and his generation embodied.

The title of another article published in October 1932, "Grandfather Liberalism," similarly underscored the inability of "old" liberal values—including parliamentarism—to respond to needs of the "new" generation of youth in Europe, including young European Jews. Like so many of his articles that tapped into ideas about youth and generational conflict, "Grandfather Liberalism" was rife with meticulously constructed contradictions. The final lines of the text predicted that liberalism would ultimately rise from the grave, even though "the old one has long been dead and buried." At the same time, however, Jabotinsky had no interest in using his article as a platform to defend parliamentarism and democracy. Instead, column after column in the article offered his readers further proof that youth had good reason to be wary of parliamentary politics. Echoing critiques of parliamentarism often invoked by Europe's authoritarian leaders, Jabotinsky's article traversed the continent, providing case after case of parliaments being paralyzed by factionalism, with political parties resorting to unsavory means to crush their opponents. In addition to demonstrating parliamentarism's deleterious effect on all Europeans, he added that Jews in particular were victims of politicians invoking liberalism to achieve their goals. Toward the end of the article, he described how the liberal value of civic equality had been appropriated and distorted by antisemites in Poland who sought to impose a numerus clausus on Jews in various professions. The principle of equality, Jabotinsky explained, was used to condemn the disproportionate representation of Jews in the arts, medicine, and law.

Significantly, Jabotinsky offered no prescription for resuscitating liberalism and parliamentarism. He did, however, have the following to say of liberalism: "In truth, its prescriptions are . . . for normal times, not times of illness. Sometimes someone becomes sick, they must have a bitter cure—whether medicine, or perhaps an operation."[63] By inserting this statement, Jabotinsky managed, as he had done in previous articles, to pave the way for taking on authoritarian measures by framing them as temporary responses to crisis. For the Revisionist movement, the "bitter cure" he anticipated would come into effect with his so-called putsch of 1933, an event that relied heavily on the youth-centered campaign Jabotinsky had conducted in the nineteen months that followed the Seventeenth Zionist Congress.

Obedient Rebels in Action: Jabotinsky's Putsch and Its Aftermath

The winter of 1933 provided Jabotinsky with the chance to put his authoritarian strategy, which relied on ideas about who youth were and how they were expected to behave, to the test. At the beginning of January, a meeting was called between Jabotinsky, the London Executive, and leading representatives of Revisionist councils worldwide, to be held in the Silesian town of Katowice. While Grossman saw the meeting as a last-ditch effort to convince Jabotinsky to respect the authority of the Revisionist Executive, Jabotinsky saw it as an opportunity to ensure that his power to determine the course of the Revisionist movement would prevail. He informed the Revisionist Executive in London that the Katowice meeting would address, once and for all, the status of the Revisionists in the Zionist Organization, as well as the scope of power he would hold in the decision-making process of the Revisionist Party.[64]

After months of rising tension within the party, Jabotinsky, the four members of the London Executive, and approximately seventy representatives from Revisionist groups worldwide convened on Monday, March 20, 1933, in a Katowice hotel.[65] One can only wonder what the meeting's delegates, arriving for the tense deliberations, made of the name of the hotel, Pod Wypoczynkiem (At Leisure). When the question of whether the Revisionist movement would remain in the Zionist Organization was put to a vote, the Revisionist council delegates largely sided with the London Executive; only thirteen of the seventy delegates supported Jabotinsky. Among the thirteen was Aharon Propes, the Biryonim leader Uri Zvi Grinberg, the veteran Revisionist activist in Palestine

Abraham Weinshal, and the Viennese journalist Wolfgang von Weisl, who had previously called for Jabotinsky to accept his destiny as a dictator. Following the vote, they were summoned to a meeting in Jabotinsky's hotel room. Joining them was David Boiko, Betar's head commander in eastern Galicia. According to Boiko—who, forty years later, provided one of the only eyewitness accounts of what took place in the hotel room—Jabotinsky confided that he sought to dissolve the Revisionist Executive and declare the movement's independence from the Zionist Organization. "We told him," Boiko later recalled, "that there was no doubt that the youth would follow him, because they were 'Jabotinsky's youth', not 'Revisionist youth.'"[66] The next day, Jabotinsky instructed Boiko to prepare to dismiss the eastern Galician Revisionist leaders from their positions in the Revisionist movement, in the event that they refused to accept the demands he presented to the Revisionist Executive. In the meantime, Jabotinsky met, behind closed doors, with members of the London Executive. The meeting lasted more than thirteen hours. Jabotinsky's request to add more members to the executive who supported secession from the Zionist Organization was rebuffed, as was his offer to agree to remain in the organization in the event that the Revisionist movement received a majority at the upcoming congress elections. The conference ended with no new resolutions, and the London Executive declared that the party's regulations would remain as they were.

As soon as the meeting ended, Jabotinsky left Katowice and traveled 120 miles north to the industrial city of Łódź. He then set into motion a plan that severely weakened the movement's democratic elements. On Wednesday, March 22, he informed Meir Grossman and the other members of the executive that they had been expelled from the movement's executive, and that he now controlled all the Revisionist organization's affairs.[67] He then sent a letter to the *Jewish Telegraphic Agency*, which in turn sent news of his decisions to Jewish newspapers worldwide.[68] Jabotinsky's letter, which later became known as the Łódź Manifesto, informed Revisionists of the decisions he had made, adding that he would soon create a temporary executive under his command that would be based in Warsaw. Of the three members of the new executive, two would be from Poland—including Betar's head commander, Aharon Propes.[69]

The language Jabotinsky used in his manifesto, and the articles written in the wake of the putsch to justify his actions, would have been deeply familiar to his Jewish audience in Warsaw and elsewhere in Poland. As citizens of an authoritarian regime, they had heard Józef Piłsudski's supporters claim at the start of the Sanacja government that authoritarian rule would ultimately ensure the eventual revival and long-term survival of democracy. Rather than speak of a split, Jabotinsky described his actions as an effort to unify the Revisionist movement. He also insisted in several articles that his action was an attempt to bring the movement *back* to its democratic foundations. Rather than let it be steered by a handful of men, Jabotinsky would "listen to the voice of the masses," and, acting in the interests of the majority of Revisionists, take on the leadership of the movement.[70] In the manifesto and elsewhere, Jabotinsky also urged Revisionist members to participate in the Eighteenth Zionist Congress. Jabotinsky's willingness to bring the party to the Zionist Congress, he explained, underscored his commitment to democracy. "A dictator," he wrote, "seeks to force his own will upon the masses. . . . I do the opposite—I am submitting myself to the will of the majority and am going to the Congress."[71] As ultimate proof of his democratic credentials, he notified Revisionist members that a plebiscite would be conducted within several weeks' time to determine whether the party's membership approved of the decisions he had made in Łódź. The plebiscite aimed to demonstrate to the Jewish public that every Revisionist member played a role in the decision-making process of the movement's leadership.[72]

Like elections in Poland and in other authoritarian countries in the region, however, the plebiscite was meant to simulate rather than implement democratic practices. Here, Jabotinsky's ambiguous definition of "youth" became crucial. On the same day that he had published the manifesto, Jabotinsky had delivered an appeal to Betar members, commanding them to "stand with pride and courage for the sturdy platform of fully unifying the entire Revisionist movement."[73] A day later, he wrote the following lines to a Grossman sympathizer in Paris: "I'll create a plebiscite, and if I'll fail—*which is doubtful if you take into consideration Betar's members over the age of eighteen*—I'll surrender and turn aside."[74] Grossman, too, focused on the role that Betar's age distribution would play in determining the results of the plebiscite. In a report published by the *Jewish Telegraphic Agency* on Jabotinsky's activity, Grossman observed, "Recently he has turned to [Brit] Trumpeldor to ask them to support the leader's mission for Revisionist goals."[75] David Boiko's account of the events that immediately followed the Katowice conference similarly underscores the role Betar played in Jabotinsky's putsch. According to Boiko, Jabotinsky sent out instructions to Propes, which were promptly cabled to Boiko. The telegram consisted of only two words, in English: "go ahead." Boiko promptly summoned Lwów's Revisionist council and told them that he had been instructed to dismiss them from their posts. In the meantime, he instructed Betar leaders to travel by motorcycle across eastern Galicia and command local Betar units to take over any offices of Revisionist councils that were not already in the youth movement's hands.[76] Without hesitation, major Polish Jewish newspapers began describing the events that were transpiring across the country as a "putsch" and a "dictator's coup."[77]

Although the putsch seems to have caught many Betar leaders in Poland off guard, they immediately rallied behind Jabotinsky. Four days after Jabotinsky had published his manifesto, Betar's weekly newspaper, *Ha-medina*, provided them with a platform to defend his actions. "Finally," the newspaper enthused on the same page that Jabotinsky's appeal was published, "the road has been found: the decisive concentration of the monistic movement around its leader in the name of one goal." True to Jabotinsky's self-presentation as a democrat, the article added, "[W]e, who know Jabotinsky as a radical democrat . . . know that . . . this very man who hated to even hear the term 'leader' did what he did because he had no other option."[78] The newspaper also featured articles in which "ordinary" Betar members begged Jabotinsky to take power in order to save the Zionist movement.[79] Downplaying the fact that Jabotinsky's putsch aimed to destroy the political influence of his opponents on the London Revisionist Executive, one article added as an afterthought, "[I]t is unfortunate that Meir Grossman and his own circle of friends did not understand the liberating deed that Vladimir Jabotinsky performed."[80] This language of liberation permeated other articles in which Betar's leaders argued that the putsch was the ultimate democratic act, empowering the masses to have their voices finally heard. In an article written just prior to the plebiscite, Propes reminded his readers that they were not Jabotinsky's passive, powerless, and mute servants. Instead, Propes insisted, "he listens to *you*: the nation speaks to him . . . he is ours, entirely ours."[81] Sure enough, when a plebiscite was staged within the movement in April, well over 90 percent of Betar members voted to approve of Jabotinsky's actions. In the months that followed, Betar leaders took over the positions previously filled by Revisionist supporters who were sympathetic to the London Revisionist Executive. In eastern Galicia, David Boiko's home base, Betar's leaders reported in 1934 that the "Revisionist" infrastructure relied almost exclusively on older Betar members, adding that thanks to their efforts, "they saved the movement after the Katowice events."[82]

Revisionist opponents of the putsch in Poland were also quick to highlight the role that Betar played in Jabotinsky's plebiscite victory. In the northeastern town of Baranowicze, for example, the city's weekly Yiddish newspaper divided the Revisionist camp into two: the youth of Betar, "compelled by a command" to vote, and on the other side, "the older and more responsible" Revisionists, who ultimately chose to boycott the vote.[83] Supporters of the putsch, too, described it as a victory for Jewish youth. Reporting on the Katowice events in Palestine, the Biryonim informed their readers that the attempts of the London Executive "to turn the movement of rebellion in the Zionist movement" into a group "whose only task would be to argue in meetings" was prevented by "youth [who] understood the spirit of the leader, and walked in his footsteps without hesitation."[84] Jabotinsky, too, looked back on the events that had unfolded in generational terms. As the dust began to settle from the putsch, and Jabotinsky turned his attention to the upcoming Zionist Congress, he wrote to veteran Revisionist activist Shlomo Jacobi to reflect on the events of the previous two months. "There's nothing to do," Jabotinsky concluded. "[Y]ou and all of your fascist generation were right about one thing: it is forbidden for leaders to be humble."[85] Jabotinsky's assessment succinctly captured the strategy that had propelled his political activity for months: by depicting himself as powerless before the force of youth, he believed that he could gain far more influence than ever before over the fate of the Revisionist movement and, he hoped, the future of the Zionist project.

Whether he would admit it or not, the very rhetorical strategies and political policies concerning "youth" that he had deployed drew him even closer to embracing the beliefs and practices of authoritarian leaders in Europe at the time. By blurring the lines between "youth" and "adult" within the Revisionist movement's policies and using this ambiguity to his advantage during the plebiscite of 1933, Jabotinsky allowed himself, like other authoritarian politicians across interwar Europe, to claim that he had upheld key procedural components of modern democracy, such as voting, even as he strove to manipulate their results. In the lead-up to the putsch, Jabotinsky used his public discussions of "generational conflict" as a platform to present to his readers arguments frequently employed by authoritarian rulers throughout Europe to justify their actions. These included assuring the public that authoritarian measures were born out of historical necessity and in the interests of national unity; that authoritarian rule would not be permanent; and that its ultimate goal was not to demolish parliamentary democracy but rather to cure it of the factionalism and corruption that had paralyzed its ability to function. No less significant were the ambiguities and contradictions that Jabotinsky had embedded within his descriptions of the behavior of youth and their role in modern politics. As much as authoritarian rulers across the continent issued bold, brash, and sweeping political declarations, they saw little need to present an ideologically seamless world to their followers. Instead, a central component of their rhetorical strategy was to blur the lines between liberty and subordination, democracy and dictatorship, submission and empowerment, and finally, restraint and extremism. The linguistic styling typical of authoritarian movements of the time was not simply one discursive approach in Betar among many, but was a crucial component of the youth movement's culture, if not its very foundation. When one sets Jabotinsky's calls in Betar's anthem for a "noble and cruel" youth in the context of the brash yet elusive linguistic style employed by leaders across the spectrum of Europe's Right, it becomes tempting to see in his construction of youth a glimmer of the "mathematical logic" he promised Gourevitch at the café in Paris that winter evening of 1932.

FIGURE 3. A Betar member welcomes Vladimir Jabotinsky to Dworzec Wiedeński, Warsaw's palatial train station, in 1932. (Photo courtesy of the Jabotinsky Institute)

FIGURE 4. Aharon Propes (1904–1978), Betar's founder and its head commander in Poland from 1929 to 1939, sits at his desk in the youth movement's office in Warsaw, 1935. (Photo courtesy of the Jabotinsky Institute)

FIGURE 5. Attending an instructor's course in 1933, Betar members from Lublin pose with rifles, likely on loan from the Polish army. (Photo courtesy of the Jabotinsky Institute)

FIGURE 6. Betar members from Żabno march in the town's annual parade, organized by Polish government officials to celebrate Poland's access to the Baltic Sea. Polish military officers participating in the parade stand to the left of the Betar youth, while to their right, civilian spectators look on. Undated photo. (Photo courtesy of the Jabotinsky Institute)

FIGURE 7. In the town of Włodzimierz (Ludmir in Yiddish, Volodymyr Volyns'kyi in Ukrainian), located in Poland's eastern borderlands, a Polish army officer provides rifle training to Betar members Avraham Amper and Sonia Haas, 1934. (Photo courtesy of the Jabotinsky Institute)

FIGURE 8. Like other Jewish youth movements in interwar Poland, Betar offered a range of recreational activities. In Suwałki, the town's Betar orchestra poses with instruments in hand, 1929. (Photo courtesy of the Jabotinsky Institute)

FIGURE 9. Four Betar members from Warsaw stand at attention during roll call at their youth movement's summer camp, 1938. By the mid-1930s, young women made up nearly half of Betar's membership in Poland. (Photo courtesy of the Jabotinsky Institute)

FIGURE 10. In 1939, twenty-six-year-old Menachem Begin (1913–1992) poses for his portrait as Betar's new leader in Poland. (Photo courtesy of the Jabotinsky Institute)

4

Poland, Palestine, and the Politics of Belonging

IT WAS A Saturday evening in late June 1933. Nearly nine hundred Jews had crowded into an auditorium in Radom, a city of some seventy thousand inhabitants in central Poland. They had come to hear Yitzhak Grinboym deliver his campaign speech for the upcoming World Zionist Congress. The tension in the room was palpable; dozens of police officers had filed in and were lined up against the wall. The previous week, Grinboym had claimed in newspapers throughout the country that Betar posed a dangerous threat to the democratic foundations of the Zionist movement.[1] In one such article, he warned the Jewish public to neither dismiss Betar's calls for a military culture to pervade Jewish civil society nor ignore the youth movement's celebration of violence. Betar's violent rhetoric was not, he insisted, merely a "game of wicked, wild children"; the youth movement's members would stop at nothing to prove that "with bullets one can dispose of people and ideas from the road" being paved by Zionists to bring about a Jewish homeland in Palestine. At the very least, he wrote, Betar members would "surely silence me with the sound of... screams and would remove me, by force, from the stage" for trying to speak out against them.[2] This was precisely what Radom's local Zionist Organization and the city's police unit feared would occur that very evening.

As Grinboym delivered his speech, everything seemed under control. But just as he concluded, nearly two hundred people throughout the auditorium sprang up from their seats, ready to follow the command of a Betar leader at the foot of the stage. Here is Grinboym, writing in Poland's most widely circulated Yiddish daily, recalling what happened next, just before he was chased out of the auditorium and a brawl broke out: "What do you think he [the Betar leader] shouted? *Nider mit di tsionistishe ferreter! Nider mit Grinboymen!* Down with the Zionist traitor! Down with Grinboym! . . . You're wrong. He shouted in Polish, *Niech żyje sanacji! Precz z opozycją!* Long live the *Sanacja*, and down with its opponents!" When a similar brawl erupted at his lecture in Lublin several days later, Grinboym recalled that "in the midst of all the shrieks and screams, one could hear sounds of [Betar members singing] 'Jeszcze Polska nie Zginęła' ["Poland has not yet perished," the opening line of the country's national anthem] and 'My pierwsza brygada'"[3]—the hymn of the First World War's Polish Legion, led by none other than Józef Piłsudski.

Grinboym was far from the only one to notice Betar's use of Polish patriotic songs and slogans. In the early 1930s, Polish police officers throughout the country were reporting to their superiors that the Zionist youth movement was placing their pledges of Polish patriotism front and center of their public activity. Some described how the youth movement's leaders marked Zionist celebrations by laying wreaths at Polish war memorials, imploring their followers to "act Polish."[4] Others recounted how local Betar units requested permission to march in parades alongside Polish scouts and soldiers during the country's national holidays.[5] Betar leaders boasted to one another of the presence of Polish military officials at their events.[6]

Betar's efforts to link Zionism with Polish nationalism became a regular feature of their activities in the early 1930s. Yet they appear to be anything but typical when read in tandem with the work of historians of modern Poland, who nearly exclusively focus on antisemitism and anti-Jewish violence as the key to understanding Polish-Jewish relations.[7] Although this scholarship correctly underscores the crucial role that antisemitism played in interwar Jewish life, its focus on moments of crisis often leaves the impression that Catholic Poles and Polish Jews were, in the words of one historian, locked "in a sociological collision course."[8] Indeed, the very term "Polish-Jewish relations," frequently used by these scholars to describe their work, implies that "Poles" and "Jews" constituted two groups whose religious, ethnic, and political borders were static, clear, and impenetrable.

Betar's activities call into question these accounts of life in Poland. At the very moment that Betar's leaders claimed to perform a distinct national identity, they modeled their ceremonies on Polish patriotic rituals, called for their members to "act Polish," and attempted to include Polish government officials as both observers and participants in their celebrations. No less significant was the reaction of the Polish government to these performances. Government officials often encouraged Betar members to participate in Polish patriotic parades. They even permitted them to join the government's paramilitary training programs, where Betar members could learn to shoot rifles. At various points, the youth movement's participants, leaders, and Polish government officials all shared the same conviction—not only was there something fundamentally "Polish" about Revisionist Zionism, but to be a young Zionist was, in many ways, to exhibit the qualities of the ideal Pole.

That is not to say, however, that Betar members, leaders, and Polish government officials shared a common understanding of what it meant for Zionists to "act Polish." Battles about the meaning of Polskość (Polishness) were as old as Polish nationalism itself. Polish political activists furiously debated whether "Polishness" could be a civic identity adopted by all future inhabitants of an independent state, or an identity that only ethnic Poles who were Catholic could possess.[9] By the 1930s, when Polish calls for an inclusive civic nationalism grew increasingly dim, these debates took on even more urgency for the country's Jews. Against this backdrop, what exactly did Betar's leaders mean when they implored their members to "act Polish"? How did their followers interpret these instructions? And what did Polish government officials make of these public performances of a Polish-Zionist alliance? This chapter takes up these questions from the diverse and often conflicting vantage points of Betar's members, leaders, and Polish government officials. In doing so, it draws attention to the dynamics and paradoxes of acculturation for young Jews coming of age in interwar Poland, as well as the complex factors at play when government officials attempted to determine the extent to which young Jews and other national minorities could be integrated into the new Polish state.

Dictation Lessons and Their Discontents

In 1929, a six-year-old boy from the city of Radom entered the first-grade class of his local public school. His teacher instructed the students to transcribe a passage in Polish. Just as he had done in *heder*, where Jewish children acquired an elementary religious education, the young boy began to write down the sounds he heard using Hebrew letters, starting from the right side of the page and moving leftward. When the teacher noticed the young boy's error, she turned to him and said, "Write from left to right, in Polish, not in Yiddish." Confused, the new student rose from his seat and asked, "Excuse me, miss, but are we Poles or are we Jews?"[10]

Recounted ten years later by the boy, now a sixteen-year-old gymnasium student invited to join Betar, this anecdote succinctly captures the power of interwar Polish public schools to transform how young Jews saw themselves. Simply learning how to write in Polish was enough to unsettle his previously held notions about who was Polish and who was Jewish. Embedded within the young student's response to his teacher was yet another question: What made a Pole and what made a Jew? Could the act of learning how to read, write, and speak in the Polish language have the power to make him Polish? These were questions that would have been deeply familiar to most young Polish Jews in the interwar period. Nearly 80 percent of the 420,000 Jewish children of school age living in 1930s Poland attended a Polish public school. In the province of Lwów—a stronghold for Betar—the number was as high as 97 percent.[11] In this province and elsewhere throughout the country, young Jews spent as many as twelve hours a week learning Polish, reading Polish literature, and listening to teachers recount the history of Polish kings, noblemen, soldiers, and politicians.[12]

The unprecedented opportunities given to these young Jews to obtain a free education, learn alongside non-Jewish students, and receive daily instruction in Polish language, literature, and history proved transformative. Not only did the Polish public school system play a crucial role in determining the linguistic preferences of Polish Jewish youth, who increasingly used Polish as a language of daily communication, but the years spent learning about Polish history and literature also shaped how Jewish youth understood who they were and where they belonged in the new Polish state. Like the young boy from Radom, other Jewish youth sought answers within the Polish public schools they attended to the question of whether they could be both Polish and Jewish.

Polish public schools under the Sanacja regime seemed to offer young Jews the promise of acceptance and integration into the Polish state. Polish government officials instructed teachers to encourage students belonging to the country's national minorities to embrace Polish literature and history.[13] They also insisted that schools stage as many patriotic celebrations as possible, from parades on Polish Independence Day to school recitals in honor of the name days (*imieniny*) of prominent Polish cultural and political figures.[14] By doing so, they hoped that the country's national minorities, particularly those living in Poland's borderlands, would identify with the Sanacja government and become loyal citizens of the country. These expectations were made clear in the new curricula designed by Piłsudski's government in the early 1930s. The Sanacja's curriculum guidelines for the study of history explained that its "emphasis on moments of active and positive participation of the minorities in Poland's state life" aimed at "strengthening in them a sense of attachment and civic responsibility with regard to the state."[15] A 1935 history curriculum instructed fifth-grade teachers, should they find themselves "in schools where there are Jewish youth," to "address more fully the participation of Jews in the struggles for independence."[16] Echoing this advice, textbooks describing national minorities in Poland's history often focused on their participation in Polish armed revolts.[17] Descriptions of Jews participating in the Polish uprising in 1794 against the partition of the Polish Lithuanian Commonwealth, or rebellions against Russian rule in 1830–31 and 1863–64, aimed to demonstrate that Polish nationalism had a tradition of inclusion and tolerance of non-Catholics. Textbooks also presented military service as the most effective route for Jewish membership in the Polish nation. A second-grade reader published in 1933, for example, described Polish soldiers coming to a village: "There are also Ukrainians, who immediately began to sing their wonderful songs. There are still others, Belarusians, who speak a musical language, and there are Jews. And all of them are Polish soldiers—good, beloved soldiers of one good, beloved Fatherland."[18]

Indeed, much of the attention that government officials lavished on public schooling stemmed from their conviction that students could serve as future soldiers who would defend the state's fragile borders from attack. By the late 1920s, Polish military officials worked closely with district school boards and local principals to prepare students for military service. In addition to providing financial and organizational support for scouting programs affiliated with the schools, local military officials offered courses in "military preparation" (*przysposobienie wojskowe*) for young men and first aid training for young women. To provide them with a taste of the honor accorded to Poland's armed forces, military units across the country invited student delegations to participate in patriotic parades alongside locally stationed soldiers.[19]

The Sanacja government's preoccupation with transforming young citizens into soldiers also left a deep imprint on the public school's literature program. Novels by such Polish romantic authors as Adam Mickiewicz and Henryk Sienkiewicz, describing seventeenth- and eighteenth-century battles against Swedes, Cossacks, and Russians, became staples of the public school classroom. Considered by Polish nationalists of every stripe to be the father of modern Polish literature, Mickiewicz wrote sweeping romantic tales of Polish military exploits and national rebirth in which Jews were a natural, integral component of Polish life. Along with his patriotic poems and plays,

Mickiewicz had also claimed elsewhere that Jews and Poles shared a mystical bond. Advocates of Jewish integration into Polish society had used these writings for decades as proof that Catholic Poles and Jews were brothers-in-arms, two oppressed nations fighting for the restoration of their homeland.[20] Mickiewicz's literature, when read within the context of the public school, reinforced the official message of the Ministry of Religion and Education that any national minority group who pledged loyalty to Poland and joined in its military struggles would be embraced by the Polish nation.

The ambitions of Polish public school officials, particularly in the eastern borderlands, were frequently hampered by a lack of finances, a shortage of qualified personnel, and skepticism among peasants about the value of education.[21] Their impact on Jewish students, however, is unmistakable in autobiographies written by Jewish youth in the 1930s. The efforts of public school officials to instill Polish patriotism are vividly described by dozens of Betar members, from a range of religious and economic backgrounds, who participated alongside several hundred young Jews in an autobiography contest sponsored by the YIVO Institute for Jewish Research. Using the pseudonym K.S.V., a young man from a town near Łódź recounted how his Polish teacher "hammered Sienkiewicz's trilogy into us until we almost broke."[22] Although he resented having to learn Sienkiewicz's account of seventeenth-century Polish military adventures by heart—a task faced by many public school students—he proudly pointed out to his readers that Polish history was his best subject. Indeed, when it came to describing their education, Betar autobiographers, along with other YIVO autobiographers, often listed Polish literature and history as their favorite subjects of study.[23] R. E., a young Betar member from the southeastern town of Horodenka, wrote with as much passion about his Polish-language teacher introducing him to Polish literature and watching Polish soldiers march during parades as he did about praying with his father and wearing *tzitzit*, ritual fringes worn by observant Jewish males.[24] For lack of a contemporary role model, he may well have recalled Mickiewicz's most famous work, *Pan Tadeusz*, which included among its protagonists an observant Jewish innkeeper in the early nineteenth century who was also a fervent Polish patriot.

Nonetheless, these autobiographies also capture the sense of confusion and frustration that many Betar members and Jewish students in general felt when they contrasted their admiration for the myths of Polish national liberation with the antisemitic behavior of their non-Jewish peers and, occasionally, school officials. Although K. S., a twenty-year-old from the town of Kozienice, described his love of learning Polish history at school, he also recalled that "in school, Christian kids used to attack the Jewish kids, and a full-blown 'war' would begin. Many would come home bloodied. The Christian students were also hurt. Such battles happened often." Even as they sat in the classroom, he added, he could still "feel their hatred."[25] Descriptions abounded in other autobiographies of Jewish students doing their best to avoid harassment from their Christian classmates by sitting on the opposite side of the classroom or avoiding the playground during recess.[26] Teachers and administrators were often depicted as indifferent, if not hostile, to Jewish students who objected to this treatment. An eighteen-year-old Betar member from a small town in the eastern province of Wołyń, for example, recounted how he was promptly expelled from school when he chose to speak up against a Polish student who had insulted him.[27] Anti-Jewish hostility could also manifest itself in more subtle but no less hurtful ways. One autobiographer from a town in central Poland described how at his graduation, the school's director kissed students on both sides of the cheek. When a young Jewish student went up to receive his grade, the teacher turned away. "We were old enough," he recalled, "to understand what such behavior meant."[28]

Although the unequal treatment of Jewish students was never enshrined in the policy of Poland's public schools, the behavior of many non-Jewish students and teachers stemmed from beliefs that were also shared and condoned by many government officials. The Sanacja's political elite, cobbled together by Piłsudski in 1926, came from a variety of groups, including several peasant parties and the right-wing Polish Christian Democratic Party, as well as from among high-ranking members of the military. They held a vast range of views concerning the country's minorities.[29] To make matters more complicated, Piłsudski never appointed a decision-making body to serve as the chief authority on the issue of nationalities, and he avoided making public statements dealing with the place of Jews in Poland.[30] As a result, government policies toward Jews and other minorities depended largely on local context and the immediate needs of Sanacja officials to consolidate their power. Practices on the ground frequently ran counter to calls for a multicultural Poland offered by some higher-ranking Sanacja officials.[31] Even as some of the Sanacja's top-tier officials promoted the notion that Jewish youth could become loyal citizens of the Polish state, they rarely claimed, as they did for Ukrainians, Lithuanians, and Belarusians, that Jews could become Polish. In official exchanges between local and national officials, representatives of the Polish government claimed that Jews were naturally predisposed to communism and were dangerously overrepresented in key sectors of the Polish economy.[32] Many officials believed a public school education would at best replace their hostility toward the Polish state with a sense of "civic attachment."

These officials were also well aware that Catholic Church officials would reinforce deep-seated beliefs among their parishioners that Jews intrinsically hated Catholics and posed a threat to the Polish state.[33] According to historian Brian Porter-Szűcs, Poland's Catholic Church was "thoroughly penetrated by paranoia over Jewish conspiracies and stereotypes about Jewish vice."[34] These beliefs were reinforced in the public schools' mandatory classes for religious instruction, where centuries-old anti-Jewish beliefs promoted by the church predominated. "Not only did the Jewish people persistently demand the death of Christ the Lord," one religious studies textbook explained, "but they and their children also took upon themselves responsibility for the innocent blood shed by Jesus."[35] Antisemitism did not always determine the nature of Polish-Jewish interactions in the interwar period, but negative and long-standing beliefs about Jews were a backdrop for many encounters between Catholic Poles and Jews. Although Sanacja officials sought to curb antisemitic violence perpetrated by the Polish ethno-nationalist Right, they did so to maintain order and their monopoly on the use of force, rather than out of any sympathy for the country's Jewish population.[36] The government never presumed it could eradicate the hostility that Poland's non-Jews felt toward Jews, nor did it attempt to do so. Officials were far more concerned with the eventual Polonization of the country than they were with nurturing a multiethnic, multicultural Polish state.[37]

Written in 1939, the autobiography of "G. S." captures the sense of confusion and frustration that many Betar members and Jewish students in general felt when they compared the ideals they encountered in their Polish language, literature, and history textbooks to the antisemitic behavior condoned by school and government authorities. In many respects, his life in Ostrołęka, a town seventy-five miles northeast of Warsaw on the edge of the Narew River, was typical of a young Jew living in a shtetl. The son of a blacksmith, G. S. offered a rich portrait of the traditional Jewish institutions and rituals that shaped the daily life of his family, from the grandeur of the town's main synagogue to the sound of his father singing a special melody for *kiddush*, a blessing over wine recited on the Sabbath and Jewish holidays. Like most of his contemporaries, however, his educational trajectory steered him beyond the town's landmarks of traditional Judaism. Although G. S. began his education at a heder, he soon transferred to a religious Zionist school, whose classes in Polish and Hebrew led many in town to brand it the "heder for heretics."[38] Soon after, he enrolled in the newly opened school established by the Tarbut educational network. Like other schools associated with Tarbut, the Ostrołęka branch became an incubator for local Zionist youth movements. A young student from Warsaw, recently returned to Ostrołęka, decided to found a Betar club within the school. Taking an oath by candlelight under the watchful gaze of Herzl's portrait, G. S. joined the group. His initial stint in the club, however, was short lived. Describing his swift departure, he explained to his readers that he knew nothing about the group's ideology or goals.

In the meantime, G. S. had his first encounter with Polish patriotic culture. Like several other Tarbut schools in interwar Poland, the Ostrołęka branch decided to march in the town's annual Constitution Day parade in May.[39] The experience, he later recalled, left a deep impression on him: "[S]tanding at attention in a line, just like soldiers . . . we energetically marched by the parade's review committee with pride, accompanied by the music of the military orchestra."[40] Soon after, he enrolled in the local Polish public school, where he was fed a steady diet of Polish patriotism. "The atmosphere in which I found myself," he confessed, "seemed entirely foreign. A new history, with fresh kings, fresh heroes, wars and nations. All of this made me bit confused and mixed up [*a bisl tsedreyt un gemisht in kop*]." While at school, he learned that the town's Betar organization, which had gone through several incarnations, had once again been resurrected. "It was obvious," he explained, that there was a "national spirit . . . dormant within me."[41] To help explain his return to Betar, he writes:

> The new school year began. The [school] director also taught us history and geography. We soon realized who were dealing with—an old Legionist, a Piłsudski supporter [*pilsudchik*]. He used to tell us about his deeds in the legion. With fervent passion, he turned to instilling within us the Polish patriotic spirit. We must love our fatherland and give it the greatest sacrifices. . . . But he also used to . . . say that the antisemitic acts being carried out by hooligans against Jews were only carried out by a few irresponsible elements. I have to say, however, that this particular lesson didn't really stick to my mind. The hateful stares of the Christians whom we encountered everywhere were too clear. . . . I clearly remember the beatings on my shoulders I used to get from the gentile scoundrels [*shkotsim*]. . . . You could bite your tongue with your teeth in anger, but you could do nothing. . . . He [the teacher] could only place the theory of loving the fatherland in our heads so long as he didn't look at the bitterness that lay in our souls.[42]

G. S.'s account captures the extent to which Jewish students' admiration for Polish patriotic culture could make their encounters with antisemitism all the more painful. No less interesting is how he wove his description of joining Betar into his descriptions of the anger, longing, confusion, and alienation he felt when learning about the "Polish patriotic spirit." Why did G. S. conceive of rejoining Betar as a potential answer to his experiences at the Polish public school?

The connection between these passages can be better understood if read in tandem with numerous descriptions by other Betar members of the youth movement's power to shape Catholic Poles' perceptions of Jews. Nearly all descriptions of the youth movement's public parades found in Betar newspapers and journals include detailed accounts of the reactions of Christian onlookers. A retrospective account of Betar's founding in the eastern town of Luboml was typical. In the early 1930s, a Betar delegation from the nearby town of Rejowiec had arrived to promote the movement. Local youth watched as Betar members, much like Polish soldiers at patriotic celebrations, marched into town with guns slung over their shoulders and an orchestra leading the way. "It is difficult," a former Betar member from Luboml recounted, "to capture the strong impression this 'Jewish army' gave ... here was a Jewish youth who knew how to defend themselves" and who received "the respect of non-Jews in town."[43] Although this account was produced decades later, it echoed the descriptions of Betar's parades that appeared in local youth movement journals during the 1930s. Time and again, these accounts repeated a magical formula: by adopting the military rituals at the center of Polish public culture, Betar members, town after town, were transforming the perceptions of Jews held by their Christian neighbors. Recounting the journey of twelve hundred Betar members in 1933 from Warsaw's Leszno Street in the Jewish district to Piłsudski Square, the city's main gathering point for Polish national celebrations, a Betar participant described how "many Christians took off their hats as the parade flags passed by."[44] "We have to show the Christians that Jews also know how to march,"[45] insisted another Betar member, as he described his local branch marching through the village of Stoczek in central Poland. By performing the roles of soldiers, he noted, Jewish youth somehow appeared to be just like Poles. Among the various descriptions of non-Jewish observers in his article, he noted, "A peasant with a horse passes by and looks at the line [of marchers]. Had he not heard them speak, he would have never believed that they were Jews." He added that the reactions of the peasant and the other non-Jews they passed by made the Betar members' "young hearts overjoyed."[46]

Equally significant was the journal article that preceded the young boy's account of his local unit's parades in Stoczek. An article entitled "Literature and Youth" offered a detailed guide to the negative perceptions of Jews shared by well-known Christian European novelists and poets. The article began, "Who hasn't seen how other nations represent Jewish youth, who hasn't seen their pictures—a shriveled little boy with two sidelocks, trembling with terror at each little blow? This is how the nations think of us. . . . Each nation is accustomed to fight and conquer and in certain cases fight and die. The Jews are only used to dying." The article's young author then turned to Houston Stewart Chamberlain's widely popular turn-of-the-century screed against Jews, *Foundations of the Nineteenth Century*, from which antisemitic movements across the continent took inspiration. The young Betar member wrote that Chamberlain was wrong to paint Jews as thieves and hucksters, but he was right to fault Jews for being "brilliant martyrs."[47]

The conspicuous presence of the approving "Christian gaze" in nearly all the parade accounts found in Betar journals—and the antisemitic views that so clearly loomed in the background—offers a glimpse into the conditions that many Betar members thought were necessary to gain the respect of their fellow citizens. Their experiences with their non-Jewish peers in Polish public schools had already made clear that emulating the idealized heroes of the Polish literary canon would not ensure their acceptance. Only if Betar members adopted Poland's public military culture while insisting on their distinctiveness as Zionists with their own homeland could they gain the respect of Catholic Poles and convince them to see Jews as brothers-in-arms. This formula had a prestigious pedigree within Zionism. The movement's founder, Theodor Herzl, and many of Zionism's subsequent leading figures in western and central Europe frequently insisted that they could only stem the tide of antisemitism by fulfilling their paradoxical desire to become just like every other nation (*ke-khol ha-goyim*) while asserting their national uniqueness.

Of the dozens of Jewish youth movements flourishing in interwar Poland, Betar appeared to many to offer the best platform to claim commonalities with Sanacja officials and the Catholic Polish majority. Although the socialist Zionist youth movement Ha-shomer Ha-tsa'ir had initially taken inspiration from the Polish scouting movement, their turn to the radical Left in the mid-1920s did not go unnoticed by the Polish government, which came to view the group as a threat to the Polish state. If Jewish youth seeking to present themselves as allies of the Polish state would have been hesitant to join Ha-shomer Ha-tsa'ir, they would have been all the more reluctant to join the Bund's socialist youth movement, Tsukunft (the Future), which by 1929 had just over ten thousand members. Although they too offered their members a vision for Polish-Jewish brotherhood—in their case, Polish and Jewish workers uniting to fight against capitalism—their outspoken critiques of the Polish government cast them as even more of a threat than Ha-shomer Ha-tsa'ir.[48] The only major youth movement other than Betar to frequently pledge its loyalty to the Polish state belonged to the Agudat Yisrael party. Their chief mandate, however, was to protect the interests of Poland's Orthodox Jews, and they often critiqued Jewish nationalism as a conduit for secularization.[49] In contrast, Betar offered a blend of scouting and military training that closely approximated the activities of Polish youth movements and insisted that these activities reinforced rather than threatened the Jewish identities of their members. Betar was, in fact, the only Jewish youth movement in Poland that combined scouting and military training, consistently and actively participated in Polish national celebrations, and used the choreography of Polish youth and military groups from Polish public events for its own national celebrations.

It is critical to note that not all Betar members followed this intellectual and behavioral trajectory. Polish public school and Polish nationalism played little to no role in the decisions of many Betar members to join the youth movement. Experiences with antisemitism in the Polish public school could propel Jewish youth to other youth movements, including Bundist and communist groups. Furthermore, as I discuss in the next chapter, many Betar members joined the movement for nonideological reasons. A brother, sister, friend, or potential romantic interest may have been a member, for instance, or the youth movement may have had the best soccer team in town. Whatever their reasons for joining, the movement provided them with opportunities to perform the characteristics and values associated with Polskość that they had been taught to revere in the Polish public school system. Equally significant was the fact that their performance of Polishness simultaneously insisted on its very uniqueness as a Zionist act. It allowed Betar's members to send a message to local Poles that even as they exhibited all the celebrated virtues of the Polish nation, they had no desire to become a member of its national community. Instead, they could take pride in their own national identity.

Betar's Leaders and the Making of the Ideal Polish Patriot

While many of Betar's members in Poland were preoccupied with the ability of Revisionist parades to capture the attention of Catholic Poles, the youth movement's leaders saw their parades primarily as a means to transform Jews into passionate Revisionists. At several points in the early years of the Revisionist movement, Jabotinsky wrote articles and delivered speeches that described how the sounds of an orchestra and the sight of hundreds of uniformed youth marching could hypnotize even the least "national" Jew.[50] Opponents of the Revisionist movement eagerly pointed to Jabotinsky's calls for Zionists to learn from the public ceremonies staged by Europe's nationalists as proof that Betar was goyish, or quintessentially non-Jewish. Much like the claims that Betar was fascist, accusations that Betar and its leaders were goyish aimed to delegitimize the movement in the eyes of the Jewish public. Significantly, however, even as Betar leaders insisted their movement was Jewish, they simultaneously embraced the epithet of being goyish as a mark of success. Indeed, the very notion that Jabotinsky did not look, speak, or act Jewish became crucial to his public persona and that of Betar. It was precisely because Jabotinsky was born and raised in Odessa's rapidly acculturating Jewish community, Betar leaders argued, that he could intuitively understand the secrets to the national success of eastern Europe's successor states better than any other Zionist leader.[51] By the early 1930s, Jabotinsky's purported demand for his followers to pay heed to "our teacher and rabbi, the gentile" had become, along with the "iron wall," one of his most oft-quoted phrases.[52]

This was a lesson that Betar's leaders in Poland took to heart. Just as the Revisionist movement had drawn on biblical legends and Jewish religious rituals when constructing Betar's culture, so too could they use the myths and rituals of Polish nationalism to entice Poland's Jews to support Revisionism. Comparing their movement's leader to Piłsudski, and its members to patriotic Poles, could also serve a purpose that references to an ancient Jewish past or current Jewish religious customs never could. One of the most frequent charges against the Revisionist movement was that it lacked a clear, concrete political program, and that its vision for a mobilized society could never be implemented. Jabotinsky's opponents depicted him as no more than a rabble-rouser, whose stubborn demeanor and penchant for incendiary proclamations rendered him utterly incapable of exhibiting the qualities of caution and compromise required of a political statesman. To counter these claims, Revisionist leaders turned to Piłsudski and his Sanacja regime as concrete proof that a nationalist, authoritarian political program could work in a newly formed national homeland. They reasoned that if Jewish traditions could provide the movement with sanctification from the past, the Polish state could provide its members with a window into Revisionism's future as a political movement in power.

One of the most frequent strategies used by Betar's leaders to cast their political program in the mold of the Sanacja regime was to liken Jabotinsky's persona and style of political leadership to that of Piłsudski. In many respects, this was an easy task. As the Sanacja regime took root, the Polish government had instituted a cult of leadership for Piłsudski. Parades were frequently staged in his honor, while students at Polish public schools were taught to see Piłsudski as the "father of the fatherland," and the "great educator of the people."[53] As I discussed in my account of the Revisionist movement's early development in Poland, these were terms that had already been attributed to Jabotinsky by his Polish Jewish adherents well before his first official visit to Poland in 1927. As Betar's activists crafted the movement's ideology and rituals in the early 1930s, its leaders embellished on the already-existing links between the two leaders. Betar and Revisionist journalists were quick to point out that Jabotinsky, like Piłsudski, founded a legion of soldiers during the First World War to fight for national liberation. Writing in *Trybuna Narodowa*, a Polish-language weekly newspaper established in 1934 by the Revisionist movement's leadership in Kraków, one such journalist encouraged the movement's members to describe Jabotinsky's Jewish Legion as "*our* First Brigade," the name given to the military unit led by Piłsudski during the First World War.[54] By continuously casting Jabotinsky in Piłsudski's image, Revisionist leaders assured Betar members that if a Jewish state came into being, Jabotinsky would conduct himself in the same manner as Poland's celebrated authoritarian leader.

Well aware of these comparisons, Jabotinsky understood that any Revisionist description of Piłsudski could be used, implicitly or explicitly, to sanctify his own leadership style. When Jabotinsky penned his eulogy for Piłsudski, who succumbed to liver cancer in the spring of 1935, his description of the Polish statesman's political behavior clearly bore the imprint of his own self-image as a politician. He began his eulogy by describing Piłsudski as a man who loathed close contact with the Polish masses. Summoning Piłsudski's voice, Jabotinsky wrote, "I want to share your troubles, I want to hear your complaints and wishes, but only from afar. And if I can bring you happiness, I'll share in your joy, but only on one condition: that even through a window, I won't hear the echoes of your applause and cries of 'Bravo!'"[55] Jabotinsky's close confidants would have heard echoes in this description of Jabotinsky's own periodic complaints about pandering to the public. Jabotinsky continued by noting that unlike Mussolini, Hitler, or Stalin, Piłsudski was reluctant to call himself a dictator. If, Jabotinsky added, Piłsudski behaved as a dictator, he only did so at the behest of his political allies, who saw no other option for Poland's political future. Here, too, one can hear in the background Jabotinsky's declarations that he had been forced by his followers to adopt increasingly authoritarian measures within the Revisionist movement.[56] Finally, Jabotinsky praised Piłsudski for refusing to create a clear doctrine for his followers. Once again adopting Piłsudski's voice, Jabotinsky wrote, "Writing theories are for those who have nothing better to do."[57] By recounting Piłsudski's supposed reticence to develop a coherent ideology for his regime, Jabotinsky sought to provide concrete evidence to his followers that his own refusal to adopt a clear stance on a range of issues would help rather than hinder the Revisionist movement's quest for political success.

The image of Piłsudski that Jabotinsky presented in his eulogy, however, was far from the only one circulating among Poland's Betar leaders. They used their eulogies for Piłsudski to further their own conflicting visions of the place of violence and dictatorship in the Revisionist quest for a Jewish state.[58] In contrast to Jabotinsky's description of Piłsudski's hostility toward leadership cults, a Revisionist leader in Kraków insisted in 1935 that a cult of leadership become a central part of the Revisionist program, precisely because "the greatness of Poland" was "unthinkable without Marshal Piłsudski."[59] While Jabotinsky's eulogy compared Piłsudski to other political statesmen, the editors of *Trybuna Narodowa* compared him to Garibaldi and other famed European "liberation fighters."[60] The fact that Piłsudski "set his heart upon fighting in advance and prepared for it" was, they wrote, his "special contribution" to the legacy of national liberation fighters. They concluded that the need to train young men for combat was "Piłsudski's truth, which lives in the legions of our Betar."[61] Rather than focus on his activities as the leader of the Polish Legions or as the Sanacja statesman, other Betar leaders emphasized his underground activity prior to the First World War. Betar activist Moshe Goldberg's eulogy claimed that the Sanacja leader's "acts of smuggling, attacks on tsarist officials and languishing in prison" were "the foundation from which Piłsudski's character began to form" and "his most important lesson for those who want to help and liberate their nation." He added that Piłsudski came to power not through the support of the Polish masses, but rather through the revolutionary acts of several hundred soldiers. Only through such a "hazardous deed," Goldberg concluded, could Zionists create faith in their cause among Jews.[62]

Just as Betar's leaders labored to construct a usable image of Piłsudski for their movement, so too did they develop models of "ordinary" Poles for Revisionist youth to emulate. Using the myth of Poland's resurrection as a model,

Betar's leaders insisted that performing the qualities associated with "Polishness" had the power to transform Jewish youth. In March 1929, at the first regional conference of Betar in the industrial city of Białystok, Aharon Propes outlined what distinguished Betar's model of behavior from other youth movements. He began by bemoaning the fact that Jewish political movements were producing too many "Einsteins," whose command of the written word was of no use to the nation. Propes continued, "When you ask the Polish farmer or the Lithuanian, Have you read Marx? He'll answer that he hasn't. Of course he hasn't, of course he doesn't know about Marx. But he knows that it is his duty to fight, to defend and to conquer, because it is his duty to sacrifice."[63] By turning "Einsteins" and the Polish or Lithuanian farmer into binary opposites, Propes articulated one of the most salient and enduring features of the youth movement's ideology: the demand to strip Jewish politics of the intellectual casuistry associated with socialism in favor of a more organic, intuitive national sentiment. In Propes's view, the Polish peasant's simplicity, intuitive sense of duty to the state, and unflinching ability to act were the keys to national liberation.[64] Local Betar leaders similarly praised the readiness of young Polish men to sacrifice their lives on the battlefield. Recounting to his fellow members in the northeastern city of Baranowicze his experience at a local parade for Poland's Independence Day, with "masses of soldiers . . . marching in their liberated land," a young Betar leader wrote in 1933 that the Polish model of national redemption proved that "for liberation one must fight with sweat and blood."[65] This was a model, leaders pointed out, that was wholeheartedly embraced by Polish youth; a 1935 Betar journal from Radom reminded its members that Polish students "were the first in liberated Poland to volunteer to go into battle and spill their blood for the fatherland" during the Polish-Soviet War of 1919–21. Like Polish youth, young Jews would serve as the "vanguard of each revolution, of each national liberation struggle"[66] faced by the Jewish nation.

Performing Revisionist Polskość: Texts, Landscapes, Parades, and Prayers

Journal articles and speeches were not the only ways in which Betar leaders sought to forge durable links for their followers between Revisionist Zionism and Polish nationalism. Betar's architects created a variety of activities designed to encourage its members to see themselves as heirs to Poland's patriotic traditions, and to perform the qualities they associated with Polskość. One of the first strategies used by Betar leaders was to instruct their members to consult textbooks published by the Polish Scouting Association and Poland's Ministry of Military Affairs.[67] These textbooks provided instructions for a vast range of scouting, sport, and paramilitary activities, from swimming and skiing to fencing, hand-to-hand-combat, and target practice. Although many of the exercises included in these textbooks could be found in Betar's own Hebrew and Yiddish handbooks, the textbooks produced by the government and Polish scouting movement served several unique functions within Betar's curriculum. On a practical level, they provided clear instructions to the growing number of Polish-speaking Betar members with little or no knowledge of Yiddish and Hebrew. No less significant was the fact that these textbooks allowed Betar members to literally perform, step by step, the same choreography that their Polish peers were engaging in.

Assigned to Betar members in 1928, the 1917 scouting handbook *Harce Młodzieży Polskiej* (Scouting Guide for Polish Youth) illustrates some of the functions these texts could serve. Betar members could easily find parallels between Betar's journals and the handbook's descriptions of how Polish youth were expected to behave. When Betar members leafed through a section devoted to Polish medieval knights, calling on young Polish men to "maintain the purity of one's words" and remain courteous to women and children, they may very well have heard echoes of Jabotinsky calling for Jewish youth to strive for hadar, a term the Revisionist leader used to denote chivalry, courteous behavior and dignity.[68] The guide also reinforced Betar's promise that scouting and military training were the keys to national liberation. Written in the final throes of the First World War, much of the 1917 textbook was in the future tense, preparing Polish youth for lives in a country that had yet to come into being. When the handbook promised its reader "becoming a citizen in the liberated Republic, you'll liberate yourself from all those defects that were imposed upon your country in slavery," Betar members would have likely recalled Zionism's promise to help Jews shed the allegedly contemptuous qualities they had accumulated in exile from the Land of Israel.[69] By allowing their members to reenact the Polish struggle for independence through this text, Betar's leaders hoped to demonstrate that the right-wing Zionist vision for a Jewish state was attainable so long as Jewish youth followed the handbook's call for sacrifice and readiness "to battle the enemy who threatens the country, whoever it may be and wherever they may appear."[70]

In addition to relying on handbooks created by the Polish scouting movement, Betar leaders strove to embed examples of ideal Polish behavior within their own curriculum guides. The first issue of *Tel Hai*, for instance, included a Hebrew translation of a story by Kazimierz Przerwa Tetmajer, a member of the turn-of-the-century Young Poland literary movement, describing cavalry waiting for the signal to attack.[71] By translating classic Polish literary texts into Hebrew, Betar leaders sought to demonstrate the cultural value of Hebrew language and literature through its ability to capture the linguistic and emotional nuances of the Polish language. In doing so, they joined a broad array of Jewish nationalists who for decades had been translating works of European literature into Hebrew and Yiddish, believing that the value of their national culture would be proved only once they could produce, or reproduce, highbrow literature.[72] No less important was the fact that these translations offered clear proof to Betar members that venerating Polish myths was an appropriate activity for young Zionists. This message was reinforced in the youth movement's instructions for group discussion. A 1932 leadership manual, for example, instructed Betar members to read and discuss Polish Nobel laureate Władysław Reymont's novels about Polish peasant life to prepare them for the existence that awaited them as new arrivals to the Yishuv.[73] With their vivid depictions of the Polish rural landscape and its inhabitants, Reymont's early twentieth-century novels may have struck Betar members as an odd set of texts to use as a guide to life in Palestine. The movement's leaders, however, could persuade them to see Reymont's depictions of the physical and spiritual resilience of Polish peasants, harvesting food on often-inhospitable soil, as the mirror image of the struggles of Jewish agricultural laborers in Mandate Palestine. Already staples in the Polish public school's curriculum, Reymont's texts, when read and discussed in the context of the Betar club, presented an image of rural Polish identity that Betar members could emulate.

If, by some chance, a Betar member might question the value of reading the work of a Polish literary giant as a blueprint for Zionist behavior, their local commander could turn to none other than Jabotinsky for an endorsement. In 1932, the Revisionist leader offered his own take on a debate raging in the Polish press about whether Adam Mickiewicz sought to organize a Jewish Legion to join British, Ottoman, and French forces in their battle against Russia during the Crimean War (1853–1856).[74] At the heart of the debate was the question of whether Mickiewicz envisioned Catholic Poles and Polish Jews as brothers-in-arms, a view wholeheartedly promoted by journalists writing in the Polish-language Jewish press.[75] Writing in *Rassvet*, Jabotinsky not only defended the viewpoint shared by most members of the Polish Jewish intelligentsia, but added a Zionist gloss to Mickiewicz's life. He insisted that the legend of Mickiewicz trying to form a Jewish military contingent during the Crimean War was historical fact and claimed that it proved that Mickiewicz was "a Zionist avant la lettre."[76] Just as Mickiewicz deemed the Polish and Jewish nations to be brothers-in-arms in the fight for an independent Poland, it stood to reason, Jabotinsky argued, that he would have supported a Jewish Legion fighting in Palestine to create a Jewish state. Thus, in Jabotinsky's view, Mickiewicz's writings, considered by many at the time to be the bedrock of the Polish literary canon, could be read as Zionist texts.

Just as Betar's leaders believed that Polish literature, when read through a Zionist lens, could attract Jewish youth to their movement, they similarly insisted that Poland's physical landscape had the power to awaken Zionist sentiments. According to the editors of *Trybuna Narodowa*, Betar leaders had chosen Kraków as the site of the movement's 1935 world conference because the city possessed its "own symbolic language ... with the walls, streets and old passageways narrating the memory of wonderful national traditions ... providing a living daily testimony to the ... miracle that occurred in Poland, gaining its freedom after centuries of enslavement." Immersed in the city's rich history, Betar members would be prepared to lead "the Jewish nation to a great, noble and proud way of life in our own country, on our own land."[77] The notion that Poland's urban and rural landscapes were invested with national significance would have been familiar to nearly all Betar members. Between the two world wars, the Polish government conducted a massive campaign to nationalize the country's ethnically diverse landscape in the eastern borderlands—from Polonizing street names to erecting statues of Polish heroes in the midst of villages and towns dominated by Belarusians, Lithuanians, Ukrainians, and Jews.[78] Throughout the country, Polish public schools and youth movements engaged in an activity they dubbed *krajoznawstwo*—"knowing the land." Through hiking and studying regional folklore and geography, they hoped to convince Poland's young citizens that the land was Polish, and that Catholic Poles were its rightful rulers.[79] As the 1920s progressed, Polish Jewish ethnographers, historians, and political activists engaged in their own version of krajoznawstwo, known as the Landkentenish movement, which sought to preserve Jewish landmarks and folklore in Poland, and to encourage a "back to nature" movement among Jews.[80]

Betar's leaders took the krajoznawstwo and Landkentenish programs one step further. Presuming that Betar members instinctively understood the power of Poland's national landscape to evoke patriotic feelings and behaviors, they asked them to imagine that Palestine's landscape would evoke the very same sentiments. For Zionist activists in Poland trying to ignite nationalist commitments for a territory more than one thousand miles away, imagination was often the only option available. Nearly all Betar's members in Poland had never set foot in Palestine. Some could read letters from relatives living in the Yishuv. On special occasions, others could hear firsthand accounts of the landscape by Zionist emissaries from Palestine, touring Poland's towns and cities to drum up financial support for their cause. Most Betar members, however, gleaned snippets of information about the region's contemporary landscape through the poetry and novels produced by Zionist activists as well as the travelogues of journalists from Poland's major Jewish newspapers. Betar's leaders argued that to create an unbreakable bond between their recruits and their ideology, it was not enough for Betar members to construct a vivid picture of the Land of Israel in their imagination. Citing popular child development theories that emphasized the importance of physical activity, Betar leaders asserted that only if Betar members immersed themselves in the natural landscape could the movement solidify its members' devotion to Zion.[81] In lieu of Palestine, Poland's landscape would have to serve as the site for this physical encounter.

Among the most popular ways for Betar's members to imagine and perform living life in Palestine were month-long summer camps, which had been coordinated by the movement since 1931. Summer colonies for urban children had been a growing phenomenon in Europe from the turn of the century. By the interwar period, summer camps had spread across the continent, operated by government authorities, local political movements, relief agencies, and other institutions with a stake in child welfare and education. Established by nearly every major Jewish political organization in Poland, and with tens of thousands of youth participating, summer camps provided movements like Betar with an opportunity to create imaginary republics of youth, in which their vision for the Jewish political future could be performed. For the Jewish playwright Zelig Lerner, a long-standing contributor to Poland's Revisionist press and the architect of Betar's summer camp program, experiential education was the only way to politicize Jewish youth. He began his 1932 summer camp handbook by arguing that "youth must have the possibility to be directly acquainted with reality, above and beyond all else, with nature" for them to embrace Revisionist ideology.[82]

Paradoxically, however, the "realities" offered by the summer camp and other outdoor experiences run by Betar were, at their heart, crafted, artificial, even theatrical experiences. Lerner's richly detailed handbook for summer camping began with instructions to local Betar leaders for how they could convince members that their journey to summer camp amounted to "going on a little adventure, traveling to a foreign land." On the day of departure, Betar members were to sing a song about the desire to return to Zion. They were then to march to the train station and sing "Hatikvah" before boarding the train to the "promised land" of the Polish countryside.[83] Upon arrival, the campers were to immediately "Hebraize" their surroundings: posters of Zionist leaders, maps of the Land of Israel, and Betar's insignia were to adorn their sleeping quarters. Lerner's daily regimen, which stretched from five thirty in the morning until nine in the evening, provided the directions for life in Palestine. Immediately after roll call and breakfast, Betar members were to spend an hour learning Hebrew. Over the course of the day, they would meet for lessons in "Palestinography," in which they could gain a deep knowledge of their homeland's landscape. At each and every step of the way, the camp's leaders were to use their imagined Palestine to "cultivate an atmosphere where discipline blossoms and grows" and contrast this environment to the alleged lawlessness of Jewish behavior in the Diaspora. For older camp members, military drilling demanded that they simulate combat in Palestine. The imaginary journey to Palestine would transcend not only geographic boundaries but temporal ones as well. Campers were frequently asked by their leaders to imagine that they had journeyed back into the ancient Jewish past. The handbook instructed leaders to tell Betar members during day trips outside the campgrounds to think of themselves as Jews wandering in the desert or Maccabeees in the Judean hills.[84]

These national narratives, however, were far from the only ones that Betar members would have associated with their excursions into Poland's landscape. Writing in the youth movement's weekly Hebrew newspaper in January 1934, a Betar leader recounted military training exercises taking place at the youth movement's annual winter instructor's course, in a small village near Warsaw. When the course's recruits were ordered to march to a nearby snow-covered hill and dig through the frost of the ground to build trenches, their leaders explained that the exercise was designed to prepare them for digging trenches in Mandate Palestine's desert.[85] While the link between the Polish winter and a desert in the Middle East was, to put it mildly, a stretch of the imagination, participants could recall the famous battles between Polish rebels and Russian troops that had taken place nearby during the November Uprising of 1831. As we saw in the celebratory descriptions of Kraków offered by Revisionist journalists, Betar leaders could envision Polish nationalist legends for particular landscapes as springboards for Betar members to imagine their own connection to Palestine.

In addition to using Poland's natural landscape to stage life in Palestine, Betar's cultural architects constructed commemorative rituals that mirrored those performed at Polish patriotic events. The most widely practiced and publicized commemorative ritual performed by Betar groups was the laying of wreaths at Polish war memorials. Public memorials had served as a rallying point for Polish nationalist activists as early as the 1870s, particularly those in Habsburg Galicia, where Polish nationalism was given relatively free reign to blossom. These monuments were envisioned by their creators as sites of pilgrimage for the stateless Polish nation; by commemorating the Polish past, they hoped to kindle and cultivate the national loyalty of Catholic Poles.[86] After the rise of the Second Polish Republic, Polish war memorials were intended to serve a similar function. Like their counterparts elsewhere in Europe, which had sprung up in the wake of the First World War, Polish memorials were often the starting or ending point for patriotic celebrations held throughout the year. During celebrations at these war memorials, soldiers and scouting groups were nearly always designated as the first groups of Polish citizens to lay wreaths. Their prominence in these rituals ensured that the ceremony would not only valorize the act of dying for one's country, but also demonstrate the military strength of the Polish nation in the present, as well as the promise of its youth to become the country's future soldiers.

Betar's leaders recognized the potential of similar ceremonies to mobilize the support of the Jewish public. First performed in Warsaw at the youth movement's inaugural world conference in 1929, the ceremony became a standard in the repertoire of newly established Betar groups making their debut in a town or city.[87] Whether in Warsaw, Kielce, Borysław, Radom, Kraków, or elsewhere, Betar members generally followed a common choreography when staging the event. Following a memorial service for Joseph Trumpeldor, Betar members would file out of the synagogue, parade through the streets of the town or city toward a war memorial, and lay a wreath. By performing a commemorative ritual that paid tribute to Jews who died fighting in the name of Zionist ideals at the very site where Polish scouts and military personnel commemorated Polish soldiers, Betar members could envision Poles and Jews as comrades in arms and view the Revisionist version of the Zionist struggle as a worthy companion to its Polish counterpart. The very nature of these memorials facilitated this process; unlike national monuments of the late nineteenth century, which generally paid tribute to a single heroic military figure, the interwar memorials attempted to commemorate the lives of tens of thousands of "ordinary" soldiers. Writing about the Tombs of the Unknown Soldier that sprung up throughout Europe in the 1920s, historian Thomas Laqueur has observed that in their attempts to remember everyone, these memorials remembered no one in particular.[88] Betar used the very ambiguity of these memorials to their advantage. Because the memorials did not specify the names of those who were to be remembered, the ceremonies staged by Betar at these sites allowed their members to conjure up, at the same time, the memory of both Polish and Zionist fighters.

Betar members were not the only constituency kept in mind by the youth movement's leaders during these war memorial ceremonies. Much like the Betar members who routinely described the "Polish gaze" as they paraded through their towns, Betar's leaders saw their public rituals as opportunities to court the support of Polish government officials. Aware that Polish state officials or informants were more likely than not to be within earshot at public gatherings of a political nature, Betar leaders in towns throughout the country could expect their declarations of loyalty to the Polish state to reach officials in Warsaw. Indeed, over the course of the interwar period, the Sanacja regime had set up an intricate network of surveillance. Deeply suspicious of national minorities, leftist activists and radical right-wing Polish nationalists, local police units and other regional government officials routinely sent letters to Warsaw's Ministry of Internal Affairs about the political activities of citizens within their midst, from protests and parades to weekly club meetings. These reports made clear that the government was taking note of Betar's public displays of Polskość. A report sent in September 1932 from the southeastern town of Hrubieszów, for example, described how Betar leaders instructed the youth movement's members to emulate Polish youth at a ceremony commemorating volunteers for the Jewish Legion.[89] Throughout 1933, local reports streamed into the Ministry of Internal Affairs that described Revisionist youth at protests against Hitler's rise to power, breaking out into song with Polish national hymns, followed by cheers for Piłsudski.[90] Government reports also noted that Betar delegations participated in the Sea Holiday (Święto Morza) ceremonies, staged to demonstrate Poland's readiness to defend its access to the Baltic Sea.[91] Betar not only promised to help protect Poland from external dangers; in other ceremonies, the youth movement's members pledged to stand in solidarity with the Polish nation against enemies *within* the Polish state. At a Betar demonstration in the southeastern city of Borysław in the summer of 1934,

Revisionist leaders asked the two thousand attendees to observe a minute of silence to commemorate the assassination of Poland's Minister of Internal Affairs, killed several days earlier by Ukrainian nationalists.[92]

Among the so-called internal enemies of the Polish state that were mentioned in government reports devoted to Betar's activities, Jewish socialist organizations stood out. These reports noted that Jewish socialist groups accused Betar of serving as the henchmen of the Polish government.[93] Jewish socialists allegedly also accused Betar of echoing and endorsing the widespread belief among Poles that socialist and communist parties were teeming with Jews. These socialist groups' accusations against Betar were not unfounded. Propes, for example, claimed in the youth movement's national journal in 1930 that it was "no secret that Jewish youth today fill the ranks of extreme Left organizations and occupy, according to their number, a very prominent role."[94] Though the percentage of Jews in Poland's left-wing political movements did far exceed the percentage of Jews in the population as a whole, Betar leaders, like Polish government officials, both mistakenly and deliberately interpreted this fact as proof that the majority of Jewish youth were under the influence of the radical Left. Government reports that described Betar's efforts to denounce socialism only reinforced the claims of the youth movement's leaders that they shared the interests of the country's political leadership.

As much as Betar leaders sought to gain the approval of high-ranking officials in Warsaw, they also devoted their energy to forging strong relationships with local Polish officials. One way in which Betar leaders reached out to local officials was by inviting them to attend their events. When Betar branches throughout the country sent updates about their activities to their movement's nationally circulated journals, they frequently reported the presence of local military and government officials. They were often sure to note, as the branch in the southeastern town of Warkowicze did in 1933, that "the most important members of the Jewish and Christian population in town attend our events."[95]

In some cases, Polish government officials took part in the ceremonies themselves. In the wake of Piłsudski's death, Jewish communities across the country staged memorial services in his honor. A report describing a synagogue service in the southeastern town of Bolechów, organized by Betar to honor Piłsudski's memory, not only provides a case study of the dual roles of participants and observers that Polish government officials could play, but also captures the innovative ways in which Betar attempted to stage Polish-Jewish brotherhood.[96] From its very beginning, the ceremony made clear to its participants that local officials supported the Revisionist cause. To open the ceremony, Bolechów's mayor delivered a speech about Piłsudski's legacy. Following the mayor, the synagogue's cantor chanted "El Maleh Rachamim," a Jewish prayer for the deceased, in Piłsudski's memory. If honoring a Catholic Polish statesman with a prayer typically reserved for Jews departed from traditional Jewish practice, what followed was equally unconventional. Immediately after the cantor finished chanting "El Maleh Rachamim," the ceremony's participants, including the government officials, joined together in singing "Boże, Coś Polskę" (God, Protect Poland). Catholic Poles considered the hymn to be an integral part of their liturgy and used it to conclude daily mass.[97] Jews singing the song at the synagogue was not without precedent; legend had it that in 1861, during synagogue services for the Jewish New Year, Jews in Warsaw sung the song in support of the short-lived Polish uprising against tsarist rule.[98] The song had achieved some popularity among acculturated Jews in interwar Poland and was sung in synagogues during ceremonies commemorating Polish national holidays.[99] By singing the hymn, Betar members sought to make clear to Polish officials that they too deemed God to be the primary agent of history, with salvation—both personal and national—in his hands. They also implied that God sanctified the Polish-Jewish brotherhood being staged by Betar and the government officials.

Although most of these ceremonies were staged on a local level, Betar's national leadership occasionally attempted to organize mass demonstrations to promote its vision of Polish-Jewish brotherhood. In the same month that the Bolechów ceremony took place, Betar's head command organized its largest ceremony yet. In July 1935, Propes sent out a circular to Betar chapters across the country, instructing members to convene in Kraków for a mass assembly to pay tribute to Piłsudski.[100] In the meantime, Betar leaders in Palestine informed the Polish ambassador in Tel Aviv that they planned to bring an urn with soil from Tel Hai, the site where Joseph Trumpeldor had been killed, to a site about ten kilometers west of Kraków's city center, where a monument commemorating both Piłsudski and Poland's struggle for independence was being constructed.

On a rainy Sunday morning in August, thousands of Betar members congregated in a sports field with Polish and Zionist flags in hand, awaiting the arrival of the urn.[101] At six o'clock in the evening, after Jabotinsky had arrived, a group of Betar members rode on motorcycles to the center of the sports field. They delivered the urn, wrapped in ribbons with colors of the Polish and Zionist flags, to Betar's leaders. Addressing thousands of Betar members, along with representatives of the city's government, Jabotinsky explained the significance of bringing the soil from Palestine to Piłsudski's mound. He described Piłsudski and Trumpeldor as kindred spirits who had at long last been united: "If only these two great figures could have met to speak with one another about the deep secret concealed in their souls. Tomorrow, in your transferring of the soil of Tel Hai to the soil of Sowiniec, they will converse with one another." Both men, he continued, would share their patriotic "feelings that lead to eternal, indestructible sacrifices on the altar of the fatherland."[102] By describing Trumpeldor and Piłsudski as mirror images of one another, Jabotinsky portrayed Revisionist Zionism as the equal of Polish nationalism.

In addition to notifying the Polish government that they were staging commemorative ceremonies for Piłsudski in Poland, Betar leaders also drew attention to their efforts to honor Piłsudski's memory in Palestine.[103] The most ambitious of these projects was a fundraiser to build an immigrant absorption center, to be named after Piłsudski, for Polish Jews in Palestine. In their appeal to gain financial support for the project, Revisionists in Poland published the following explanation of its significance:

> When Jewish newcomers from Poland enter into the building, they will be reminded of the dear and beloved Marshal. Inside the building, they will find an atmosphere of true, living, fervent patriotism, free from chauvinism, but at the same time free from compromises; they'll find there the national iron will for independence, whose greatest teacher was Piłsudski. And they will remember a country that raised them and generations of their ancestors . . . their love will last and will never change towards that country . . . their beloved old Fatherland.[104]

The appeal nicely captures the messages about Polish nationalism that Betar leaders intended to instill in their members. By describing Piłsudski as their teacher, and his model of nationalism as the example to emulate, Betar members could envision themselves as both Zionists and ambassadors of Poland, bringing the best of Poland to Palestine. No less significant were the lessons that Revisionist leaders claimed Piłsudski imparted to their youth movement. Readers of the appeal would have heard echoes of Jabotinsky's "iron wall" slogan in Piłsudski's alleged call for his nation to maintain an "iron will" that was "free from chauvinism but at the same time free from compromises."[105] The implicit reference to national enemies invited readers to compare the Polish government's relationship to its country's national minorities with the relationship of Yishuv Jews to the region's Arab inhabitants. Readers may well have recalled the Polish government's 1930 violent "pacification" campaign in eastern Galicia, aimed at crushing the activity of Ukrainian irredentist organizations in the region. By 1935, the Polish government had banned the self-government of Ukrainian villages, placed them under military rule, and meted out collective punishments for acts of terrorism. The Revisionist appeal's call for a tolerant but unyielding nationalism implied that the Revisionist position on Palestine's Arabs echoed the Polish government's promise to protect its national minorities, even as they defended their right to rule over their country. Finally, by describing the enduring love of Revisionists for the "old Fatherland," the appeal permitted Betar members to express Polish patriotism while making clear that their future lay in Palestine.

Brothers-in-Arms beyond the Parade?

When Betar's leaders set their sights on Polish government officials, they not only sought to capture their hearts and minds. From the beginning, theirs was a battle for financial and tactical support. Permission to join the government's paramilitary training programs was considered the most coveted prize. In 1927, Piłsudski had ordered the formation of a National Agency for Physical Education and Military Preparation (Państwowy Urząd Wychowania Fizycznego i Przysposobienia Wojskowego, hereafter PW). Spearheaded by the Ministry of Military Affairs, the agency aimed to create a new cadre of young recruits for the army. It also sought to provide basic training to the country's civilians, particularly in the borderlands, in the hopes that they would form voluntary paramilitary defense units to protect Poland's borders. With branches throughout the country, the organization provided financial support as well as sports and military instruction to Polish schools and youth movements such as the Polish Scouting Association, the Sokół Gymnastics Society, and the Rifleman's Association (Związek Strzelecki). By 1929, more than 265,000 youth movement members in Poland had participated in PW programs.[106]

The incentives provided by the Polish government to join PW were coupled with threats to paramilitary youth movements that refused to do so. The Polish government made clear that any paramilitary organization that did not join PW would be forbidden to use weapons while training its members—if they were permitted to convene at all. Indeed, as much as the agency sought to provide military training to young citizens of the Polish state, its founding also served as a pretext to exert greater control over groups like the Polish Scouting Association and dismantle any paramilitary youth group that opposed the Sanacja regime. Military officials were instructed to be particularly vigilant about curbing the military training activities of the youth movements of national minorities. Simultaneously, however, some government officials entertained the possibility of including national minorities in PW groups and wrote of the potential of the agency, much like public schools, to transform them into loyal citizens.[107]

It was against this backdrop that Betar leaders sought to gain access to PW's resources. As soon as Betar held its first conference in December 1927, the youth movement's leaders reported that its members in Warsaw had begun to enroll in their local PW units.[108] In the two years that followed, Betar units sought training within local PW units, from the central city of Radom, the Galician cities of Stryj and Stanisławów, to the small town of Boremel in the province of Wołyń.[109] In February 1929, Betar's command in Warsaw announced that a government official from PW would supervise a course to teach Betar leaders the basic principles of military combat and defense.[110] Throughout the 1930s, dozens of local Betar branches reported that they had received support from their local PW councils in towns like Otwock and Ostrów-Mazowiecka, as well as in larger cities such as Lublin, Kalisz, Przemyśl, and Lwów. Betar members were provided with guns and ammunition as well as training by an officer of the Polish army to decipher maps, create battle plans, and use firearms.[111]

Training under the supervision of Polish officers was not the only benefit afforded to Betar groups that joined PW units. Their participation also gave them the privilege of marching with guns alongside Polish soldiers during Polish patriotic celebrations—a privilege that Betar members and Polish government officials were sure to note in their reports of these events.[112] Marching with weapons in hand alongside Polish soldiers provided many Jewish youth with the chance to prove to their non-Jewish peers, as well as to themselves, that the Polish army saw them as worthy partners in national demonstrations of strength, honor, and sacrifice. In some cases, Betar's public displays of an alliance with PW officials could also provide the movement's leaders with increased prestige and power among local Jews. Ya'akov Hetman, a Betar leader in the eastern borderland town of Luboml, was the only Jew to be appointed to his local PW council, which included representatives of the town's community council, the police, and locally stationed military officials. Reflecting on his time on the council, Hetman later recalled, "I became a sort of unofficial representative of the town's Jews to the authorities.... Suddenly I found myself, a young eighteen-year-old man, representing the local Jews by the power of my position as a Betar captain."¹¹³ While Hetman's retrospective account may be inflated, it nonetheless provides a window into the types of power Betar members and leaders believed they could attain through personal interactions with Polish government officials.

That is not to say, however, that Polish government officials always offered support to Betar, or that they never viewed the youth movement with any suspicion. Despite the Polish government's attempt to centralize its decision-making process on matters of military training, the question of whether a youth movement could join a local PW unit was often left to provincial or district committees. The final decision could rest with either a local representative of the Ministry of Education or the Ministry of Military Affairs, or a city official or town councilman. An exchange of letters between PW representatives and provincial officials in the province of Lublin demonstrates the contingencies involved in whether a Betar unit was granted government support. In 1931, the regional director of PW notified provincial officials of Betar groups in the towns of Biłgoraj, Hrubieszów, and Tomaszów-Lubelski wanting to join their program, and asked them to verify whether "from the perspective of loyalty to the country, their presence would be harmful."¹¹⁴ Although the Lublin regional government had received directives five years earlier describing Betar as loyal to the Polish state, a provincial official responded that the movement was "connected to the Zionist movement, whose negative stance towards the country [Poland] and its government is well-known"; their participation in the PW units, he concluded, would be "entirely inadvisable."¹¹⁵ What exactly was "well-known" about Zionist beliefs and behaviors was left unsaid; historians can only guess at what evidence the Polish government official drew on to conclude that Zionists were a threat to the Polish state. To many Polish officials, Zionism was but one more example of a separatist nationalist movement within their midst. He may well have recalled the efforts of Zionist leader and Polish Sejm deputy Yitzhak Grinboym in 1922 to help organize the National Minorities' Bloc, a parliamentary coalition of Jewish, Ukrainian, German, and Belarusian candidates united in their opposition to Poland's polices toward minorities.¹¹⁶ The provincial official may have also known that Jabotinsky claimed common cause with Ukrainians prior to the First World War.¹¹⁷ With the number of Ukrainian terrorist attacks rising in the eastern borderlands— the very region where Betar had its stronghold—Polish government officials might have been particularly skittish about the prospect of having another armed national minority in their midst. The provincial official, like many of his contemporaries in the Ministry of Military Affairs, might have also believed that Jews being trained by the Polish army—whether as soldiers or as volunteers in local defense corps—were communists in disguise.[118] Noting that the participation of Betar in PW would set a precedent for other Zionist movements to flood into the organization, the provincial official's fear of socialist Zionists gaining access to arms was likely the decisive factor in determining his response.

The haphazard nature of these decisions infuriated officials in Warsaw's Ministry of Internal Affairs. In November 1933, the ministry convened a meeting with representatives from various government ministries to determine, once and for all, whether Betar could participate in government-sponsored paramilitary units. The officials also aimed to reach a consensus on whether to ban Brit Hahayal, the Revisionist movement's new organization for Jewish veterans of the Polish army. Their concerns were triggered by the increasingly successful efforts of the Polish radical Right to vilify the Sanacja among the Polish population. Over the summer, Polish ethno-nationalists had pointed to Betar's close connections to the Sanacja as proof of the government's "Jewification" and claimed that the youth movement called for "terrorizing Polish society, revolutionary upheaval ... and the creation of Judea on Polish soil."[119] Deeply sensitive to accusations that they did not represent the national interests of Poles, government officials struggled to balance the perceived benefits of supporting Betar's pledges of Polish patriotism with the need to mobilize support among the Catholic Polish masses.

Gathered in Warsaw's Ministry of Internal Affairs, representatives from Poland's counterintelligence, paramilitary training units, Ministry of Education, and Warsaw's city council sought to reach an "authoritative decision" on Revisionist youth and put an end to what they characterized as the "chaos" of their previously uneven and uncoordinated decisions. Yet the variety of solutions proposed at the meeting to end their public relations crisis made clear that creating consensus would be a difficult task. Some officials insisted that any lenient policies toward Jewish youth would set a dangerous precedent for other national minorities. Vehemently opposing the creation of a Revisionist reservist organization, a representative of the Ministry of Internal Affairs warned, "[F]irst a Jewish organization, tomorrow a Ukrainian organization or Belarusian Organization—it is unacceptable."[120] Others approved of Betar's existence but warned against integrating them into the government's paramilitary training units. A representative from the Ministry of Religion and Public Enlightenment insisted that any scouting training conducted by Jewish youth should take place in special Jewish units under the sole supervision of the

Polish Scouting Association. He also urged those in attendance to forbid Jewish public school students from enlisting in Betar. His positions reinforced his ministry's long-held view that Jewish youth in public schools were, on some level, the property of the Polish state, an elite whose loyalty would be compromised by contact with a Jewish political organization. His proposal also highlighted how public school officials sought to cultivate loyalty rather than integration. His suggestion to create separate Jewish units within the Polish Scouting Association implied that it was inconceivable to integrate young Polish Jews with their Catholic Polish peers. Of all officials present at the meeting, one lone voice from the Ministry of Physical Education and Military Preparation welcomed Betar's participation in the organization without hesitation.

Betar leaders also occasionally expressed uncertainty and unease about the relationship—both symbolic and real—that they were cultivating with the Polish government. While local Betar leaders frequently wrote into their nationally circulated journals with news of their units receiving training from PW officials, not one article ever appeared in these journals describing their training in detail. The journal's editors had good reason to be reticent about providing written accounts of Betar members training with weapons. Published evidence of their reliance on the Polish government would have highlighted the fact that the movement did not have sufficient personnel or equipment to provide military training to Jewish youth. Furthermore, Betar leaders were constantly walking a fine line between claiming commonalities with the Polish national struggle and insisting that Betar was emphatically Jewish. When Betar journals described the military training of the movement's members, they most often emphasized how their activists were producing a new and distinct national culture—from the creation of a Hebrew military lexicon to newly created emblems, insignia, and uniforms.

The movement's anxiety about producing a unique national culture occasionally shaped how its leaders described Polish culture. Although at times keen to offer detailed reports celebrating their presence in Polish patriotic parades, at other times, they felt the need to assure their members that their interactions with Poles and Polish culture were not attempts to dissolve Jewish distinctiveness. In 1935, for example, a *Trybuna Narodowa* article lampooned the secular Jewish poet and satirist Julian Tuwim, who had recently written that Jews were in large part to blame for the antisemitic beliefs of Poles. The article opened by mocking Tuwim for his attempts to "no longer [be] a Jew but a one-hundred-percent member of the Polish nation."[121] What was particularly interesting about the article was its definition and assessment of assimilation. Defined as "a natural process that takes place within social or territorial boundaries of different ethnic groups," the article argued that assimilation was "a positive agent for the exchange of values between the spirits of different nations—but it can never be permitted to lead to the disappearance of a living nation."[122] In contrast to most Zionist leaders of the period, who used the word "assimilation" solely as a pejorative term to signal the absence of Zionist national consciousness, this article insisted that the value of assimilation—defined here as the adoption of the attitudes and behaviors of other nations—depended on its outcome. This definition of assimilation implicitly condoned Betar's use of the iconography and choreography of Polish patriotic culture, all the while allowing the movement to look on Tuwim and other "Polonized" Jews with derision.

In tandem with the cultural anxieties provoked by Revisionists' intimate engagement with Polish culture, they also grew uneasy when faced with government decisions they opposed. Although Revisionist leaders had insisted as early as 1928 that they would not weigh in on debates about Poland's domestic politics, they did not always express unconditional and unadulterated praise of the Polish government's policies.[123] The mounting anxiety they felt about Poland's domestic policy toward Jews came through in their response to the government's new constitution in April 1935. Approved by Piłsudski less than one month before his death, the constitution gave the president the power to choose his successor, all ministerial posts, and one-third of the members of the senate. Parliament could be dissolved at any point by the president, and votes could take place in the absence of the opposition. These changes effectively stripped power from the legislature. On the one hand, the Revisionist movement praised the government's decision to further limit the power of the parliament and strengthen the authority of the president. On the other hand, however, they expressed concern that the new laws would significantly reduce the number of Jews who could fill posts in the parliament. While the article "extended its widest congratulations" for the constitution's "principle of equality for all its citizens,"[124] it added that Jews would only offer their full support for the new constitution if the government fulfilled this principle in practice. They had good reason to be skeptical. In the halls of the Polish parliament, ethno-nationalist deputies increasingly urged the government to restrict the political rights of Jews.[125] Outside of the Sejm, young Jews, particularly those at universities, were among the main targets of widespread and widely popular outbreaks of anti-Jewish violence led by ethno-nationalist Polish youth movements.

As a movement claiming that Poland's Jews and Catholics not only shared common interests but also possessed the same noble traits, Betar was an inevitable target of antisemitic campaigns. In 1934, a right-wing Polish newspaper accused Betar of being an anti-Polish movement, citing as proof articles written by Jabotinsky nearly two decades earlier, in which he had denounced Polish nationalists for their antisemitism. His response to these claims, published in the Yiddish daily *Der Moment*, walked a fine line between maintaining his movement's praise of the Sanacja and criticizing the behavior of Polish nationalists. He began by describing his "great, even romantic love for Poland" as a young man, and even claimed that his empathic writings on Polish nationalism in Russian-language periodicals led one famous Polish journalist to praise him publicly for his "ability to understand the Polish soul." Years later, he continued, he greeted Piłsudski's coup d'état as nothing short of a miracle. The article ended, however, by warning Poles that in the eyes of the "civilized world," many modern-day Polish nationalists were threatening to turn the Polish nation from a people who were "one of the most beautiful symbols of a suffering nation"[126] into a nation loathed for its intolerance. This marked the first time since the rise of the Revisionist movement that Jabotinsky publicly declared that not all iterations of Polish nationalism were worthy of praise. If the meaning of "Polishness" had once encompassed a spectrum of attributes from which Betar could draw, Jabotinsky created a vision of Polskość that presented two starkly opposed modes of believing and behaving—one beautiful, noble, and appealing, the other loathsome and morally repugnant.

But it was precisely through Jabotinsky's description of two Polish nationalisms that Betar members could persist in their performances of Polishness. Echoing similar claims by Polish Jewish leaders and the few members of the Polish intelligentsia who remained sympathetic to Jews, Jabotinsky described Mickiewicz's inclusive vision of the Polish nation as the original driving force behind Polish national aspirations. By doing so, he allowed Betar members and leaders to envision themselves as both the defenders and the ambassadors of an authentic Polish nationalism, rather than as foolish proponents of a vision of Polish-Jewish brotherhood that could never be realized.

Not all Betar's leaders, however, were willing to adopt Jabotinsky's depiction of Polish nationalism, and some believed that his response to the rise of antisemitism in Poland was too tame. We will have occasion to meet some of these activists in the final chapter of this book, where I trace Betar's relationship with the Polish government and the youth movement's responses to Polish antisemitism following Piłsudski's death. Yet the rise in antisemitism was not the only reason Betar members might not readily accept the analogies between Polish nationalism and Zionism presented by the youth movement's leadership in their periodical literature and rituals. At the start of this chapter, we met a young man from Radom who had asked his teacher at Polish public school whether writing from left to right made him Polish. We return to his autobiography. After attending a Betar meeting with a friend from school, they began to discuss the Revisionist program:

> My schoolmate claimed that Palestine must be liberated, not bought. He said that a Jewish Legion must be created and it must go to battle. He gave Piłsudski as an example. I didn't think at the time that the Revisionist movement was bad, but . . . the Piłsudski example seemed ridiculous to me. . . . Piłsudski fought on his own territory with the support of thirty million Poles, while barely several million non-Poles were in Poland. For every Jew in Palestine there were three Arabs. I thought that the Revisionist movement was on a wild goose chase.[127]

Betar's national leadership in Warsaw were well aware that their detailed scripts for how to believe and behave were not always accepted by their followers or potential recruits. As the movement expanded, they worked strenuously to intervene in the activities of their branches, to ensure that their ideological labor would bear fruit. Perhaps most challenging of all, in their view, were the branches in small towns across eastern Poland, which seemed far from their reach in Warsaw. It is toward these towns, and Betar's efforts to transform them, that we now direct our attention.

5

Taming the Shtetl

IN THE SPRING of 1932, a devastating report arrived to Betar's headquarters at 6 Leszno Street in Warsaw. Its author, who chose to remain anonymous, claimed to have inspected more than forty of the youth movement's branches in towns across eastern Galicia. Each assessment was more scathing than the next. The town of Zabłotów's "terrible" Betar branch on the Polish-Romanian border had no leader; youth movement members in Sądowa Wisznia were "[n]asty material. They don't even know if there's a difference between us and [the socialist Zionist] Ha-shomer ha-tsa'ir"; Betar youth in Stary-Sambór, "completely infected" by other streams of Zionism, had abandoned Revisionism; and the Jewish youth of Chodorów, with a population of less than five thousand, had somehow managed to establish two rival Betar organizations. Of their interactions, all the report could muster were four words: "wars, riots, police intervention."[1]

Although the report's characterization of provincial Jewish youth as ideologically inept at best and traitors at worst was far from charitable, it saved its most vicious critique for Betar's leaders in Warsaw. Its author blamed Betar's head command, with the twenty-eight-year-old Aharon Propes at its helm, for the anarchy reigning in southeastern Poland. In the critic's view, Propes and his colleagues in Warsaw had undertaken no serious initiatives to bring the youth movement's members into line. Given that Betar's leaders from towns and cities alike considered Jewish youth in provincial towns to be the lifeblood of their movement and the key to their success, these accusations were difficult for them to ignore. According to the internal census conducted by the youth movement in 1930, no more than 10 percent of its members lived in Warsaw or its nearby towns. Most lived at least two hundred miles away, in Poland's eastern borderlands. More than a quarter of the youth movement's members lived in eastern Galicia, which included the country's southeastern provinces of Lwów, Stanisławów, and Tarnopol. Nearly one-third lived northward in the eastern borderland provinces of Wilno, Nowogródek, Polesie, and Wołyń, which Betar leaders proudly described as the "fortress of the Revisionist movement."[2] In all these provinces, the vast majority of Betar's members lived in market towns.[3] Their numerical strength made the reports of their unruly behavior all the more worrisome. Above all, these accusations threatened to expose the inability of the movement to uphold its promise to transform Jewish youth into a disciplined unit, ready at a moment's notice to carry out Jabotinsky's commands. Against this backdrop, Betar's head command in Warsaw spent much of the 1930s struggling to tighten its grasp over youth movement clubs in hundreds of provincial towns across eastern Poland, as well as in towns in the country's central region.

They were not alone in their efforts to "tame" the Jewish inhabitants of Poland's small towns, who made up as much as 40 percent of the country's Jewish population. Many of the anxieties and ambitions expressed by Betar's leaders in Warsaw were shared by Polish Jewish activists across the political spectrum. They too perceived vast benefits to be gained by extending their reach beyond the country's urban centers, where their periodical presses and executive leadership were headquartered. Inspired by long-standing stereotypes about Jewish life in small towns, they envisioned their efforts as the culmination of a noble quest, launched nearly a century before, to "modernize" shtetl Jews. This chapter explores the origins of these ambitions, as well as the techniques of mobilization devised by Betar's urban activists to tame their members and change their worldviews and behaviors. Above all, it maps the tense interactions between these urban activists and the young Jews living in the provincial towns the activists sought to transform. In telling this story, the chapter reveals the limits of using the triumphant ideological proclamations and meticulous political prescriptions emanating from Poland's urban centers as a key to understanding modern Jewish politics in interwar Poland. By paying attention to the struggles of Betar activists to enforce their national vision for Jewish youth, we gain an unprecedented view of their fraught and often fruitless efforts to contend with a social, economic, and political landscape that was largely beyond their power to control, let alone transform.

Imagining the Shtetl

In the spring of 1933, Betar activist B. Goldanski set out to write an exposé on the youth movement's activities in provincial towns across Poland. Published in the pages of *Ha-medina*, his searing critique characterized thousands of provincial Jewish youth as lazy and perpetually whining buffoons. To justify these generalizations, Goldanski explained, "[T]he *entire* group of Betar branches in small towns resemble one another, whether in the nature of their membership, the level of their spirit, or in the form of work that occurs."[4]

What inspired Goldanski to imagine Poland's provincial towns and their Jewish inhabitants in such stark and sweeping terms? There were, to be sure, traits that one could reasonably expect to find in most Jewish communities in provincial towns across central and eastern Poland. Goldanski and his readers might have called to mind a Jewish population making up 50 percent or more of the town's inhabitants, using Yiddish as their daily vernacular; a bustling marketplace and stalls in the center of town, where Jews, among them butchers, bakers, shoemakers, tailors, carpenters, cobblers, and other skilled-trade workers, would sell their wares to peasants from nearby villages; and a variety of Jewish religious institutions to serve local needs, including a ritual bath, a burial society, a synagogue, smaller prayer houses known as shtiblekh, and centers of religious learning, such as the heder for young children and the beysmedresh for more advanced study for men. Yet no provincial town was exactly like another. Jews living in towns nestled in the mountainous region of southeastern Galicia inhabited a landscape vastly different from Jews living in towns in the mostly flat, unforested terrain of central Poland or in the swampy marshlands and forests of the eastern provinces of Wołyń and Polesie. On market days in towns of central Poland, such as Jędrzejów, Krosno, and Dąbrowice, Jews would cater to the surrounding Catholic Polish peasant population; hundreds of miles east, Jews would serve a predominantly Belarusian-speaking peasant population in the north, and Ukrainian-speaking peasants in the center and south. If Jews from the town of Bakszty, in the northeastern province of Nowogródek, would have traveled to the town of Łask in western Poland, they may very well have strained at first to understand the dialect of Yiddish spoken by the region's inhabitants. Jews often insisted on the uniqueness of their particular town's local customs, from patterns of religious observance and dress to types of food.[5]

Goldanski was in good company when he chose to ignore these differences and treat the "shtetl Jew" as a distinct social type. For nearly a century, Jewish social, cultural, and political activists working in eastern Europe had found it useful to envision the lives of Jews living in provincial towns in a similar fashion. Around the mid-nineteenth century, when some of the region's advocates for the Jewish enlightenment (*haskalah*) turned to fiction to popularize their views, they envisioned provincial towns as the ideal setting to critique everything they deemed wrong with traditional Jews, from their religious superstitions, pedagogy techniques, and occupations to their habits of language, dress, and hygiene. Proponents of the haskalah branded each town, no matter its size, a shtetl, or "little town": ramshackle, diminutive, dilapidated, simultaneously tragic and comic, its inhabitants to be lampooned, pitied, despised, and ultimately rescued.[6] By the 1880s, even as the architects of modern Yiddish literature began to meld components of the haskalah program's modernizing agenda with the various concoctions of populism, socialism, and nationalism circulating at the time in eastern Europe, they continued to turn to the shtetl as their muse. Their portrayals of shtetl life often dramatized their own journeys beyond traditional Jewish life in small towns, frequently vacillating between critiquing traditional Jewish society and celebrating the shtetl as an idyllic bastion of communal intimacy and resilience.[7] Many Jewish political activists, however, expressed far less ambivalence when they ventured into these towns at the turn of the century to mobilize support. Armed with stereotypes about the "shtetl mentality" cultivated in Yiddish literature, they insisted that backwards small-town Jews, trapped in their rotting towns, could achieve redemption through the particular political programs they peddled. In an effort to win their support, Jewish political clubs in larger urban centers, such as Warsaw, Białystok, Wilno, and Odessa, invested time and effort in helping Jews from nearby provincial towns establish newspapers, libraries, and voluntary associations.[8] Joined on the eve of the First World War by Jewish philanthropic organizations seeking to promote health and education, these activists envisioned their organizations as vehicles that could bring the best of modernity to the shtetl.

In the wake of the First World War, which ravaged many of the provincial towns of central and eastern Poland and generated a wave of expulsion and emigration, urban Jewish political activists considered their work all the more urgent. As the 1920s progressed, dozens of Jewish organizations headquartered in Warsaw boasted that they had outposts in hundreds of small towns in central and eastern Poland. Among them were schools run by the Tarbut secular Zionist Hebrew education network, health clinics organized by the Society for Safeguarding the Health of the Jewish Population (Towarzystwo Ochrony Zdrowia Ludności Żydowskiej, TOZ), vocational training courses sponsored by urban Jewish philanthropists in Poland and abroad, and youth movements established by political parties. While Jewish activists from Warsaw and other major urban centers traversed the towns of central and eastern Poland, Polish government officials were attempting to "civilize" their eastern borderland regions. They drew a link between the alleged "backwardness" of its landscape and buildings to the national indifference of its Polish-speaking inhabitants and hoped that their efforts to modernize the towns and villages of the region through technological and pedagogical expertise would in effect Polonize a region dominated by Belarusians, Lithuanians, and Ukrainians.[9] Other political activists across interwar Europe were similarly sponsoring rural welfare and education programs with nationalist goals in mind.[10] The popularity of these programs, coupled with the century-old legacy of Jewish social activism in small towns, gave Zionist activists in Warsaw good reason to believe that their efforts to bring "modernity" and "progress" to the shtetl would encourage local Jews to begin to think in national terms and mobilize for the Zionist project.

Betar activists harnessed the extensive repertoire of shtetl images produced by Jewish activists before them to justify their mission to tame Poland's *shtetlekh*. The youth movement's leaders insisted that the very backwardness of Jewish life in Poland's provincial towns impeded the Revisionist project. Many focused on the alleged ignorance bred by shtetl life, which they claimed made it all but impossible for young Jews to transform into disciplined soldiers for the future Jewish state. Goldanski, who had portrayed shtetl youth as bumbling fools, urged his readers to express compassion and patience; the fact that Jews in provincial towns "lack the most elementary knowledge," he explained, meant that they "*cannot* understand what it means to submit to a command."[11] Propes, too, portrayed shtetl Jews, along with Polish Jews at large, as nearly impossible to mobilize. He described the attendees of the first world conference of Betar in 1929, many of whom had traveled from dozens of the youth movement's outposts in provincial towns, as "wild masses, without content, without form too—haphazardly strewn together fools, and I asked myself: can one do anything in Poland? It would have been better that there would have been nothing there rather than what I found."[12] Moshe Goldberg, describing himself as a westernized "folklorist" and "ethnographer," used the pages of *Ha-medina* to recount his journeys to "the most castaway [*farvofnste*] Polish shtetlekh to which one can barely travel only after surviving the seven circles of hell." There, he quipped, Betar members "create their own original 'intelligentsia language,'" teeming with spelling errors, gibberish phrases, and misused words in Yiddish and Hebrew. If Betar allowed this language to persist, he warned, the youth movement's members would never be able to implement, let alone understand, the tenets of Revisionist Zionism. Goldberg hoped that by displaying the mangled words of shtetl Jews to Betar activists, his article would ignite within them "a fiery desire to teach, teach and teach once more these youth from the villages and shtetlekh."[13]

To compliment their images of forlorn shtetl youth desperate for rescue, Betar's urban leadership encouraged their youth movement activists to envision themselves as powerful agents of modernity who could tame the Jewish masses. They depicted Jewish youth in provincial towns as wild but pliant. In a letter addressed to Betar activists setting off to visit the youth movement's branches in provincial towns across Galicia, their coordinator warned, "[I]n every location there are quarrels, disputes, intrigues, a lack of leaders, a lack of activity, a lack of culture, and what else is not missing from there." Simultaneously, however, he enthused, "Before you is human material that no one has seriously attempted to mold, and it's in your hands now to give it form." The coordinator likened the nationalization of Galicia's youth to taming the wild, unsanitary terrain of the region, and to curing a physical illness. Referring to the youth movement's members, he wrote, "Betar . . . which grew dramatically and quickly, is full of mud and muck . . . it's not a dangerous illness, but rather like measles, which . . . they'll overcome if they follow the instructions of the doctor." If, he continued, the region's youth voiced any objections to his instructions, Betar's doctor-emissaries would "mercilessly destroy the rotting site, and rebuild to mend the gap."[14]

Mobilizing the Shtetl

To tame Betar's members in provincial towns across Poland and convince them to conceive of themselves in national terms, the youth movement's leaders launched an ambitious program. One of their first tasks was to create an organizational structure that would help convince Betar members that they belonged to more than just a local youth club, but a broader national community whose leaders wielded the power to transform their lives. This was no small feat for the youth movement's "world leadership," which was made up of no more than a handful of impoverished eastern European Jewish men in their early twenties, who crowded around Jabotinsky in Paris. Branding themselves the military "officers" of the "Betar Authority" (Shilton Betar), they asked the youth movement's members to imagine themselves as citizens of a militarized state. In the summer of 1932, twenty-two-year-old Moshe Yoelson, a founding member of the first Betar branch in Riga, traveled through Poland to ensure that the youth movement's branches adopted the "Authority's" organizational model.[15] Hebrew terms describing state and military power were to permeate the ranks of the movement. The headquarters of Betar in each country were to take on the title of *netsivut*, or "the command." Poland's netsivut was expected to supervise several regional commands (*mifkadot galiliyot*), where activists from a province's urban center would supervise the activities of towns within their orbit. Each leader of a local Betar nest (*ken*) was a commander (*mefaked*), whose task was to oversee the various subsections within their branch, divided by age and gender. A cluster of several subsections within a local nest were to be known as battalions (*gdudim*). Members of Betar branches were asked to conceive of themselves not only as soldiers, but as members of a national family as well. Avoiding the term "comrade," which was popular among socialist Zionist movements, Betar's leaders instructed their followers to address one another as brother (*ach*) and sister (*achot*).[16]

Soon after Yoelson's visit to Poland, the officers of the Betar Authority in Paris announced that they would begin to produce identity cards for the youth movement's members that would "testify to the citizenship of the young man or woman in Betar."[17] Described by Benjamin Lubocki, one of the Authority's members, as the "Betar passport," he explained to the youth movement's members in Poland that the documents proved that "Betar [is] *one* camp, *one* will—it truly is its own country among all the countries of the world!"[18] The identity card campaign sought to instill in Jewish youth a sense of belonging to a unified, disciplined national community. By using the language of citizenship, Betar's architects encouraged their followers to fantasize that their leaders were already running a Jewish state. The identity cards also served as a pretext to "tax" Betar's members with an annual "passport fee," which would go directly to the Authority in Paris. Lubocki reminded Betar youth in Poland that "the citizens of our very own Betar country are conscientious enough to understand that the government of our country cannot exist if its citizens do not pay its taxes."[19]

The campaign to unite the youth movement's members as "citizens" under the care and command of the Betar Authority also provided a pretext for Propes's efforts to eradicate the youth movement's regional divisions, which mirrored those of most Zionist organizations in Poland. By 1930, three Revisionist executive leadership councils were operating simultaneously in Warsaw, Kraków, and Lwów. They differed in significant ways. Much like other Zionist activists operating in the region that was formerly Congress Poland, many of the Revisionist movement's executive leadership in Warsaw were born and raised in Yiddish-speaking and religiously observant homes. In contrast, Kraków and Lwów's Revisionist leadership, much like other urban Zionist activists in Galicia, comprised a cadre of Jewish journalists, lawyers, engineers, and dentists, most of whom had been raised speaking Polish at home and had attended Polish-language gymnasia. In the regions of former Congress Poland, Zionist leaders had earned the reputation of pursuing a politics of confrontation with the Polish government; in contrast, Zionist leaders in the regions of western and eastern Galicia tended to favor a more conciliatory approach toward Polish officials.[20] Along with other members of the netsivut in Warsaw, Propes viewed these divisions as yet another roadblock to enforcing discipline within the movement. In the winter of 1931, he demanded that Betar's leadership in western and eastern Galicia subordinate themselves to Warsaw.[21]

In a further effort to ensure that local customs did not interfere with the Warsaw netsivut's directives, its members sought to ensure that Betar's clubhouses operated independently, beyond the reach of the town's non-Revisionist organizations. Much like other Zionist youth movements in Poland, many of Betar's clubs initially convened in the buildings of more established Zionist organizations, meeting in the gymnasium of the local Maccabi athletics club, the classrooms of the Tarbut Hebrew school, or even the offices of the town's Zionist Organization. To safeguard Betar's members from the diverse ideologies that circulated in these spaces, the youth movement's leadership encouraged Jewish youth to rent two rooms near the center of town, where they could operate independently and construct their own miniature "Betar country."[22] By wresting local Betar groups from locations where non-Revisionist ideology might circulate, netsivut activists also sought to ensure that their youth movement clubs were more than just sites of leisure and recreation. Propes insisted the Betar ken was "not [merely] a meeting place for Hebrew youth," where people "want to rest, to speak with acquaintances, play ping pong or even sing something."[23] In the introduction to Betar's first detailed guidebook for setting up a branch, the twenty-five-year-old netsivut member Isaac Remba, who supervised the authority's cultural programming from 1934 onward, argued that the very construction of the club space would inspire Betar members "to adjust ... to [Betar's] foundational values: order, precision and discipline," ideals "foreign to the Jew of the diaspora."[24] In contrast to the shtetl's "mud and muck," the Betar clubroom was to be clean and rationally organized. Moshe Goldberg, the guidebook's author, who had previously ridiculed the "intelligentsia language" of small-town Betar activists, imagined the youth movement's members immersing themselves in Revisionist ideology the moment they crossed the threshold of their clubrooms. Straight ahead, they would behold the Jewish Legion's menorah emblem plastered to the wall, with the words "Tel Hai" at its base. Below the menorah were pictures of Herzl,

Trumpeldor, and Jabotinsky. To step into the club was to enter a miniature Land of Israel: the surrounding walls would be adorned with posters, sketches, and photographs of Mandate Palestine, from Tel Aviv's buildings to Zionist pioneers making the desert bloom. Above the images, slogans across the wall would remind Betar members of their sacred tasks: "No matter, it is good to die for our country!," "Hebrew youth, speak Hebrew!," "The Land of Israel for the People of Israel!," and "In blood and fire, Judah fell, in blood and fire, Judah will rise!"[25]

Goldberg also imagined one of the walls would be devoted exclusively to a board on which all commands (*pkudot*) from Paris, Warsaw, and the regional command would be posted. Betar's Warsaw activists envisioned the commands hanging from the board as the lifeline between them and members scattered across Poland's provincial towns.[26] Taking advantage of Poland's recently centralized postal service, members of the netsivut would send typed commands to Betar branches by mail. Local commanders were expected to fill out a slip within the envelope to confirm receipt of the command. They were also instructed to list how many members of the branch attended the weekly general meeting on Saturday afternoons, during which the commands were to be recited.[27] When asked by Warsaw's leadership to measure their success, regional commanders competed with one another to list the greatest number of letters received and sent.[28]

Poland's new postal service also played a pivotal role in allowing Betar's Warsaw activists to send educational bulletins to their local branches. Bulletins with titles such as *Our Work* (*'Avodatenu*) or *The Betar Leader* (*Madrikh Betar*) provided an exhaustive list of instructions for the various activities that Warsaw's leaders envisioned would take place within their youth movement's clubrooms. Claiming pedagogical expertise, Warsaw's activists crafted elaborate schemes for Betar leaders in provincial towns to implement. Every evening from Sunday to Thursday, Betar members were expected to assemble in the ken for between ninety minutes and two hours, with the youngest members arriving for the earliest session at 6:30 p.m.[29] The authors of these bulletins mapped out how each of these meetings would help transform their members into ideal Revisionists. Like other Zionist youth movements in Poland and elsewhere, Betar described each element of its curriculum as *hachshara* (preparation) for emigration to the Land of Israel. Betar envisioned three different types of hachshara for its members to undertake: cultural, professional, and military. Local Betar leaders were expected to use the educational bulletins from Warsaw as their guides for fulfilling these various preparation activities.

Like the shtetl reform activists who preceded them, the authors of Warsaw's educational bulletins envisioned their youth movement's "cultural preparation" program as the antidote to the negative effects of traditional Jewish institutions of education. A member of Betar's command in Warsaw claimed that their leaders had to undo the learning habits of Jewish youth traumatized by "being enclosed in a small and narrow heder," where instructors "stuffed them with abstract teachings far from daily reality." He warned Betar leaders not to follow the examples of the religious educators with whom they had studied; the "verbosity" (*verbalizmus*) typical of young men studying in heder and yeshiva would "be the death sentence of the [Betar] educator's work."[30] The Warsaw activist called on Betar's local leaders to turn instead to the advice offered by German and American pedagogical experts for constructing lessons that were rational, organized, and appealing. Published in 1935, the Warsaw netsivut's curriculum guide similarly insisted on the Western pedigree of Betar's pedagogical techniques, breathlessly citing Plato, Gottfried Wilhelm Leibniz, Herbert Stern, and Stanley Hall as inspirations for each component of cultural programming.[31] Encouraged to perform the role of modern pedagogical experts in the shtetl, local Betar activists were also asked to think of themselves as enlightened schoolteachers, assembling appropriate reading material far in advance and building each lesson on the one that preceded it.[32]

The curriculum guides for "cultural preparation" (*hachshara tarbutit*) designed by Betar's activists in Warsaw set out to combat the allegedly sweeping ignorance they had observed in their visits to Poland's provincial towns. Much like the leaders of other Zionist youth movements, Betar's sought to emphasize the modern, interactive style of their pedagogical approach by describing their lessons as *sihot*, or discussions. On at least two evenings between Sunday and Thursday, Betar groups were expected to assemble in the ken for sihot. The pedagogical approach adopted by the sihot guides sought to encourage a "free" conversation among Betar members while ensuring that they absorbed the ideological messages of the lesson. Nervous that youth movement leaders in provincial towns might stray from the boundaries of Revisionist ideology, Betar activists in Warsaw frequently crafted scripts for their local leaders to recite during these discussions. The topics of these scripts spanned from Jewish history and politics to the geography and demography of Mandate Palestine.[33] The sihot could also be used as a platform to introduce Betar members to topics that seemed, at first glance, outside the boundaries of Zionist activity. In the northeastern province of Nowogródek, for example, a member of the region's command not only created conversation scripts on the political heroes and enemies of Revisionism, but also included sessions on Aesop and the history of Greek mythology.[34] In a similar vein, Remba suggested that Betar leaders conduct sihot concerning Daniel Defoe's popular adventure novel *Robinson Crusoe*, as well as the works of Edmondo De Amicis and Jules Verne. Insisting that European literature was a gateway to Jewish nationalism, Remba argued that conversations about the heroic figures in these books would ultimately "educate the pupil in the spirit of Hebrew heroism and develop within him feelings of love and devotion towards his nation."[35]

Other Betar leaders similarly viewed their members' embrace of "European culture" as a critical component of their transformation into Zionists. Yosef Krelman, a member of Betar's command in Warsaw, vividly illustrated to Betar members in 1934 how efforts to transform the behavior of shtetl Jews could make their members simultaneously more Zionist and European. Betar's members, he explained, had two options: to remain the "barbarian, an Asian [*azyat*] . . . brutal, tactless, crudely pushing himself into places he shouldn't go, wearing a dirty, greasy suit" or to become the "one hundred percent European . . . noble, courageous, healthy, well educated, well mannered, with a feeling for aesthetics—in a word, a gentleman." Only after Betar members completed this internal civilizing mission—from using toothbrushes to keeping their houses neat and orderly—could they undertake their great task to "extend and plant the very foundational principles of European civilization" in Mandate Palestine. To remind them that this quest was deeply Zionist, Krelman noted that Jabotinsky himself had coined the Hebrew term "hadar" to embody the values of the "gentleman" who would help Jews prove that their nation was "an organic part of European culture and European civilization."[36]

In addition to sihot, there were other means to bring about this civilizing mission. In one of Betar's earliest instruction bulletins circulated across Poland, an activist in Warsaw suggested that the youth movement's members hang a checklist on their clubhouse wall with the names of the group's members and the books they were expected to read. The sample checklist consisted of *Don Quixote, David Copperfield*, and a book of legends about India translated into Hebrew.[37] Betar's leaders also envisioned their literacy program as a recruiting and publicity tool. In a 1935 guidebook for cultural training, Betar members were encouraged to devote three weeks to reading and analyzing a book. They were then expected to invite their town's Jewish population to a "literary trial" of the book's author, characters, and themes.[38] Popular among youth movements of the time, literary trials were conceived as theatrical performances where an audience could watch young Jews, in the roles of lawyers, judges, and witnesses, display their literary prowess. By having members perform their command of literature, Betar leaders hoped to showcase the fruits of their "civilizing mission," and in doing so, gain more supporters among the town's residents. To further convince the town's inhabitants to view the Betar club as a cultural destination, Betar's activists in Warsaw encouraged local Betar leaders to establish libraries filled with books in Hebrew, Yiddish, and Polish.

Even Hebrew instruction within the youth movement's branches, which took place twice a week, could serve the dual function of "nationalizing" shtetl Jews as future citizens of a distant Jewish state while turning them into more "civilized" Europeans. On the one hand, the use of Hebrew to describe their activity allowed Betar members to mark their clubrooms as national spaces: meetings became *asefot*, hikes became *tiyulim*, and military drilling became *mishtar*. Betar's Hebrew-language instruction guides, like those of other Zionist movements in Poland, taught Jewish youth to mark the landscape of Mandate Palestine as exclusively Jewish by learning the names of biblical landmarks, cities, and settlements in which Jews concentrated and Zionist activists operated. At the same time, however, Hebrew classes could also be designed to reinforce the youth movement's civilizing mission in Poland: a lesson devoted to Hebrew words for the home focused on "tools for hygiene," such as a toothbrush and soap.[39]

Echoing the language used by activists in TOZ and other health agencies of the era, Betar activists insisted to their followers that "physical culture" (*tarbut ha-guf*), from hygiene and nutrition to clothing and physical exercise, was inextricably connected to their psychological well-being and intellectual enrichment. Educational bulletins from Warsaw provided instructions for Betar members to combat the dirt, filth, and disease associated with life in the Diaspora in general, and small-town life in particular. Members of Betar's netsivut imagined the youth movement's members as ambassadors of hygiene and etiquette in their small towns. Writing in Madrikh Betar, an educational bulletin for the youth movement's leaders, one activist explained how the lessons they taught their followers could extend throughout the shtetl. The youth movement's members were expected to demonstrate respect toward their teachers, rabbis, and other figures of authority, avoid any events in town that disrupted public order, and ensure that order and cleanliness reigned in their homes, schools, streets, and even local theaters. No matter the location, Betar members were commanded to see themselves as "warriors" with the power to "repair all of the spoils" in their town.[40]

As part of Betar's efforts to embody and promote cleanliness, the youth movement's members were expected to don their meticulously maintained dark navy blue pants or skirts, brown shirts, black ties, military caps, and pins bearing the Jewish Legion's emblem during any public activity. Propes imagined that Betar's uniform had the power to help erase the social and economic differences among young Jews in small towns. "The uniform," he mused, "changes people; it makes them forget everything that is outside of Betar, all the differences in social rank, in economic situation, in education, in character ... creating [instead] one complete family."[41] Propes was not alone in envisioning Betar's power to combat social and economic tensions among Polish Jews. To prove that Zionism could flourish without fomenting class conflict, Betar's leaders in Warsaw claimed that their program would appeal to every economic sector of Polish Jewish society, from water carriers and peddlers to the sons and daughters of doctors and factory owners.[42] To help achieve this end, Propes strongly discouraged the growth of Masada, a relatively small Revisionist organization for gymnasium students, who generally came from wealthier homes.[43] In their youth movement's publications, members of Warsaw's netsivut showcased instances in which students and workers could be found in the same Betar club.[44]

The netsivut's members sought not only to diminish economic tensions among Polish Jews, but also to regulate the economic activity of Betar youth through the netsivut's "professional preparation" (*hachshara miktso'it*) program. Above all, netsivut members sought to take control of economic endeavors that had been initiated by Betar groups in provincial towns and villages without the leadership's consent. In 1931, the Zionist Organization decided that young Jews who had received training in agriculture within hachsharot, or training farms, were best suited to receive certificates for immigration to Mandate Palestine.[45] By the time Propes had arrived in Warsaw in 1929, several members of Betar groups in central and eastern Poland had already banded together to establish hachsharot in farms, stone quarries, and lumber yards in the hopes that the Zionist Organization would grant them these certificates. By 1933, between fifteen hundred and two thousand Betar members were working in as many as ninety hachsharot operating in the youth movement's name.[46]

The attitude of Warsaw's Betar leaders toward these hachsharot was ambivalent at best. Like many of their contemporaries in the Zionist movement, Betar's leaders insisted that Jewish youth needed to acquire new vocational skills before immigrating to Mandate Palestine. At the same time, however, they feared that the activity taking place within their hachsharot threatened to undermine the central tenets of the Revisionist movement. Jabotinsky had insisted for years that he was the champion of Jewish merchants and tradesmen, and he had frequently critiqued the Zionist Organization for giving pride of place to agricultural workers as prospective immigrants to Palestine. Even worse was the idealized hachshara lifestyle promoted and popularized by the Zionist Left. In the imagination of popular Labor Zionist organizations such as He-Halutz (the Pioneer), hachsharot were not only sites to transform the economic profile of Jews, but also utopian communes where egalitarianism could freely flourish.[47] Betar's activists in Warsaw feared that if left unchecked, their youth movement members would use hachsharot to experiment with the ideals and lifestyles promoted by socialist Zionists. No less dangerous was the threat of youth who were utterly indifferent to Zionism but desperate for work flooding the ranks of Betar's hachsharot. Charged with the task of supervising Betar's hachsharot, Warsaw's netsivut member Yosef Chrust warned Betar's regional commanders in March 1933 that these youth would become "dangerous, explosive material" that would "permanently damage our organization from an ideological standpoint."[48] Even though no more than 5 percent of Betar members were working in hachsharot, Propes similarly described the desire of others within the youth movement to join hachsharot as "a sin with no penance ... a path [that will lead toward] the liquidation of Betar."[49]

Two months later, Betar's leadership in Warsaw sent out a command to the youth movement's branches that outlined how they would exert further control over the hachsharot. In an effort to distinguish Betar's hachsharot from those of the Zionist Left, they were to be called "battalions," whose "commanders" were to be appointed by the netsivut. Rather than cultivate an egalitarian society, the task of the battalion would be to prepare its members for "conscription" into similar battalions operated by Betar in Mandate Palestine.[50] To ensure the ideological integrity of Betar's hachsharot, Warsaw's head command insisted that the only Betar members who could join a hachshara were those who had passed an exam conducted by the netsivut and had reference letters from their local commanders attesting to their "ideological purity, preparedness, responsibility and morality." Only Warsaw's netsivut would have the power to establish a hachshara or determine when its members could leave.[51]

Hachsharot were not the only local initiatives of Betar branches that the netsivut sought to "tame." Betar leaders also strove to ensure that the military training conducted by local Betar branches was firmly within the grasp of the netsivut. During the first three years of Propes's activity in Warsaw, the military training of Betar members was a haphazard affair and largely the result of local initiative. In the towns of Biała Podlaska and Podwołoczyska, for example, Betar members reached out to local Jewish veterans of the Polish army to teach them the basics of military drills.[52] As we have already seen, others turned to paramilitary programs run by local Polish military officials for assistance. Although Propes and others in Warsaw's netsivut were grateful for the support of the Polish military, they simultaneously sought ways to ensure that these activities reinforced Betar's ideology. Betar's leaders in Warsaw also sought to present themselves as military experts in their own right.

Spearheading the task to prepare a cadre of military experts within the youth movement was Yirmiyahu Halperin. Born in 1901 in Smolensk but raised in Ottoman Palestine, Halperin had fought alongside Jabotinsky in the 1920 Jerusalem riots. In 1928, he helped Abba Achimeir establish a military training school for Tel Aviv's Betar members. Three years later, Jabotinsky urged him to come to Europe, where he would supervise the training of Betar leaders across the continent. Arriving to Warsaw with his wife in the fall of 1931, Halperin rented several houses in the nearby village of Zielonka to establish a national school for Betar leaders. Halperin taught his recruits from across the country how to march, dig trenches, conduct first aid, engage in hand-to-hand combat, and use firearms.[53] In addition to running the national school for several more years, Halperin coordinated similar programs elsewhere in Poland, including Białystok, Straszów, Przemyśl, Lublin, Łódź, Ludmir, and Baranowicze.[54] Running two to three weeks, these courses drew together provincial youth from branches across their region. The presence and participation of Polish military officials in these courses allowed Betar members to gain legal access to firearms. Much like the activity in Betar's newly constituted hachsharot, Halperin's military courses also provided his recruits with training to be experts in Revisionist ideology and culture. The military graduates of these courses would be given the title lieutenant commander (*segen mefaked*). They were expected to bring their skills back to their local branches, where they would conduct at least three hours of military drills a week. In addition to these courses, Halperin founded a sailor's training program in 1934. Operating for four years in an Italian naval academy in the seaside town Civitavecchia, the academy drew several dozen Betar members annually from across Europe, with the largest contingent from Poland.[55]

The efforts of Betar's leaders in Warsaw to gain greater control over the military training of their followers unleashed another set of questions. By 1933, Betar activists reported to their leaders in Warsaw that Jewish women made up more than 40 percent of the youth movement in Poland and were demanding military training.[56] The netsivut saw the popularity of their youth movement among young Jewish women more as a cause for concern than celebration. Much like other Zionist movements of the era, Betar had invested little effort in creating a blueprint for what an ideal woman political activist might look like.[57] The heroes of Zionist behavior offered by the Revisionist movement, from Herzl to Trumpeldor, were almost exclusively male. The characteristics they celebrated as Zionist, including chivalry, courage, and military might, were typically identified as masculine qualities and the exclusive domain of men. Betar's leadership in Warsaw expressed deep reservations about promoting these values among Jewish women. Their suspicions about women's participation in Zionist politics were inextricably linked to contemporary debates across Europe about the roles and rights of women in politics. In interwar Poland, doubts about the value of Jewish women's political activism were not harbored solely by the members of traditional Jewish organizations, such as the Agudat Yisrael party, which claimed that the laws of Judaism protected and prevented women from participating in public life.[58] In many of the country's daily Jewish newspapers, journalists from across the political spectrum debated whether women possessed the physical or mental capacity of men to participate in politics.[59] Much was at stake in these debates. Despite unprecedented educational opportunities for young women in interwar Poland, their political status remained uncertain. Jewish women had the right to elect government officials at the local and the national level, but they were forbidden from participating in elections for Jewish community councils (*kehilot*) and denied the right to hold positions of leadership within them.

When Betar's leaders, much like most of their colleagues in the Polish Jewish Zionist press, addressed the "women question," they set their focus on the supposed dangers of women's full participation in political activity. Between 1932 and 1933, Betar's educational bulletins presented several articles describing the dangers of women participating in the youth movement's programs alongside men. In one such article, Betar activist Yosef Krelman warned, "I would not be exaggerating if I said that all young women in Betar, or, more accurately, all young women in the Zionist youth movement, are sick with a deep and dangerous psychological illness . . . our young women would very much want, if it was in their power, to turn into men. The young woman imitates the way in which he talks, walks, and moves. . . . [T]his is how the popular and well-known spectacle of the she-male was created; according to her sex, she is a woman, but according to her character she appears as a horrific mixture of masculine and female qualities. There is no charm, beauty, or advantage to such a type."[60] Krelman and other leaders in Betar traced the origins of this "sickness" to the socialist movement, which they claimed sought to destroy the Jewish family unit in the name of women's emancipation.[61] He claimed that Betar aimed "to minimize the number of such young women," not only in Betar, but in Polish Jewish society at large.[62]

Betar's male leaders were not the only ones to express these sentiments. Among the most devoted advocates of segregating Jewish women and men in Betar was Helena Libertal. A founding member of Betar in Riga, Libertal, who completed her doctorate at the University of Vienna, was the only woman to play a role in crafting Betar's curriculum. In an article published in one of Warsaw's educational bulletins, she warned that Betar was attracting women who sought to use military exercises to uproot their femininity. To emphasize the danger she perceived in permitting women to fully participate in Betar's activities, Libertal insisted that their behavior was "no more than assimilation. The very same assimilation that appears to us with all its ugliness, with all its betrayal to the nation and to the soul of man."[63] Libertal warned that the presence of women in Betar was particularly dangerous when they assumed positions of leadership. She feared that young boys, who naturally longed to imitate their leaders, would begin to adopt feminine traits, making them unfit to serve as the nation's warriors.

Libertal and Betar's leaders in Warsaw, hard at work on the movement's educational bulletins, envisioned their version of Zionism as a corrective to the gender confusion created by modern politics. Just as Zionism promised to help effeminate Diaspora Jewish men restore their masculinity, so too would it help masculine Jewish women reclaim their womanhood. To do so, the educational bulletin's writers proposed several programs to cultivate and protect women's "natural instincts." One Betar leader suggested that the youth movement train Jewish women to be gardeners and educators, roles "that are suitable to the character of woman and her feelings of love and compassion."[64] Another leader wrote that the Betar woman's "cultural preparation" program would teach her to "strive to develop her sense of aesthetics, to be beautiful, to wear tasteful dresses, not ugly ones."[65] Doing so, he argued, would help inspire Betar's young men to behave in a chivalrous fashion. Like others in the Zionist movement, many of Betar's leaders believed that the primary task of Jewish women in politics was to facilitate the character development and political activity of men. When it came to military training, Betar's educational bulletins envisioned young women as nurses, tending to wounded soldiers. Above all, the greatest contribution Betar's women could give to the battlefield was to become mothers who would educate their sons to fight and die for their nation. Through these proposals, Betar's leaders strove to limit the political participation of women to raising, supporting, or inspiring young men. These proposals conformed to most right-wing nationalist movements throughout Europe at the time, whose leaders insisted that they sought to promote rather than overthrow traditional gender roles.[66]

At the same time as Betar's leaders were devising intricate and elaborate curricula to uplift the shtetl, from its cultural life and economic structure to relations between its young men and women, they were no less preoccupied with creating ways in which to monitor and enforce the implementation of their directives. To ensure that their members conformed to their expectations, Betar's leadership in Warsaw trained a cadre of activists to serve as inspectors of the youth movement's branches across Poland.[67] Drawn initially from the ranks of Halperin's instructor's school in Zielonka, this group of "Betar inspectors" were expected to tour provincial towns across Poland to monitor the activities of local branches. Leaders in Warsaw's head command expected these inspectors to stay in one location for four to seven days. In addition to conducting an evaluation of the branch's activities, the inspectors were instructed by their superiors to provide an activity plan that would last between one to two months.[68] They were also expected to demand ten złoty, which was to be immediately deposited into the netsivut's bank account. In return, the inspector would grant the branch an "official" certificate permitting it to operate. The inspector's permission certificate and inspection report were just two of dozens of documents created by the Betar's leaders in Warsaw to project an image of a finely tuned, powerful bureaucracy that could effectively monitor the activity of its followers.

As Propes began to coordinate the visits of Betar inspectors, Warsaw's netsivut announced, at the end of 1932, that it would begin to conduct exams testing the skills of Betar members across the country.[69] The youth movement's members were warned that failure to pass these exams would prohibit them from receiving one of the immigration certificates to Mandate Palestine allotted to Betar by the Zionist Organization. The exam would test the ability of Betar members to speak Hebrew and use firearms, as well as their knowledge of Revisionist ideology. In yet another effort to create a document that bestowed on them further authority, Warsaw's Betar leadership informed their followers that those who passed the exam would also receive a "Betar visa," which would ensure that if and when they arrived in Mandate Palestine, they would be welcomed into the ranks of Betar's local battalions.

In addition to inventing incentives for Betar's members to obey the leadership's commands, the netsivut devised methods to deter their followers from straying from the programs created in Warsaw. The youth movement's educational bulletins included extensive discussions of how local leaders could punish Betar members for misconduct. No breach of protocol was too small to ignore. "If you silently pass over a small sin," Warsaw's netsivut warned them, "the pupils will see the weakness of their educator, and it will motivate them to commit a grave sin."[70] The netsivut occasionally invented specific punishments for particular "sins." Betar members who had not purchased uniforms, for example, were forbidden to stand at roll call with their friends during their branch meeting.[71] Most often, however, the netsivut left it to the discretion of the local leader to determine what constituted a serious infringement, which could result in suspension or expulsion from the movement. Betar members were warned that any acts of "discipline breaking" they committed would permanently blemish their record in the youth movement. Any infringement of the youth movement's rules was to be recorded on the offender's identity card.[72]

The netsivut also warned the youth movement's members that they could face collective punishment. Failure to contribute to a fundraising drive for the youth movement could result in being publicly humiliated in Betar's newspapers.[73] Warsaw's Betar leadership boasted that they had the power to forbid local branches of their youth movement from operating. The pages of Betar's educational bulletins frequently reminded the youth movement's members that Warsaw's netsivut could stop sending them commands and periodicals and, at the very worst, could appeal to local government officials to revoke the club's right to operate. Thus "Command 51," published in April 1933, notified Betar members that in two months' time, the netsivut would publish a list of Betar branches who had paid for the "Betar passport." "No Betar branches will be exist," the command warned, "except for those who are on this list."[74]

Drawers, Pins, and Sleighs

One of the hundreds of Betar branches to receive such threats was five hundred miles east of Warsaw, deep in the province of Wołyń's northern forests. Established in the mid-nineteenth century as an agricultural colony by Tsar Nicholas I, Osowa Wyszka's several hundred inhabitants were nearly all Jewish. It took no more than fifteen minutes to walk through the town. Along its five narrow dirt roads, one could find a brick kiln, flourmill, and factory for tanning hides. Toward the center of town stood a Polish public school, three prayer houses, and a dozen small shops run by tailors, shoemakers, and carpenters. In the spring, knee-high reeds would sprout from the muddy soil surrounding the town's roads. During the warm and humid summer months, peasants from nearby villages, along with some of the town's Jews, would harvest its fields of wheat and barley. Local craftsmen with an entrepreneurial spirit would have to travel at least seventy miles with their horse-drawn carts to reach the cities of Pińsk or Równe to peddle their wares.[75]

Betar's leaders in Warsaw could not have imagined a more eager recipient of their circulars and instruction guidelines than the young man in Osowa Wyszka who chose the pseudonym "Sufferer 1001" for his submission to the YIVO autobiography contest in 1939. He recounted how the expanding networks between his town and the country's cities were conduits for his political awakening. Although he had yet to leave Osowa Wyszka by the age of fourteen, he was already an avid reader of Warsaw's Yiddish daily, *Haynt*, which arrived in town thanks to five of its residents sharing one subscription. As if to vindicate Jabotinsky's strategy of using incendiary prose in his newspaper columns to mobilize support, Sufferer 1001 explained to his reader, "What was written in *Haynt* about the provocative Betar youth especially jumped out at me, and precisely because of this, the party awakened even more interest in me."[76] The youth movement, he continued, had only recently been founded by a town resident who had learned of Betar's existence during his stay in the northeastern city of Grodno, where he had sought out work. Convinced that time in Poland's cities could provide access to political knowledge that was difficult to obtain back home, Sufferer 1001 eagerly awaited the return of his brother from Warsaw, where he was enrolled in a rabbinical seminary. Upon his older brother's arrival in Osowa Wyszka, the autobiographer recounts, "I decided to make use of the months he was here to gather information about world politics in general and the situation of Jews specifically.... [H]e explained things to me that I had no idea about.... After my brother went on his way, I joined Betar."[77] In addition to pointing out how the flow of people to and from cities contributed to his town's political life, Sufferer 1001 also noted the importance of Poland's postal network. He recounted to his readers that one of the first political activities he chose to undertake was to voraciously read the pamphlets mailed to their club by the youth movement's headquarters in Warsaw.

Had they read his account of discovering and promoting Betar in Osowa Wyszka, the members of Betar's head command in Warsaw would have likely pointed to his prose as proof that their efforts to extend their control into the farthest reaches of provincial Poland were bearing fruit. They would have also looked approvingly at Sufferer 1001's account of his political conversion: placing Betar's ideology and activists front and center of his recruitment narrative, he described being beguiled by provocative prose and inspired by youth movement activists from larger towns and cities. The story he told of his sister's political adventures, however, was another matter altogether. Several years before his quest to promote Betar, his sister had founded a local branch of the socialist Zionist youth movement Ha-shomer Ha-tsa'ir. It was a far cry from the revolutionary utopia envisioned by the movement's activists in Warsaw. "The town's organization," Sufferer 1001 explained, "had an entirely different character than that of the general organization.... [I]t was forbidden to enter the clubhouse without a head covering, and the boorish members of the organization believed that Ha-shomer was a religious organization. They couldn't fathom that it would be possible for a Jewish organization not to be religious."[78] Instead of engaging the members of Ha-shomer Ha-tsa'ir in discussions about the fundamentals of class conflict and proletarian revolution, his sister led conversations on how to rebuild the Holy Temple in Jerusalem as speedily as possible. When the youth movement's headquarters in Warsaw sent her instructions, she simply stuffed them into a drawer at home. When Sufferer 1001 discovered these circulars, he got wind of the movement's socialist and antireligious program. He told no one of his discovery; protecting his sister was more important to him than exposing the truth to the local members of Ha-shomer Ha-tsa'ir.

Sufferer 1001's account of how his sister defied the expectations of her youth movement's leadership is just one among dozens recounted by Betar members from provincial towns across Poland who submitted their life story to YIVO's autobiography contest. These autobiographies offer a glimpse into how Betar members understood and explained their attraction to the youth movement, how they interacted with the directives of their leaders in Warsaw, as well as the reasons some of them decided to abandon the organization. In myriad ways, the autobiographies demonstrate how the flow of people, goods, and ideas among villages, small towns, and cities did not guarantee a seamless transmission of political attitudes and behaviors from urban centers. Instead, the accounts lay bare how the very dynamics that animated the lives of Polish Jewish youth in provincial towns and, in many cases, the country at large defied the national myths and scripts so carefully crafted by political activists in Warsaw—Zionist or otherwise.

Part of what made the ambitious and demanding curriculum created by Warsaw's Betar leaders impossible to fulfill was that it was utterly tone deaf to the daily economic challenges of the youth movement's members. By the age of thirteen, most Polish Jewish youth, regardless of their location, were either hard at work or seeking whatever meager employment they could scrape together. Woven within their accounts of joining Betar are descriptions of their desperate search for work—as locksmiths, milk carriers, bootmakers, dressmakers, and watch or harness makers. With bleak economic conditions in the early 1930s, many if not most parents in provincial towns saw no other option but to force their children to contribute to the family income. This was all the more necessary in the wake of a parent's death, a not infrequent occurrence among the Betar autobiographers.[79] Shielding school-aged children from work was often a luxury parents could not afford. F. J., recalling his early childhood in Ostrowiec, a large town in central Poland on the Kamienna River, described his struggle, at nine years old, to work at the local dye factory while attending public school. The dye stains on his hands so repulsed his teacher that he was frequently barred from setting foot inside the classroom.[80] The multiple demands on young Polish Jews made it difficult to fulfill Betar's expectations for attending evening meetings throughout the week.

The autobiographers' descriptions of their economic lives also cast doubt on the claim of Betar's leaders in Warsaw that they had managed to erase the economic fault lines dividing Polish Jews by uniting workers and students within the same youth movement branch. Instead, the accounts highlight how economic standing often played a decisive role in determining the political movement young Jews chose to join. Writing in Wieluń, a large town in the province of Łódź, the twenty-one-year-old "K.S.V." recounted why he and his brother began to visit the town's main Zionist club: "I don't know why we went there and not elsewhere. Maybe there wasn't anything else around. Either way, we were from a middle class family, maybe we wouldn't be let in elsewhere."[81] For Jews in Poland, the notion that one's economic standing was linked to other aspects of one's life was all too familiar: houses of prayer, for example, often catered to distinct occupational groups. While an autobiographer from Ołyka, a town surrounded by the forests of Wołyń, informed YIVO that his town's Betar group consisted exclusively of poor religious youth, an autobiographer from a middle-class home in Zaleszczyki, 170 miles south, confessed, "I had no idea what goals . . . Betar sought to achieve. I joined it because I was assimilated—although this was never said out loud."[82] These accounts not only demonstrate how the socioeconomic configuration of each Betar branch depended on local context, but they also highlight how levels of religious observance could serve as criteria to determine the composition of the membership.

When Betar's autobiographers described their encounters with political ideology, many defied the ideological scripts for national recruitment created by Betar's leaders in Warsaw. In contrast to the wild, ignorant, and politically unblemished masses that Propes had imagined as potential recruits, many had several years of political experience behind them. The son of Hasidic parents, "K. S." joined Betar in his hometown of Kozienice in central Poland only after several years of membership in the town's communist movement. During his time in the movement, he read Russian socialist literature voraciously, participated in the movement's underground activity, and even spent time in a Polish prison. Several years later, when Trotsky was excommunicated from the Communist Party and rumors spread that Soviet agents had instigated Palestine's Arab-Jewish riots in 1929, K. S. decided to join Betar.[83]

If Betar members like K. S. described an ideological trajectory that contradicted the scripts of recruitment from Warsaw, others made clear that Revisionist ideology played little to no role in enticing them to join the youth movement. Writing some three hundred miles southeast of Kozienice, in the town of Horodenka, a twenty-year-old man recounted that his childhood pastime of "playing soldier," not Revisionist ideology, had inspired him to enlist in Betar. Joining the youth movement had an added advantage: while marching two by two in the street, he and his friends could confide in one another about the town's girls beyond the prying eyes of parents.[84] A young woman from Jezierzany, a small town about sixty miles north of Horodenka, similarly insisted that ideology had nothing to do with her decision to join Betar. By the time she described her induction into Betar, she had already recounted her harrowing memories of the First World War as a young child: the death of her mother when she was five years old; her completion of elementary school at thirteen years old; and her time at a local trade school, where she fell in love with one of the students. Immediately after describing her heartbreak when she realized her love was not reciprocated, she recounted the efforts of two Zionist youth movements, Betar and the socialist but anti-Marxist Gordonia, to court her support: "It was fashionable among us at the time to join a party. I was invited to Gordonia and Betar. My mind was agitated with the question, where should I go? I was entirely uninterested in either of their programs. After some deliberation I enrolled in the Revisionist organization. I was more quickly captivated by the beautiful menorahs [Betar's pins] than the small pins of Gordonia, and the way Betar marched, I even liked their shirts more than those of Gordonia. I consider myself to be a 100% Revisionist woman."[85]

Ideology could even be a negligible force in the lives of Polish Jewish youth who strove to rise through the ranks of the movement's leadership. Among the contestants to submit an autobiography to YIVO in 1934 was "Modestus," a young man living in the northeastern town of Bereza Kartuska, in present-day Belarus. After reading Marx, Lenin, Trotsky, Ahad Ha'am, and the nationalist literature of "reborn nations" across Europe, he concluded that Jews had to "strive for a pure nationalism with no socialist games."[86] Despite the echoes of Revisionist ideology in his reasoning, his decision to join Jabotinsky's ranks was ambivalent at best. As if to insist that he was not anchored to Revisionism, he informed his reader that if there was another youth movement closer to his worldview, he would join it. It was also no accident that he chose to explore politics by entombing himself in piles of Zionist books and brochures in the town's Jewish library. The library offered refuge from the previous tumultuous months, in which he had carried out a secret relationship with Maria, a young Catholic woman in the city of Chełm. Their romance took a turn for the worse when Maria discovered she was pregnant. Modestus described finding a note she had written soon after:

> I picked it up with trembling hands, and when I read it, I froze like a pillar of salt: "My beloved ... I have decided to leave Chełm and travel with my aunt to the village. I want to have an abortion. If everything works out and falls into place, we'll see each other soon. And if it doesn't work out, I don't want to spoil your life or mine (here, there were trails of [her] tears [on the page])—and we won't see each other ever again. Consider me dead, and don't look for me. From the one who will love you until the day she dies, Maria."[87]

He never heard from her again. His efforts to find her were fruitless. In the meantime, his deeply pious grandfather threatened to kick him out of his home if he continued to commit transgressions. Even reading a secular newspaper was grounds for punishment. Heartbroken and desperate to flee, Modestus contemplated suicide. News of a Betar instructor's course in Baranowicze, some seventy miles northeast, offered an escape. "[B]ecause I could no longer continue to live in this poisonous atmosphere," he explained, "I decided to leave, at least for a few weeks. I gathered the little money I earned from giving private classes and I travelled to Baranowicze for three weeks. [T]here, my harassing thoughts didn't command over me."[88]

K.S.V., the young man from Wieluń, similarly avoided the language of national obligation promoted by Betar's leaders in Warsaw when describing his ascent to the leadership of his town's Betar branch. Like many other young Polish Jews, he had been drawn into the youth movement by his sibling. "I must confess," K.S.V. wrote, "that I consider the time which I spent in the organization, *notwithstanding its ideological character*, and only regarding its social components, to be the best and richest in my life."[89] Reflecting on his time as a Betar leader, he noted, "I developed spiritually and morally in many respects; I worked hard to improve myself, and I can say that I was happy, I enjoyed myself very much, and I learnt a lot."[90] Whether in a mandolin orchestra, on a soccer team, or at a summer camp, many other YIVO autobiographers echoed K.S.V.'s descriptions of the joy they experienced engaging in their youth movement's leisure activities. He also described the social status he enjoyed as Betar's leader. Becoming branch leader, he explained, was like "becoming a big-shot" and made him feel all the more respected by his peers.[91] While a confluence of factors, such as fun, friendships, family, and a sense of power, kept K.S.V. within Betar's ranks—at least for some time—ideology was nowhere to be found in his recruitment narrative.

Autobiographers who ultimately abandoned Betar also have much to tell us about the limits of the netsivut's efforts in Warsaw to shape how ideology was transmitted and interpreted. The young woman from Jezierzany, who had chosen Betar over Gordonia for its pins and uniforms, had this to say of her departure from the youth movement:

> Every night, I visit the club. They hold lectures where they tell me about Trumpeldor: how he fell as a sacrifice for the fatherland; and in his honor, people want to found a legion, and Jabotinsky, who is as heroic as Trumpeldor, will take his place. We will expel all of the Arabs from the country and create a Jewish majority. Later, I was told about the foundations upon which they want to build the national home. Each person must think only of themselves, so that they can become rich . . . and not accept any Arab workers, but only care for the Jewish ones. The lecturer gives an example of [such] egoism; a few girlfriends are walking. Suddenly, a [horse-driven] sleigh passes by, and one of them wants to take it. This girl will certainly leave her girlfriends . . . [to] ride on the sleigh.
>
> At this point, a voice inside me began to protest. No, I wouldn't do that. . . . I wouldn't leave all my girlfriends . . . either all of us would go on the sleigh, or none of us would. He wasn't right. . . . He keeps saying that

we have to kick out the Arabs, [but] they are also human beings... people also want to kick Jews out from every country in the exact same way and deny them the capability of living ... that is also inhumane. Something about what he said regarding each person having to only care for themselves also didn't sit right with me.... I want to be rich, happy... but other people also have the same desires. Is it not unfair that I should have and they should not?"[92]

This account is as elusive as it is illuminating. Far from transparent reflections of the past, the autobiographical narratives presented by Betar's apostates were often shaped by whichever ideological worldview they endorsed at the time of writing. Upon leaving Betar, the young woman in Jezierzany immediately enlisted in the socialist Bund's youth movement, Tsukunft. It would not be difficult to hear echoes in her account of how Tsukunft depicted the Revisionist movement's program. Nonetheless, if we can entertain that there is some truth in her account of the Betar lecturer, the passage can provide a remarkable map of how Revisionist ideology could be transformed when interpreted by the youth movement's members. While Betar activists in Warsaw were careful to avoid any calls to expel Arabs from Palestine, the Betar leader in Jezierzany seemed to have no reservations about declaring that their expulsion was a fundamental goal of the movement. The lecturer's efforts to translate the Revisionist movement's economic program into terms palatable to young Jews similarly displayed a degree of creative license that would have likely made Betar's leaders in Warsaw shudder. They had little power to police how leaders in provincial towns interpreted and promoted the movement's ideology. Had members of Warsaw's netsivut perused the autobiographies submitted to YIVO, they would have been no less horrified to discover the numerous cases in which ideology played no role in the decision of their members to abandon the movement. Just as dramatic clubs, sports teams, and the prospect of romance could draw Jewish youth into a political movement, these incentives could also entice them to seek greener pastures.

Even if an autobiographer could claim steadfast commitment to Betar's ideology, it did not guarantee the survival of their local youth movement branch. Numerous challenges could paralyze the activity of a Betar branch or extinguish it altogether. We return, once again, to Osowa Wyszka. Sufferer 1001 had embraced Betar's ideology; collected the movement's circulars, periodicals, and pamphlets for distribution; and enlisted local youth for his cause. Yet his group swiftly collapsed. He insisted that its demise had little to do with the youth movement's program but was rather the result of endless bickering and petty contests for power. Tellingly, he attributed his peers' behavior to their inability to shake off the "traditional" mentality they had been raised to embrace in the shtetl. "Just like in a beysmedresh," he lamented, "everyone here wanted to be the 'master of knowledge,' and everyone was convinced that they deserved to give the instructions."[93] A former resident would later recall a different reason for that branch of Betar's dissolution: its leader allegedly decided to become a communist.[94] Although Betar would be resurrected in town several years later—a common fate among Polish Jewish youth movements—Sufferer 1001 would not be found within its ranks.

Reports from the Field

Much like Sufferer 1001, members of the netsivut directed their wrath toward local Betar activists when they sought to explain why their efforts to tame provincial Jewish youth were bearing such little fruit. Their first targets were the members of the regional commands set up by Moshe Yoelson in 1932. The netsivut had envisioned the activists in these command centers as local emissaries who would fulfill their demands. Regional commanders, however, often diverged from the instructions issued to them from Warsaw. The question of agricultural training in hachsharot was particularly divisive. Despite Warsaw activists envisioning the hachsharot as dens of depravity, many regional commanders saw little need to transform the training centers they had established. They reasoned that the benefits of using the hachsharot to draw local youth into the movement far outweighed any danger of a socialist ethos creeping into them. Warsaw's netsivut was baffled by the pushback they received to their demands that they militarize the hachsharot or abandon them altogether. At a meeting of Poland's regional commanders in 1933, an infuriated member of the netsivut scolded the provincial emissaries. Driven by "narrow local patriotism," he reported, "not only did [they] not help us with assembling hachshara battalions, but [they also] occasionally interfered with the netsivut in this work."[95]

The most ferocious pushback to the netsivut's instructions came from regional leaders in eastern Galicia. Responding to Propes's demand that they subordinate themselves to Warsaw, leaders in Lwów turned in September 1931 to Revisionist leaders in London to intervene. Taking a cue from other Zionist organizations in Galicia, they presented themselves as heirs to a tradition of enlightened and sophisticated political activism forged by Zionist leaders in the

Habsburg Empire. They mocked Zionists of Warsaw as heirs of the backwards politics of the Russian Empire. The members of Warsaw's netsivut, they claimed, "do not want to honour law and justice, the foundations of every cultured society, and using the brute force of their act of violence [Gewaltsreich], they want to infiltrate those who have never been in a subordinate position to Warsaw."[96] The London Executive tried to mollify the eastern Galician leaders, insisting that they had no intention of "robbing the autonomy" they had enjoyed.[97] The regional leaders' frantic protest proved partially successful. Although Propes ultimately managed to strengthen the contacts between eastern Galicia's Betar commanders and the netsivut in Warsaw, the leaders in Lwów continued to exercise autonomy by running their own hachsharot.[98] As Revisionist leaders would later recall, tensions between Betar's leaders in Warsaw and those in Galicia would continue to sporadically erupt throughout the 1930s.[99]

Regional commanders were no more successful than the netsivut in controlling their subordinates. Members of Lublin's regional command bluntly informed the netsivut in 1932 that all their energies had been committed to dealing with rivalries between local branches of their movement. As a result, they reported, it was all but impossible to carry out the orders issued by Warsaw's Betar leadership.[100] As the national coordinator of Halperin's instructor's schools, which sent emissaries to Betar branches across Poland, Avraham Axelrod was an obvious target for local branches to direct their complaints. Born and raised in a small town near Wilno, he was one of the first graduates of the youth movement's instructor's school in 1932. Overwhelmed by the volume of complaints about the behavior of the youth movement's peripatetic instructors, Axelrod took to the movement's nationally circulated newspaper to accuse them of exhibiting an "idiotic pride" when interacting with the commanders of the local branches in their province.[101]

Even Axelrod, the very man charged with serving as the netsivut's primary emissary, was proving problematic to Betar leaders in Warsaw. In letters from Warsaw's netsivut to the twenty-year-old activist, Betar leaders seethed with frustration and anger. "We are astounded," one typical letter began, "that we haven't received to date any reports about your visits to the branches." The letter continued by scolding him for remaining in the eastern city of Łuck, rather than following the itinerary provided by the netsivut for his visits to Betar's branches. The author saved his greatest outrage for the handwritten postscript to his typed letter: "Why aren't you organizing the monthly taxes [of the Betar branches], and you haven't even paid off one of your debts. Pay off your debts immediately!!! Help us in the work [we need to do], which I do not have to remind you of!!!"[102] The young man had no problem responding in kind. In reply to one of Axelrod's letters, Propes quipped, "Instead of lecturing me, coming up with suggestions would be more helpful."[103] Another letter from Axelrod so offended netsivut members that they informed him that until he learned to address them with respect, they would refuse to pay attention to his requests.[104]

If the netsivut struggled to tame the very people they relied on to extend their program into Poland's provincial towns, they were all the more helpless to enforce the directives they offered in their pamphlets, circulars, and commands. In 1935, Betar's netsivut members observed that the instructions they had provided for organizing local branches continued to fall on deaf ears. They complained that despite the nearly three years that had passed since they had launched a campaign to make Betar organizations conform to the organizational blueprints provided by Warsaw, "a terrible confusion of forms and structures" continued to reign in the youth movement, which was "harming many aspects of Betar's work, but above all, its discipline."[105] No one branch's leadership structure, system of registration, or punishment criteria seemed to match the other. No less appalling to the netsivut was that Betar's branches were sending letters to Warsaw written in Yiddish rather than Hebrew.[106] Like most other Zionist movements, Betar leaders denigrated Yiddish as a disfigured language of the Diaspora; celebrated Hebrew as the authentic, pure language of the Jewish nation; and claimed to be at the vanguard of the battle to make Hebrew the primary spoken language of Jews.[107]

The persistence of Yiddish in Betar branches was viewed by netsivut members as just one indication that their cultural directives were making little inroads in the provincial clubs. They attributed the failure of their bloated cultural curriculum guidelines to the fact that many Jewish youth erroneously saw the Betar club as a place to relax and have fun, rather than as a school and fortress for Revisionist ideology. A typical report from the field was offered by Krelman, the Betar leader who had previously called on Jewish youth to abandon their "Asian" ways. After conducting several inspections of Betar branches in provincial towns, he reported that Betar members tended to come and go as they pleased, rather than observe the schedule posted on the wall by their local commanders. Instead of conducting meetings with curriculum guidelines in their hands, "they talk, they schmooze, they roughhouse, they joke around, they chatter."[108] Other Betar activists in Warsaw wondered if the members of the youth movement's provincial branches had even bothered to read the movement's educational literature and commands in the first place.[109] They suspected that Betar members all but ignored the ideological gloss that the netsivut provided to the soccer matches, dramatic clubs, singing, and dancing that took place within the framework of the youth movement. In some cases, the failure of ideology to leave a decisive imprint on Betar branches could produce unexpected alliances with other youth movements. Betar leaders were not the only ones to be alerted to such ideological transgressions. In a letter to Ha-shomer Ha-tsa'ir's headquarters from the youth movement's branch in the northeastern town of Mołczadź, for example, members explained the strategy they had adopted to avoid arousing the interest of the local Polish police, who had been instructed to keep tabs on socialist movements. By sharing the same clubhouse as the town's Betar branch, the Ha-shomer Ha-tsa'ir branch had led the police to think both organizations were one and the same.[110] Surprisingly, the letter included no apology or explanation for why they had chosen Betar, of all organizations in town, as an ally in their effort to avoid being the subject of police surveillance. The letter also hints at the ways in which the challenges faced by Betar's leadership in Warsaw to enforce their ideology in provincial towns were by no means unique.

Even with evidence that Betar members in provincial towns were reading their directives and blueprints, netsivut members could not guarantee that their prescriptions for transforming Jewish youth would be readily accepted. Occasions when Betar members could publicly challenge these directives were rare. Although Betar's newspapers were happy to provide a platform for netsivut activists to scold the youth movement's provincial branches for any transgressions, they rarely published articles from local Betar members directly challenging directives from Warsaw. The one notable exception was instigated and sanctioned by none other than Jabotinsky. Prompting him to permit Betar's members to have their voices heard were the proposals circulating in the netsivut's periodicals about the place of young women within the youth movement. Long before Betar's establishment, Jabotinsky had articulated his support for women's suffrage.[111] Taking to the pages of *Ha-medina* in the spring of 1933, he opposed calls to ban all coeducational activities within the movement. As for the ideal role of women in Betar, he confessed, "[N]ot everything is clear to me, and neither myself, nor any of the men that participate in the work of Betar will clarify this [question] completely: the young women of Betar will discover for themselves the identity and content of their special tasks."[112] Published only one week before the Łódź Manifesto, Jabotinsky's call for women to participate in the youth movement's conversation about the "women question" allowed him not only to reassert his long-standing reputation as a supporter of women's political rights, but also to present himself as a democratic leader, encouraging rather than stifling debate.

The young Polish Jewish women who read Jabotinsky's article interpreted it as an invitation to participate in a conversation that had, to that point, been almost entirely the preserve of Betar's male leadership. In the weeks that followed, young Jewish women from provincial towns across Poland sent articles on the women question to the youth movement's head office in Warsaw. Nearly all of them challenged Betar leaders' assumptions about and approaches to the question. Some of these young women may have drawn inspiration from women activists in other Zionist movements who wrote in Jewish daily newspapers or party periodicals to challenge the gender norms of the movement.[113] Writing in April 1933, a young woman from a small town near Białystok scolded Betar's leaders for expressing panic about a problem that did not even exist. "There is no need," she wrote, "to fabricate a special 'woman's question' in Betar, nor should one be terrified of this so-called [sexual] assimilation."[114] Others, like Batya Kremer, a member of a hachshara near the town of Kostopol in eastern Galicia, urged Betar's leaders to move past their fantasies about the supposed threat posed by women and focus instead on the real challenges they faced. "The problem," she explained, "is that men in Betar despise women.... [W]e are not counted in Betar's leadership, none of us get the opportunity to develop our organizational abilities and use our intelligence.... Are we really incapable of doing anything more than cooking, washing and sewing? Is it really true that nature has degraded us?"[115] Other women echoed Batya's claim that they were sidelined during club meetings and prevented from obtaining positions of leadership.[116]

The women who wrote into Betar's newspapers took particular issue with the fact that their participation in the movement's self-defense training was being called into question. In one such article, a young woman insisted, "It is not enough for young women [in Betar] to prepare for family life, to serve the nation as a mother and a woman. Young women must learn how to perform, hand in hand with young men, the difficult tasks of building the [Jewish] state.... Just like male Betar members [Betarim], we need military training.... [W]e need to know how to use weapons."[117] Other articles similarly insisted that military training would not prevent Jewish women from fulfilling their traditional gender roles as mothers and educators.[118] Ultimately, Betar's leaders in Warsaw decided that it was best not to intervene in how each provincial branch decided to address the women question. Instruction guidelines for military training remained conspicuously silent on which activities could be conducted with both men and women. The role models devised for women—from mothers and educators to armed revolutionaries—were diverse enough to allow the membership to select whichever ones conformed with local and personal attitudes toward the place of Jewish women in politics.[119]

Of all the projects devised by Betar's netsivut to tame the shtetl, their efforts to extract money from Jewish youth in provincial towns proved the most disastrous. Nearly half of the commands issued by the youth movement consisted of leaders begging or demanding that Betar members pay their dues to Warsaw. Like their members, Betar's leaders in Warsaw were not immune to the economic crisis pushing Polish Jews even deeper into poverty. As they struggled to cover the costs for centralizing the movement, the netsivut, perpetually strapped for cash, sunk into debt. The netsivut's members repeatedly warned that the movement's activity would grind to a halt unless they received "taxes" from the provinces.[120] Describing the withholding of membership dues as a "crime with no penance," a desperate Propes announced to Betar's members in 1933 that the netsivut would "impose severe sanctions, in order to put an end to the anarchy that has reigned to this day regarding this matter."[121] In one week alone in the winter of 1932, the netsivut announced that it planned to cut off contact with eighty Betar branches.[122] Regional commanders, too, issued similar warnings. In the winter of 1934, Zvi Bregman, a member of Baranowicze's regional command, issued a barrage of threats: "[W]e will not be in touch with you, you won't receive our circulars, we won't let your brothers go to hachsharot and we will publish your names, and the names of your commanders, in a special circular, and we will also try to publish them within the commands of the netsivut."[123]

Bregman's most powerful threat was undoubtedly his claim that Betar members who failed to pay their taxes would be forbidden to attend hachsharot. Failure to join one of the hachsharot prevented them from being eligible to receive certificates issued by the Zionist Organization to immigrate to Mandate Palestine. The promise of gaining a certificate had convinced many Betar members to remain within the movement. This was even the case for Axelrod; the netsivut repeatedly promised him that if he fulfilled his tasks, they would help him obtain an immigration certificate.[124] But Betar's members and lower-tier leaders would quickly discover how little power the netsivut actually possessed to obtain immigration certificates to Palestine. As early as 1929, the Revisionist movement accused the Zionist Organization of deliberately withholding certificates from Betar members, favoring instead Labor Zionist youth. In the four years that followed, Revisionist leaders unsuccessfully lobbied the Zionist Organization's leadership to afford Betar's members a fair share of the certificates. They demanded greater representation in the Zionist Organization's local Land of Israel offices (misradim ertsisra'elim), which were responsible for distributing certificates allotted by the British and for providing information and aid for immigration to Palestine. With their demands unmet by the spring of 1932, Poland's Revisionist leadership decided to cease collecting money for the Zionist Organization's primary fundraising bodies, the Jewish National Fund (keren kayemet le-yisra'el) and the Foundation Fund (keren ha-yesod). Ever the admirer of sweeping publicity stunts, and determined to weaken the Zionist Organization, Jabotinsky called on Betar members in the fall of 1933 to instigate a mass protest against the certificate distribution system. This protest, he claimed, was directed against not only the Zionist Organization, but also the British government's restrictive immigration policies toward Jews. Notifying them that Betar's leaders would no longer participate in the Land of Israel offices' distribution of certificates, he commanded the organization's members to refuse any certificates offered to them by local representatives of the Zionist Organization.[125]

Jabotinsky's call to protest put the netsivut's claims of power in jeopardy. The very effectiveness of their threats depended on whether Betar members believed that their leaders could facilitate the immigration of Jewish youth to Mandate Palestine. In an effort to salvage their semblance of power, Jabotinsky's Betar Authority in Paris issued a command informing Betar members that the youth movement would circumvent the Zionist Organization by obtaining hundreds of certificates from private employers in Palestine. In addition to asking Betar branches to draw up lists of prospective immigrants, the netsivut warned them that any Betar member who accepted a certificate from the Zionist Organization would be immediately thrown out of the youth movement.[126]

Jabotinsky was ultimately unable to obtain the certificates he had promised Betar's members. In January 1934, the Zionist Organization officially banned Betar members from receiving certificates.[127] If the netsivut in Warsaw could have previously relied on baiting Polish Jewish youth with the promise of a certificate, they were now left with little to prove their power. They had to inform Betar members that their pleas for certificates from the netsivut were useless. Desperate members of Betar from provincial towns traveled to the netsivut in Warsaw, hoping they might be able to receive a certificate in person. They too were turned away.[128] All Propes could offer Betar members in 1934 was the promise that once Jabotinsky's demands for mass immigration were heard by the British, the netsivut would lead Betar's members from Poland to Palestine. Those who paid their taxes to the youth movement, he added, would be first in line. Until that point, he confessed, "we have no other choice but to wait! To wait patiently until our total victory!"[129] Propes's admission of helplessness and calls for patience were a far cry from the confident tone he and other netsivut members had exuded in the curriculum guidelines they had developed to tame Betar's members. In the years to come, several of Betar's leading figures would increasingly direct their efforts toward helping thousands of their followers find passage to the Yishuv illegally, most often by ship, arriving to Palestine's shores under the cover of dark.[130]

While Propes and his colleagues in the netsivut may have ultimately been the ones to be tamed, other leaders within Betar benefited from the increasing desperation and helplessness of the youth movement's members. From its inception in 1930, the Brit Ha-Biryonim rejected patience as a political value and diplomacy as a means to achieve Zionist goals. The failure of the netsivut in its battles with the Zionist Organization over granting Betar members certificates only reinforced the Biryonim's convictions. Its members insisted that the only way the youth movement could help bring about a Jewish state was through the creation of an elite cadre of revolutionaries. The Betar leaders who increasingly supported the Biryonim's views joined a steadily rising number of Jewish youth in Poland who found in radical politics a response to the sharp rise in antisemitism and worsening economic conditions within the country.[131]

Several of the leading Betar activists to endorse the revolutionary ethos of the Brit Ha-Biryonim were also entrusted with training Poland's leadership for the youth movement. Among them was Yirmiyahu Halperin, who had taken on the task of providing military instruction to Betar's members. In contrast to Jabotinsky, who owed much of his success to presenting himself as an articulate and refined European statesman, Halperin was idolized by Poland's Betar youth for his muscular, rugged physical features, stern character, and reputation as a fearless fighter in Palestine.[132] In a letter to Avraham Axelrod, who had waited years for the netsivut to grant him a certificate, Halperin confided, "Axelrod, I want to reveal a secret to you. I hope that our instructor's organization will one day be the nucleus for the *real* Betar, that very power upon which we'll be able to rely in a difficult hour."[133] The young instructors under Halperin's command would be trained not only to engage in self-defense, but to initiate attacks as well. The nature of the attacks he envisioned, and their implications for the youth movement's vision of life in both Poland and Palestine, would push Betar even further beyond Jabotinsky's grasp.

6

Terror

IT WAS ONLY once doctor Arie Alotin walked through the doors of Jerusalem's Hadassah Hospital on Friday, June 16, 1933, that he realized why he had been called in at eleven o'clock at night. There, lying on a table in the corridor, covered in his own sweat and blood, was Haim Arlosoroff, one of the most powerful Labor Zionist leaders in Mandate Palestine. He had been walking on a Tel Aviv beach with his wife, Sima, only hours before when two men had approached them. One carried a flashlight, the other, a gun. The bullet had cut through an artery in Arlosoroff's abdomen. By the time Dr. Alotin began surgery on his still-conscious patient, it was too late. During an attempt to transfuse blood after sewing the artery shut, Arlosoroff lost consciousness and died.[1]

Three days later, Sima Arlosoroff was brought into an office of the Mandate Palestine Police Criminal Investigations Division. The officers had lined up sixteen men, standing side by side, for Mrs. Arlosoroff to scrutinize. The chief inspector later reported that about two-thirds of the way into the line, she nearly collapsed when she locked eyes with a heavy-set man, twenty-seven years of age. He had been picked up that day at the Jerusalem apartment of Abba Achimeir. The police officers permitted the young man under arrest to send one telegram. Soon afterward, some fifteen hundred miles away, in a city known in Yiddish as Brisk, a telegram operator began transcribing the young man's message to his parents: "Be calm. I'm innocent."[2] The telegram, along with telegrams from Jewish leaders in Mandate Palestine reporting the event, quickly spread throughout Poland: Avraham Stavsky, a member of Betar in Poland who had arrived in Palestine only three months ago, was accused of murdering Haim Arlosoroff.

News of Arlosoroff's death and Stavsky's arrest shocked Zionists worldwide and thrust Poland's Betar into the public spotlight. Labor Zionist leaders in

Poland and in Palestine leapt at the opportunity to use the murder as proof that Jabotinsky's youth movement posed a threat to Jews worldwide. The Zionist project would collapse, they claimed, unless they put an end to the system of youth politics that had lifted Jabotinsky to power, with its provocative rhetoric and promises to harness the wild temperament of young Jews. If left unchecked, they warned, Jabotinsky's Polish Jewish youth would continue to import the violent tactics of Europe's radical Right to Mandate Palestine.

With information, goods, and people flowing faster than ever between Poland and Palestine, Jabotinsky had to contend with more than just the claims of Betar's rivals that his youth movement was importing the political radicalism of Europe into the Yishuv. The porous boundaries between Poland and Palestine also made it increasingly difficult for Jabotinsky to withstand challenges to his leadership from within his own movement's ranks. Emboldened by Jabotinsky's expulsion of his movement's moderate executive leadership during the putsch of March 1933, Palestine's Brit Ha-Biryonim launched a campaign to export their radical views to Poland. Traveling through the country's towns and cities, the group urged Polish Jewish youth to prepare themselves to engage in acts of revolutionary violence to liberate Palestine from British rule. Some were even calling for Polish Jews to draw a lesson from the Biryonim's program in Palestine and stage retaliatory attacks against antisemitic rioters in Poland. In the coming years, as Jewish life became increasingly bleak in Poland and in Palestine, the youth movement's supporters and opponents fought to determine whether acts of radicalism by Jewish youth should shape the destiny of Jews in both locations.

At stake for Polish Jews consumed by these debates were two burning issues. The first was Jabotinsky's brand of youth politics. Did the provocative and ambiguous prose of Zionist leaders like Jabotinsky, who presented his young followers with an array of contradictory interpretive possibilities, help or hinder the Zionist project? Jabotinsky, too, would increasingly question whether his initial vision for youth politics would be the key to the creation of a Jewish state. The second issue with which they wrestled concerned the geographic borders of Zionist politics. Even if a Zionist living in Poland and one in Palestine might claim to share the same beliefs, to what extent could they look to one another's behaviors as models to emulate? Did the unique conditions of crisis in both locations demand that Zionists adopt different tactics in each one? Or did Zionism possess a behavioral code and formula for defending Jews and Jewish interests that transcended geographic boundaries? These questions lay at the heart of the movement's increasingly fierce and frequent debates about the effectiveness of terrorism: could assassinating political leaders or targeting civilians prove useful to the Zionist cause?

Prelude to Murder

Although the Arlosoroff murder stunned Polish Jews, it was not the first time they had received news of a bloody confrontation between left-wing and right-wing Zionists. In the summer of 1932, the Revisionist movement in Palestine formed their own workers union to rival the Labor Zionist Histadrut, which dominated the Yishuv's Jewish labor market. In the months that followed, a series of violent clashes in Jerusalem, Petah Tikva, and elsewhere in Mandate Palestine erupted between Revisionist workers and members of the Histadrut. In November 1932, these violent clashes spilled into Poland. On the outskirts of the northeastern city of Baranowicze, members of a tree-felling hachshara run by the socialist Zionist organization He-Halutz accused Betar members of stealing their work. The brawl that ensued left one Betar member in critical condition.[3]

In the wake of these brawls, leaders of the Zionist Left and Right accused one another of instigating the violence. Labor Zionists described Revisionist workers as a "gang of hoodlums" who sought to launch a "holy war."[4] Jabotinsky accused the Histadrut of launching "pogroms" and urged Betar members to continue "destroying, step by step, the rule of the traitors."[5] By the spring of 1933, when a new wave of brawls erupted in Palestine, Revisionist leaders claimed that left-wing Zionists were collaborating with antisemites to harm Betar members. The popular thirty-seven-year-old radical poet Uri Zvi Grinberg, who had returned from Palestine to Poland to edit the Revisionist movement's Yiddish weekly newspaper, accused Labor Zionists in Palestine of teaming up with Palestinian Arab workers to attack Betar youth.[6] The editors of *Ha-medina* reported that Jewish socialists were recruiting antisemitic farmers in Poland to attack members of Betar: "[T]he time will come," they warned, "when real pogroms will take place by ordinary Christians who were organized . . . by the sons of Israel."[7] The Nazi seizure of power in the winter of 1933 provided Betar leaders with yet another opportunity to compare the Histadrut with an antisemitic movement. Yirmiyahu Halperin claimed that the Histadrut's participation in the violent clashes with Palestine's Revisionists brought "to mind the most recent events in Germany—with the difference that the scoundrels in Germany haven't yet started to spill the blood of babies and young girls."[8]

If anyone on the Zionist Left were to embody the alleged link between Nazi Germany and the Histadrut in 1933, it was Haim Arlosoroff. Throughout the spring of that year, Arlosoroff led negotiations between the Zionist Federation of Germany and the Nazi government to help facilitate the emigration of German Jews to Palestine. Negotiations between Zionist leaders and Nazi officials ultimately led to the Ha'avara (Transfer) agreement, which allowed German Jews to emigrate to Palestine with greater ease, so long as they provided their capital and assistance to export German products to the Yishuv. Like many other Zionist leaders who had called for a global boycott of German goods, Jabotinsky saw the negotiations as an ineffective way to help German Jews and a dangerous precedent for Zionist collusion with the Nazi government. When news of the negotiations went public, Revisionists staged a press conference in Warsaw, where they accused Arlosoroff of "cold bloodedly" announcing that "he was prepared to make a pact with Hitler, at the very moment when every Jew stands in battle against Hitler."[9] Uri Zvi Grinberg called on his Polish Jewish readers to "carry this news to all Jewish homes . . . the call should spread throughout the nation, 'Get off the Jewish stage, Dr. Arlosoroff!'"[10] Wolfgang von Weisl, a leading Revisionist activist in Palestine and a staunch supporter of the Brit Ha-Biryonim, allegedly told Betar members that had Arlosoroff been on trial for the negotiations, he would have received a death sentence.[11]

Leaders on the Zionist Left were only too happy to respond in kind to Revisionist accusations that they resembled Nazis. After years of comparing the Revisionist movement's leader to Mussolini, they found a new nickname for Jabotinsky: Vladimir Hitler.[12] The brown hue of Betar's uniforms quickly became associated with shirts worn by the Nazi Party's paramilitary squad, the Sturmabteilung. By linking right-wing Zionism to Nazism—in effect, accusing the Revisionist movement of being no different than the most powerful antisemitic threat facing Jews in Europe—the Zionist Left hoped to convince Revisionist supporters to abandon the movement in droves. They also sought to ensure that the Jewish public would view Revisionists, and not Labor Zionists, as the chief culprits of the violent clashes in Mandate Palestine between left-wing and right-wing Zionist workers.

Had the descriptions of the Revisionist movement as the Jewish equivalent of the Nazi Party remained the preserve of the movement's opponents, Jabotinsky might have been able to dismiss these claims as cheap and even comical attempts to discredit Betar. In one such attempt, he wrote that the Polish Jewish public could just as easily look at Betar's brown shirts and think of dark chocolate, rather than Nazi militiamen.[13] Several activists within Betar, however, were publicly arguing that there was much to admire in Nazism. In the very same party newspaper informing Mandate Palestine's Jews of Jabotinsky's putsch, the radical Abba Achimeir had gone so far as to suggest that the Revisionist movement had a great deal to learn from the Nazi Party.[14] Days later, Jabotinsky wrote to a supporter in Paris, urging him to reach out to Betar members in Germany to put an end to their declarations of admiration for Nazism. He insisted that "despite the enthusiasm of millions [in Germany] that is impressing our [Jewish] youth," Nazism was no more than "a type of cheap ... assimilation." "[E]very flattery to the [Nazi] government and its people, or to their ideas," he warned, were "criminal acts."[15] In his strongest letter yet to the editors of Palestine's Revisionist newspaper, Jabotinsky threatened to shut down the publication, throw its editors out of the party, and cut all personal ties with them if they continued to publicly praise Hitler.[16] Significantly, the letter was entirely devoid of the ambivalent language and mixed messages that had characterized some of his previous exchanges with the Biryonim.[17] His articles on Nazism addressed to Polish Jewish youth similarly left little room for interpretation. "Even if it appeared in *Hazit Ha'am*," he warned Poland's Betar members in the Yiddish daily newspaper *Der Moment*, "don't waste time on trying to 'understand' the enemy's soul.... [O]ne must first annihilate the enemy; then the historian can come along and 'understand' as much as he desires."[18]

If the putsch two months beforehand had proved to Jabotinsky that mobilizing ideas about youth could reap tremendous political rewards, his experiences in the following months served as a stark warning that the linguistic flexibility that had previously served him well had its limits. In an age of increasing radicalism, the burgeoning power of "youth"—both imagined and real—posed a threat to Jabotinsky's role as the ultimate arbiter of how the movement turned its political rhetoric into practice. In the months to come, the notion that Jewish youth held this power would ultimately lead Jabotinsky and numerous Jewish politicians in Poland to question whether they had gone too far in giving youth pride of place in modern Jewish politics. It would take Arlosoroff's stroll along a beach in Tel Aviv to convince them that youth politics was not only dangerous but deadly.

Youth Politics on Trial

By the time news of Haim Arlosoroff's murder reached Warsaw, Labor Zionist leaders from Palestine had already spent several weeks tirelessly campaigning in Poland for the upcoming elections to the Zionist Congress, set to take place in Prague in August 1933. Among them was David Ben-Gurion, the powerhouse leader of the Histadrut union and chairman of the Worker's Party for the Land of Israel (Mapai). He had arrived in Poland determined to prevent the Revisionists from capturing the votes of Polish Jews, who made up the majority of congress voters. While devastated by the news of their colleague's death, Ben-Gurion and other Labor Zionist leaders saw in Avraham Stavsky's arrest—and the subsequent arrest of several other Betar members in Palestine—the ingredients for the perfect publicity campaign to defeat the Revisionist movement at the congress elections. Labor Zionists and their sympathizers used the Yiddish daily *Haynt* to launch their attack. Playing on already growing fears in Poland about the growing political extremism of young Polish Jews, they presented Arlosoroff's murder as the violent manifestation of a generational conflict within the Zionist movement. This claim allowed them to take aim at the system of youth politics Jabotinsky had cultivated within Betar. Depicting themselves as veteran Zionists defending democracy and parliamentarism, Labor Zionists portrayed Revisionists as a band of young terrorists who sought to bring the violent ethos of Europe's radical Right to Palestine. What followed on the pages of *Haynt* was a public trial of Jabotinsky's "youth politics."

To portray themselves as the guardians of time-honored Zionist practices, Labor Zionist activists turned Arlosoroff into a symbol of a bygone era. Eulogies by Labor Zionists and their sympathizers portrayed the thirty-four-year-old Arlosoroff as the custodian of the political mores of generations of Zionist leaders before him. He was hailed as a symbol of the Western political tradition, a leader poised to continue the traditions of reason, statesmanship, and parliamentarism cultivated by his predecessors.[19] The same journalists and political leaders juxtaposed their descriptions of Arlosoroff with their depictions of Stavsky. In the days following his arrest, journalists from Warsaw set off to his hometown of Brisk to find out more about the Betar member. Reports that reached the offices of *Haynt* in Warsaw offered a portrait of a youth who was Arlosoroff's diametric opposite. According to reporters, Stavsky was a stocky, impulsive, and brutish delinquent. Besides being charged with gambling, "ruining" the lives of women, and brawling in the streets with young Jewish socialists, Stavsky was most remembered for the gun slung at the side of his waist.[20] Taking stock of this portrait, one of *Haynt*'s founding editors, Avrom Goldberg, described Stavsky as a "sick" and "lawless youth," an "insane fanatic, a true product of our dark diaspora."[21]

Like Goldberg, other *Haynt* journalists emphasized that the assassination of Arlosoroff was the result of Betar members importing "foreign" European models of nationalist violence to Mandate Palestine. To make their case, they drew on long-standing fears among many Polish Jews about the Polonization of Jewish youth. In an article calling on the Jews of Poland to reassess the state of Zionist politics, *Haynt*'s Y. M. Nayman told readers that "the murderer of Arlosoroff ... shares the same mentality of Niewiadomski," referring to the radical Polish nationalist who had assassinated Poland's first president, Gabriel Narutowicz, in 1922.[22] "One has the impression," another *Haynt* journalist reported several days later as he met Betar members from a town in the northeastern province of Nowogródek, "that one finds oneself in a circle of none other than—yes, let us say it—Endek [right-wing Polish nationalist] youth. The argumentation of Betar youth is so similar to that of the Camp of Great Poland [Obóz Wielkiej Polski]," a radical Polish nationalist organization that had been banned four months beforehand by the Sanacja government. The older youth who led Betar's branch in the shtetl, he continued, believed "that Hitler's program will cure Germany and that Hitler has returned authority and esteem to his fatherland.... They, just like the Endecja, appropriated Hitler's program, only without the Aryan Paragraph."[23]

Inextricably bound to their descriptions of Betar members as violent radicals was the question of who bore responsibility for their actions. Some argued that Jewish youth were victims of political indoctrination and that Jabotinsky bore responsibility for the murder. "Gone is the old Jabotinsky, the democratic leader," wrote prominent Polish Jewish journalist Bezalel Katz in an open letter to the Revisionist leader; "now, he is carrying himself away [*mitgerisn zikh*] with a mass of naïve, innocent and directionless [*unerfarene*] youth, who leap to call the leader holy and blindly follow his will."[24] Taking the image of the authoritarian leader one step further, *Haynt*'s resident humorist Moshe Yustman entitled his own article condemning Betar "The Messiah of the Knife." Devoid of any of Yustman's signature humor, the article described Jabotinsky as a self-styled messianic figure instructing his followers to commit acts of murder.[25] Several months later, to mark the tenth anniversary of Betar, Yustman reiterated his portrayal of Betar members as naïve youth who had been corrupted by Revisionist ideology. As members of the Revisionist movement, he wrote, Jewish youth "drunk with high-sounding slogans ... drunk with egoism, with megalomania" were "educated in the reckless ... spirit of terror and lawlessness, of brutal arrogance against the honorable old Zionist workers."[26]

If some *Haynt* journalists described Betar youth as passive and vulnerable victims of political indoctrination, others used the Arlosoroff murder to illustrate the excessive power given to Jewish youth to determine political ideology and behavior on the "Jewish street." *Haynt*'s journalists insisted that much of the generational conflict threatening to unravel the Zionist project could be attributed to the dangerous ways in which young Jews interpreted the proclamations of their leaders. "What the 'leader' clothed in a literary manner of speaking [*redensartn*]," *Haynt* writer M. Kleynman observed, "the Revisionist boys [*yinglekh*] translate into their own language, according to the language of their culture."[27] Concluding his open letter to Jabotinsky, Bezalel Katz wrote, "I ask you openly and politely: do you still have it in mind, after seeing how your students translate your words, to go on the same path of [calling for] 'breaking' and 'slaughtering'?"[28] Katz's use of the term "breaking" called to mind an article published by Jabotinsky a year earlier, in which he demanded that Revisionists "break" the monopoly of the Histadrut in Palestine's Jewish workforce.[29] Although Jabotinsky later insisted that the term "break" had nothing to do with condoning violence against the Left, the article's title was widely interpreted by the Zionist Left as a clever way in which to incite Betar youth to violence without having to claim responsibility for their actions.[30] Focusing on Jabotinsky's call for Betarim "not to stop in the face of danger when leading the battle for the upcoming election campaign," another *Haynt* article noted, "this expression ... is so general, too elastic, that ... Betarim ... can interpret it differently and say that first, they must destroy the meetings [of the Left]." "Such a call," the article continued, was "an open and clear call to his members to perform acts of violence and terror" which would turn "Jewish Poland into a bloody battlefield."[31]

While Labor Zionists could point to no explicit calls made to attack Arlosoroff, Betar had certainly left a sufficient trail of articles to convince Jewish readers that it was not altogether impossible that Stavsky had committed the crime. It was this trail that Labor Zionists would repeatedly point to over the course of Stavsky's trial. Labor Zionists relied heavily on these articles to make their case against voting for Revisionists at the Eighteenth Zionist Congress. In the weeks that followed the murder, *Haynt*, along with Labor Zionist publications in Poland, presented numerous collages of quotes taken from articles written by Jabotinsky, Abba Achimeir, Uri Zvi Grinberg, Wolfgang von Weisl, and other activists on the Zionist Right.[32]

Betar's leaders and members were faced with a formidable challenge. Not only had Labor Zionist activists in Poland gained the sympathy of *Haynt*, the country's leading Yiddish newspaper, but they had also skillfully linked Arlosoroff's murder and Stavsky's arrest with deep-seated concerns expressed within the country about a generational conflict between Polish Jewish youth and their elders. Ironically, the youth-centered rhetoric of the Labor Zionists' campaign against the Revisionists provided the very formula for Jabotinsky's response. Jabotinsky was no stranger to using concepts of generational conflict to convince the Jewish public to support the politics of the Zionist Right. He saw that discussions about the dangers of Jewish youth transposing the political extremism of Europe onto Palestine's soil had touched a raw nerve with the Polish Jewish public. He also observed that discussions about reining in the political power of youth could help cast the Revisionist movement as a responsible political party that sought to restore peace and order in Jewish public life. Rather than devote their time to addressing the barrage of accusations leveled against Stavsky and the Betar youth movement as a whole, Jabotinsky and other activists on the Zionist Right chose instead to echo and at times amplify the very fears that Labor Zionists were articulating about the future of Jewish youth as political actors. The crucial difference, however, lay in whom the Revisionists deemed responsible for both corrupting Jewish youth and inciting them to perform acts of violence. In the eyes of Jabotinsky and other Betar activists, the culprits of terror were Labor Zionist leaders.

The first crucial step Jabotinsky needed to take to affirm Betar's innocence was to eulogize and praise the fallen Zionist leader. Although Revisionists had previously vilified Arlosoroff, Jabotinsky praised him as "a serious and honest servant of his nation and his conscience; principled and conscientious in every aspect of his work, decent and polite even in his polemics, which is a great rarity in his political camp."[33] Here and elsewhere, readers familiar with Jabotinsky's work would have been able to hear echoes of how the Betar leader described his own political behavior. Jabotinsky also noted that Arlosoroff allegedly insisted in his final moments that his murderers were not Jewish.[34] According to Jabotinsky, Labor Zionists who were convinced of Stavsky's guilt were not only betraying their fallen colleague, but also exploiting his death in order to undermine the very ideals he had fought for throughout his political career. The campaign against Stavsky, he argued, was no more than an attempt to direct attention away from the fact that "they [Labor Zionists] were beating up children in Tel Aviv, in Haifa, in Petah Tikvah, in Kfar Saba, even here in Baranowicze."[35]

Jabotinsky rallied several of his colleagues at the Yiddish daily *Der Moment* to help him place the blame on the Zionist Left for the rising internecine violence within the Zionist movement. Like their counterparts at *Haynt, Der Moment* journalists viewed this violence as a foreign import. "Twenty years ago," mused Shaul Stupnicki, a well-known *Moment* journalist, "we could not have imagined such behavior; we could have only imagined it among the Macedonians in the Balkans. There, one did not fight with arguments, but with the dagger, with the grenade in hand."[36] Reflecting on the attacks of Labor Zionist youth on members of Betar in Mandate Palestine several months later, Jabotinsky asked his readers in *Der Moment*, "You think that our homeland is called 'The Land of Israel'? This is according to geography, not ethnography. Its true name is 'Macedonia #2.'"[37] The Internal Macedonian Revolution Organization was notorious not only for its internal fighting, but also for its guerilla tactics and assassinations of European officials, including the beheading of Bulgaria's prime minister in 1923. By employing the image of Macedonia—which had long served western European observers as a synonym for primitive, barbaric political behavior—*Der Moment* sought to both condemn the behavior of Labor Zionist youth, and affirm the "Westernness" of Zionist political culture.[38]

Like their counterparts at *Haynt*, Revisionist sympathizers in *Der Moment* drew on widespread fears about the Polonization of Jewish youth in order to convince their readers that Jewish youth posed a dangerous threat to the practice of Jewish politics. A day after Stupnicki's warning about Macedonian politics was published, *Der Moment* reported that in Raciąż, a small town north of Warsaw, left-wing Zionist youth joined Polish socialists in their attack against Betar members, shouting together, "Beat the bourgeois Jews!" Tellingly, the very title of the article dramatized the Polonization of Jewish youth by interspersing Polish in its Yiddish headline: "One shouts 'Bić Żydów!' [Beat the Jews] and attacks Revisionists!"[39]

Echoing their opponents once again, Revisionists offered ambivalent assessments of whether young Jews were to blame for the crisis unfolding within the Zionist movement. In an article explaining the effect of the Zionist Left's alleged reverence of class conflict, Jabotinsky warned, "They [Labor Zionists] make an ideal and religion out of it, they hammer these teachings into the young heads of thousands of children. . . . And a generation is coming of age, for whom the Jewish middle class . . . are nothing more than a collective vampire."[40] Other writers at *Der Moment*, however, refused to depict Jewish youth as innocent victims of indoctrination. Many of *Der Moment*'s writers wrote of the danger of young people "translating" the provocative language of the Jewish Left into acts of violence. Rather than accuse Jewish youth of being naïve, a letter to the editor from the southeastern town of Mizocz accused the writers of *Haynt* of being completely unaware of how incendiary their work could be when read and interpreted by young Jews. The letter suggested that the writers of *Haynt* "should trouble themselves to send their ambassadors to the small shtetlekh, where youth are divided between the Revisionists and the Left." Only then could they be convinced "of the destruction that the 'Zionist' *Haynt* brought into the Zionist camp, and into each Jewish house where children belong to different Zionist political groups." Were it not for Zionist leaders in shtetls across the country, the letter continued, "Jewish blood would pour in the streets of every shtetl."[41] The next day, as if to confirm the warning of the letter published a day beforehand, the headline of *Der Moment* read, "Jewish Youth are Drowning in Blood!" and reported that Haynt's articles had "provoked youth and brought bloodshed" in Lwów, Łódź, Pińczów, and Główne.[42]

As the end of the summer approached, and the Eighteenth Zionist Congress in Prague drew closer, the sense of panic among *Haynt* and *Der Moment* journalists dramatically intensified. Often described by Zionists as the "parliament of the Jewish people," the biannual Zionist Congress was envisioned by journalists from both newspapers as a crucible for the democratic political traditions of Zionism. They insisted that through voting and parliamentary debate, the Zionist movement could present itself as the most capable Jewish lobbying force to come to the aid of German Jewry. Their reporting on the congress, however, confirmed their deepest fears about the "conflict of generations" that had seized the Zionist movement. For the journalists of *Haynt* and *Der Moment*, the congress was the death knell of democracy and parliamentarism in the Zionist movement and a victory for extremist politics, with youth at the helm. In the days leading up to the congress elections, both newspapers accused Zionist youth groups of sabotaging voting stations throughout Poland.[43] During the congress, Labor Zionist leaders condemned Jabotinsky as the commander of young terrorists and the chief culprit of the Arlosoroff murder. In one typical speech, Berl Katznelson, a founding member of the Labor Zionist movement and the editor of its daily newspaper, *Davar*, declared, "among us sits a delegate who called his students to fight the Histadrut not with resolutions and not with parliamentarism, but with barricades in the street, with fire and blood.... [J]ust as Arlosoroff fell as a victim, so too may we ... pay for our convictions with our life."[44]

Haynt's reporters supplemented their summaries of such statements with their own commentary about the "invasion" of the politics of youth during the congress. Reporter Ezriel Carlbach's description of the congress's attempt to formulate a public response to the Third Reich provides a vivid account of how the conflict of generations was enacted on the "parliament" floor. Carlbach recounted how members of Betar stormed the auditorium during the most widely anticipated session of the congress. Just as the delegates were about to issue a declaration of protest against Germany,

> suddenly, out of nowhere, a scream, a whistle. I turn around. I see Jabotinsky sitting among his excited "gang" [*khevre*]. He sits, as usual, with folded hands and somewhat stooped, quietly paying attention to what's happened. I look and I do not understand . . . agitated youth are about to conduct "adventures" . . . but how can he, Jabotinsky, sit among them, encircled by them, in the very moment when they are about to make ruins out of the last little demonstration that we have left [against the Nazis]. How does he allow these youths, with their whistling and with their wasteful screams, to destroy the historical moment, when for the first time the Jewish parliament raises its voice against Hitler? . . . He sits, keeps quiet, lightly smiles, as his "soldiers" jump, dance, clap . . . whistle, beat, tear apart, while the Zionist Congress tries to read its declaration against Hitler. It was a shocking moment. We could, in that very moment, lose any last bit of hope in the maturity of the Jewish people.[45]

On the same day of Carlbach's report, *Der Moment* published its own sensational story of youth invading the congress. Described in a front-page headline as "the shameful scandal in the Congress building," Jabotinsky and his wife, the newspaper reported, were surrounded by members of Ha-shomer Ha-tsa'ir.[46] Members of Betar, the report continued, arrived soon afterward to protect the couple. To the astonishment of *Der Moment*'s reporters, a socialist Zionist began the brawl by beating a Revisionist delegate, described as a "veteran of the Zionist movement."[47] *Der Moment* could not have found a more vivid portrait of the conflict of generations that they perceived to be at the heart of the congress's failure. As the summer of 1933 drew to a close, the conflict of generations was no longer merely rhetorical but had become a physical conflict between the old and the young.

Jabotinsky on Trial

By the time Stavsky's trial had come to an end in late July 1934, nearly twelve months had passed since the pandemonium of Prague's Zionist Congress. Throughout the intervening year, violent clashes between youth movements of the Zionist Left and Right persisted in both Poland and Palestine. So too did fervent debates about the threat of violent youth to Jewish politics. The year had also seen dozens of dramatic turns during the murder trial, including accusations of false testimony, fabricated evidence, and an initial death sentence for Stavsky from Haifa's district court. Ultimately, however, the chief justice of Mandate Palestine's Supreme Court found that the testimony of Arlosoroff's wife was not sufficiently corroborated by other evidence. Reporters hoped that with the verdict cast and Stavsky freed, tensions between the Zionist Left and Revisionists would subside, and that calm would return to Jewish communities in Poland and in the Yishuv.[48]

The journalists, however, had good reason to be skeptical. Despite repeated claims from both movements that they were the victims, rather than the perpetrators, of youth movement violence, Zionist leaders of the Left and the Right continued to offer deliberately ambiguous instructions to their followers about whether they could use force against their opponents. Mapai's leadership, for example, published a circular in March 1934 entitled *The War against Revisionism*. They urged their party's members to "use all of the strength of our organization and its physical might" to "force [Revisionists] into [a state of] fear and inferiority"—and, at the same time, "to weigh deeds and their consequences" and "refrain from individual and group guerrilla attacks (even if they are justified)."[49] Jabotinsky similarly offered instructions that both condoned and condemned the use of force. In one typical article responding to claims in the winter of 1934 that Betar members were launching attacks on Labor Zionist groups in Poland and in Palestine, he wrote, "I demand from my young comrades: stop ... [I]t is in our interest that the custom to beat other Jews should remain a 'monopoly' of the Red camp." Jabotinsky's call to his members to refrain from violence, however, was tempered by the following lines:

> One can't live only with the theory [of nonviolence] in a time when other Jews are beating my young comrades every week in every town in every colony of our Homeland, the Land of Israel.... It would be foolish, in such a situation, to demand a humanly impossible moral principle: Let them hit you, let them even hit your friends, and sit and be silent. I say openly, in such a situation, with such people around us, the entire question of physical repression loses its "ethical" character.[50]

Much like his claims about the inability of democratic ideals to be upheld in an age of political crisis, Jabotinsky was arguing that, in the name of self-defense, ethical considerations could be rendered null and void.

Jabotinsky's implicit approval for actions he would never explicitly condone only increased the popularity of the Brit Ha-Biryonim, whom he had called "my beloved sons" (*b'nei libi*) during the Arlosoroff trial.[51] As the court proceedings progressed, the admiration of Poland's Betar members for the radical Revisionists grew exponentially. Arrested and imprisoned for his alleged role in inciting Stavsky to murder Arlosoroff, Abba Achimeir quickly became a celebrated martyr within the youth movement. At the same time as Betar's newspapers began to glorify Achimeir, they increasingly published articles on how to conceal weapons and engage in guerilla fighting.[52] Paying tribute to this change in a December 1933 issue of Betar's journal for instructors, a member of the youth movement's head command insisted, "National extremism without mercy or compromise—that is the chief characteristic of Betar. . . . Betar is an extremist, revolutionary organization, and we shouldn't be embarrassed by these terms. . . . So long as Betar fans the flames of extremism, the fire of a national revolutionary ethos, the movement will grow, from soldier to soldier."[53] Although the Biryonim and their supporters continued to publicly pledge allegiance and obedience to Jabotinsky, they were clearly providing interpretations of Jabotinsky to Betar members that rendered obsolete the Revisionist leader's more temperate political statements. In one typical example, Betar's summer camp coordinator Zelig Lerner justified his call for revolutionary activity by noting that "The Head of Betar said that if it was possible to bring about the redemption of Israel with the power of the devil, he would not recoil from doing so. . . . And if 'national extremism' is the name of the Devil—may his name be blessed."[54]

Even though Jabotinsky did not want to compromise his image as a youthful rebel, he nonetheless sought opportunities to restore his reputation as a capable political statesman and democratic leader. His opportunity arrived in the spring of 1934, when Pinhas Rutenberg, the founder of the Palestine Electric Company, initiated efforts to broker a "peace agreement" between the Zionist Left and Right. The prospect of negotiations with Ben-Gurion did more than just provide Jabotinsky with the opportunity to present himself as a peace broker within the Zionist movement. A negotiation, he hoped, would also result in the Zionist Organization issuing immigration certificates to Betar's members once again and, in so doing, lessen the temptation of Betar members to endorse an armed revolt against British rule.[55]

In the last two weeks of October, Jabotinsky met with Ben-Gurion in London to flesh out the conditions for the agreement. Significantly, the incendiary language that both Ben-Gurion and Jabotinsky had employed throughout the

Stavsky trial in their youth movements' publications was entirely absent from their correspondence to one another in the months that followed. Instead, Jabotinsky gushed to Ben-Gurion about how pleased he was to have received a letter from him that began with "My dear friend." Jabotinsky's attention to language in these letters underscored his exhaustion with the polemics he had conducted the previous year. Referring to Ben-Gurion's warm greeting, Jabotinsky confessed, "I've already forgotten this language," and quickly added, "it's surely a sign and prophecy for a new era, and I will try with all my efforts to ensure that this era will arise, or at least will begin."[56] Equally significant were the ways in which Jabotinsky used the letter to subtly critique the trappings of youth movement politics both leaders had adopted. Although, Jabotinsky wrote, he was skeptical that "ordinary" Histadrut members shared Ben-Gurion's willingness to negotiate, "it's not important[;] what's important is that . . . the minds that put the finishing touches on the ideology, the minds that are in the elite of the movement understand you."[57] Jabotinsky's statement about who ultimately mattered in the world of politics was a far cry from the claims of his disciples that his greatest skill as a political leader was to both embody and pay heed to their voices. Just one week after his fifty-fourth birthday, Jabotinsky published a circular to branches of the Revisionist movement informing them—to their great surprise—that a preliminary agreement had been reached concerning violence and employment competition between Revisionist and Histadrut workers. In clear and stern prose, he insisted, "we emphasize the need to remove violence from our national life—in all conditions, no matter what. Now this idea will be accepted by all factions in the Zionist movement, and your honor demands that you become the more faithful keepers of this cultural law."[58]

For a fleeting moment, it appeared as if Jabotinsky's swift transformation from tireless warrior against socialism to peace negotiator would be welcomed by Betar's leaders in both Poland and Palestine. In the week following Jabotinsky's letter, Betar leaders pledged that they would accept the agreement and carry it through completely, despite being skeptical of the Zionist Left's intentions.[59] But promises to uphold the agreement quickly dissipated. With members of both the Left and the Right rejecting the initial agreements forged by their leaders, the politics of behind-closed-doors statesmanship, negotiation, and compromise could not overcome the hatred that Jabotinsky and Ben-Gurion had fomented among their ranks throughout the previous years. Embarrassed by the reaction of his followers, Jabotinsky informed his longtime supporter Shlomo Jacobi that he had all but given up on the prospects of reaching a lasting agreement, and that he would spend the remainder of his time trying to salvage negotiations with the Zionist Organization to issue Betar members immigration certificates.[60] Here, as well, Jabotinsky's efforts at political statesmanship produced few results. The Zionist Organization, he reported, continued to postpone conversations with him about granting Betar members certificates for immigration.[61]

With the world conferences of both Betar and the Revisionist movement rapidly approaching in Kraków, it appeared as if Jabotinsky would be facing his movements' delegates empty handed. Achimeir's popularity was at an all-time high, and Jabotinsky knew that the conference, held only steps away from the crypt where Poland's kings and queens were buried, could potentially crown a future leader for Betar. To retain his standing in the youth movement, Jabotinsky was faced with the daunting, nearly impossible task of defending his ability to represent youth while simultaneously publicly undermining the provocative political rhetoric that had defined his youth politics for years.

Jabotinsky did all he could to make his case in the three days of speeches that preceded the general debate. On Tuesday evening, January 8, 1935, he walked onto the stage of Kraków's Stary Teatr (Old Theater), located in the heart of the city's main square. Before an audience of two hundred delegates, two thousand members of the public, and hundreds more crowded around the theater, he took aim at the Biryonim's calls for revolt. His arguments not only critiqued the Biryonim's worldview, but also the very ambivalent, contradictory prose that had typified the Revisionist movement's youth discourse for years. "The foundation of the Revisionist movement's politics," he explained, "is logic. If we demand from the Mandate Government that it should introduce a government that favors Jewish colonization, we cannot, at the same time, present the impression that any one of us wants to do away with them."[62] The next day, at the opening of Betar's conference, which consisted of nearly all the same delegates as the previous day, Jabotinsky needed to prove that his plea for logic did not amount to a rejection of Betar's military ethos. From the moment he walked into the conference room, delegates could see him making his case. For the first time in his political career, he was not wearing a suit and tie at a Revisionist conference. Instead, he was dressed in a Betar uniform, providing visual proof that he was a youth in spirit.[63] After being unanimously "elected" by Betar's delegates to maintain his position as the head of Betar, he declared, "I feel a great love for the Revisionist movement, but an even greater love for Betar. The Revisionist movement are the branches of a tree, and Betar are its roots."[64] In the speech that followed, he invoked the revolutionary rhetoric of the Biryonim to describe the putsch of 1933:

> What does the word "putsch" mean? Putsch means revival. . . . Often, we have to begin by carrying out such acts because we have to take a leap [*shprung*], even when we aren't sure whether this leap will work. . . . [W]e are a revolutionary movement, and revolutionary movements must go through experimental phases. . . . We must be conquerors and take what we can take. Betar was not founded to be passive. [It was founded for] conquest, battle, and *old ideals* for new achievements.[65]

Jabotinsky's description of the putsch aimed to prove to Betar's members that he did not want to diminish the movement's revolutionary fervor, so long as it was directed toward the "old ideals" for which he stood.

No matter how intricate, Jabotinsky's performance did little to prevent the unprecedented onslaught of criticism from within Betar's ranks that was unleashed on him during the general debate the following evening. The first speaker, a Betar delegate from Romania, set the tone by declaring, "[T]his is the first time I feel bad attending a Revisionist conference." His worst fears, he continued, had materialized: Revisionist leaders were attempting to use Stavsky's release from jail to seek peace and compromise with their enemies—a move, he added, that was no more than an opportunistic bid to gain the approval of the mainstream Jewish public. He then turned directly to Jabotinsky: "One makes peace after a victory, but after an attack, or when you're overcome by exhaustion, is that the reason for peace? Does one not believe anymore in our stubborn resilience? Simply for certificates, we resigned from our battle with the Zionist movement, which Jabotinsky once told us to 'break.'" The delegate's comments made plain that Jabotinsky had betrayed the very polemics he had employed for years within the movement. The reference to Jabotinsky's exhaustion, in contrast to Betar's "stubborn resilience," drew attention to the fact that their leader was aging. Betar's leaders from Poland echoed these views. "We stand firm with our leader Jabotinsky," a delegate from Warsaw began. "But one has to see the situation clearly. In the movement there are old men, who are looking for comfort and rest. But we want to lead the movement on revolutionary paths."[66]

It was only fitting that the most eloquent of Betar's leaders to criticize both Jabotinsky's negotiations with the Zionist Left and his critiques of the revolutionary violence promoted by the Biryonim came from the same city in which Stavsky had been born and raised. The son of a prominent Zionist activist,

Menachem Begin and his two older siblings had initially been members of Ha-shomer Ha-tsa'ir, until their father insisted they join Betar following the Zionist socialist youth movement's turn to the radical Left. In 1931, upon completing a high school degree in his town's Polish gymnasium, Begin moved to Warsaw to begin studies in law. Continuing his activity in Betar, he quickly rose through the leadership ranks of the movement. He served first as Betar's regional commander in the eastern province of Polesie. By 1933, he was a member of Betar's head command in Warsaw. Despite the lanky, gaunt appearance of the twenty-year-old, Betar's leaders saw him as a compelling enough presence to enlist him to travel throughout the country promoting the movement at Zionist gatherings.[67] At the end of 1933, impressed with his rhetorical skills, the editors of the Revisionist movement's journals invited him to contribute articles. One year later, he published a pamphlet on Betar's ideology, directed toward Jewish parents.[68] His ambitions within the movement were no secret. In honor of the holiday of Purim, in the winter of 1934, the youth movement's national newspaper included caricatures of thirteen Betar leaders. Begin's tiny caricature, buried in the bottom lefthand corner, depicted him as a short and puny child, weighed down by massive glasses, trying to get the attention of the others by exclaiming, "I'm going to become big!" The double entendre of the accompanying caption, simultaneously mocking Begin's ambition and his height, was likely not lost on the newspaper's readers.[69]

From the moment he joined Warsaw's head command, Begin demonstrated his devotion to the Brit Ha-Biryonim. Several weeks after Jabotinsky's putsch, Begin appended his name to a list of signatures of Betar leaders in Poland who supported Achimeir's views.[70] Although none of his early articles explicitly celebrated radical violence, they echoed themes repeated time and again by the Biryonim. He described the increasing desperation of Jewish youth in the face of immigration restrictions, the rising threat to Polish Jewish youth of the Jewish Left, and the need for Betar's leadership to exercise greater discipline.[71] In his first article for *Ha-medina*, he praised the "revolutionary attitude" of Poland's Revisionists and called on the movement to embark on "a new, wide, road of national, redemptive *deeds*."[72] Given that he had pledged to his readers that Betar would "rescue the souls of Jewish youth from the red drug which they [the Left] wants to poison them with," the peace agreement understandably came as a shock.[73]

Taking the floor at the conference, Begin opened his remarks by taking aim at the ideological ambiguity that had characterized Betar's youth politics for several years. After calling on every delegate to address fundamental questions about the nature of their movement, he insisted, "Our position on all questions must be effective and clear." He continued by critiquing the negotiations between the Revisionists, the Histadrut, and the Zionist Organization as "diplomatic gambles" that "in the *real* reality [*in di eymese virklikhkayt*] cannot be realized." Turning directly to Jabotinsky, he framed his critique of the leader as the expression of an unbridgeable gap between the attitudes and behaviors of a father and his sons. "Mr. President may forget the attacks of Ben-Gurion.... [T]hat is his own prerogative. But we, his children—we will never forget how much filth Ben-Gurion used [*benutzt*] against the president—our father." While this pledge of filial loyalty allowed Begin to present his critiques as a defense of Jabotinsky, the comments that followed cast Jabotinsky's authority into question. While insisting that he was not a member of the Brit Ha-Biryonim, Begin continued, "We must, however, recognize that besides the president, we have yet another teacher, who has already transformed into a legend. Let us not efface this very legend, because it is a legend of suffering and pain, of heroism and resilience, and of imprisonment."[74] By implicitly casting Achimeir as a direct competitor of Jabotinsky, Begin sought to make clear to the Revisionist leader that his opposition to the Biryonim would jeopardize the hold he had on the Betar youth movement.

If the aftermath of the conference was any indication, Jabotinsky took Begin's words to heart. Eager to prove that he had no intention of rescinding his support for the movement's radical leaders, he published an article in *Der Moment* in early February that began, "[A]t the Kraków conference there were a few Maximalists; too few for my taste. Every one of us has maximalist sentiments ... and what they say and what they do is often (but not always) a true echo of everyone's feelings."[75] The article assured readers that Jabotinsky would encourage the Biryonim to promote their views within the Revisionist movement, so long as they did not call for the formation of a separate organization. His approach to the Biryonim's promotion of violence underscored his increased resignation to their ideals. After the article criticized the Biryonim's provocative language against the British Mandate—dubbed by Jabotinsky as "stylistic heroism"—Jabotinsky wrote, "If a maximalist does something, they have to be prepared to suffer alone; the party won't take responsibility.... [I]f someone used their fists in a situation in which it is illegal to do so, or if they broke someone's bones, when one should not—he [the *biryon*] should know exactly what he's doing and not fear to suffer [the consequences]."[76] Although Jabotinsky's warning made clear that these behaviors were beyond the pale of permissible "official" Revisionist behavior, it also did not constitute a sweeping condemnation of these activities. Instead, it presumed that the Biryonim's supporters would engage in acts of violence, while absolving Jabotinsky of responsibility for their behavior. Equally significant was how the conference's events were covered by the youth movement's national journals. No direct reference to the general debate, or to any ideological discord whatsoever, appeared in Betar's press. Jabotinsky was likely supportive of the journals' efforts to present his youth movement as more unified than ever before.

When one moves beyond the political prose of Betar's journals to look instead at Jabotinsky's correspondence, a different story emerges. At first, Jabotinsky insisted to friends and supporters that the conference was an invigorating experience—enough to make the failure of his negotiations with Ben-Gurion a blessing rather than a curse for the movement.[77] Even as he assured his sister that he would not permit the Biryonim to establish a new organization within the Revisionist movement, he insisted that the "Maximalist spirit" was valuable because such "moods" were "spontaneous and erupt on their own."[78] The decisions made under his supervision by Betar's head command reflected his continued efforts to harness the "Maximalist spirit." Menachem Begin was promoted to head of Betar's Organizational Department, which would determine the structure of Betar groups throughout Poland. One year later, he would spend five months as Betar's interim leader in Czechoslovakia. Responding to an angry letter sent by Propes, Jabotinsky even seemed resigned to the fact that a power shift was occurring within Betar. "How," Jabotinsky asked Propes, "are you not ashamed to write that I apparently 'don't take your opinion into account'? I do indeed take it into consideration ... but even I cannot always behave according to my worldview."[79] By the time Jabotinsky wrote this letter, in February 1935, he was in Montreal, at the beginning of a speaking tour lasting several months, with the clamor of Revisionist movement politics in Poland no more than a distant echo.

As Jabotinsky wove his way through a series of cities on North America's East Coast, he was met with half-empty auditoriums. His name, he complained, just didn't have the "magnetic attraction" that it carried in eastern Europe.[80] Not that he minded the calm. In the same letter addressing the position of the Biryonim in the movement, Jabotinsky told his sister that his trip to the United States would give him time to rest; when he left the auditoriums, he enthused, "no one will be permitted to come towards me."[81] Time away from the political chaos of the past two years would allow him to write his autobiography, which he jokingly referred to as his "mythography."[82]

Tellingly, his autobiography described him as a devout proponent of liberal ideals.[83] He also found time to complete a semiautobiographical novel, *Piatero*, about a group of upper-middle-class Jewish adolescents in fin-de-siècle Russia.[84] Perhaps it was in writing these works—each in their own way reflecting on his adolescence, long gone by—that Jabotinsky began to give himself permission to admit to the failings of the previous months. His unlikely confidant was none other than David Ben-Gurion. From Chicago, Jabotinsky wrote:

> I don't know if I'm going to send this letter once it's completed . . . perhaps you'll read these lines with eyes that have changed. I fear I have also changed somewhat. I'll admit, for example, that when I received the news of the postponement of the agreement, there was a sort of inner whisper within me that said these words—"[T]hank God we've been exempted from this." . . . And yet . . . I learned in London to value the man Ben-Gurion and his works. . . . There are generations, now, that don't know your [ideological] meanderings and did not participate in your quest for truth. . . . There seems to be a new characteristic among our present-day youth, Jewish and Gentile alike, who refrain from delving into matters and are inclined towards "yesses" or "no's" that are bold, simple, basic and brutal. Of these two threads they seek the one that is thicker, or more shiny; and that love which in the past moved you to moderate, and moderate once more the proportions [you put] in the [ideological] combinations, they call it casuistry or a lack of might—or even worse. With what then will you fight this brutality, with what concoction? Will you try to teach them your beliefs? I doubt whether this generation is capable of understanding them. This generation is very "monistic"—[p]erhaps this is no compliment, but it is definitely a fact. Or perhaps, you won't fight them, you'll go with the stream [of the movement], in part hoping that the stream will reach a point that is so absurd that it will cure itself, or in part [you believe you'll be] going with the stream without this hope?[85]

Although Jabotinsky was addressing Ben-Gurion's relationship to the Histadrut's membership, he might as well have been describing the challenge he felt bearing down on him that winter. Plans were under way to create the New Zionist Organization; under Jabotinsky's direction, it would compete with the Zionist Organization for the support of the Jewish masses. Would he "go with the stream," renounce his democratic persona, his occasional calls for restraint, and his penchant for diplomacy, all the while hoping that the Maximalists' program would quickly unravel when put into action? Would he fully accept the Maximalist platform without looking back? Or would he ultimately reject, in no uncertain terms, the Maximalist calls for revolutionary violence and leave the world of politics? Whatever choice he would make, one thing was clear. Jabotinsky's once firm belief that he possessed the power to steer the course of his youth movement by using provocative political prose had been shaken. The final phrase of a *Der Moment* article he wrote the previous year captured it best: "[T]he children of Betar are children of iron—even stronger than the steel typewriter that raised them."[86]

"Defense through Attack"

Jabotinsky's power to shape the beliefs and behaviors of his followers continued to wane in the final years of Betar's activity in interwar Poland. These years saw a dramatic shift in debates within the youth movement, and the Zionist movement at large, about the use of force. The Zionist Left and Right had been preoccupied with violent clashes between them. As the 1930s progressed, they increasingly debated whether acts of retaliatory violence against non-Jews could serve Zionist interests. This shift was prompted by the rise of attacks against Jews in both Europe and Mandate Palestine. By the time Betar's leadership had met in Kraków for the Second World Conference, Jews in Nazi Germany had been banned from government service and editorial positions, denied the right to practice law, and restricted in their access to German public schools. Nine months following the conference, the Nuremberg Race Laws had stripped them of their citizenship. Germany's anti-Jewish legislation fired the imaginations of statesmen across eastern Europe, who crafted laws of their own designed to exclude the Jews within their midst. In the years that followed Józef Piłsudski's death in 1935, the Polish government adopted a slew of antisemitic measures. Leading members of the ruling government bloc introduced legislation to restrict Jewish employment and ban the kosher slaughter of animals. Felicjan Sławoj-Składkowski, in his inaugural speech in the Polish parliament as prime minister in July 1936, offered the following formula for the Polish campaign against Jews: "Economic struggle yes [*owszem*], but no [physical] injury."[87] Radical Polish nationalists, in contrast, expressed little reservation about the use of violence. In addition to spearheading economic boycott campaigns against Jews, they frequently attacked Jewish students, store owners, and passersby. By the fall of 1939, more than one thousand Jews had been wounded, and dozens killed, in antisemitic attacks.[88]

Although Jewish life in Europe looked increasingly grim, it was in Mandate Palestine that Jews faced the most immediate threat to their lives. In April 1936, following a series of violent clashes between Jews and Palestinian Arabs, members of the Palestinian elite established the Arab Higher Committee to spearhead an organized rebellion. Leading a general strike of Palestinian Arab workers, they demanded that British officials halt Jewish immigration, prohibit land sales to Jews, and establish a democratic government to be dominated by Mandate Palestine's Arab majority. By the summer, the strike was giving way to armed attacks by guerrilla fighters against British officials and Palestine's Jews, who now made up nearly one-third of Mandate Palestine's population. Violence intensified from the summer of 1937 onward, after the British publication of the Peel Commission Report calling for the partition of Palestine and the establishment of two independent states, Jewish and Arab. Armed with guns, grenades, and bombs, Palestinian Arab fighters attacked Jewish settlements and staged terrorist attacks in public meeting places, resulting in the deaths of more than three hundred Jewish civilians.

Zionists were deeply divided concerning how best to respond to this wave of violence. Labor Zionists initially insisted on a policy of *havlaga*, or "self restraint." They argued that Jews should only take up arms in self-defense and refrain from committing acts of revenge. Such attacks, they argued, would only put the Zionist project in further jeopardy by encouraging British officials to view Zionists as no different than Palestinian Arab guerrilla fighters.[89] By refraining from counterattacks, they reasoned that they could demonstrate to the British that they desired peace and order and possessed a moral integrity lacking among Palestinian Arabs. The call for havlaga was adopted by most Jewish communal organizations in Mandate Palestine. British officials rewarded this approach by providing military training to thousands of Haganah members through the establishment of the Jewish Settlement Police in May 1936.

Not all Zionists within the Yishuv, however, endorsed the policy of havlaga. As early as 1931, several members of the Haganah formed a splinter group known as the Haganah Bet, which eventually became known as the Irgun, the National Military Organization (Irgun tsva'i le'umi). Its original leader, Avraham Tehomi, called for a more forceful response to Palestinian Arab attacks and insisted that his new organization, in contrast to the Haganah, be independent from Labor Zionist control. Although the Irgun was not officially a Revisionist organization—its original supervisory committee also consisted of representatives from the General Zionists, Mizrahi, Agudat Yisrael, and the Jewish State Party—many of its members were affiliated with Betar. The Arab Revolt of 1936 reinforced the bonds between the Revisionist movement and the Irgun. In December 1936, an agreement was reached between Tehomi and Jabotinsky, stipulating that Jabotinsky would become the supreme commander of the Irgun and that the organization would not act against the interests of the New Zionist Organization. Tehomi, however, expressed deep reservations about the agreement and returned to the Haganah in April 1937, taking with him at least a quarter of the Irgun's members. Those who remained were nearly all members of Betar. They viewed the policy of havlaga with disdain and called for Jews in Mandate Palestine to undertake acts of retaliation.

The Irgun and Betar's attitudes toward retaliation were not shaped solely by developments in Mandate Palestine. Their embrace of retaliatory violence was partially inspired by conversations within the Revisionist movement about how to respond to antisemitism in Poland. It was in Poland, not Mandate Palestine, that a right-wing Zionist leader first presented a blueprint for Jews to engage in acts of radical violence. This proposal did not come from the fringes of Betar but from Yirmiyahu Halperin, the leader charged with coordinating the military training of its members. Although Halperin had close connections to the Biryonim in Mandate Palestine, upon his arrival to Poland in 1931, he initially presented himself as a faithful ambassador of Jabotinsky's more temperate statements on the role of violence in the Zionist movement. Like Jabotinsky, Halperin emphasized that the youth movement's military training program should aim, above all, to teach Jewish youth how to defend themselves. Echoing Jabotinsky's claim that military training inspired young Jews to be chivalrous and well mannered, Halperin had urged Betar members to aspire to be "gentlemen" and "sportsmen" who would abide by a strict ethical code. His first handbook for military training, published in 1931, focused primarily on how to stand at attention, march in parades, read maps, and use basic Morse code. The only weapons to make any appearance were sticks and stones.[90]

It would take events in Poland, not Palestine, to push Halperin to voice support for retaliatory attacks in both locations. Halperin's arrival in Poland coincided with a surge in antisemitism and anti-Jewish violence across the country. At the start of the 1931 academic year, right-wing Catholic Polish student organizations launched a series of anti-Jewish riots at their universities. Beating, stabbing, and occasionally killing Jewish students, they hoped to put pressure on the Polish government to impose a quota restricting the admission of Jews to the country's institutions of higher learning. Their efforts culminated several years later with university-sanctioned "ghetto benches" that separated Jewish students from their non-Jewish peers. Similarly violent attacks on Jewish students were taking place in universities across Austria, Germany, Romania, and Hungary. As Halperin spoke to Jewish university students, he observed that they felt powerless in the face of university administrators, government officials, and police. All these officials, they believed, were passively or actively supporting the actions of the antisemitic student organizations. He was no less struck by the fact that Jewish students were terrified of retaliating because they feared that doing so would only encourage antisemitic youth to stage further attacks on Jews throughout the country. The only response they could envision was to launch a protest movement that would try to convince the international community to exert pressure on European governments to condemn antisemitism and protect Jewish students.[91]

Halperin decided that the calls for revolutionary violence promoted by the Biryonim in Palestine could prove helpful to beleaguered Jewish youth in Poland and elsewhere in Europe. In the winter of 1933, he used the youth movement's weekly newspaper *Ha-medina* as a platform to present a radical new manifesto for the use of force within the movement. To accompany his proposal, Halperin provided a provocative title: "Defense through Attack" (*Hagana be-hatkafa*). Halperin insisted in his proposal that protests and political diplomacy were futile. Nor would the establishment of Jewish self-defense groups deter antisemitic rioters. Halperin argued that anti-Semitic rioters would only stop attacking Jews if they were terrified of a vicious response from their victims. He called on Betar members to form small, clandestine vigilante groups and launch retaliatory attacks against anti-Semitic students. Drawing on the biblical injunction "an eye for an eye, a tooth for a tooth," Halperin urged Jewish youth to abandon restraint and embrace the very same tactics used by their opponents. These youth, he explained, would prove once and for all that Jews would no longer "suffer quietly and shut up."[92]

His Hebrew-language guidebook for military training, published in Warsaw the following year, was even more provocative. Spanning one hundred pages, the guidebook was devoted to the techniques of guerrilla fighting. In the wake of an antisemitic attack, Betar members were expected to coordinate underground cells. Catching their opponents by surprise in streets, alleyways, or homes, they would attack and vanish into the civilian population before their enemies could respond. He provided his readers with detailed instructions for how to use knives, brass knuckles, grenades, and guns. If their opponents abandoned the ethics of war, they too could use every means possible to achieve their goals. Halperin paid special attention to the psychological damage these surprise attacks could inflict. He explained that the only way a minority population could triumph against a powerful and armed majority was if they instilled panic, despair, and demoralization among them. To do so, the guidebook described various theatrical techniques Jewish youth could employ to surprise their enemies and generate publicity in the press. Whether by wearing masks or shouting distinctive rallying cries, these tactics would, in Halperin's words, instill "fear in the presence of terror."[93] Even though Halperin's handbook departed from Jabotinsky's more temperate comments regarding the use of force, the Revisionist leader saw little need to intervene in Halperin's activities. In the same year that Halperin's guidebook was published, Jabotinsky congratulated him for the success of his military training program and assured him that he would continue to play an important role in the youth movement's affairs.[94]

Halperin's guidebook is striking not only because it is the first guide published by a Zionist movement to provide a blueprint for terrorist activity, but also because it highlights how conversations among Zionists about anti-Jewish violence in Europe were intertwined with their conversations about Mandate Palestine. Tellingly, Halperin saw little need in his guidebook to specify where Betar members should engage in partisan warfare. At several points in the text, Halperin would move abruptly from an example of anti-Jewish violence in Europe to one in Mandate Palestine. His descriptions of Jewish retaliation strategies similarly blurred the lines between the *Yishuv* and Europe.[95] By deploying this deliberately ambiguous language, Halperin encouraged Polish Jewish youth to blur the lines between Poland and Palestine when thinking about how to respond to anti-Jewish violence. In the wake of anti-Jewish riots in Poland, some Betar leaders began to echo Halperin's calls for retaliatory violence. "There will be a cost for spilling Jewish blood!" warned Betar leader Yosef Klarman in the aftermath of the infamous Przytyk riots of March 1936.[96] Borrowing one of Jabotinsky's most famous phrases, Klarman insisted to the readers of Warsaw's Revisionist weekly that only if Polish Jews forged an "iron wall" of protection would Catholic Poles refrain from committing acts of violence against them. "In the Land of Israel," he added, young Jews "sang in the face of the British, 'we won't move from here.' At this very moment [armed Jewish] forces in locales across Poland repeat this with a double dose of stubbornness."[97]

Although several Betar leaders from Warsaw echoed Klarman's calls for confrontation with Catholic Poles and the Polish government, their voices soon became out of sync with official Revisionist policy. One month following the Przytyk riots, Jabotinsky began to meet with Polish government officials, among them the prime minister and leading members of the Foreign Ministry. He sought to gain their support for his "Evacuation Plan," which called for 1.5 million Jews to emigrate from eastern Europe to Mandate Palestine over the course of ten years. Jabotinsky expected that Betar's leaders in Poland would echo his statements seeking to establish a clear distinction between Catholic Polish antisemitism and Nazism. In contrast to Nazi Germany's rabidly racist ideology, Jabotinsky argued, Catholic Polish hostility toward Jews could be described as the "antisemitism of things," a natural and inevitable product of a severe shortage of jobs and resources in a country plagued by a population surplus.[98]

Polish government officials responded warmly to Jabotinsky's overtures. One year before Jabotinsky's campaign, they had made clear their desire to make the mass emigration of Polish Jews official policy by transferring issues related to Poland's Jews from the Ministry of Internal Affairs to the Ministry of Foreign Affairs. Polish officials were already hard at work exploring various locations across the globe where their country's Jewish population could potentially resettle. They envisioned Jabotinsky's campaign as yet another avenue to pursue their program to reduce their country's Jewish population significantly and expand their political strength in the Middle East.[99] Among the Revisionist movement's admirers was foreign minister Józef Beck; Wiktor Tomir Drymmer, who was in charge of the Division of Emigration Policy in the Foreign Affairs office; Count Edward Bernard Raczyński, Poland's ambassador in the United Kingdom; and Witold Hulanicki, Poland's consul general in Jerusalem. Between 1936 and 1938, their support took several forms. On the international diplomatic front, Polish officials endorsed the Evacuation Plan at the League of Nations. In Poland, they attempted to facilitate the emigration of Revisionist youth by subventing the cost for passports and transportation out of Poland. They also attempted to intervene in the activities of the Zionist Organization, urging them to provide more immigration certificates to Polish Jewry. Discussions regarding the military training of Irgun members from Mandate Palestine were initiated in the winter of 1938. The following year, Polish military officials conducted a training course near the southern town of Andrychów for twenty-five Irgun members from Mandate Palestine. In addition to providing military training, the Polish government also supplied some arms and ammunition to Irgun members.[100]

Some historians have argued that this instance of Polish-Jewish cooperation was primarily a "marriage of convenience" between Revisionist Zionists, who sought military training and supplies, and Polish government officials, who were happy to endorse activities that could hasten the mass emigration of the Jews within their midst.[101] Others have suggested that this alliance also testified to the mutual affection shared by Polish government officials and right-wing Zionist activists.[102] To be sure, there is no dearth of official Revisionist texts from these years that praise Poland and cite Piłsudski as an inspiration for the establishment of the Irgun.[103] As late as May 1939, Betar's leaders were publishing articles with titles such as "Two Fatherlands" and calling for Betar members to make "sacrifices for their Polish fatherland, as well as for the rebuilding of the Jewish State in Palestine."[104] These texts, however, provide only a partial view of the diverse attitudes of Betar's leaders and members toward the Polish government and the country's Catholic Polish population. Given the vested interests of the Revisionist movement in maintaining a good relationship with Polish officials, it was Revisionist policy to keep criticism of the Polish government far from public view. Well aware that the Polish government forbade the formation of vigilante groups to combat anti-Jewish violence, journalists writing in the Revisionist press were also careful to avoid describing local cases of Revisionist youth defying government regulations.

Decades later, former Betar members writing in memoirs and memorial anthologies for their hometowns expressed none of these reservations.[105] Recalling his years as a Betar leader in Tomaszów Mazowiecki, Leon Markowicz noted that his local youth movement branch turned to Yirmiyahu Halperin's textbook for inspiration to respond to an outbreak of antisemitic riots in 1938. Describing his efforts to train Betar's members, Markowicz noted that the textbook not only taught "how to organize the defense of settlements . . . in the Land of Israel, but also how to organize self-defense from rioters in the Diaspora." As if to showcase his group's implementation of Halperin's instructions for surprise attacks, Markowicz recalled the shock of antisemitic rioters "at the sight of the quick response of our boys, who appeared suddenly, as if underground."[106]

Two hundred miles to the east, in the town of Luboml, Betar's local leader Ya'akov Hetman, who had previously boasted of his relationship with Polish government officials, organized an armed response to antisemitic riots. When rioters began to attack elderly Jews on Sabbath evenings, Hetman echoed Halperin's insistence that violence against Jews in Poland merited the same response as violence against Jews in Palestine. The "act of standing upright," he argued, "was not limited by geographic borders, and . . . the readiness to fight could not be reduced to a matter of the future alone, or to the Land of Israel alone." "It was obvious," he added, "that we had to 'pay back' the attackers."[107] Hetman's account not only described instances of retaliation, but also illustrated the inability of Betar leaders to legislate the behavior of their followers in the heat of violent clashes that were, by their very nature, unruly, unscripted, and unpredictable. Describing a confrontation with rioters, he recalled that two Betar members broke an unspoken rule not to inflict life-threatening wounds. When two Polish rioters were stabbed by Hetman's men and sent to the hospital in critical condition, police officials placed the blame for the violent clashes squarely on Betar. The youth movement's members were no longer permitted to march in Polish patriotic parades or participate in government-sponsored military training programs, as they had done in the past.[108] Although their accounts of confrontations with Polish antisemitic rioters can neither be taken at face value nor deemed representative of the Revisionist movement as a whole, the recollections of former Betar members nonetheless alert historians to the dangers of presuming that the public declarations of Polish-Jewish brotherhood by the movement's leadership accurately reflected the beliefs and behaviors of all its members.[109]

On the Gallows

Shalom Tabacznik would die with Jabotinsky's name on his lips. This was, at least, how the twenty-five-year-old Betar member envisioned his death when he wrote to friends from his prison cell in Palestine.[110] In the final days leading up to his execution in the summer of 1938, Tabacznik did all he could to let people know that his entire life had been devoted to obeying Jabotinsky's commands. In letters to family and fellow Betar members, and in notes scribbled on the walls of his prison cell, he insisted that Jabotinsky's poems and articles had offered clear guidelines for his life and impending death. Ten months beforehand, he had heeded Jabotinsky's call for the mass emigration of Polish Jewry. Leaving his hometown of Łuck, a city in Poland's eastern borderlands, Tabacznik began a journey taken by as many as seventeen thousand Polish Jews in the late 1930s, to immigrate illegally to Palestine with the help of Revisionist and Irgun activists, among them Avraham Stavsky.[111] Once Tabacznik arrived, he obeyed Jabotinsky's instructions for newly arrived Betar members and joined a small Revisionist work battalion in Rosh Pina, a Jewish settlement in the Upper Galilee. To shed his diaspora past, he took on the name Shlomo Ben Yosef. When a friend was shot dead by a Palestinian Arab assailant, Ben

Yosef may have called to mind Jabotinsky's injunction to be proud, noble, and cruel. Joined by two other Betar members, he threw grenades and fired shots toward a bus carrying twenty-four Palestinian Arab civilians.

Although Ben Yosef's mission was a failure—the grenades never went off, and the bus driver swerved in time to miss the bullets—he took comfort in the fact that he would be the first Jew executed by Mandate Palestine's British authorities. To his mother and friends, he wrote, "I can't tell you how happy I am that I've been given the chance to die in the Land of Israel. . . . I never dreamed that I would die such a heroic death."[112] He would have likely been pleased that dozens of young Jews in Palestine spent the weeks following his execution carrying out reprisal attacks of their own. Jabotinsky had sent a telegram to Irgun activists in Mandate Palestine to "invest heavily" should Shlomo Ben Yosef be executed.[113] They interpreted Jabotinsky's command as they saw fit, staging shooting attacks and setting off bombs in Arab buses, marketplaces, and coffee shops. In one month alone, nearly ninety Palestinian Arab civilians were killed.

Ben Yosef's selective reading of Jabotinsky was far from unique. Like other Betar members coming of age in Poland, he had been encouraged to "translate" Jabotinsky's ambiguous prose in ways that best matched the needs of the hour for the Zionist movement. When he scribbled lines from Jabotinsky's Betar anthem on the walls of his prison cell, he avoided its second verse, which called for chivalrous behavior. Instead, he wrote the anthem's third verse, which urged Betar's members to "die or to conquer the mountain."[114] Irgun supporters in Poland similarly pruned Jabotinsky's prose for endorsements of their activity. Published in Warsaw, the underground movement's Yiddish newspaper *Di Tat* (The Deed) included articles that described Jabotinsky's philosophy as "two eyes for one eye and an entire mouth of teeth for one tooth," and quoted Jabotinsky's description of the Irgun as "the strongest form of protest" for the Jewish people.[115]

The newspaper's editor was Natan Friedman-Yellin, a Betar activist from Grodno who had joined the youth movement's national executive leadership after arriving in Warsaw in 1933 to study engineering. In November 1937, he was introduced to twenty-nine-year-old Avraham Stern, an Irgun operative in Mandate Palestine who originally hailed from Suwałki, a town near Białystok. By the time he arrived in Warsaw, Stern was already gaining a reputation among Betar's members as a revolutionary poet. In one poem, written in 1934, he mused, "today [I write] on paper, tomorrow on the torso of a man."[116] His 1932 poem "Anonymous Soldiers" described the readiness of bands of armed

Jews to defend and conquer their homeland during "red days of riots and blood." It served as the Irgun's anthem and was integrated into Betar's official songbook several years later.[117] Stern had arrived in Warsaw to negotiate with Polish government officials to provide the Irgun with military training and aid. Although he had allegedly traveled with a letter of recommendation from Jabotinsky in hand, he confided to Friedman-Yellin that he rejected the Revisionist leader's continued commitment to diplomacy, as well as his reluctance to declare a revolt against the British. Stern spoke instead of forming Irgun cells in Poland without Jabotinsky's authorization. He envisioned building an army, some forty thousand strong, that would illegally immigrate to Mandate Palestine and launch a revolt against British rule.

Friedman-Yellin eagerly accepted Stern's request that he travel to Betar branches across the country and establish Irgun cells.[118] He was joined soon after by Avraham Amper, a twenty-one-year-old Betar leader from Ludmir. Friedman-Yellin, describing his travels by train for weeks on end in the summer of 1938 to recruit Irgun members, recalled that Betar's members were anxious to know whether Jabotinsky approved of their activity. "[I]n order to prevent a psychological conflict within themselves," he recalled, "I would answer them in a somewhat vague fashion: Ze'ev Jabotinsky was, as was known, the chief decision maker of the Irgun, and he determines its policies. But it is not his obligation to personally intervene in every aspect of the organizational activity."[119] Believing that Jabotinsky had sanctioned their activity, Irgun cells throughout Poland raised money for the underground organization's activity in Palestine and began to improvise their own training. In Łuck, cells of no more than five to six members conducted rifle training in the name of the Irgun rather than Betar.[120] An Irgun cell in Baranowicze practiced spying on strangers and concealing weapons at large public events.[121] By August, nearly twenty-five members of these cells had received training with Irgun representatives from Mandate Palestine.

Despite Friedman-Yellin's promise to Betar members, both in person and in the pages of *Di Tat*, that Jabotinsky had given his blessing for the establishment of Irgun cells in Poland, the Revisionist leader's relationship with the underground organization was fraught with tension. At the start of the 1936 Arab Revolt, Jabotinsky endorsed the policy of havlaga, warning that Zionist acts of retaliation against Palestinian Arabs would antagonize the British.[122] In the revolt's first days, he also voiced moral concern over rumors that Betar members had attacked Palestinian Arab workers in Tel Aviv.[123] As the revolt persisted, however, Jabotinsky voiced increasing support for retaliatory violence, even if its targets were civilians. His change of heart was the product of multiple factors. He was pushed, in part, by his followers in Betar and the Irgun. By 1938, Betar leaders across Poland were increasingly demanding that Jabotinsky endorse their belief that armed revolt against Palestinian Arabs and British officials was the only option available to Zionist youth. These demands were coupled with their scathing critiques of Jabotinsky's efforts to promote the Revisionist cause through mass petitions and diplomacy. Despite its promise to rival the Zionist Organization, Jabotinsky's New Zionist Organization remained poorly organized, underfinanced, and largely ineffective.

In addition to his concern that his power over Betar's members was weakening, Jabotinsky also feared appearing politically impotent as the Irgun's leader. Given that the Irgun was waging its battles hundreds of miles away from their "supreme commander," his role in the organization was largely symbolic. Often, the only option available to him was to weigh in on attacks carried out by Irgun members in Palestine after they had already occurred. Although he saw value in their activities, he also feared, and rightly so, that some of the Irgun's leadership sought a complete break from his authority. Jabotinsky had long believed that the Zionist struggle had to be waged on multiple fronts, and that he could lead each of these endeavors. His belief had led to a scenario in which he was constantly having to juggle the multiple personas he had adopted for his various roles, whether as president of the New Zionist Organization, as head of Betar, or as supreme commander of the Irgun.

Jabotinsky refused to give up on believing in his ability to be both rebel and statesman. Ever the political chameleon, he followed the strategy he knew best: he continued to issue deliberately contradictory and ambiguous instructions to his followers. At Betar's Fourth World Conference in September 1938, held in Warsaw just weeks after Shlomo Ben Yosef's execution, Jabotinsky vigorously protested calls from some of the delegates to abandon the politics of diplomacy and wholeheartedly endorse a war for national liberation against British officials and Palestinian Arabs. The most heated exchange took place between Jabotinsky and the now twenty-five-year-old Menachem Begin. Declaring the era of political diplomacy a thing of the past, Begin insisted that the conference delegates revise the fourth clause of the youth movement's oath, written by Jabotinsky four years beforehand. Instead of the phrase "I will train in order to fight in the defense of my people, *and I will only use my strength for defense*," Begin proposed, "I will train to fight in the defense of my people *and to conquer the homeland*." In a lengthy response, Jabotinsky referred to Begin's calls for armed revolt against the British as "the squeaking of a door, with no sense and no benefit."[124] One audience member recalled that Jabotinsky's rebuke brought Begin to tears.[125] He likely expressed relief when his rendition of the oath was overwhelmingly approved by Betar's delegates.

Jabotinsky's now famous exchange with Begin is often quoted by historians to portray the conference as a showdown between two worldviews—one calling for revolt against the British and endorsing attacks that targeted civilians, and the other calling for cooperation with the British and moderation in the use of force.[126] Yet Jabotinsky made sure, as he had done in the past, to offer the conference's participants another version of himself to obey. At a banquet held in Shlomo Ben Yosef's honor that very same evening, Jabotinsky presented an approach to guerrilla violence that radically differed from the one he had articulated in his confrontation with Begin. In his speech to the conference delegates, Jabotinsky proclaimed Ben Yosef to be Betar's ambassador: "[H]e arrived to show the entire world what our movement is. Not only in worldview and spirit, but also in real deeds."[127] Addressing the fallen Betar member, Jabotinsky then declared, "I, as head of Betar give you ... and to your two friends the command to go the way of the King and do what you did."[128] With these words, Jabotinsky provided his followers permission to believe that he sanctioned terrorist attacks that targeted Arab civilians.

Jabotinsky's actions in the coming months make it difficult to discern whether he was attempting to harness, tame, or empower his internal opposition. In an effort to retain whatever waning power he had, he likely believed that all these approaches would be helpful. In an agreement struck in February 1939 between Jabotinsky and representatives of the Irgun, known as the Paris Agreement, Jabotinsky appointed the Irgun's commander, David Raziel, as the head of Betar in Palestine. In exchange, he asked that Irgun activists refrain from interfering with Betar's activities in Europe and in the United States, and instead restrict their independent activity outside Palestine to raising funds and purchasing ammunition and weapons. A representative of Betar's leadership in Warsaw, under Jabotinsky's command, would be responsible for recruiting and training Irgun members from within Betar's ranks. Aharon Propes would have welcomed Jabotinsky's efforts to place Betar's interactions with the Irgun under his direct supervision. Even though he opposed the policy of havlaga, Propes had fought for months against the establishment of Irgun cells within Betar, fearing a challenge to his authority. Propes was also viewed by the underground organization's sympathizers as too moderate, even though he celebrated on *Ha-medina*'s pages the Irgun's targeting of Arab civilians.[129] Perhaps out of exasperation with Irgun activists who, despite the Paris

Agreement, continued to organize cells within Betar, Propes decided to take a leave of absence from his role as head commander of Betar in Poland in order to help organize the youth movement in the United States. Propes suggested that his position be filled by Shimshon Yunitchman. A former Betar leader in Poland, Yunitchman was the head commander of the youth movement in Mandate Palestine and was heavily involved in the Irgun's attacks. Only when Yunitchman refused the position was Menachem Begin considered as an alternative.[130] By March 1939, Jabotinsky replaced Propes with Begin. Three months later, Jabotinsky was visiting Irgun training camps in Poland and sharing with Irgun operatives his dream to arrive by boat with its members to Palestine's shores, where they would launch a revolt.[131]

Historians have relied on testimony from Jabotinsky's close collaborators for proof that these decisions were made with great reluctance, and that Jabotinsky retained moral misgivings about the Irgun's activities.[132] Yet Jabotinsky's letters and articles on the eve of the Second World War only partially substantiate these claims. Though Propes and Begin had butted heads in the past, Jabotinsky's extant correspondence contains no hint of regret regarding Begin's appointment as the head of Betar in Poland.[133] In several letters, he spoke optimistically of a rapprochement between the New Zionist Organization and Irgun representatives.[134] What scant criticism of the Irgun exists within these letters focuses on instances in which they defied the Paris Agreement by engaging in independent political activity in Europe and the United States.[135] Their battle tactics were another matter altogether. When weighing in on their targeting of civilians, he occasionally offered words of praise and blessing.[136]

In one notable exception in June 1939, he wrote to Irgun commanders in Palestine to urge them to refrain from conducting any attacks that deliberately targeted women, children, and the elderly. The letter followed news he had read in the *London Times* that four Palestinian Arab women were shot in their homes by Jewish assailants. Jabotinsky's letter also insisted that the perpetrators of the attack, if they were indeed Irgun members, be punished by their superiors.[137] That same day, he wrote to members of the New Zionist Organization Executive that the time was ripe for them to reach out to the British colonial secretary and ask that Jabotinsky be granted permission to enter Mandate Palestine so that he could exercise his "moral influence" on members of the Irgun. He urged his executive to tell the British official that he sought to convince Irgun members to cease their acts of retaliation.[138]

Yet four days later, Jabotinsky published the following lines on the front page of *Ha-medina*:

Today, in the summer of 5699 [the Jewish calendar year corresponding with 1939], there is no need to renew the childish argument over the moral value of havlaga and retaliation [*t'guvah*]: every Jew in the land [of Israel] and the Diaspora will wholeheartedly be pleased with every act of retaliation . . . and anyone who says they are not pleased is a liar . . . [We are told,] "Don't you dare punish the innocent"; [this is] such superficial and hypocritical prattle. In war, in each war, in every single war, are not both sides innocent? What crime did the "enemy" soldier setting out to be my opponent commit—this pauper, like me, a slave, like me, conscripted by force? If a war will break out [in Europe], we will unanimously demand a sea and land embargo on the enemy, to starve their citizens with their innocent women and children; and after the first aerial attack on London and Paris, we will expect an aerial attack on Strasbourg and Milan, in which there are also many women and children. There is no war other than war against innocents . . . every war is damned, no matter its form. Defense and attack together, and if you don't want to harm the innocent—die. And if you don't want to die—shoot and don't chatter.

It was because of this elementary lesson taught to us by Ben Yosef that I called him my teacher.[139]

Had Jabotinsky changed his mind in a mere four days? Did he really believe that targeting women and children was necessary to the survival of the Zionist project in Mandate Palestine? Or was he merely telling Betar's members what he believed they wanted to hear? Was his proposal to reach out to the British colonial secretary for a visa a desperate attempt to find a way to curb the Irgun's terrorist activity, or a cunning attempt to exploit the crisis in order to gain passage to Palestine? The answers to these questions are, as always, left for his readers to decide.

Even though the Revisionist movement counted only several thousand members in Palestine, the Irgun's military actions played a pivotal role in propelling the debate about the use of force within the Yishuv. As the revolt progressed, the approaches first developed by Betar's leaders and members, and later implemented by the Irgun, became increasingly compelling to Zionists across the political spectrum. Just as Jabotinsky and the Revisionist movement had done for a decade, they too began to wrestle with how to blur the lines between defensive and offensive military actions. Although Labor Zionists in Palestine insisted that they maintained a "purity of arms," military groups under their auspices increasingly initiated violent clashes with Arabs.[140]

Under the command of British officer Charles Orde Wingate, Labor Zionists in Special Night Squads, established in 1938, used collective punishment when engaging in counterinsurgency activity in Palestinian Arab villages suspected of harboring perpetrators of attacks on Jewish communities. Labor Zionists would have adamantly denied the claim that they were reproducing the practices of the Zionist Right. But when the moment arrived for the "native born" young Jews of Palestine to join underground Labor Zionist battalions that at times targeted civilians, they had at their disposal an arsenal of thousands of articles from Betar's journals that offered moral justification for employing violence against Palestine's Arab population.

As they faced an onslaught of terrorist attacks launched by Arab fighters, Jewish leaders in Palestine increasingly adopted one of the central messages of Betar: in a world where Jews constantly feared for their lives, they would only survive if they struck back and, at times, struck first. If this message was attractive to young Jews in Palestine in the late 1930s, it would be all the more compelling to them in the years that followed, when the friends and family they had left behind in Europe—including the vast majority of Betar's members—suffered a fate far more horrific than Jabotinsky, or any other Jewish leader on the eve of the Second World War, could have ever imagined.

Epilogue

ON SEPTEMBER 2, 1939, Polish president Ignacy Mościcki received a telegram sent by Vladimir Jabotinsky. Barely twenty-four hours had passed since the Third Reich's invasion of Poland. Over one million German soldiers were marching toward Warsaw, and Luftwaffe planes were raining bombs over the capital. Deploring Germany's "suicidal aggression," Jabotinsky spoke "in the name of the movement which years ago was among the first to realize Poland's mission as one of the world's great powers, and conceived of the providential connection between the renaissance of the Jewish Palestine State and the triumph of Poland." He called for God's blessing on Poland and its soldiers, "of all creeds, united in loyalty and sacrifice."[1]

Many Betar members made good on their movement's pledges to defend the Polish state. In Sosnowiec, a city near the Polish-German border, several local Betar members joined the town's Catholic Polish youth in a hastily organized civilian defense battalion.[2] Bracing themselves for attack, Betar members in Sanok, a small city in the south, between Poland's eastern and western borders, helped set up bomb shelters and dig trenches.[3] One hundred and fifty miles east, Betar members in the town of Bursztyn joined a self-defense unit organized by Catholic Poles who feared that the surrounding Ukrainian population would take advantage of the power vacuum and try to seize control. They were met instead by Soviet forces, who controlled the eastern half of the Polish state by the first week of October and would remain there until German forces launched Operation Barbarossa in June 1941.[4]

Menachem Begin also called for solidarity with Poland. Days before the war broke out, he allegedly proposed to a Polish officer that a Jewish brigade be established within the Polish army to help fend off a German attack.[5] By September 6, with German troops nearing the outskirts of the city, Menachem and his wife, Aliza, fled Warsaw. Traveling with several other Betar activists, they headed toward Lwów by train. Nearly all the members of Betar's national leadership in Warsaw followed suit. They set off once again one month later. Traveling by train some four hundred miles north, they arrived in Wilno, now officially crowned Vilnius by the Lithuanian forces who remained in the city until Soviet troops took hold in August 1940. Of the nearly fifteen thousand Jewish refugees pouring into the city from German and Soviet-occupied Poland, about five hundred were Betar members.[6]

The flight of Betar's leaders from Warsaw was far from exceptional. With rumors circulating that German troops were executing prominent Polish and Jewish political activists, many leaders of Jewish youth movements were on the run.[7] As time passed, however, many of these activists chose to return to German-occupied Poland and to their followers, with the hope of organizing underground activity. Yet Betar's national leadership, whose calls for military training, underground action, and revolt had far outmatched those of any other Zionists between the two world wars, refused to return. When Perets Lasker, the only member of the netsivut who remained in Warsaw, met some of his former colleagues immediately after the war, he told them that he could not forgive them for their abandonment of Betar's members in Poland's besieged capital.[8]

Betar leaders who had recently arrived in Palestine from Poland were among their fiercest critics. Shimshon Yunitchman, who a year before had been offered Begin's leadership position in Poland, likened his behavior to that of a captain abandoning his ship.[9] In Palestine for several months before heading to the United States, Aharon Propes scolded Begin for demanding that the Yishuv's Betar leadership help him obtain visas to Palestine. Reminding Begin of his duty to lead Betar's members, he added, "[Y]ou are obligated to remain in the Diaspora and your new exile, together with the ranks, until the final moment."[10] Begin intimated that Propes was preventing him from going to Palestine because of their political differences. Infuriated, Propes retorted that even the Maximalists in the Yishuv, in whose name Begin had challenged Jabotinsky at the 1938 conference in Warsaw, believed that he should be among the very last to immigrate to Palestine.[11] Troubled by these accusations, Begin convened a meeting of the youth movement's leadership and proposed that they return to German-occupied Poland. His suggestion was rejected.[12]

Propes was also rankled by Begin's claim that the Zionist movement had nothing to gain from encouraging their members to join the Allied war effort. By the winter of 1940, Jabotinsky was in the United States, campaigning for the creation of a Jewish army, one hundred thousand strong, to fight alongside the Allies. He echoed the calls of other prominent leaders in the Zionist movement, who urged their followers to join the British government's war effort despite the white paper issued in May 1939 rejecting the creation of a Jewish state and severely restricting Jewish immigration and land purchase in Palestine. After years of protesting against British rule in Mandate Palestine, Begin insisted that there was little benefit to joining the Allied effort and suggested instead that the youth movement's members wait and see how the war unfolded.[13] Writing to Begin in the winter of 1940 from New York, Propes pleaded, "It's not the same as 1914; only one side has declared a war of destruction [hashmada] against the Jews."[14]

Right-wing Zionists in Palestine were also debating whether to join the British war effort. Although the Irgun had launched several attacks against British targets in the wake of the white paper, many of its members decided to heed Jabotinsky's command to enlist in the British Army. Others called for right-wing Zionists to continue their attacks on British officials in Palestine. Among them was Avraham Stern. Breaking ranks with the Irgun, he formed his own underground group, Lohamei Herut Israel (Fighters for the Freedom of Israel), which would come to be known by its acronym, Lehi, He was joined by scores of Polish Jewish immigrants in Mandate Palestine who had first entered the universe of right-wing Zionist activity through their participation in Poland's Betar.[15] They fantasized that a sprawling Jewish state from the Nile to the Euphrates would emerge in the wake of their war for national liberation. To fund their attempts to assassinate British officials, they robbed banks and kidnapped wealthy Jews, holding them for ransom. Convinced that the British Empire's enemies were natural allies of the Zionist movement, Lehi leaders reached out to Fascist Italy in the spring of 1940 and to the Third Reich in the winter of 1941. German and Italian officials rejected these overtures. One year later, Stern was gunned down in a Tel Aviv apartment by British police, who had found him hiding in a closet. Lehi's command would soon be taken over by Natan Friedman-Yellin, formerly the editor of Warsaw's *Di Tat*. He was joined by Israel Scheib (later Eldad), a former Tarbut schoolteacher and Betar leader in Wilno, and Yitzhak Jeziernicki, a Betar member who had emigrated from Warsaw to Mandate Palestine in 1935 and joined the Irgun soon after.[16]

Begin shared none of Stern's interest in forging a relationship with the Axis powers. He focused his energies instead on seeking passage to Palestine.[17] Eager to demonstrate that he still cared about the fate of Betar's members in German-occupied Poland, he wrote to Jabotinsky in June 1940 and asked whether the Revisionist leader could funnel money to Betar branches under Nazi rule. In the same letter, he and Yosef Glazman, Betar's leader in Latvia, requested help to obtain visas for their immigration to Mandate Palestine.[18] Jabotinsky's response is not recorded, but judging from letters he sent from the United States in the same month, he felt utterly helpless to intervene in the fate of his followers in occupied Europe.[19] He died two months later, on August 3, succumbing to a heart attack at a Betar summer camp in Hunter, New York.

On the very same day as Jabotinsky's death, Red Army troops and tanks invaded Vilnius. Six weeks later, Menachem Begin was arrested on the outskirts of the city by the NKVD (People's Commissariat of Internal Affairs). He had managed to obtain exit visas to Palestine just days beforehand; Begin's wife and several others associated with Betar put them to use. After months of imprisonment and interrogations, Begin was sentenced to eight years in Siberian labor camps.[20]

His sentencing proved to be his salvation. German troops invaded Vilnius just days after his departure. In the coming year, fate would intervene once again in Begin's favor. As German forces began their advance toward Moscow in June 1941, Stalin hastily sought out new allies among former enemies. One month later, the Soviet Union signed a pact with the Polish government-in-exile in London. Tens of thousands of Polish prisoners of war held in Soviet camps were released. Among them was General Władysław Anders, who had served as chief of staff for the Polish army in the mid-1920s. Anders was tasked with forming a Polish army, which under Soviet supervision would fight alongside Allied forces. Along with tens of thousands of prisoners of war and exiles from Poland in the Soviet Union, Begin joined the Anders army, which came under British command when its soldiers arrived in Iran in March 1942. Traveling westward through Iraq and the Transjordan, they reached the Jordan River several weeks later. At least in this instance, Jabotinsky's description of a "providential connection" between Poland and Palestine seemed to bear some truth. When Begin set foot for the first time on Palestine's soil in May 1942, he did so in a Polish soldier's uniform.

The deadliest year for Europe's Jews under German occupation was 1942. In the same month that Begin arrived in Palestine, Schutzstaffel (SS) doctors and soldiers performed their first selection of victims for Auschwitz-Birkenau's gas chambers. In the spring and summer months, German soldiers began to empty the ghettos of Kraków, Lublin, and Lwów, sending their Jewish inhabitants to the killing centers of Bełżec and Chełmno. By the end of the summer, more than a quarter of a million Jews in the Warsaw ghetto had been brutally rounded up and murdered in Treblinka, a death camp some fifty miles away. By the year's end, Jews from the across nearly all of German-Occupied western Europe were being forced into cattle cars destined for Nazi killing centers in Poland. By the spring of 1943, nearly one million Jews in regions under former Soviet control had been murdered by Einsatzgruppen units and local collaborators. Most were shot in mass graves dug in valleys and forests near their homes.

Like other Polish Jewish immigrants to Mandate Palestine, Betar members were left to grasp at whatever information they could about the fate of their families and European Jewry as a whole. In the months that followed Begin's arrival in Tel Aviv, Palestine's Revisionist daily *Ha-mashkif* (the Observer) published articles about Jews who remained in Nazi-occupied Europe, drawing on newspapers from England, updates from the World Jewish Congress headquarters in Geneva, and reports from Jewish relief organizations that had initially been granted limited access to ghettos through the Red Cross. Although readers learned of starvation, appalling sanitary conditions, and massacres, they had yet to discover the extent of the devastation.[21] Information was so scant that in October 1942, *Ha-mashkif* drew material from a newspaper published in the Third Reich to report on the situation of Jews in Brisk, Begin's hometown. Fearing for his parents and siblings, he had never stopped trying to establish contact with them. Had he read the article about Brisk, he would have been assured that most of its buildings were left intact, that its Jewish population was being kept alive, and that they were working as forced laborers for the German war effort.[22] *Ha-mashkif*'s editors had no way of knowing that just days before the article's publication, German troops had initiated their liquidation of the Brisk ghetto. By the end of the year, most of its inhabitants, among them Menachem Begin's mother, Chasia, had been executed in pits outside the town. His father and older brother had been murdered the year before, one of five thousand Jewish men taken outside the city limits and killed in June 1941.

By the end of November 1942, word had reached the Yishuv of the Nazis' systematic attempts to annihilate Europe's Jews.[23] Propes might have expected that this news would convince Begin to accept his earlier demand to call on Betar members to join Britain and the Allied forces in their war against the Nazis. Instead, news of Hitler's war of annihilation only strengthened Begin's resolve to fight the British. In February 1943, he wrote to readers of the Revisionist press in Palestine that "the annihilation of Europe's Jews is not just the result of the wickedness of Germans but also [the result of] the closing of the gates of our homeland by the British, who in so doing, prevent rescue and redemption."[24] Begin insisted that the only way to save the remaining Jews of Europe was to revolt against the British in Mandate Palestine and establish a Jewish state. One year later, as the new commander of the Irgun, Begin launched the underground organization's revolt against the British. Between 1944 and 1948, Begin would repeatedly invoke the Holocaust to vilify the British and justify the Irgun's activities against them.[25] Under his command, the Irgun sabotaged oil pipelines and telephone lines, planted roadside mines targeting British military and police vehicles, bombed British government buildings, and killed British soldiers in retaliation for the arrest and execution of Irgun members.

Like other Zionist leaders in Mandate Palestine, Begin's use of Zionist ideology to help come to terms with the personal and collective traumas of the Holocaust influenced how he depicted its victims.[26] Drawing on long-standing Zionist characterizations of Diaspora Jews as weak and passive, many of them argued that Europe's Jews bore some responsibility for their fate, and that the most of them were "sent to the slaughter" without protest. Begin used these images of Jewish passivity as a foil for the Irgun's fighters, whom he depicted as brave, fearless warriors who had abandoned any vestiges of their Diaspora mentalities the moment they had set foot on Palestine's soil.[27]

His initial reaction to the Warsaw Ghetto Uprising in April 1943 is instructive. When German forces entered the ghetto on the morning of April 19 with the intention of liquidating its Jewish inhabitants, they were met with armed resistance. For nearly one month, members of underground organizations, armed with grenades, guns, and Molotov cocktails, fought against German SS and police units. The uprising was led by two separate underground organizations established in the summer of 1942. The Jewish Combat Organization (Żydowska Organizacja Bojowa) was founded by three left-wing Zionist youth movements and was later joined by Bundist and Communist activists. A somewhat smaller group known as the Jewish Military Union (Żydowski Związek Wojskowy) drew much of its support from Betar activists. Acquiring some of their weapons from a private arms dealer with ties to the Polish underground, members of ŻZW, numbering between 100 and 160, fought for three days in one of the first battles of the uprising. The fighting took place in Muranowska Square, which lay on the northeastern edge of the ghetto.

During the battle, they likely raised a Polish and Zionist flag over one of the ghetto's buildings. Fleeing through a tunnel to the Aryan side of Warsaw following the battle, most of the surviving fighters were captured and executed by German forces.[28] As soon as news of the uprising reached Mandate Palestine, left-wing and right-wing Zionists made competing claims over who had initiated and led the revolt.[29] Begin took pride in the uprising and insisted that it had been led by Revisionists. At the same time, however, he urged his readers in 1946 to remember that the uprising was an exception, and that "hundreds of thousands of Jews in the capital of Warsaw were sent to the slaughter *without protest.*"[30]

Many Betar members who survived the Holocaust sought to ensure that their resistance activity against Nazi rule was on public record. Survivors of the ghetto in Łachwa, a small town in the northeastern region of the former Polish state, recalled that members of various Jewish youth movements were organized into an underground cell by Yitzhak Rochczyn, the leader of the local Betar branch. In the six months of the ghetto's existence, Rochczyn's group, with the assistance of Łachwa's Judenrat, stockpiled axes, knives, and iron bars. When German forces and a police unit comprising Ukrainians and local Belarusian residents entered the ghetto to liquidate its inhabitants, the Judenrat's leader set fire to his council's headquarters, signaling the start of the revolt. The underground attacked, killing six German soldiers and eight policemen. Although the ghetto's fence was breached, and approximately one thousand Jews managed to escape, most of Łachwa's Jewish inhabitants were eventually tracked down and killed.[31]

Survivors from the ghetto in the town of Buczacz, which lay three hundred miles south, recalled failed attempts at an uprising by three underground movements, one of which included Betar members from the nearby town of Tłumacz.[32] Others recalled how Betar members in Białystok cooperated with activists from other youth movements in their resistance activity.[33] Betar members who had served in partisan units throughout German-occupied Poland submitted their biographical information to the archive of the Revisionist movement in Tel Aviv, determined to ensure that they too would be remembered for resisting Nazi attempts to annihilate Europe's Jews.[34] At times, Revisionists had to curate their narrative of resistance in the interests of maintaining their movement's prestige. Revisionist survivors of the Vilna ghetto, for example, could describe Betar values as an inspiration for the youth movement's leader in Latvia, Yosef Glazman, to help found the United Partisans Organization (Fareynigte partizaner organizatsye), bringing together socialist Zionists, communists, and Betar members. Few would draw attention to the fact that the head of the Vilna ghetto's Jewish Police, who actively attempted to suppress resistance activity, happened to have been a Revisionist sympathizer before the war.[35]

Relations between Revisionist activists and Catholic Poles during the Holocaust were subjected to even more creative historical curation. In the late 1950s, a small group of Poles who claimed to be former members of the Polish underground convinced Revisionist chroniclers of the Holocaust that they had served as the patrons of the Warsaw ghetto's Jewish Military Organization. For decades, their story—now painstakingly examined and discredited by historians Laurence Weinbaum and Dariusz Libionka—was accepted by Revisionist activists and was seen by some as a symbol of Polish-Jewish brotherhood.[36] Relations between the Revisionist movement, the Polish underground, and Poland's government-in-exile were far more complex. The surge in Catholic Polish antisemitism accompanying the final years of the Second Polish Republic had already dampened the admiration many Betar members felt for the Polish national liberation narrative. Upon arriving in Palestine, some of them preferred to draw inspiration from European nationalists who did not include antisemitism as a core component of their worldview. Among these Betar members was Yitzhak Jeziernicki, who adopted the Irish-inspired codename Michael when he became one of the three main leaders of Lehi in 1943. Disposing of his Polish-sounding last name, he opted instead for the Hebrew-sounding Shamir, the name with which he was sworn into office several decades later as Israel's seventh prime minister.

Nonetheless, some Betar leaders who arrived in Mandate Palestine as wartime refugees continued to invoke legends of Polish national liberation to inspire their followers. The arrival of the Anders army in Palestine further fired the imaginations of Betar activists writing for *Ha-mashkif*. As they had done in the past, they claimed that Polish and Jewish nationalists shared parallel fates: just as Catholic Poles struggled to overthrow the foreign rule of Nazis in Poland, so too were Zionists in Palestine fighting to cast off the yoke of the British Empire. Catholic Poles were once again presented as models to emulate.[37] Several months after the Anders army reached Palestine, former leaders of the Revisionist movement in Poland sent a telegram to the country's government-in-exile in London, in which they announced their desire to once again forge an alliance. A group of Revisionist activists established close ties with Polish troops stationed in Palestine, serving in the Intelligence Service and Document Bureau.[38] These connections likely played a role in the Polish army's decision to grant Menachem Begin a leave of absence, from which he never returned.

This "alliance" was tenuous from the beginning. The Polish government did not want to endanger its relations with the British, who viewed Revisionists as rebels. Nor did Polish officials want to close off the possibility of gaining financial support from Jewish organizations who opposed right-wing Zionism. Within several months, relations between the Polish government-in-exile and Revisionist Zionists soured. In the first half of 1944, Revisionist activists in London voiced public support for Jewish soldiers who had defected from the Anders army to protest the rampant antisemitism within its ranks. Among those who supported their demand to be transferred to British units was Yirmiyahu Halperin, who had spent the war years promoting the creation of a Jewish army under Allied command. Viewing their defection as an opportunity to promote his cause, Halperin declared that the Polish government-in-exile "cannot be trusted with the restoration of Polish liberty, for unlimited liberty for such a Government must mean unlimited persecution and misery for all the minorities in Poland."[39] Officials from the Polish government-in-exile were infuriated by Halperin's response, as they were by the refusal of Revisionists and other Zionists to echo their concerns over the Soviet Union's territorial aspirations in Poland.[40]

Relations between Revisionists and Polish officials only worsened in the aftermath of the war. Keenly aware of the demographic boost that Holocaust survivors could bring to Mandate Palestine's Jewish population, and anxious to protect survivors from further antisemitic violence, Zionist activists launched a clandestine network for illegal immigration known as Beriha (Escape). Betar and Irgun activists played an active role in these efforts, which ultimately brought approximately 250,000 Jews from Europe to Palestine.[41] Zionists simultaneously made their case to the international community for the establishment of a Jewish state, insisting that Europe's Jews were doomed if they returned to their former places of residence. Their fears were reinforced when more than forty Holocaust survivors were murdered by Catholic Poles during a pogrom in Kielce in April 1946. Begin not only echoed these fears, but also linked the antisemitism that fueled the pogrom with British rule in Mandate Palestine. Broadcasting on the Irgun's underground radio, he provocatively declared, "Obviously, it was the Polish rioter who pushed the knife into the hearts of our brothers; but their hearts were brought closer to the knife. The name on the knife—the British exterminator."[42] Begin also made sure to describe all the Kielce pogrom's victims, irrespective of their political beliefs, as Zionists who had anxiously awaited the opportunity to return to their homeland.

Some leaders within the ranks of the Zionist Right began to seek alliances elsewhere. By July 1944, Polish military officials reported that Revisionists were meeting with Soviet officials in London and in the Middle East to court their support for the establishment of a Jewish state in Mandate Palestine.[43] Former Betar members who had joined the ranks of Lehi called for right-wing Zionists to dispose of their long-standing hostility toward communism and forge an alliance with the Soviet Union.[44] Polish officials who were once deemed allies transformed into enemies. Even Witold Hulanicki, the Polish consul in Jerusalem who had helped Avraham Stern and the Irgun acquire arms and military training, was not safe. He was assassinated by Lehi members in February 1948.[45]

By the time Hulanicki was assassinated, three months had already passed since the outbreak of a vicious civil war between Jews and Palestinian Arabs. The war followed the United Nations General Assembly vote on November 29, 1947, to partition Palestine and establish a Jewish and an Arab state. In the first stages of the civil war, Palestinian Arab fighters and volunteers from neighboring Arab states appeared to have the edge, taking hold of major roads, attacking Jewish settlements, and laying siege to Jerusalem. By the spring, the thirty-five thousand members of the Haganah, two to three thousand Irgun members, and three to five hundred Lehi fighters outnumbered Arab combatant units, who were suffering from a lack of arms, training, and coordination. During the second stage of the civil war, Jewish forces launched an offensive in April 1948 to take over strategic areas, gain control of main towns and internal lines of communication, and secure border areas in preparation for the anticipated invasion of Arab armies following the establishment of the state of Israel. The leadership of Lehi and Irgun units taking part in this offensive were dominated by former Betar members from Poland, and Polish Jews made up approximately one-third of their rank and file.[46] Many of these fighters had arrived in Palestine only months beforehand from displaced persons' camps in Europe.[47]

Despite the profound differences between Poland and Palestine, many of them would had have had little difficulty drawing links between their prewar past and their experiences during the war for Israel's establishment. The rivalry that raged between Betar and Labor Zionists in the interwar period continued to persist. In the preceding years, relations among the Irgun, Lehi, and Haganah alternated between hostility and cooperation. Between November 1944 and March 1945, the Haganah had declared an "open season" on Irgun and Lehi members, confiscating their weapons, interrogating them, and occasionally handing them over to the British police. When the Second World War came to an end, the Haganah changed its course, no longer viewing cooperation with the British to be politically expedient. In October 1945, they formed a pact with the Irgun and Lehi to join in a Hebrew Resistance Movement (Tenuat Ha-meri Ha-ivri) and attack British targets. The Haganah disbanded the movement in June 1946 in the wake of the Irgun's bombing of the King David Hotel, which served as a British military and administrative headquarters. The casualty toll of ninety-one people was deemed by the Haganah to be beyond the pale of acceptable resistance activity. When civil war broke out at the end of 1947, the Haganah once again reached out to the Irgun and Lehi. In the first stage of the civil war, they did not clash with one another and occasionally coordinated their actions against Arab militias and civilians.

Tensions came to a head once again in April 1948 during a joint campaign to break through the siege of Jerusalem and destroy Arab militia bases in nearby villages. On the morning of April 9, some 130 Irgun and Lehi members set out to conquer the village of Deir Yassin. Even though the inhabitants of Deir Yassin had previously refused to host Arab irregular units in their village, the Irgun and Lehi had gained approval for their operation from the Jerusalem command of the Haganah. At the start of the battle, an Irgun truck carrying a megaphone to warn the village inhabitants to surrender and leave halted or overturned at a ditch some thirty meters away. It was unclear whether any of the villagers heard the announcement. Facing sniper fire, five members of the Irgun and Lehi were killed, and thirty more were wounded. Under cover fire from Haganah machine gunners stationed nearby, they advanced from house to house, using grenades, rifles, submachine guns, and explosives. More than one hundred civilians were killed inside their homes or as they tried to escape or surrender. News of the massacre quickly spread throughout Palestine and precipitated the further flight of between two hundred thousand and three hundred thousand Palestinian Arabs from their homes in the two months that followed.[48] The mainstream Zionist leadership and Haganah immediately condemned the massacre.

Recalling the events at Deir Yassin two years later in his memoir about the Irgun, Menachem Begin lamented the deaths of the village's civilians. He insisted that the Irgun's members had met fierce resistance from Deir Yassin's inhabitants, had scrupulously observed "the traditional laws of war," and had delivered a "humane warning."[49] "I am convinced, too," he added, "that our officers and men wished to avoid a single unnecessary casualty in the Dir Yassin [sic] battle."[50] Lehi ideologue Israel Eldad recalled the event in an entirely different light.[51] Deir Yassin's roots, he argued, could be traced to the editorial offices of Warsaw's *Di Tat*, where he, along with other Betar and Irgun activists, had worked to mobilize support among Polish Jews for their activities during the Arab Revolt. Melding together the ancient Jewish past, his Zionist activism in Poland, and his participation in the 1948 war, he felt no need to deny that a massacre had taken place at Deir Yassin and saw little value in claiming that the Irgun and Lehi's actions were in the name of self-defense. Instead, he mused, "In the editorial offices of *Di Tat*, the ground is being prepared for the future conquest of Deir Yassin; *the laws of revenge*—as good for our day as for the days of Joshua Bin Nun and King David—are being taught."[52]

Relations between the Zionist Left and Right only worsened in the months that followed. On June 1, 1948, just two weeks after the declaration of Israel's independence and the ensuing attacks by Jordanian, Syrian, Egyptian, Iraqi, and a handful of Lebanese troops, a reluctant Menachem Begin signed an agreement with the newly formed Israeli government to integrate the Irgun's members and weapons into the newly established Israel Defense Forces (IDF). Despite the agreement, David Ben-Gurion, now the State of Israel's prime minister, feared that Begin was plotting a coup d'état. His fears were stoked when he received news two weeks later that the *Altalena*, an Irgun ship carrying 850 immigrants, along with a massive supply of rifles and ammunition, had set sail from France and was headed toward the fledgling new state. Begin negotiated with IDF official Yisraeli Galili as the ship approached Israel's shores, requesting that 20 percent of the arms be given to Irgun units in Jerusalem. Galili agreed to this request but rejected Begin's suggestion that the remainder of the arms go to Irgun units in the IDF.

When Ben-Gurion received word from Galili that Begin was potentially attempting to form a private army, he called on the IDF to take any action necessary to prevent the *Altalena*'s cargo from falling into the Irgun's hands. The ship arrived on June 20 to a beach about thirty miles north of Tel Aviv. As hundreds of Irgun supporters began to offload the weapons, IDF troops surrounded the beach and ordered them to surrender. By the evening, the IDF had opened fire at Irgun supporters on the beach and chased after the *Altalena*, which had set sail toward Tel Aviv. The following day, IDF soldiers battled Irgun members on the beaches of Tel Aviv and shelled the ship, causing it to explode. Clashes between the IDF and Irgun fighters spilled onto Tel Aviv's streets. That evening, Begin delivered an address on the Irgun's radio station in which he commanded his men to cease fighting and, in doing so, prevent a civil war. By the time calm was restored, three IDF soldiers and sixteen Irgun supporters had been killed. Among those killed on the doomed *Altalena* was Avraham Stavsky, accused some fifteen years earlier of nearly starting a civil war between Labor Zionists and Revisionists by murdering Haim Arlosoroff. Stavsky was killed only fifty yards from the site where Arlosoroff had been shot.

―――

Of all the memories of prewar life in Poland invoked by Betar's Polish Jewish alumni to justify their political activity in the State of Israel, their recollections of Jabotinsky proved the most important. This was especially true for Menachem Begin. Some ten months after his arrival in Mandate Palestine, he wrote to Jabotinsky's widow, Anya, to announce the birth of his son. He proudly revealed that his son's first name, Ze'ev, paid tribute to the Hebrew first name of her late husband, whom he described as his "immortal father." He promised that he and his wife, Aliza, would "perpetuate the name of our father not just by giving his name to our children, but also through the total fulfillment of his aspirations." This goal, he added, was "the essence of our entire life."[53] The letter would be the first of many instances in which Menachem Begin would position himself as Jabotinsky's chosen son and heir apparent, entrusted to bring the ideals that had captivated the hearts and minds of thousands of Polish Jewish youth to fruition in the State of Israel.

If Jabotinsky's prose was open to multiple interpretations in his lifetime, it was all the more flexible following his death. As the Irgun's commander, Begin reconstructed Jabotinsky's biography to justify the underground organization's revolt against the British. Ignoring Jabotinsky's treasured self-image as a statesman, Begin described his "father" as a "man of war from his first appearance on the public stage until the very last days."[54] Portraying Jabotinsky as a steadfast opponent of the British, Begin reminded listeners of the Irgun's underground radio station that the founder of Revisionism was the only major Zionist leader to be tried, imprisoned, and exiled from his homeland by British officials.[55] Begin also cast aside Jabotinsky's more moderate comments concerning the use of violence, depicting him instead as "the father of revolutionary theory and rebellious action."[56]

Although Begin's declarations about Jabotinsky's attitudes toward rebellion resonated with many of his peers on the Zionist Right, others balked at his attempts to portray himself as the natural heir of the Revisionist leader. Founded by Begin just one week before the *Altalena* was shelled, the Herut (Liberation) Party had won only 14 of 114 seats in Israel's first parliamentary election in 1949.[57] The party lost half of these seats in the following election. Many veteran activists in the Revisionist Party and in the Irgun believed that Begin was unfit to serve as the head of Herut. Yirmiyahu Halperin, now living in Eilat, called for Begin to step down.[58]

Perhaps most damning of all was the reaction of Vladimir Jabotinsky's son to Begin's leadership. Born in 1910, Eri Jabotinsky had spent much of his adolescence in Paris with his parents. He moved in 1935 to Mandate Palestine, where he was an active leader in Betar. During the Second World War, Eri was in the United States, where he joined Hillel Kook's Bergson Boys group in fundraising for the Irgun and campaigning for the rescue of European Jewry.[59] Along with Hillel Kook and Shmuel Merlin, his former Irgun colleagues in the United States, Eri saw Judaism as an ossified remnant of the Diaspora past that would harm the new Jewish state. They insisted that the Herut Party embrace a radically secular agenda. Begin, by contrast, had a deep respect for Jewish tradition and believed that Eri's proposals would alienate many potential voters. Eri viewed Begin's declared commitment to tradition as shallow populism, a cheap effort to gain the support of new immigrants pouring into the country. Following the second Herut conference, Jabotinsky's son left the party that claimed to perpetuate his father's legacy. He was joined by several former Maximalist Revisionists. In his letter of resignation, addressed to Begin, Eri urged him to stop using his father's name to promote the party.[60] He presumed that Begin's quest for political power was doomed to fail, and that he would fade into oblivion.

Begin, of course, ignored Eri's request. Nearly thirty years later, after numerous twists and turns in his political career, Jabotinsky's name was still on his lips when he became Israel's first right-wing Zionist prime minister.[61]

Jabotinsky never lived to see the birth of the State of Israel or the triumph of the Israeli Right. But his ghost continues to roam the streets of Israel. Zionists of every persuasion invoke his name to justify their views on a staggering array of issues facing Israeli society, from the role of the rabbinate in legislating the lives of Israel's Jewish citizens and the status of women in civic life to the repercussions of economic inequality. Above all else, Israelis turn to Jabotinsky's prose in search of solutions to the Arab-Israeli conflict. How, they ask, would Jabotinsky have responded to the geopolitical threats facing Israel and the Middle East? What would he have made of Israel's decision to dismantle its settlements and withdraw its military from Gaza in 2005, but to continue to rule over the West Bank? How would he have responded to acts of political violence against civilians carried out by Israelis and Palestinians alike?

Perhaps the most powerful testament to Jabotinsky's persistent presence in conversations about the Arab-Israeli conflict comes from debates among politicians within the increasingly fractured Israeli Right. Its leaders continually produce contradictory interpretations of his legacy to provide legitimacy for their competing views. When Prime Minister Ariel Sharon sought to justify to Israelis the disengagement from Gaza in 2005, he turned to Jabotinsky's prose, including a passage from a 1915 essay insisting that settlement was not an "end in and of itself."[62] Opponents of disengagement responded to Sharon's speech by citing passages from Jabotinsky's prose highlighting his territorial maximalism.[63] Inspired by Jabotinsky's articles promising the equal treatment of an Arab minority within a future Jewish state, president Reuven Rivlin has argued for extending citizenship to Palestinians in the West Bank while retaining Israeli control in the area.[64] In contrast, Avigdor Lieberman, who describes his party, Yisrael Beitenu, as "a national movement with the clear vision to follow in the brave path of Ze'ev Jabotinsky,"[65] has called for a two-state solution that would include a population transfer of Palestinian citizens of Israel and Jews living in the West Bank. He could easily turn to Jabotinsky's musings in 1940 on the potential merits of Arab emigration from the future Jewish state.[66] Lieberman has also called to strip Palestinian citizens of Israel of their citizenship if they do not publicly pledge loyalty to Israel as a "Jewish and democratic state." Referring to Israeli Palestinians at a conference in March 2015 devoted to the future of Israeli politics, Lieberman mused, "[T]hose who are against us, there's nothing to be done—we need to pick up an ax and cut off his head. Otherwise we won't survive here."[67] A spokesman for the party quickly "clarified" Lieberman's comments by noting that he was, in fact, "paraphrasing Jabotinsky, who said that we should be very generous to those who stand with you and cruel to those [who] physically stand against you."[68] Israeli journalists appalled by Lieberman's statements assembled passages from Jabotinsky's writings, accusing him of betraying the founder of right-wing Zionism's commitment of protecting minority rights.[69]

Had Jabotinsky observed his acolytes and opponents at war over his legacy, he would have discovered that his political prose remains just as elusive as he had intended it to be between the two world wars. From its founding, the Revisionist movement aimed to appeal to a broad constituency and collected a range of supporters with differing views. To maintain his leadership of this diverse political base, Jabotinsky maintained an ideological dexterity in his journalistic output and public appearances. He did not hesitate to offer ambiguous or contradictory messages to his followers. Even as he condemned radicals within his movement as reckless rebels, he often offered them more ambivalent instructions to pursue. Even as he insisted that he was a fierce proponent of democracy and liberalism, he raised doubts, in full public view, about the ability of these political ideals to serve the national interests of an increasingly endangered Jewish population. His followers in interwar Poland and Mandate Palestine had ample room to interpret him as they saw fit. The tensions and contradictions that characterize Jabotinsky's public and private statements are, perhaps, the key to his staying power.

Although Jabotinsky continues to fascinate Israelis, his Polish Jewish followers receive scant attention. Israelis express little interest in the lives of Polish Jews between the two world wars. Few on the Israeli Right would be aware of the social and political conditions in interwar Europe, and in Poland in particular, that helped right-wing Zionism gain a mass following. Fewer still would recall that many of Jabotinsky's followers were drawn to him not simply because he stood out on the "Jewish street," but because he bore a striking resemblance to several political leaders on the European Right. When Reuven Feldschuh, Betar's first national leader in Poland, insisted in the 1920s that Zionists should "refuse to [be] led by the leash of democracy,"[70] he likely had more in mind than the dangers of democracy in Mandate Palestine, where Jews were a minority. Like other Betar leaders, he would have also had in mind Poland's Sanacja regime, whose authoritarian leaders insisted that democracy needed to be suspended, or at the very least postponed, to create a strong unified state and defeat the nation's enemies.

When Polish Jewry enter the historical imagination of Israeli politicians, it is to commemorate their tragic fate. The Holocaust looms large in Israel and plays a critical role in government-led efforts to build and maintain Israeli national identity.[71] The horrific deaths of Jews during the Holocaust are often depicted as proof of the danger and futility of Jewish life in the Diaspora. Those who claim to be Jabotinsky's heirs insist that he had foreseen this danger. When they invoke Polish Jewry, they most often recall a speech Jabotinsky delivered in August 1938 to a Jewish audience in Warsaw. Promoting his Evacuation Plan, Jabotinsky pleaded, "I warn you incessantly that a catastrophe is coming closer ... that you, dear brothers and sisters, do not see the volcano which will soon begin to spit its all-consuming lava.... Let anyone save himself as long as there is still time, and time there is very little."[72] To sustain the myth that Jabotinsky predicted the Holocaust, his supporters ignore his correspondence and public speeches in the winter, spring, and summer of 1939, which make clear that he was convinced that the Third Reich's army was weak and would be unable to launch a full-scale war across the continent. When he conceived of catastrophe, Jabotinsky mostly imagined antisemitic attempts to destroy the economic life of Jews, not a systematic program for genocide.[73]

Among those on the Israeli Right to invoke Jabotinsky and the fate of Polish Jewry during the Holocaust is Prime Minister Binyamin Netanyahu. As Israeli and Palestinian leaders were meeting to negotiate the terms for the 1993 Oslo Accords, Netanyahu, who had recently been appointed the leader of the Likud party, used Jabotinsky's speech in August 1938 to offer a stern warning. Just as Betar members in Poland had done decades before, he lifted a passage from Jabotinsky's speech, placed it in a new context, and in doing so reshaped its meaning. Netanyahu began by recalling his first visit to Poland in 1987. Reflecting on his visit to Auschwitz-Birkenau, he asked, "How did an entire people arrive at a state where they were herded quietly to the slaughter, unable to resist the monstrous assault on their persons and their collective existence?"[74] Polish Jewry, he continued, bore some responsibility for the horrors that awaited them:

> As the doctrines of modern pacifism emerged, many Jews rushed to embrace them, pretending they could transform into a universal virtue what had always been a unique vulnerability of the Jews. That the Jews "would not" (could not) resort to arms, that they would not "demean" themselves by "stooping to violence," was taken to be a clear sign of their moral superiority over other peoples who were not similarly constrained. Once leading segments of Jewish opinion in Europe had transformed Jewish weakness into a positive good, the Jewish people's chances of escaping its fate reached a new low.

Immediately following this passage, Netanyahu writes, "Of all Zionist leaders, Jabotinsky was virtually alone in seeing where all this was leading." It is here that he brings his readers to Warsaw, 1938, where Jabotinsky, in Netanyahu's rendition, stands before "Poland's three million Jews, almost none of whom were to survive the war."[75] With Netanyahu's careful selection and placement of the speech, Jabotinsky's call for Polish Jews to save themselves is no longer just a call for emigration. It is a blistering critique of "Jewish pacifism" and a call to arms.

Netanyahu has Jabotinsky posthumously endorsing Netanyahu's vision for the history and legacy of Jews in Poland. Polish Jewry, in Netanyahu's view, were not only to blame for failing to flee Poland to the Jewish state-in-the-making. No less tragic was the "fact" that "the Jewish people remained largely docile during the period between the two world wars, as their patrimony and national rights were progressively whittled away and as millions of their fellow Jews were being imperiled."[76] In Netanyahu's retelling, Jabotinsky's message to Polish Jewry in 1938 is also a critical warning to Israelis: surrounded by hostile neighbors and internal threats, Jews have no other choice but to live by the sword and be prepared to unleash violence against their enemies within and beyond the state's borders. If they refuse to do so, they will be fated, like Polish Jewry, to bear some responsibility for their own annihilation.

At least on the legacy of Polish Jewry, the various factions of the Israeli Right seem to agree.

NOTES

Introduction

1. According to the 1931 government census, which relied on linguistic criteria, Poles constituted 68.9 percent of Poland's population, with Ukrainians making up 13.9 percent, Jews 8.6 percent, Belarusians 3.1 percent, and Germans 2.3 percent. The remaining 3.2 percent comprised Lithuanians, Russians, Czechs, and *tutejszi* (locals), those without a defined national identity. See Porter-Szűcs, *Poland in the Modern World*, 126–27.

2. File 16, p. 95, collection 1183/0, in Archiwum Akt Nowych (Archive of Modern Records), Warsaw (hereafter AAN).

3. "Lochem ha-machteret she-hegi'a la-tsameret" *Ma'ariv la-no'ar*, May 31, 1977; Begin, "Sheloshah devarim," 249–51; Dolev, "Leilot levanim, re'ayon 'im Menachem Begin, *Ma'ariv la-no'ar*, June 10, 1977; and Shilon, *Begin: A Life*, 93, 265–66.

4. Begin, "Sheloshah devarim," 249. Begin's biographers tend to accept his depictions of life in Poland. See Grozbard, *Menahem Begin*, 13–25; Hirschler and Eckman, *Menachem Begin*, 17–26; Gervasi, *Life and Times*, 80–81, 87; and Perlmutter, *Life and Times*, 24–41.

5. These membership numbers are taken from records of the Revisionist Party in 1933, the same year as Begin's speech in Kobryń. See *Igrot*, December 1 1933, 13, cited in Shtain-Ashkenazi, *Betar be-erets Yisra'el*, 3.

6. See file 12t.11, p. 200, in AMZHP/1537, collection 2/1378/0, AAN; and file 14, p. 197, Mf1749, collection 2/1380/0, AAN.

7. See, for example, file 3, p. 72, in collection 1186/0, AAN.

8. File 12t.11, p. 199a, 2/1378/0, AAN. See also "Tsu der idisher efentlikhkayt in radom," *Haynt*, June 29, 1933.

9. For overviews of the Sanacja's policies and practices, see Polonsky, *Politics in Independent Poland*, 147–390; Rothschild, *Piłsudski's Coup d'Etat*, 157–372; and Paruch, *Myśl polityczna obozu piłsudczykowskiego*.

10. Shtain-Ashkenazi, *Betar be-erets Yisra'el*, 3; and Remba, *Shnatayim*, 2.

11. See, for example, Koestler, *Arrow in the Blue*, 115–20; and Weizmann, *Trial and Error*, 63.

12. For a concise biography of Jabotinsky, see Halkin, *Jabotinsky: A Life*. For an overview of the Revisionist movement, see Shavit, *Jabotinsky and the Revisionist Movement*; and Shindler, *Rise of the Israeli Right*, 1–228.

13. Jabotinsky, "Oyfn pripetchik," *Haynt*, October 16, 1931.

14. "Trumpeldor's yortsayt," *Haynt*, March 2, 1928; "Shir Betar," *Hazit Ha'am*, March 22, 1932. For an analysis of the anthem, see Naor, "Jabotinsky's New Jew," 144–48.

15. In 1918, only thirty thousand Jews lived in the western provinces of Poznań, Pomorze, and Silesia, formerly under German rule. See Mendelsohn, *Jews of East Central Europe*, 18.

16. Ezra Mendelsohn's work remains the most useful introduction to Jewish politics in Poland between the two world wars. See ibid., 43–83; Mendelsohn, "Jewish Politics in Interwar Poland," 1–19; and Mendelsohn, *On Modern Jewish Politics*, especially 63–78.

17. On Jewish participation in the Polish parliament, see Rudnicki, *Żydzi w parlamencie II Rzeczypospolitej*.

18. For a detailed case study of the activity of Zionist emissaries from Mandate Palestine in interwar Poland, see Yona, "Nihyeh kulanu halutsim," 9–71, 160–302.

19. Engel, "Poland from 1795 to 1939," 1400.

20. Shtain-Ashkenazi, *Betar be-erets Yisra'el*, 4. The Revisionist movement fared somewhat better during elections to the Elected Assembly (Asefat ha-nivharim), a representative organ of Jews in Mandate Palestine, winning 10,189 votes. See Shavit, *Jabotinsky and the Revisionist Movement*, 43.

21. See, for example, Livezeanu, *Cultural Politics in Greater Romania*; Hanebrink, *In Defense of Christian Hungary*; Ward, *Priest, Politician, Collaborator*; and Michlic, *Poland's Threatening Other*, 69–130.

22. For a panoramic view of collaboration between Nazis and radical right-wing groups across Europe, see Friedländer, *Years of Extermination*, 166–78, 212–32, 372–73, 640–42.

23. Paxton, *Anatomy of Fascism*, 9. On Jewish life in Fascist Italy, see Klein, "A Persistent Past," 40–90. By the late 1930s and through the Second World War, antisemitism had become a prominent feature of Italian Fascist policy. See Gordon, "Race," 296–316; Zimmerman, *Jews in Italy*, 71–208; and Rodogno, *Fascism's European Empire*, 368–74.

24. Edwards, "Foreign Office and Fascism," 153–61; Shorrock, "France and the Rise of Fascism in Italy," 591–610; Diggins, "Flirtation with Fascism," 487–506; and Mazower, *Dark Continent*, 63–77.

25. Useful surveys of the disintegration of parliamentary democracy across eastern Europe in the 1920s can be found in Polonsky, *Little Dictators*; and Rothschild, *East Central Europe*.

26. Czechoslovakia was the famous exception to this trend.

27. Wróbel, "Rise and Fall of Parliamentary Democracy," 110–64.

28. Brykczynski, *Primed for Violence*. Warsaw's Jews were well aware of the interplay between democracy and antisemitism long before the establishment of the Second Polish Republic. On the role of democratization in exacerbating relations between Catholic Poles and Polish Jews in the Russian Empire in the wake of the 1905 revolution, see Ury, *Barricades and Banners*, 214–60.

29. See, for example, Walicki, *Ruch syjonistyczny*, 133–48; Rudnicki, *Żydzi w parlamencie II Rzeczypospolitej*, 223–41; and Aleksiun, "Regards from My Shtetl," 57–71.

30. On the Sanacja's public "purification" campaign, see Plach, *Clash of Moral Nations*; and Hein, *Der Piłsudski-Kult*.

31. For brief introductions to fascist ideology in Mussolini's Italy, see De Grand, *Italian Fascism*; and Morgan, *Italian Fascism*.

32. This list does not intend to provide an iron-clad definition of fascism. For attempts to arrive at such a definition, and some of the debates they have generated, see Paxton, *Anatomy of Fascism*; Payne, *Fascism*; and Griffin, *Nature of Fascism*.

NOTES TO INTRODUCTION 257

33. The best-known work to identify boundaries separating authoritarianism from fascism is Linz, *Totalitarian and Authoritarian Regimes*. Sociologist Michael Mann argues that the differences between authoritarianism and fascism were of degree, not kind. See Mann, *Fascists*, 42–48.

34. See Stanley Payne's essays comparing Mussolini and Hitler's regimes in Payne, *Fascism*, 42–104. See also Corni, "State and Society," 279–95.

35. On these debates, see Rogger, "Afterthoughts," 575–89; De Felice, *Interpretations of Fascism*; Griffin, *International Fascism*, 1–39; and Paxton, *Anatomy of Fascism*, 3–23.

36. See Paxton, "Five Stages of Fascism," 4–7; and Paxton, *Anatomy of Fascism*, 15–18. Paxton's approach challenges the widely held view that one can identify an ideologically coherent "essence" of fascism. Among the most well-known works to take the approach that Paxton challenges are Griffin, *Nature of Fascism*; Sternhell, Sznajder, and Asheri, *Birth of Fascist Ideology*; Payne, *History of Fascism*; Eatwell, *Fascism*; and Laqueur, *Fascism*.

37. See, for example, Mussolini, *Doctrine of Fascism*, 11–12, 21–25; and Riley, *Civic Foundations of Fascism*, 3–6.

38. Most accounts of the Revisionist movement's history written by its sympathizers are embedded within biographies of Jabotinsky. See Ben Baruch, *Z'abotinski, lohem ha-umah*; Nedava, *Z'abotinski be-hazon ha-dor*; Schechtman, *Rebel and Statesman*; Schechtman, *Fighter and Prophet*; and Katz, *Z'abo*. For histories of Betar and Revisionism written by former leaders of these movements, see Schechtman and Benari, *History of the Revisionist Movement*; and Ben-Yerucham, *Sefer Betar*. The best-known popular history of Revisionism that aimed to discredit the movement is Brenner, *Iron Wall*. For scholarly studies that seek to uncover a comprehensive Revisionist philosophy, see Bilski Ben-Hur, *Kol yachid hu melekh*; and Kaplan, *Jewish Radical Right*.

39. Shavit, *Me-rov li-medinah*; Shavit, *Jabotinsky and the Revisionist Movement*; Heller, "Ha-monizm shel ha-matara o ha-monizm shel ha-emtsa'im?," 315–69; Heller, *Stern Gang*, 1–58; Zouplna, "Vladimir Jabotinsky and the Split within the Revisionist Union," 35–63; Weitz, "Revisionist Movement and Democracy," 185–204; Shindler, *Triumph of Military Zionism*; Shindler, *Rise of the Israeli Right*, 79–191; and Natkovich, *Ben 'ananei zohar*.

40. I borrow this term from Shindler, *Rise of the Israeli Right*, 97.

41. For examples of these approaches, see Heller, *Stern Gang*, 6; Zouplna, "Vladimir Jabotinsky and the Split within the Revisionist Union," 36, 51; Shindler, *Triumph of Military Zionism*, 199–212; and Capkova, "Piłsudski or Masaryk?," 211.

42. Stanislawski, *Zionism and the Fin de Siècle*, 116–202.

43. Jabotinsky, "Yo, brekhn," *Haynt*, November 4, 1932.

44. Ya'akov Na'or, in "Hemshekh erev zikhronot betar Grodno," collection T-32/271, Goldstein-Goren Diaspora Research Center Archive, Tel Aviv (hereafter DRC).

45. Yosef Klarman, "Hadar," *Madrikh Betar*, October 1933, 24.

46. Jabotinsky, *Ra'ayon betar*, 3.

47. See, for example, "Der yudisher Mussolini," *Naye Folktsaytung*, January 4, 1929; "Tsum fashistishn onfal," *Bafrayung Arbeter Shtime*, October 26, 1928; "Nider mitn fashistn revisionism," *Bafrayung Arbeter Shtime*, October 28, 1932; and "Oyb nisht nokh nideriker," *Unzer Frayhayt*, November 1932, 1. On the rise of the phrase "Vladimir Hitler" among Labor Zionists, see Teveth, *Ben-Gurion*, 414–15.

48. Y. Grinboym, "Untern frishn ayndruk," *Haynt*, July 11, 1933.

49. Ben Shlomo, "Jabotinsky ferbreytet zayn operatsions baze," *Haynt*, July 17, 1933.

50. "Ongehoybn zikh di yuvl-fayerungen fun yidishn legion," *Der Nayer Veg*, August [date unknown], 1932, 15; "Di legion-fayerungen in poyln," *Der Nayer Veg*, September 18, 1932, 15.

51. See, for example, file 12t.11, p. 163, AAN; and file 3, p. 72, in collection 1186/o, AAN.

52. For descriptions of the event, see "Der betar kinus in kroke," *Ha-medina*, September 9, 1935.

53. On these paramilitary programs, see Odziemkowski, *Armia i społeczeństwo*, 87–98; and Kęsik, *Naród pod bronią*, 81–96.

54. For a detailed account of interactions between the Polish government and the Revisionist movement between 1935 and 1939, see Weinbaum, *Marriage of Convenience*; and Tzur, "Yechasim mesukanim," 390–402.

55. See, for example, Melzer, *No Way Out*, 15–94; Heller, *On the Edge of Destruction*, 77–142; Rudnicki, *Obóz Narodowo Radykalny*; Tomaszewski, "Role of Jews in Polish Commerce," 141–57; Michlic, *Poland's Threatening Other*; and Polonsky, "Why did they hate Tuwim and Boy so much?," 189–209.

56. Porter-Szűcs, *Faith and Fatherland*, 295–314.

57. Rudnicki, "Anti-Jewish Legislation in Interwar Poland," 148–70.

58. Moss, "Thinking with Restriction," 205–24.

59. See especially Landau-Czajka, *Syn będzie Lech*. On the increasing use of Polish among Jews in interwar Poland, see Steffen, *Jüdische Polonität*, 49–56; and Heller, *On the Edge of Destruction*, 211–32.

60. For a discussion of the Polish public school system and acculturation, see Bacon, "National Revival, Ongoing Acculturation," 71–92; Kassow, "Communal and Social Change in the Polish Shtetl," 39–55; Martin, *Jewish Life in Cracow*, 121–49; Bassok and Novershtern, "Ma'arakhot ha-hinukh," 736–51; and Kijek, "Świadomość i socjalizacja polityczna," 255–304.

61. Kijek, "Was It Possible to Avoid 'Hebrew Assimilation'?," 111.

62. Mendelsohn, *Jews of East Central Europe*, 18.

63. Shanes, *Diaspora Nationalism and Jewish Identity*, 46–69.

64. Mendelsohn, *Jews of East Central Europe*, 21. For a detailed description of the differences and clashes between Zionist activists from Galicia and those from Congress Poland, see Mendelsohn, *Zionism in Poland*, 91–110, 146–47, 178–85, 213–22, 300–310.

65. For the case of Eastern Europe, see Mendelsohn, *On Modern Jewish Politics*, 103–8.

66. Y. Grinboym, "Yalduti," 55, cited in Mendelsohn, *Zionism in Poland*, 345. When writing in Polish, Grinboym would spell his last name "Grünbaum." For consistency, I have chosen in this book to use the transliterated spelling of his name used in Yiddish- and Hebrew-language publications.

67. See, for example, Mendelsohn, *On Modern Jewish Politics*, 104; and Yona, "Nihyeh kulanu halutsim," 174.

68. Nur, *Eros and Tragedy*, 1–43.

69. Kijek, "Was It Possible to Avoid 'Hebrew Assimilation'?," 117–32.

70. The concept of Gegenwartsarbeit, that is, "work for the present" to help obtain rights for Jews living in the Diaspora, was first incorporated into the Russian Zionist Federation's program in 1906. On the pragmatic uses of expressing Polish patriotism in the Polish-language Jewish daily press, see Landau-Czajka, *Polska—to nie oni*, 98–119.

71. Ibid., 118–30.

72. I borrow the phrase "ticket of admission" from Lichtenstein, *Zionism in Interwar Czechoslovakia*, 3.

73. Landau-Czajka, *Polska—to nie oni*, 101, 120.

74. Weinbaum, *Marriage of Convenience*; and Snyder, *Black Earth*, 58–76.

75. Shamir, *Summing Up*, 2, 6.

76. Seweryn Liwa, "Dwie Ojczyzny," *Chad-Ness*, May 1939, 13.

77. See, for example, "Protokol shel ha-pgishah ha-rishonah ha-glilit shel Brit Trumpeldor," March 1929, folder P153-2/1, Archives of the Jabotinsky Institute (hereafter JI), Tel Aviv; and "Pilsudski ha'emtan," *Metsuda*, June 10, 1938. See also Ya'akov Shavit's pioneering article on the Revisionist movement's use of "Polish models" for inspiration. Shavit, "Politics and Messianism," 229–46.

78. Yosef Klarman, "Fun vokh tsu vokh," *Unzer Velt*, March 13, 1936.

79. Esden-Tempska, "National and Civic Education," 299, 301.

80. Paruch, *Od konsolidacji państwowej*, 93–360.

81. Rezmer, "Służba wojskowa Żydów," 97–110; Michlic, *Poland's Threatening Other*, 88–93; and Ciancia, "Poland's Wild East," 117–18.

82. See, for example, Henschel and Stach, "Nationalisierung und Pragmatismus," 165–86; Stach, "Minderheitenpolitik der Zweiten Polnischen Republik," 394–412; Schenke, *Nationalstaat und nationale Frage*; and Mironowicz, *Białorusini i Ukraińcy*.

83. See, for example, Cohen, *Politics of Ethnic Survival*; King, *Budweisers into Czechs and Germans*; Judson, *Guardians of the Nation*; Zahra, *Kidnapped Souls*; and Ciancia, "Poland's Wild East." For a useful overview of this approach to nationalism, see Judson and Rozenblit, "Constructing Nationalities in East Central Europe," 1–18. For studies of Jewish nationalism adopting this approach, see Shanes, *Diaspora Nationalism and Jewish Identity*; Klein-Pejšová, *Mapping Jewish Loyalties*; and Lichtenstein, *Zionism in Interwar Czechoslovakia*.

84. There is a vast literature on this topic for Britain, France, and Germany. On European efforts to mobilize youth, see Gillis, *Youth and History*, 95–183. On education, see Maynes, *Schooling in Western Europe*. On France, see Alaimo, "Shaping Adolescence in the Popular Milieu," 419–38. On Germany, see Peukert, *Grenzen der Sozialdisziplinierung*; Elkar, "Battle for the Young," 92–104; and Linton, *Who Has the Youth, Has the Future*. On Britain, see Gillis, "Evolution of Juvenile Delinquency in England," 96–126.

85. Pomfret, "Youth Movements in Europe," 139–42. On the Wandervogel, see Laqueur's classic study, *Young Germany*. On French Catholic youth organizations, see Whitney, *Mobilizing Youth*. On the Boy Scouts in Britain, see Springhall, *Youth, Empire, and Society*. On the Polish case, see Sikorski, *Szkice z dziejów harcerstwa polskiego*.

86. Whitney, *Mobilizing Youth*, 17–29; Donson, *Youth in a Fatherless Land*; and Wohl, *Generation of 1914*.

87. The text most frequently cited in the interwar period on the value of crowd psychology and propaganda was Le Bon, *Psychologie des foules*. See Nye, *Origins of Crowd Psychology*; Fritzsche, *Rehearsals for Fascism*; and Rossol, "Performing the Nation," 616–38.

88. For a broad overview of these movements, see Kligsberg, "Di yidishe yugnt-bavegung," 137–228. For histories of several of these movements, see Oppenheim, *Tenuat he-haluts be-Polin*; Hertz, *Di geshikhte fun a yugnt*; Bacon, *Politics of Tradition*, 118–41; Jacobs, *Bundist Counterculture*, 8–61; Kaniel, *Yomrah u-ma'as*, 75–178; and Tzur, *Lifnei bo ha-afelah*.

89. Important new studies of Jewish youth in interwar Poland include Kijek, "Świadomość i socjalizacja polityczna"; and Yona, "Nihyeh kulanu halutsim."

90. In addition to the work of Kamil Kijek and Rona Yona, see Steinlauf, "Jewish Politics and Youth Culture in Interwar Poland," 91–104; Landau-Czajka, *Syn będzie Lech*; Kaniel, "Ben hilonim, mesoratiyim ve-ortodoksim," 75–106; and Moss, "Negotiating Jewish Nationalism," 390–436.

91. On the autobiography contest and YIVO's Youth Research Division, see Kirshenblatt-Gimblett, "Coming of Age in the Thirties," 1–104; Cała, "Wstęp," 18–50; Kijek, "Max Weinreich," 25–55; Bassok, "Mavo," 7–25; and Kuznitz, *YIVO and the Making of Modern Jewish Culture*, 149–54.

92. An important exception to this trend is the work of Samuel Kassow. See Kassow, "Community and Identity in the Interwar Shtetl," 198–220; and Kassow, "The Shtetl in Interwar Poland," 121–39.

93. On Jewish women in interwar Poland, see Bacon, "Woman? Youth? Jew?," 3–28; Mickute, "Modern, Jewish, and Female"; and Mickute, "Making of the Zionist Woman," 137–62.

94. On the autobiographies' accounts of factors drawing Jewish youth into particular political movements, see Steinlauf, "Jewish Politics and Youth Culture in Interwar Poland," 91–104; Kirshenblatt-Gimblett, Moseley, Stanislawski, introduction to *Awakening Lives*, xi–xlii; Bassok, "Tenu'ot ha-no'ar ha-yehudiyot," 769–79; and Kijek, "Świadomość i socjalizacja polityczna," 533–81.

95. Mendelsohn, "Jewish Politics in Poland," 10.

96. See, for example, Zahra, *Kidnapped Souls*; and Bjork, *Neither German nor Pole*, 59–71.

97. See Paxton, *Anatomy of Fascism*, 121; Neumann, *Communist Youth League*; and Kunicki, *Between the Brown and the Red*, 20–27.

98. See, for example, Karl Mannheim's 1928 essay "The Problem of Generations," 276–322.

99. Weinreich, *Der veg tsu unzer yugnt*, 9. See also Heller, *On the Edge of Destruction*, 237–40.

100. Weinreich, *Der veg tsu unzer yugnt*, 207–19; on political radicalization among Polish Jewish youth in the 1930s, see Kijek, "Świadomość i socjalizacja polityczna," especially 629–47, 682–717.

101. Schatz, "Jews and the Communist Movement," 17.

102. On the various conflicts between Tse'irei Mizrahi (Mizrahi Youth), the Torah ve-Avoda (Torah and Work) movement, and the Mizrahi organization, see Kaniel, *Yomrah u-ma'as*, 86–89.

103. Ben-Eliezer, *Making of Israeli Militarism*, ix–50. See also Shapira, *Land and Power*, 219–370; and Goldstein, *From Fighters to Soldiers*.

Chapter 1: Jabotinsky Encounters Polish Jewish Youth

1. "Powitanie Żabotyńskiego w Warszawie," *Dziennik Warszawski*, February 18, 1927, 4.

2. Vladimir Jabotinsky to Yoanna (Anya) Jabotinsky, February 19, 1927. Jabotinsky's letters are located in collection A1-2, JI. Many are available online: http://www.jabotinsky.org.

3. Vladimir Jabotinsky to Yoanna (Anya) Jabotinsky, March 10, 1927, in A1-2, JI.

4. Jabotinsky to Shlomo Jacobi, March 22, 1927; and Jabotinsky to Aharon Zvi Propes, March 25, 1927, both in A1-2, JI.

5. Vladimir Jabotinsky to Yoanna (Anya) Jabotinsky, March 21, 1927, in A1-2, JI.
6. "Protocols of the Revisionist Executive, Paris, 1925–1929," in G1/2, JI.
7. Vladimir Jabotinsky to Yoanna (Anya) Jabotinsky, February 27, 1927, in A1-2, JI.
8. Fritzsche, *Rehearsals for Fascism*; Ross, "Mass Politics and the Techniques of Leadership," 184–211; Grant, *Propaganda and the Role of the State*; Verhey, "Some Lessons of the War," 99–118; Canning, "Culture of Politics—Politics of Culture," 576–80; and Rossol, "Performing the Nation," 616–38.
9. Shukman, *War or Revolution*, 62–63. For overviews of the Jewish Legion's activity during the First World War, see Elam, *Ha-Gedudim ha-'ivriyim*; and Keren and Keren, *We Are Coming, Unafraid*.
10. On Weizmann's diplomatic activity during the First World War, see Reinharz, *Chaim Weizmann*.
11. Jabotinsky to various institutions of the Yishuv in Eretz Yisra'el, May 5, 1920, in A1-2, JI.
12. Jabotinsky, "Hefker," 103.
13. Ibid., 102, 105.
14. Ibid., 105.
15. Gra'ur, *Kitve Ze'ev Z'abotinski*, 202–35.
16. Zouplna, "Beyond a One-Man Show," 401–32.
17. Jabotinsky, "On the Iron Wall (1923)," 257–63.
18. Menachem Brem, interview with Aharon Zvi Propes, April 6, 1977, in EP-13, JI.
19. Jabotinsky, "Ha-Hashmona'i ha-riga'i," 191.
20. A. Disentchik, "Di fareynikte yugnt, antviklung un mehus fun Brit Trumpeldor," *Massuot*, January 10, 1928, 5–6; and Ben-Yerucham, *Sefer Betar*, 1:30–34.
21. Jabotinsky to Paul Diamant, December 8, 1923, in A1-2, JI.
22. Ibid. Emphasis mine.
23. Jabotinsky to Ya'akov Hoffman, September 14, 1924, in A1-2, JI.
24. Jabotinsky to Abraham Recanati, September 15, 1924, in A1-2, JI.
25. Eliav, *Zikhronot min hayamin*, 23.
26. "Sefer ha-protokolim shel yeshivot va'ad ha-rashim ba-histadrut 'al shem Yosef Trumpeldor," April 20, 1926–December 7, 1926, in B29-2/2, JI.
27. *Conference des sionistes revisionnistes, tenue à Paris du 26 au 30 Avril 1925* (Thessaloniki: l'Association des Sionistes revisionnistes de Salonique, 1925), in G1-18, JI.
28. Executive council meeting, May 15, 1925, "Sefer ha-protokolim shel yeshivot va'ad ha-rashim ba-histadrut al shem yosef trumpeldor," in B29-2/2, JI.
29. See collection of protocols and decisions from the First World Conference of the Revisionist Movement, G1-18, JI.
30. Natkovich, *Ben 'ananei zohar*, 17–48, 103–11, 159–64; and Shindler, *Rise of the Israeli Right*, 14–31.
31. "Basta," *Rassvet*, June 28, 1925, 3–5; and Zouplna, "Beyond a One-Man Show," 425.
32. Jabotinsky to Oscar Gruzenberg, November 12, 1925, in A1-2, JI.
33. Jabotinsky, *Ma rotsim tsionim revizyonistim?*, 20.
34. "Hartsa'ah be-migrash ha-macabi be-tel aviv," *Davar*, October 31, 1926.
35. Schechtman and Benari, *History of the Revisionist Movement*, 42.
36. "Resolutions," in *Conference des Sionistes Revisionists*, 30–36.

37. Jabotinsky to Meir Grossman, July 7, 1926, in A1-2, JI.

38. "Yediot ahronot," *Doar Hayom*, May 13, 1925.

39. Katz, *Lone Wolf*, 2:993–98.

40. "Hartsa'a la-no'ar be-ulam kolno'a be-tel aviv," *Ha'aretz*, October 31, 1926.

41. Vladimir Jabotinsky to Yoanna (Anya) Jabotinsky, October 26, 1926, in A1-2, JI.

42. Jabotinsky to Zvi Bonfeld, December 6, 1926, in A1-2, JI.

43. On German Jewish perceptions of eastern European Jews, see Aschheim, *Brothers and Strangers*.

44. "Protocols of the Revisionist Executive, Paris, 1925–1929," G1/2, MJ.

45. Jabotinsky to Shlomo Jacobi, September 11, 1925, in A1-2, JI.

46. Many Zionist spokesmen in Congress Poland opposed Jabotinsky's outspoken criticism of Polish nationalists. They feared that his critiques of Polish nationalism, as well as his warning that the region's Jews might throw their support behind Russians should Polish anti-semitism persist, would only further convince Polish nationalists of the danger of Jews within their midst. See Engel, "Ha-she'elah ha-polanit veha-tenu'ah ha-tsiyonit," 59–82. For Jabotinsky's articles, see "Homo Homini Lupus," *Oddeskie novosti*, July 18, 1910, published in Hebrew in Eri Jabotinsky, *Ketavim*, 9:255–65; and "Resistance," *Rassvet*, March 15, 1913, 5–9; March 22, 1913, 8–11; April 4, 1913, 23–27.

47. Vladimir Jabotinsky to Yoanna (Anya) Jabotinsky, October 5, 1925, in A1-2, JI.

48. Police report, pp. 40, 47, HM2/8665.2, in Central Archives for the History of the Jewish People, Jerusalem (hereafter CAHJP).

49. Ibid.

50. Jabotinsky to Aharon Propes, March 25, 1927, in A1-2, JI.

51. On Jewish-Ukrainian relations during this period, see Abramson, *Prayer for the Government*.

52. Police report, p. 58, HM2/8665.2, CAHJP.

53. Sikorski, *Szkice z dziejów harcerstwa polskiego*, 7–50.

54. Baden-Powell, *Scouting for Boys*; and Collins, *Character Factory*.

55. Małkowski, *Scouting jako system wychowania młodzieży*, 9.

56. Between the two world wars, Piłsudski's opponents on the Polish Right contested the sacralization of the Polish Legions. They focused instead on the wartime diplomatic campaigns of their leaders, which resulted in the inclusion of a demand for the restoration of an independent Poland in Woodrow Wilson's Fourteen Points. On the mythologization of the Polish Legions, see Biskupski, *Independence Day*, 7–21.

57. Kała, *W służbie Ojczyznie*.

58. Guż, "Realizacja programu przysposobienia wojskowego," 33–49.

59. See Mendelsohn, "From Assimilation to Zionism in Lvov," 521–34. It is critical to note that not all members of the acculturated Galician Jewish intelligentsia followed this political trajectory. Some opted instead for supporting the Polish Socialist Party (PPS). As Joshua Shanes has argued, many of these young Jews were politically promiscuous, frequently changing party affiliations. He has also demonstrated that the early leaders of Jewish nationalism in the region were also drawn from young Jews who had been raised in traditional homes. See Shanes, *Diaspora Nationalism and Jewish Identity*, 46–69.

60. Mintz, *Havle ne'urim*; Elkana Margalit, "Social and Intellectual Origins of Hashomer Hatzair," 25–46; and Nur, *Eros and Tragedy*, 1–29.

61. "Hashanim ha-rishonim be-Galitsyah," 6.
62. Police report, pp. 22–33, HM2/8665.2, CAHJP.
63. Bader, *Darki le-tsiyon*, 52.
64. Police report, p. 54, HM2/8665.2, CAHJP.
65. Glerter, "Kehillat Stanislawow," 291.
66. "Sprawozdanie sytuacyjne z ruchu zawodowego i społeczno-politycznego na terenie województwa stanisławowskiego za miesiąc czerwiec, 31 lipca 1925 r," Komenda Województwa Policji Państwowej w Stanisławowie, in file 1, 2019/0, AAN.
67. Ibid., 59; and Glerter, "Kehillat Stanislawow," 291.
68. "Ekronot brit ha-no'ar ha-ivri al shem Yosef Trumpeldor," *Massuot*, April 13, 1927, 16.
69. "Regulamin wewnętrzny, Związku Zrzeszeń Harcerzy Żydowskich im. Josefa Trumpeldora w Polsce," August 26, 1927, in B33-4/2, JI.
70. Over the course of his career as a Zionist activist, Feldschuh altered the spelling of his last name several times. In Polish-language documents, he occasionally used Feldszu or Feldszuh. When writing in Hebrew, he frequently used his nom de plume Reuven Ben-Shem. In the citations of his articles and pamphlets that follow, I use the name attached to each document. For consistency, I use Feldschuh in the main body of my text.
71. See Weinbaum, "Shaking the Dust Off," 7–44; and Prokop-Janiec, *Polish-Jewish Literature in the Interwar Years*, 16, 209–10.
72. Nur, "Relevance of Countercultures," 37.
73. See Shapira, "Black Night–White Snow," 144–71.
74. Zait, *Ha-utopia ha-shomrit*, 180–96.
75. Ben-Shem, *Yugend tsionizm*, 1.
76. Ha-shomer Ha-tahor/Ha-le'umi, "Biuletin #1," November 1927, file 4137, RG DD1, Central Zionist Archives, Jerusalem (hereafter CZA).
77. Reuven Ben-Shem, "Kana'ut," *Derekh Ha-shomer Ha-le'umi*, December 1927, 3–6.
78. See, for example, Ya'akov Rechtman and Aharon Kaplan, "Ha-shomer ha-tahor/ha-le'umi, ma hu?," *Derekh Ha-shomer Ha-le'umi*, December 1927, 9–13; Aharon Kaplan, "Ha-shomer ha-tahor (ha-le'umi) ve-hist. ha-tsioni," *Derekh Ha-shomer Ha-le'umi*, July 1928, 6.
79. Ben-Shem, *Betar be-Polanyah*, 7.
80. Corrsin, *Warsaw before the First World War*, 33.
81. See Silber, *Le'umiut shonah, ezrahut shavah!*
82. Perelman, *Moje przeżycia, spostrzeżenia*, 20.
83. Ibid., 3–19; and Perelman, *Rewizjonizm w Polsce*, 1–2.
84. Perelman, *Moje przeżycia, spostrzeżenia*, 20–25; and Perelman, *Rewizjonizm w Polsce*, 2–5.
85. Perelman to Jabotinsky, December 16, 1923, cited in Perelman, *Moje przeżycia, spostrzeżenia*, 31–32.
86. "Fun volominer 'hashachar,'" *Haynt*, April 22, 1925; and "Di fon fayerung fun gdud 'hashahar,'" *Haynt*, June 10, 1925.
87. "Di lag ba-omer fayerungen fun yudisher yugend in varshe," *Der Moment*, May 22, 1925.
88. Perelman, *Rewizjonizm w Polsce*, 8–9.
89. *Haszachar*, September 26, 1926, 2–5, 16–20 in PR1-124, JI.
90. Ibid., 11–15.

91. Perelman to Jabotinsky, December 16, 1923, cited in Perelman, *Moje przeżycia, spostrzeżenia*, 31–32.

92. Jabotinsky to Perelman, January 2, 1924, in A1-2, JI.

93. Jabotinsky to Ya'akov Cahan, August 21, 1925; December 30, 1925; April 22, 1926; July 27, 1926; August 11, 1926; September 9, 1926; September 24, 1926; and December 18, 1926, all in A1-2, JI.

94. Perelman, *Rewizjonizm w Polsce*, 47–53.

95. "Di rezolutsyes fun der 1-ter land-konferents fun di tsionisten-revizionisten in Poyln," *Haynt*, December 29, 1926.

96. Perelman, *Rewizjonizm w Polsce*, 52–58.

97. Rothschild, *Piłsudski's Coup d'Etat*, 47–154; and Polonsky, *Politics in Independent Poland*, 97–186.

98. Polonsky, *Politics in Independent Poland*, 186–233; Rothschild, *Piłsudski's Coup d'Etat*, 157–308; and Plach, *Clash of Moral Nations*.

99. Hein, *Der Piłsudski-Kult*, 46

100. Mazower, *Dark Continent*, 59.

101. See, for example, Bacon, "Poznanski Affair," 135–43.

102. Gitelman, *Century of Ambivalence*, 70–86. On efforts to create a Sovietized Jewish culture, see Gitelman, ibid., 88–113; Shneer, *Yiddish and the Creation of Soviet Jewish Culture*; and Shternshis, *Soviet and Kosher*.

103. See, for example, "Sprawozdanie Tygodniowe no 19, 6.5.28 do 12.5.28r," Wydział Bezpieczeństwo Publicznego, in Komisariat Rządu m. st. Warszawy, Wydział Bezpieczeństwo Publicznego, 109–10, 2/1402/297/VII-2, AAN.

104. Walicki, *Ruch syjonistyczny*, 133–48; and Rudnicki, *Żydzi w parlamencie*, 223–41.

105. "Sprawozdanie sytuacyjne za miesiąc wrzesień 1926 r," file 10, group 475/0, in Archiwum Państwowe w Warszawie (National Archives of Warsaw; hereafter APW).

106. *Haszachar*, 7.

107. Vladimir Jabotinsky to Anya Jabotinsky, March 10, 1927.

108. Ibid., February 19, 1927.

109. Ibid., February 27, 1927.

110. Jabotinsky to Ya'akov Cahan, March 4, 1927, in A1-2, JI.

111. Jabotinsky to Shlomo Jacobi, March 5, 1927, in A1-2, JI.

112. Ibid., May 8, 1927; and Jabotinsky to Ya'akov Hoffman, July 13, 1927, both in A1-2, JI.

113. Jabotinsky to the Hashmona'i Student Organization, November 14, 1927, in A1-2, JI.

114. Ya'akov Cahan to Vladimir Jabotinsky, May 22, 1927, in A1-3/15, 31, JI; and October 16, 1928, in A1-3/16/2, 73, JI.

115. Shavit, *Jabotinsky and the Revisionist Movement*, 37.

116. Grinboym quoted in Mendelsohn, *Zionism in Poland*, 263–64.

117. Ibid., 265–66.

118. Jabotinsky, "Anahnu ha-burganim," 211–17. On Jabotinsky's use of the term "bourgeoisie," see Shavit, *Jabotinsky and the Revisionist Movement*, 285.

119. Jabotinsky, "Der yuval gedank," *Haynt*, May 20, 1927; "Der Kremer," *Haynt*, June 5, 1927.

120. Jabotinsky, "Tguvot le-'inyane ha-yom," 222–25, originally published in *Rassvet*, June 5, 1927, 4–5.

121. Shindler, *Rise of the Israeli Right*, 69–79; and Goren, *Ha-imut ha-kove'a*.
122. "Wł. Żabotyński wśród dziennikarzy warszawskich," *Dziennik Warszawski*, February 20, 1927.
123. Ibid.
124. Jabotinsky, "Homo Homini Lupus"; "Resistance," *Rassvet*, March 15, 1913, 5–9; March 22, 1913, 8–11; April 4, 1913, 23–27.
125. Adolf Nowaczyński quoted in "Nowaczyński-Żabotyński," *Dziennik Warszawski*, February 24, 1927, and in "Nowaczyński o Żabotyńskim," *Nowy Dziennik*, February 27, 1927, 10.
126. Vladimir Jabotinsky to Anya Jabotinsky, February 27, 1927
127. Jabotinsky to Ya'akov Cahan, March 6, 1927, in A1-2, JI.
128. Jabotinsky to Aharon Propes, October 8, 1925, in A1-2, JI.
129. Ibid., March 25, 1927.
130. "Wł. Żabotyński wśród dziennikarzy warszawskich," *Dziennik Warszawski* 18 February 1927; "Wywiad sportowy z Żabotyńskim," *Dziennik Warszawski*, February 25, 1927.
131. Jabotinsky, *Samson the Nazarite*, 200–201.
132. See, for example, Stanislawski, *Zionism and the Fin de Siècle*, 221–27; Horowitz, introduction to *Vladimir Jabotinsky's Story of My Life*; and Natkovich, *Ben 'ananei zohar*, 179–200.
133. Jabotinsky to the youth of Włocławek, March 29, 1927, in A1-2, JI.
134. "A lokh in unzer natsionaler ertsiung," *Haynt*, December 26, 1927.
135. "2-ter tsuzamenfar fun tsionistn-revizyonistn in poyln, di groyse rede fun Vl. Jabotinsky," *Haynt*, December 30, 1927.
136. "Barikht iber di ershte poylishe ve'idah brit trumpeldor," *Massuot*, February 20, 1928, 3. See also "Di konferentz fun brit trumpeldor (haszahar)," *Haynt*, December 27, 1927; and "Din ve-heshbon fun der 1-ter konferentz fun 'brit trumpeldor' ('ha-shachar) in poyln," *Cyjon*, January 20, 1928, 10–12.
137. M. Lejzerowicz, "Nokh der konferentz," *Cyjon*, January 20, 1928, 2. Emphasis mine.
138. Ibid.
139. "Barikht iber di ershte poylishe ve'idah brit trumpeldor," 3–4.
140. Ibid., 5.
141. Ibid.
142. M. Lejzerowicz to the Revisionist Executive in Paris, April 7, 1929, in G1-9/9, JI.
143. Moshe Yoelson to Vladimir Jabotinsky, December 4, 1928, item 208, in A1-3/16/3, JI. See Betar Supreme Command, Correspondence with the World Executive, September 29, 1929; March 12, 1930; April 28, 1930; May 20, 1930; and September 18, 1930, in G2-4/1, JI.
144. Lubotzky, "Le-irgun ha-hanhaga ha-olamit be-atid," *Igrot Livne Betar*, October 12, 1928, 2.
145. "Zirkular 8, Union Des Sionistes-Revisionistes-Zentralburo," April 20, 1928, in G1-4/4, JI.

Chapter 2: Little Fascists?

1. Moshe Yoelson, "Die erste Weltpegischa der Brith-Trumpeldor, Warschau, 1–4.1.1929," in B1-14/14, JI; "Di impozante fayerlikhkayt fun brit-trumpeldor in varshe mit der bateyligung fun ze'ev jabotinsky," *Haynt*, January 1, 1929; "Der tsuzamenfar fun brit trumpeldor in varshe,"

Der Moment, January 1, 1929; "Nekhtige brit-trumpeldor-fayerungen in varshe," *Haynt*, January 2, 1929; "Światowa konferencja Org. 'Brith Trumpeldor,'" *Nowy Dziennik*, January 3, 1929; "Wszechświatowy Zjazd Org. Młodz. 'Brith Trumpeldor' w Warszawie," *Chwila*, January 5, 1929, 9; and "Ha-pgishah ha-'olamit ha-rishonah li-mfakde betar," *Igrot Livne Betar*, July 15, 1929, 3.

2. "Jabotinsky makht shtimung far der 5-ter aliya," *Naye folktsaytung*, January 2, 1929.

3. "Ph-leysh!," *Naye Folktsaytung*, January 4, 1929; "Der yudisher Mussolini," *Naye Folktsaytung*, January 4, 1929; and "Jabotinsky makht shtimung far der 5-ter aliya."

4. "Tsum fashistishn onfal," *Bafrayung Arbeter Shtime*, October 26, 1928.

5. See, for example, "Nider mitn fashistn revisionizm," *Bafrayung Arbeter Shtime*, October 28, 1932; and "Oyb nisht nokh nideriker," *Unzer Frayhayt*, November 1932, 1.

6. Quoted in H. Libertal, "Di roymishe yugnt," *Tel Hai*, May 2, 1930, 11.

7. Emma, "Pionirtum un verkraft (der brit trumpeldor)," *Tsiyonistishe Bleter*, July 26, 1929, 186.

8. The term was used by Betar members in Węgrów, describing the hostility they encountered in town from other Jewish organizations. "Fun unzer bavegung," *Tel Hai*, May 2, 1930, 15.

9. Ortega y Gasset, "Sobre el Fascismo" (1927), quoted in Passmore, *Fascism*, x.

10. Paxton, *Anatomy of Fascism*, 14.

11. Jabotinsky, "Trumpeldor's yortsayt."

12. D. Stabiecki, "Vos zaynen mir, mir revizyonistn?," *Der Emes*, November 20, 1928, 6–7.

13. Nietzsche, *Beyond Good and Evil*, 260.

14. Stabiecki, "Vos zaynen mir, mir revizyonistn?"

15. On the place of these ideals in Italian fascism, see Payne, *Fascism*, 42–51, 68–87; Payne, *History of Fascism*, 80–128; Lyttelton, *Seizure of Power*; and Mann, *Fascists*, 93–137.

16. Mussolini, *Doctrine of Fascism*, 19.

17. De Grand, *Italian Fascism*, especially 138–63.

18. Mussolini, *Doctrine of Fascism*, 11–12, 21–25.

19. Diary of Moshe Friedman, p. 10, in P-32, DRC.

20. Ze'ev Shem Tov, *Igrot Livne Betar*, September 12, 1928, 2.

21. Ze'ev Shem Tov "Le-birur ha-ra'ayon," *Igrot Livne Betar*, December 12, 1928, 4.

22. Ben-Yerucham, *Sefer Betar*, 1:281.

23. M. Lejzerowicz, "Di drite alpoylishe landes-konferents fun di tsionistn-revizyonistn," *Der Emes*, February 20, 1929, 5.

24. "Hatsa'at takanon brit ha-no'ar ha-ivri al-shem Trumpeldor," December 1929, in P153-3/1, JI.

25. "Din ve-heshbon fun dem 2-tn alpoylishn tsiyon. revizionistishn tsuzamenfar," *Tsiyon*, January 20, 1928, 7.

26. Ben-Shem, *Betar be-Polanyah*, 7.

27. "Fashistishn gevalt zikh araynreysn keyn nitso," *Haynt*, April 29, 1924; "Khuliganishe onfaln fun antisemitishe student oyf yuden," *Der Moment*, June 29, 1927; and "Der blutiger dinstik in varshe," *Der Moment*, May 2, 1928.

28. "Musolinis sharfe erklerung gegen antisemitizm," *Haynt*, November 23, 1927.

29. See, for example, "Fartraybt di idishe kolonizatsye dem araber fun bodn?," *Tel Hai*, April 1, 1930, 13; and Ya'akov Cahan's speech at the Third All-Polish Revisionist Conference, reported in Lejzerowicz, "Di drite alpoylishe landes-konferents," 2–3.

30. Ben-Shem, *Betar be-Polanyah*, 4.

31. Vladimir Jabotinsky to Meir Grossman, January 10, 1929, in A1-2, JI.

32. Yoelson, "Die erste Weltpegischa der Brith-Trumpeldor," in B1-14/14, JI.
33. Jabotinsky, "Vegn militarizm," *Haynt*, January 15, 1929.
34. Jabotinsky, "Brit Trumpeldor," *Rassvet*, January 27, 1929, cited in Nedava, *Ha-revizyonizem ha-tsiyoni be-hitgabshuto*, 294–98.
35. Jabotinsky, "Zionist Fascism," *Zionist*, June 25, 1926.
36. Jabotinsky to Weizmann, July 21, 1922, in A1-2, JI.
37. Jabotinsky to Mussolini, July 21, 1922, in Alfonso Pacifici Archive, P172/110, CAHJP. The letter is cited in Pinto, "Between *imago* and *res*," 93.
38. Wolfgang von Weisl to Jabotinsky, January 20, 1927, in A1-3/15, JI; Abba Achimeir to Jabotinsky, October 25, 1928, in A1-3/16/2, JI; and Haim Vardi to Jabotinsky, May 30, 1929, in A1-3/17/2, JI.
39. Achimeir to Jabotinsky, October 25, 1928.
40. Jabotinsky to Meir Grossman, November 28, 1928, in A1-2, JI.
41. Zelig Lerner, "Rekhtlekhe gevaldtetikayt," *Tel Hai*, February 1930, 4.
42. "Rozmowa z wodzem rewizjonizmu," *Chwila*, January 4, 1929, 11. See also "Ha-bhirot be-polin," Nedava, *Ha-revizyonizem ha-tsiyoni be-hitgabshuto*, 273–75, originally published in *Rassvet*, March 18, 1928.
43. Jabotinsky to Miriam Lang, August 27, 1930, in A1-2, JI.
44. Jabotinsky to Haim Vardi, May 2, 1929, in A1-2, JI.
45. See Hart, *Social Science and the Politics of Modern Jewish Identity*; and Hart, "Introductory Essay."
46. Gordon, "Race."
47. "Ha-geza' she-baruah," *Doar Hayom*, May 24, 1929, 2.
48. On the rise of the Histadrut, see Tahor, "Histadrut," 473–508. For a concise and insightful history of Ben-Gurion's rise to power, see Shapira, *Ben-Gurion*.
49. Jabotinsky to Joseph Schechtman, May 30, 1929, in A1-2, JI.
50. Jabotinsky to Chaim Blilowski, May 2, 1929, in A1-2, JI.
51. *Report of the Commission on the Palestine Disturbances*, 145.
52. For a fascinating anatomy of the riots and their impact, see Cohen, *Year Zero*. For Cohen's take on Jabotinsky's response, see 221–22.
53. Jabotinsky to Alexander Poliakov, August 28, 1929, in A1-2, JI.
54. "Brif tsu der eksekutive," *Haynt*, September 9, 1929; "Jews in Palestine: Revisionists and the Mandate; To the editor of the *Times*," *London Times*, September 6, 1929; Jabotinsky to Richard Lichtheim, September 17, 1929, in A1-2, JI; "Matsavenu," *Doar Hayom*, October 4, 1929; "Vos iz geshen un vos hot gemuzt geshen," *Der Nayer Veg*, October 13, 1929; and "She'elot ha-bitahon," *Doar Hayom*, October 17, 1929.
55. Jabotinsky to Lichtheim, September 17, 1929; and Jabotinsky to Meir Grossman, October 18, 1929, in A1-2, JI.
56. Jabotinsky, "On the Iron Wall (1923)," 257–63.
57. "Dvar jabotinski el ha-Yishuv 'al matsav ha-tsiyonut," *Doar Hayom*, December 24, 1929.
58. Jabotinsky, "On the Iron Wall (1923)," 258. When addressing British officials and the English-reading public from the mid-1930s until his death in 1940, Jabotinsky on occasion affirmed that the Revisionist movement was committed to protecting the minority rights of Palestinian Arabs in a future Jewish state. See, for example, Jabotinsky, *The Jewish War Front*, 212–220.
59. "Dvar jabotinski el ha-Yishuv 'al matsav ha-tsiyonut."

60. Halkin, *Jabotinsky: A Life*, 167.
61. "Yoman," *Tel Hai*, December 1, 1929, 3.
62. Ibid.
63. "Pkudah alef: Tsu ale kenim fun Betar in Poyln," February 26, 1929, in B33-4/2, JI.
64. I. Dralicz, "Tsu aykh (A briv tsu di bney betar)," *Tel Hai*, December 1, 1929, 3.
65. Propes, *Eynike onvayzungen*.
66. See Trumpeldor's reprinted 1918 program for He-Halutz, "Hehalutz, zayn mehus un zayne oyfgabn," republished in *Massuot*, April 1, 1928, 3–10.
67. Ibid., 7–8.
68. Ibid., 9.
69. Zerubavel, *Recovered Roots*, 39–47, 84–95, 147–77.
70. Jabotinsky, *Story of the Jewish Legion*, 90.
71. Jabotinsky, "Shalosh he'arot," *Massuot*, April 1, 1928, 10.
72. Trumpeldor, "He-Halutz," 8.
73. Jabotinsky, "Vegn militarizm."
74. Merchavia, *Likrat Ha-medina*, 8.
75. Ibid., 13.
76. H. Merchavia, "Mitokh sihot," *Tel Hai*, December 1, 1929, 13.
77. Propes, *Eynike onvayzungen*, 6
78. Propes, *Dos lebn fun yosef trumpeldor*, 2.
79. "Betar un di bavegung eretz-yisrael ha'ovedet," *Tel Hai*, August 1930, 9.
80. See, for example, "11 Adar 1920–11 Adar 1930," *Tel Hai*, March 7, 1930, 1; and "Ahim va-ahayot!," ibid., 3.
81. "Di erefnung fun'm velktlekhn tsuzamenfar fun 'brit trumpeldor,'" *Haynt*, January 3, 1929.
82. "Chaluc w pojęciu Trumpeldora," *Jardenu*, [date unknown], 1931, no pagination, in B33-6/6, JI.
83. "Ve-sha'atnez lo ya'aleh aleha," *Haynt*, January 18, 1929.
84. Merchavia, *Likrat Ha-medina*, 4–5.
85. Merchavia, "Me'az ve'ad henah," *Tel Hai*, March 7, 1930, 5.
86. "Midivre Yosef Trumpeldor," ibid., 10.
87. Jabotinsky, "Trumpeldor's yortsayt," i–vi.
88. Ibid., iv–v.
89. Ibid., iii.
90. Ibid., ii.
91. Ibid., i–ii.
92. Jabotinsky, "Garibaldi," *Tel Hai*, December 1, 1929, 10–12. Originally published in *Oddeskie novosti*, January 14, 1912.
93. Lejzerowicz, "Kidush hashem," *Tel Hai*, March 7, 1930, 7.
94. Ibid. Emphasis mine.
95. See, for example, Shapira, "Religious Motifs of the Labor Movement," 250–71; and Myers, *Reinventing the Jewish Past*.
96. The use of synagogues by Zionist political activists extends into the late nineteenth century; early Zionist activists in Russia used the break between afternoon and evening prayers to present their views to the synagogue congregation. See Goldshtain, *Ben tsiyonut medinit le-tsiyonut ma'asit*, 53–60.

97. "Fun unzer bavegung."
98. "Ken betar varkovich," in P153-3/9, JI.
99. Shapira, "Religious Motifs of the Labor Movement," 259.
100. Ben-Szem, *Tarshim tokhnit ha-'avodah*, 2–3; and Ben-Szem, *Yugend tsionizm*, 1–27.
101. "Di erefnung funm veltlikhn tsuzamenfar."
102. The prohibitions appear in Leviticus 19:19 and Deuteronomy 22:5 and 22:9–11.
103. "Ve-sha'atnez lo ya'aleh aleha," *Haynt*, January 18, 1929.
104. "Der yovel gedank," *Haynt*, May 20, 1927; see also "Di sotsiale filozofie fun tanakh iberkhazrungen," *Haynt*, April 26 and May 6, 1932.
105. See, for example, Y. Almoni, "Ha-sindikalizm ha-fashisti be-italia," *Madrikh Betar* October 5, 1933, 31–36; and H. Melech Merchavia, "Ha-medina ke-matara sofit," *Mishmar Ha-yarden* 9 (1935).
106. "Hora'ot le-avodah," *'Avodatenu* [month unknown] 1931, 13–14.
107. "Unzer manhig," *Madrikh Betar*, April 1933, 16–17.
108. Fishman, *Rise of Modern Yiddish Culture*, 108.
109. A. Goldin, "Yehuda ha-makabi," *'Avodatenu*, December 1932, 14.
110. Propes, "Hannukah," *Tel Hai*, December 25, 1929, 5.
111. The original account is found in the first book of Maccabees, written in the latter half of 2 BCE.
112. Propes, "Hannukah." In the original text, the passage that begins with "lit the menorah" is set in bold typeface and a larger font.
113. Ibid.
114. See, for example, "Unzer yugend," *Der Emes*, August 17, 1928; "Protokol der 8, Sitzung Mittwoch, den 13, August 1930," in Ha-ve'ida ha-olamit ha-4: protokolim ve-hahlatot, 10–14.8.1930, G2-7/1/3, JI; Propes, "Brit hatsohar un betar," *Tel Hai*, August 1930, 4; and *Brit Trumpeldor*, 45.
115. M. Buchweitz, "Faszyzm, socjalizm, a antysemityzm," *Trybuna Narodowa*, June 2, 1936; and "Albion czy Roma," *Chad-Ness*, January 1938.
116. See, for example, a local journal from Wołożyn in 1929, which contained several articles that retold the myth of Trumpeldor's death in order to promote these values. *Degalenu: Yarhon le-inyanei ha-noar ha-tsiyoni* (1929), in B33-6/7, JI. See also "Unzer ideal," in *Le-matara* (Tarczyn: undated), and "Yidishe kinder," in *Unzer Vort* (Stoczek: n.p., 1931).
117. "'Tsum shand slup' Sefer Hahayim shel havrei brit ha-shomer 'hashahar' be-vilna, 1927–1930," p. 100, in B33-5/2, JI.
118. "Korespondentsies," *Der Emes*, February 20, 1928, 19.

Chapter 3: Obedient Children, Reckless Rebels

1. Gourevitch, "Jabotinsky and the Hebrew Language," 594; and E. Jabotinsky, *Avi, Ze'ev Z'abotinski*, 13–14.
2. "Shir Betar." The term for "decay" (*afar* with the letter ayin) was also used in the Hebrew Bible to refer to ashes.
3. Gourevitch, "Jabotinsky and the Hebrew Language," 594.
4. Classic studies on youth as a cultural category include Ariès, *Centuries of Childhood*; and Gillis, *Youth and History*.

5. Remba, *Shnatayim*, 14; *Tel Hai*, June–July 1930, 17–18, and July 1931, 15.

6. See, for example, Jabotinsky, "Shatnez lo ya'ale alekha," *Haynt*, January 18, 1929; Jabotinsky, "Vegn militarizm," *Haynt*, January 25, 1929; Jabotinsky, "Ven di velt iz yung geven," *Haynt*, January 23, 1931; and Jabotinsky, "Oyfn pripetchik," *Haynt*, October 16, 1931.

7. Propes, "Unzer firer," *Tel Hai*, October 1930, 3.

8. Telegrams addressed to Jabotinsky between October and November 1930, in A1-3/18/3, JI.

9. For examples of Jabotinsky's early complaints about the Revisionist movement's growth, see Jabotinsky to Ya'akov Hoffman, July 13, 1927; Jabotinsky to Richard Lichtheim, August 14, 1927; and Jabotinsky to Shlomo Gepstein, July 27, 1929, all in A1-2, JI. On the movement's financial woes, see Jabotinsky to Yaakov de Haas, February 7, 1928; Jabotinsky to Shlomo Jacobi, March 24, 1928; Jabotinsky to Wolfgang von Weisl, January 29, 1931; and Jabotinsky to Meir Grossman, February 4, 1931, all in A1-2, JI. For examples of conflicts within the Revisionist executive leadership, see Jabotinsky to Grossman, July 9, 1930; July 13, 1930; and October 25, 1930; Jabotinsky to the London Revisionist Executive, July 27, 1930, and November 9, 1930, all in A1-2, JI.

10. Zouplna, "Vladimir Jabotinsky and the Split," 38–39; and Robinson, *Se'arah mesaya'at*, 27–30.

11. See, for example, M. Grossman, "Geferlekhe shtimungen," *Der Emes*, November 20, 1928; and M. Grossman, "Mir un di tsionistishe organizatsye," *Der Nayer Veg*, May 15, 1932.

12. See, for example, Jabotinsky to Grossman, October 25, 1930, and March 19, 1931; Jabotinsky to J. Machower, January 25, 1931, and March 6, 1931; and Jabotinsky to Lichtheim, March 20, 1931, all in A1-2, JI.

13. Shavit, *Jabotinsky and the Revisionist Movement*, 37.

14. See, for example, "Polityka Weizmana czy nowy kurz Żabotyńskiego?," *Nasz Przegląd*, July 5, 1931; and "Ani ma'amin Żabotyńskiego," *Chwila*, July 8, 1931.

15. *Jewish Telegraphic Agency*, July 6, 1931.

16. "Revisionists Return to Congress after Quitting Amidst Uproar," *Jewish Telegraphic Agency*, July 13, 1931.

17. "Split in Revisionist Party as Jabotinsky Takes Six Months Leave of Absence," *Jewish Telegraphic Agency*, July 17, 1931.

18. Zouplna, "Vladimir Jabotinsky and the Split," 47–49.

19. Jabotinsky to Eliyahu Ben Horin, September 17, 1931, in A1-2, JI.

20. Wolfgang von Weisl to Jabotinsky, January 20, 1927, in A1-3/15, JI; von Weisl to Jabotinsky, January 14, 1928, in A1-3/16, JI; Abba Achimeir to Jabotinsky, October 17 and October 25, 1928, in A1-3/16, JI; and von Weisl to Jabotinsky, January 17, 1931, in A1-3/19, JI.

21. *Hazit Ha'am*, August 9, 1932.

22. Abba Achimeir, "Ha-sa'ir le-'azazel," *Tel Hai*, December 1, 1929, 6; "Kfar Saba," *Tel Hai*, July 1930, 10; Achimeir, "Al regel achat," *Madrikh Betar*, September 1932, 3–4; and Uri Zvi Grinberg, "Uri Tsvi Grinberg medaber," *Ha-medina*, February 1932, 5.

23. *Baranovitsher Vokh*, October 28, 1932.

24. Jabotinsky to Shlomo Gepstein, October 16, 1930; Jabotinsky to Lichtheim, March 20, 1931; and Jabotinsky to Baruch Weinstein, December 29, 1931, all in A1-2, JI. On the Biryonim serving as "accelerators," see Jabotinsky to Weinstein, May 26, 1932, in A1-2, JI.

25. Jabotinsky to Grossman, January 26, 1932; Jabotinsky to the Revisionist Executive in London, January 28, 1932; Jabotinsky to Alexander Ponianski, May 26, 1932, all in A1-2, JI.

26. Jabotinsky to Grossman, May 30, 1929, in A1-2, JI.

27. See Jabotinsky, "Vegn avanturizm," *Haynt*, February 26, 1932; and "Vayter vegn avanturizm," *Haynt*, July 29, 1932.

28. Jabotinsky to Y. H. Yeivin, August 9, 1932, in A1-2, JI.

29. "Tsveyte zitsung fun der velt konferentz," *Der Nayer Veg*, September 10, 1932, 11. Interestingly, the article omits Achimeir's reference to Oswald Moseley, the British Fascist leader, to whom Achimeir attributes this statement; see "Generaldebatte 30 August 1932," in G2-7/4/3, JI.

30. Alexander Aker, "Be'ene Betar ve-ha-metsiut be-moledet," *Madrikh Betar*, January 1933, 15–17.

31. "Vegn Aktivizm," *Ha-medina*, April 2, 1933, 4. Emphasis mine.

32. Tuvia Techlin, "Tsum aktivizm," *Ha-medina*, March 19, 1933, 4.

33. Natkovich, *Ben 'ananei zohar*, 210–28, 267–72.

34. Teveth, *Ben-Gurion*, 414–15.

35. M. Gantsnberg, "Di betsiyung tsvishn betar un brith ha-tsohar," *Der Nayer Veg*, vol. 7 [no date legible], 1932, 18; M. Grossman, "Unzer hov tsu der revizionistisher yugnt," *Der Nayer Veg*, November 27, 1932, 4.

36. For examples of uses of the term "generational conflict" in interwar France, Germany, Britain, and Italy, see Dowe, *Jugendprotest und Generationenkonflikt*, 113–208. On "generational cohorts" as a social construct, see Wohl, *Generation of 1914*; Bessel, "Front Generation," 121–36; and Whitney, *Mobilizing Youth*. For a collection of articles from the interwar period theorizing the existence of generational cohorts and the conflict of generations, see Esler, *Youth Revolution*.

37. More than seven thousand Betar members in Poland participated in the survey. See "She'elonim snif Polonia," in B1-10, JI.

38. *'Avodatenu: din ve-heshbon*, 17–19.

39. Propes, "Brit hatsohar un betar." See also "Yoman"; and "Di revizionistishe konferentz," *Biuletin shel betar be-Polin: 'Avodatenu* [month unknown] 1931, 3.

40. Feldschuh to Grossman, February 11, 1931, in P59-2/89/15, JI. See also Lipman to the London Executive, November 26, 1931, in G2-5/38, JI.

41. Undated letter from Moshe Lejzerowicz in a collection of letters sent to the Central Revisionist Office in Paris between 1925 and 1929, in G1-9, JI.

42. Ibid.

43. "Protokol der 8, Sitzung," in G2-7/1/3, JI.

44. Ibid.

45. Propes, "Brit hatsohar un betar"; and David Melamed, "Betar ve-hatsohar," *Tel Hai*, December 25, 1929.

46. Jabotinsky, "Ha-no'ar shel ha-tsiyonut ha-hertslela'it," *Doar Hayom*, August 29, 1930.

47. *Brit Trumpeldor*, 71–72.

48. Jabotinsky, "Ha-no'ar shel ha-tsiyonut ha-hertsela'it."

49. Jabotinsky to the General Secretary of Betar's Command, July 30, 1931, in A1-2, JI.

50. Jabotinsky to London Revisionist Executive, August 17, 1931, in A1-2, JI.

51. "Musar ha-atsma'ut," *Ha-medina*, September 25, 1931, 2.

52. Jakób Rothmann to London Revisionist Executive, September 5, 1931, in G33-1/10, JI.

53. Kunicki, *Between the Brown and the Red*, 20–27.

54. Lejzerowicz to the London Revisionist Executive, August 23, 1931, in G2-5/38, JI.

55. Jabotinsky, "Zionist-Revisionists in Poland: To the Editor of the *Times*," *London Times*, January 26, 1932.

56. Ibid.

57. This sentence is found in the original letter sent by Jabotinsky to the editors of the *Times*, January 6, 1932, but it was excised by the editors. A copy of the original letter is located in the Jabotinsky Institute's online archives.

58. Jabotinsky, *Zamelbukh far betarisher yugend*, 32–40.

59. Jabotinsky, "Vegn avanturizm."

60. "Mittwoch den 31, August 1932, Herr Vl. Jabotinsky," in "Protocols and Decisions of the 5th World Revisionist Conference, 28.8–3.9 1932," in G2-7/4/3, JI. Interestingly, an account of Jabotinsky's speech that appeared in *Der Nayer Veg*, the Revisionist journal edited by Meir Grossman, added several words and lines that do not appear in the original recording of his speech in the conference protocols. This includes Jabotinsky's insistence that he was "unconditionally loyal to the democratic form of the Revisionist organization." *Sefer Betar*, the official party history of the movement, added the following line to his speech: "I stand with all my strength by the democratic nature of our movement." See Ben-Yerucham, *Sefer Betar*, 1:425.

61. Jabotinsky, "Prakim fun a rede," *Haynt*, September 9, 1932.

62. Jabotinsky, "A dor realistn," *Haynt*, February 19, 1932.

63. "Zeyde liberalism," *Haynt*, October 14, 1932.

64. Jabotinsky to the London Revisionist Executive, January 2, 1933, in A1-2, JI.

65. See "Ha-mo'atzah ha-'olamit be-Katowits," 34, in G2-7/5, JI.

66. Interview with David Boiko, "Ha-mo'atzah ha-olamit shel ha-tsohar be-Katowits," February 8, 1971, 1, EB4, JI. See also Schechtman, *Fighter and Prophet*, 166–70. Unlike Boiko, Schechtman insisted that Jabotinsky had not reached a decision about the putsch until after the Katowice conference.

67. Jabotinsky to Grossman, March 22, 1922, in A1-2, JI.

68. "Jabotinsky Suspends Revisionist Executive Following Conference," *Jewish Telegraphic Agency*, March 23, 1933. See also Jabotinsky to Members of the Revisionist Movement, March 22, 1933; and Jabotinsky to Betar members, March 22, 1933, both in A1-2, JI.

69. At the time, Propes had been on a brief hiatus as commander of Betar in Poland, but he was reinstated following the events of March 1933.

70. Jabotinsky, "Kruz," *'Avodatenu*, April 1933, 3.

71. "Der zin fun plebisit," *Der Moment*, April 16, 1933. See also "Kruz rosh Betar," *Ha-medina*, March 26, 1933; and "Oyfruf fun Ze'ev Jabotinsky tsu di revizionistn," *Ha-medina*, March 26, 1933.

72. "Kruz nasi ha-tsohar," *Ha-medina*, April 10, 1933.

73. Jabotinsky to Betar members, March 22, 1933.

74. Jabotinsky to Israel Trivus, March 23, 1933, in A1-2, JI. Emphasis mine.

75. "Text Eines vom Londoner Büro der JTA Mitgeteilten Telegramms, datiert 23 März 1933," 106, in G2-7/5, JI.

76. Boiko interview, 2, in EB4, JI.

77. "Majer Grossman o zamachu dyktatorskim Żabotyńskiego," *Nasz Przegląd*, March 24, 1933; and "Grossman przeciw puczowi Żabotyńskiego," *Chwila*, March 25, 1933.
78. "Ha-tokhnit ha-makhri'ah," *Ha-medina*, March 26, 1933.
79. L. Lipshitz, "Ver zol firn?," *Ha-medina*, March 26, 1933.
80. Ibid.
81. Propes, "Unzer," *'Avodatenu*, April 1933, 2.
82. *'Avodatenu: din ve-heshbon*, 19.
83. "Erklerung," *Baranovitsher Vokh*, April 23, 1933.
84. "Darko shel Jabotinsky—derekh hatsohar!" *Hazit Ha'am*, March 28, 1933.
85. Jabotinsky to Shlomo Jacobi, May 13, 1933, in A1-2, JI.

Chapter 4: Poland, Palestine, and the Politics of Belonging

1. Y. Grinboym, "A deklaratsye," *Haynt*, June 21, 1933; "Groys is di kharpe, brenend di shand," *Haynt*, June 21, 1933; "'Al ha-dam ha-shafukh: Mikhtav galui el betar," *Ba-derekh*, June 22, 1933; and "Haim Arlosoroff," *Haynt*, June 28, 1933.
2. Grinboym, "'Al ha-dam ha-shafukh."
3. Grinboym, "Untern frishn ayndruk," *Haynt*, July 11, 1933.
4. See, for example, file 12t.11, p. 200, in AMZHP/1537, collection 2/1378/0, AAN; and file 14, p. 197, Mf1749, collection 2/1380/0, AAN.
5. See, for example, file 3, p. 72, in collection 1186/0, AAN.
6. "Ongehoybn zikh di yovel-fayerungen fun yidishn legion," *Der Nayer Veg*, August [date unknown], 1932, 15; and "Di legion-fayerungen in poyln," *Der Nayer Veg*, September 18, 1932, 15.
7. Among the most recent studies that exemplify this approach are Michlic, *Poland's Threatening Other*; Weeks, *From Assimilation to Antisemitism*; and the essays in Blobaum, *Antisemitism and Its Opponents in Modern Poland*.
8. Stauter-Halsted, "Jews as Middleman Minorities," 57.
9. For a survey of these debates, see Porter, *When Nationalism Began to Hate*.
10. "L. J.," folder 3841, pp. 148591–92, RG 4, YIVO Institute for Jewish Research, New York. While heders were traditionally male-dominated learning institutions, a heder education for young girls, particularly in lower levels of learning, was not uncommon by the First World War. In interwar Poland, Orthodox Jewry experienced considerable innovation regarding the religious education of Jewish women. By 1938, the Beis Ya'akov network of schools, affiliated with the Agudat Yisrael movement, provided Jewish education for nearly thirty-eight thousand girls. Most of these institutions were afternoon programs for Jewish girls who studied in Polish public schools in the mornings. See Kaniel, "Beys Yankev"; and Bacon, "Agudat Israel."
11. To assess the impact of the interwar Polish public school system on Poland's Jews, historians generally cite data provided by a government statistics bureau for the school year of 1934–35. See "Uczniowie Żydzi w szkołach powszechnych," *Biuletyn Ekonomiczno-Statystyczny: Materiały i cyfry z życia ludności żydowskiej w Polsce*, September 1937; and Samuel Chmielewski, "Stan szkolnictwa wśród Żydów w Polsce," *Sprawy Narodowościowe* 11 (1937): 44, table 8.
12. Sienkiewicz, *Atlas Historii Żydów Polskich*, 297. For a discussion of the school system and Jewish acculturation, see Bacon, "National Revival, Ongoing Acculturation," 71–92; Martin,

Jewish Life in Cracow, 121–49; Bassok and Novershtern, "Ma'arakhot ha-hinukh," 736–51; and Kijek, "Świadomość i socjalizacja polityczna," 255–304.

13. For general histories of the interwar Polish public school system, see Trzebiatowski, *Szkolnictwo powszechne w Polsce*; Garbowska, *Szkolnictwo powszechne w Polsce*; and Zloch, *Polnischer Nationalismus*, 209–52. On minorities in these schools, see Mauersberg, *Szkolnictwo powszechne dla mniejszości narodowych*.

14. Juśko, *Szkolnictwo powszechne w powiecie tarnowskim*, 217–25; and Wojtas, *Learning to Become Polish*, 284–322.

15. MWRiOP, *Program drugiego stopnia, Historja*, 16, quoted in Esden-Tempska, "National and Civic Education," 299.

16. MWRiOP, *Program drugiego stopnia, Historja*, 6, quoted in Esden-Tempska, "National and Civic Education," 303.

17. Esden-Tempska, "National and Civic Education," 278.

18. Mikulski and Saloni, *W Lipkach*, 136, quoted in Esden-Tempska, "National and Civic Education," 301.

19. Odziemkowski, *Armia i społeczeństwo*, 87–98; and Kęsik, *Naród pod bronią*, 81–96.

20. Steffen, *Jüdische Polonität*, 125–42.

21. Benecke, *Die Ostgebiete der Zweiten Polnischen Republik*, 247–67.

22. "K.S.V.," p. 21, folder 3644, RG 4, YIVO.

23. See "R. E.," folder 3571, RG 4, YIVO; "K. S.," p. 11, folder 3814, RG 4, YIVO; and "Esther" in Shandler, *Awakening Lives*, 323.

24. "R. E.," folder 3571, RG 4, YIVO.

25. "K. S.," p. 11, folder 3814, RG 4, YIVO.

26. See, for example, "Maks Einhorn," p. 16, folder 3652, RG 4, YIVO; "K.S.V.," p. 13, folder 3644, RG 4, YIVO; "G. S.," p. 51, folder 3515,RG 4, YIVO; and "L. J.," p. 148593, folder 3841, RG 4, YIVO. See also Max Weinreich's classic study of these autobiographies, *Der veg tsu unzer yugnt*, 186–89, 197–201.

27. "S. H.," p. 7, folder 3511, RG 4, YIVO.

28. "K.S.V.," p. 22, folder 3644, RG 4, YIVO.

29. Paruch, *Od konsolidacji państwowej*.

30. Ibid.; Rudnicki, *Równi, ale niezupełnie*, 116–34.

31. Żblikowski, "Poles and Jews in the *Kresy Wschodnie*," 41–53; Rudnicki, "Anti-Jewish Legislation in Interwar Poland," 148–70; and Henschel and Stach, "Nationalisierung und Pragmatismus," 165–86.

32. Rezmer, "Służba wojskowa Żydów," 97–110. On the widespread belief that all Jews were Bolsheviks in disguise, see Michlic, *Poland's Threatening Other*, 88–93. On Polish government perceptions of Jewish economic control, see Ciancia, "Poland's Wild East," 117–18.

33. On the Catholic Church and antisemitism, see Michlic, *Poland's Threatening Other*, 82–88, 98–100; and Porter-Szűcs, *Faith and Fatherland*, 295–314.

34. Porter-Szűcs, *Faith and Fatherland*, 273, 291.

35. Białowąs, *Pan Jezus wśród ludzi*, 43, 47, quoted in Landau-Czajka, "Koledzy czy wrogowie," 9.

36. Krzywiec, "Czy państwo w Polsce pomajowej było czynnikiem antyżydowskim," 372.

37. Henschel and Stach, "Nationalisierung und Pragmatismus," 182–86.

38. "G. S.," p. 4, folder 3515, RG 4, YIVO.

39. On encounters with Polish patriotic culture at Tarbut schools, see ibid., 51; file 3, p. 104, in collection 1181/0, AAN; and Kijek, "Was It Possible to Avoid 'Hebrew Assimilation'?"

40. "G. S.," p. 51, folder 3515, RG 4, YIVO.

41. Ibid., 68.

42. Ibid., 68–69.

43. Ya'akov Hetman, "Betar be-Luboml," in P153-3/9, 1, JI.

44. "Impozanter tsug fun der brit yugnt iber di varsh. gasn," in B33-2/1, JI.

45. Y. Oyslerner, "A beytarisher oysflug," *Unzer Vort* (1931), 21, in B33-6/7, JI.

46. Ibid., 22.

47. M. Wodinski, "Literatur un yugnt," *Unzer Vort* (1931), 9.

48. On the relationship of the Bund with the Polish Socialist Party, see Brumberg, "Bund and the Polish Socialist Party," 75–97.

49. On the Agudat Yisrael, see Bacon, *Politics of Tradition*.

50. Jabotinsky, "Vegn militarizm," *Haynt*, January 25, 1929.

51. See M. Lejzerowicz, "Ha-holem ve-halohem," *Tel Hai*, October 1930, 4.

52. "Ha-veida ha-olamit ha-revi'it: Protokolim ve-hahlatot," in G2-7/1/3, JI. See also Almoni, "Mehanekh ha-am," *Tel Hai*, October 1930, 5; and Z. Lerner, "Nihye ke-hol ha-goyim," *Ha-medina*, March 30, 1934, 2.

53. Hein, *Der Piłsudski-Kult*, 139–50.

54. "Nasza 'Pierwsza Brygada,'" *Trybuna Narodowa*, November 8, 1935; "Związek Sjonistów Rewizjonistów, organizacja na terenie Polskiej," November 29, 1926, file 23, in collection 29/215/0, Archiwum Narodowe w Krakowie (National Archives of Kraków; hereafter ANK); and "MSW do wszystkich panów starostów," November 5, 1926, in HM2/8561.8, CAHJP.

55. Jabotinsky, "Fun der vaytns," *Morgn Zhurnal*, June 3, 1935.

56. Vladimir Jabotinsky to Anya Jabotinsky, February 27, 1927; Jabotinsky to Members of the Revisionist Party, March 22, 1933; Jabotinsky to Betar members, March 22, 1933; "Der goyrel fun revizionizm," *Der Moment*, March 26, 1933, 3; and "Der zin fun plebitsit," *Der Moment*, April 16, 1933.

57. Jabotinsky, "Fun der vaytns."

58. Shavit, "Politics and Messianism," 235–40. On representations of Piłsudski in the Polish-language Jewish daily press, see Landau-Czajka, *Polska—to nie oni*, 164–83.

59. A. Laufgang, "Problemy kulturalno-wychowawcze w Hacoharze," *Trybuna Narodowa*, January 25, 1935.

60. See also Yosef Klarman, "Der mentsh fun belvedere," *Ha-medina*, May 28, 1935; "Nad trumną Józefa Piłsudskiego," *Trybuna Narodowa*, May 17, 1935; and "Ku czci pamięci marszałka Piłsudskiego," *Trybuna Narodowa*, July 12, 1935.

61. "W dniu imienin Józefa Piłsudskiego," *Trybuna Narodowa*, March 22, 1935.

62. Moshe Goldberg, "Yosef Pilsudski," *Ha-medina*, May 28, 1935.

63. "Protokol shel ha-pgisha ha-rishonah ha-glilit shel Brit Trumpeldor," March 1929, in P153-2/1, JI.

64. Ibid.

65. Barukh, "Hag ha-shihrur shel ha-'am ha-polani," *La-nitsahon: Iton darga alef ken betar baranowicze*, December 6, 1933, 4.

66. Moishe Lindenboym, "Frayhayts kempfer," *La-nitsahon: Iton mukdash le-hagigat yovel he-asor li-tsirat betar be-Radom*, January 1935, 10.

67. Lerner's summer camp manual, for example, instructed Betar members to consult the following works: *Podręcznik Przysposobienia Wojskowego* (date and place of publication unknown); Lewakowski, *Terenoznawstwo i kartografia wojskowa*; Sliwinski, *Sygnalizacja*; and Wyrobek, *Harcerz w polu*. See Lerner, *Mahanot kayits/Zumer Lagern*, 78.

68. Schreiber and Piasecki, *Harce Młodzieży Polskiej*, 21; Jabotinsky, "Hadar," *Cahiers du Betar* 7 (1931): 8–10; and *Brit Trumpeldor*, 49–50.

69. Schreiber and Piasecki, *Harce Młodzieży Polskiej*, 24.

70. Ibid.

71. "Ha-parashim ha-yeshanim," *Tel Hai*, December 1, 1929, 9.

72. Moss, "Not the *Dybbuk* but *Don Quixote*," 196–240.

73. "Di formen fun der idisher kolonizatsiye in erts-yisroel: A sikha far darga bet un darge gimel," *'Avodatenu*, February 1932, 9.

74. Steffen, *Jüdische Polonität*, 130–36.

75. On Mickiewicz's rendition of Polish-Jewish mysticism and messianism, see Haumann, "Adam Mickiewicz," 247–59.

76. Jabotinsky, "Evreiskaia legion mitskievitcha," *Rassvet*, September 11, 1932. One month later, a Polish Jewish journalist in *Chwila* had similarly described Mickiewicz as a Zionist. See H. Hescheles, "Sjonista Adam Mickiewicz," *Chwila*, October 17, 1932.

77. "Na otwarcie konferencyj," *Trybuna Narodowa*, January 4, 1935.

78. Ciancia, "Poland's Wild East," 28–62, 103–41.

79. Poland's Ministry of Education designed textbooks especially for this task. See, for example, Radliński, *Krajoznawstwo*; and Gajówna, *Krajoznawstwo*.

80. Kassow, "Polish Jews and the Landkentenish Movement," 241–64.

81. See, for example, Libertal, *Sefer ha-nesharim*, 12–13, 21–22, 30–31; Lerner, *Mahanot kayits/Zumer Lagern*, 3; and Isaac Remba, "Ha-tsa'ad ha-rishon," *Madrikh Betar*, November 1932, 21–23.

82. Lerner, *Mahanot kayitz/Zumer Lagern*, 1.

83. Ibid., 5, 12.

84. Ibid., 49–51.

85. Avraham Rozenfeld, "Tsvishn okopes: Reportazh fun kurs fun madrikhim in zielonka," *Ha-medina*, January 31, 1934.

86. On the importance of national commemoration ceremonies in the creation of Polish nationalism, see Dabrowski, *Commemorations and the Shaping of Modern Poland*; and Biskupski, *Independence Day*, 46–82.

87. "Nekhtige brit-trumpeldor fayerungen in varshe," *Haynt*, January 2, 1929; "Ha-pgisha ha-'olamit ha-rishona le-mifkadei betar," *Igrot Livne Betar*, July 15, 1929, 3; "Kinus fun betar fun kielcer galil in radom," *Der Nayer Veg*, August [date unknown], 1932, 18; "Di legion fayerungen in poyln," *Der Nayer Veg*, September 10, 1932, 15; file 12t.11, p. 200, 2/1378/0, AAN. For retrospective accounts of the ceremony, see the memoir drafts of Aharon Propes, 2–3, P183-2/1, JI; *Sefer Radom* (Tel Aviv: Irgun yots'e Radom be-Yisra'el, 1961), 201–2.

88. Laqueur, "Memory and Naming in the Great War," 150–67.

89. File 14, p. 197, Mf1749, 2/1380/0, AAN.

90. File 12t.11, p. 163, 2/1378/0, AAN.

91. Ibid., 138.

92. "Poświęcenie sztandaru Betaru w Borysławiu," *Trybuna Narodowa*, June 17, 1934.

93. See, for example, file 12t.11, pp. 198a and 199, 2/1378/0 AAN.

94. A P—S, "Oyf falshe vegn," *Tel Hai*, February 1, 1930, 7.

95. *Di Velt*, October 4, 1933, 15.

96. "Listy z kraju," *Trybuna Narodowa*, July 5, 1935, 8.

97. On the significance of "Boże, Cós Polskę" for Polish Catholics, see Porter-Szűcs, *Faith and Fatherland*, 226–27, 234.

98. Polonsky, *History of the Jews in Russia and Poland*, 105; and Bartal and Opalski, *Poles and Jews*, 42, 47, 157.

99. Martin, *Jewish Life in Cracow*, 24.

100. "Ku czci pamięci maszałka Piłsudskiego," *Trybuna Narodowa*, July 12, 1935.

101. For descriptions of the event, see "Der betar kinus in kroke," *Ha-medina*, September 9, 1935; "W skrótach," *Haneszer*, August–September 1935, 50; "Mowa wł. Żabotyńskiego na Złocie Betaru w Krakowie," *Trybuna Narodowa*, August 16, 1935, 4; and I. Rodal, "Gdy groby mówią do siebie Reportaż z krakowskiego zlotu Betaru," *Trybuna Narodowa*, August 16, 1935, 4.

102. "Z'abotinski no'em lifne ha-noar ha-le'umi," *Ha-yarden*, August 28, 1935.

103. "Listy z kraju," *Trybuna Narodowa*, July 5, 1935.

104. "Dom im. J. Piłsudskiego w Palestynie," *Trybuna Narodowa*, June 21, 1935, 7.

105. Ibid.

106. Odziemkowski, *Armia i społeczeństwo*, 100. See also Kęsik, *Naród pod bronią*, 72–101; Rozwadowski, *Państwowy Urząd Wychowania Fizycznego i Przysposobienia Wojskowego*; and Ignatowicz, *Przygotowanie obronne społeczeństwa w polsce*, 124–47.

107. On the fear of armed irredentist paramilitary activity among adolescent national minorities and the prospect of making them loyal citizens of Poland through PW participation, see "Kuratorjum Okręgu Szkolnego Wołyńskiego do Pana Wojewody Wołyńskiego w Łucku, w sprawie udziału mniejszości narodowych w pracy PW," December 6, 1927, I.300.69.23, Centralne Archiwum Wojskowe (Central Military Archives), Warsaw (hereafter CAW); and "Spraw udziału mniejszości narodowych w pracy PW," November 23, 1928, I.300.69.23, CAW.

108. "Din ve-heshbon," *Der Emes*, January 20, 1928, 7.

109. "Korespondentsies," *Der Emes*, September 28, 1928, 13; "Do pana wojewody w kielcach Radomski starosta powiatowy," Urząd Wojewódzki Kielecki, Wydz. Bezpieczeństwa, file 3158, in MSW/100/0, Archiwum Państwowe w Kielcach (National Archives in Kielce; hereafter APK); "Fun unzer bavegung," *Tel Hai*, February 1, 1930, 15; and "Do pana wojewody w Stanisławowie 3 Lutego 1930r," in HM2/8652, CAHJP.

110. "Fun tsentrale instruktorn shule in varshe," *Der Emes*, February 20, 1929, 19.

111. "Algemayner iberblik iber di tsen yerige tetigkayt fun brit trumpeldor in radom," *La-nitsahon: Iton mukdash le-hagigat yovel he-asor li-tsirat betar be-Radom*, January 1935, 26; "Betar arbet in poyln," *Ha-medina*, March 5, 1933, 8; Remba, *Shnatayim*, 11; and "Z ruchu betarowego w Środkowej Małopolsce," *Trybuna Narodowa*, August 31, 1934, 7.

112. See, for example, "Listy z kraju," *Trybuna Narodowa*, June 22, 1934, 8; "Sprawozdanie Sytuacyjne: Sytuacja ogólna dla wszystkich mniejszości narodowych," July 9, 1933, file 3, p. 72,

collection 1186/0, AAN; "Wyczynki z dziennika obozowego K. I.," *Jardenu*, October 1932; and "Khaveyrim shraybn fun di shtet un shtetlekh," *Di Velt*, May 30, 1933, 14.

113. Hetman, "Betar be-Luboml," p. 2, P153-3/9, 1, JI.

114. "Do Pana Wojewody Lubelskiego w Lublinie," September 14, 1931, 1138/26, in Urząd Wojewódzki Lubelski Wydział Społeczno-Polityczny, 1919–1939, Archiwum Państwowe w Lublinie (National Archives in Lublin; hereafter APL).

115. "Lubelski Urząd Wojewódzki do Dowóztwa Orkręgu Korpusu Nr. II. Okręgowy Urząd WF I PW," September 29, 1931, 1138/26, APL. For the 1926 government report describing the Revisionist movement's loyalty to the Polish state, see "Wojewoda Lubelski do Panów Starostów Województwa Lubelskiego," November 24, 1926, 492, collection 35/403/0, APL.

116. On Grinboym and the National Minorities' Bloc, see Mendelsohn, *Zionism in Poland*, 213–22.

117. Kleiner, *From Nationalism to Universalism*.

118. Rezmer, "Służba wojskowa Żydów," 97–110.

119. "Starosta Grodzki Częstochowski do Pana Wojewody Kieleckiego w Kielcach," August 14, 1933, file 20495, p. 383, in UWK1, RG 100, APK.

120. "Ustosunkowanie się władz do stowarzyszeń żydowskich uprawiających W.F.i.P.W.," November 9, 1933, file 3420, pp. 249–54, in UKW1, RG 100, APK.

121. "Do Juljana Tuwima," *Trybuna Narodowa*, July 26, 1935, 4.

122. Ibid.

123. D. Lerner, "Unzer landes-politik," *Der Emes*, November 20, 1928, 4–5.

124. "Konstytucja polska z 23 marca," *Trybuna Narodowa*, March 29, 1935.

125. Rudnicki, "Anti-Jewish Legislation in Interwar Poland," 158.

126. Jabotinsky, "Fun tog bukh," *Der Moment*, November 23, 1934, 4.

127. "L. J.," p. 148600–148601, folder 3841,RG 4, YIVO.

Chapter 5: Taming the Shtetl

1. Betar Authority in Paris to Betar Commission in Warsaw, March 30, 1932, B33-1/1, JI.

2. "Ha-mifkadot ha-gliliyot," *Hoveret Betar: 'Avodatenu*, December 1932, 14.

3. "She'elonim snif Polanyah, 1930," B1-10, JI.

4. B. Goldanski, "Unzere kennim in di shtetlekh," *Ha-medina*, April 10, 1933, 7.

5. For useful overviews of Jewish lives in provincial towns across modern eastern Europe, see Katz, *The Shtetl*; Kassow, "Community and Identity in the Interwar Shtetl," 198–220; Kassow, "The Shtetl in Interwar Poland," 121–39; Pinchuk, "The Shtetl," 495–504; and Shandler, *Shtetl*, 7–50.

6. Bartal, "Imagined Geography," 179–92.

7. For an introduction to literary renditions of the shtetl, see Miron, *Traveler Disguised*; Miron, *Image of the Shtetl*; and Roskies, *Jewish Search for a Usable Past*, 40–66.

8. Veidlinger, *Jewish Public Culture in the Late Russian Empire*.

9. Ciancia, "Poland's Wild East."

10. See, for example, Bucur, *Eugenics and Modernization in Interwar Romania*, 187–209; and Zahra, *Kidnapped Souls*.

11. Goldanski, "Unzere kennim in di shtetlekh." Emphasis mine.

12. Aharon Propes, ʿAvodatenu, July 1932, 1.
13. Moshe Goldberg, "Dos beytarishe folk redt," Ha-medina, January 6, 1935, 14–15.
14. Yirmiyahu Halperin to Avraham Axelrod, March 29, 1932, in P-14/3, JI.
15. "Bi-tnuʾat ha-noʾar," Ba-derekh, September 29, 1932.
16. Goldberg, Der beytarisher ken, 7–10.
17. Shilton Betar, circular 1, September 9, 1932, in B2-7/1, JI.
18. Lubocki, ʿAvodatenu, December 1932, 3.
19. Ibid.
20. On these regional differences, see Mendelsohn, Zionism in Poland, 91–110, 146–47, 178–85, 213–22, 300–310. On regional differences within the Revisionist movement, see Shechter, "Yeme Neʾurim," 10.
21. Propes, circular 13, March 18, 1931, in G2-5/40, JI.
22. Propes, Eynike onvayzungen, 15; and Schelles, Praca kulturalno wychowacza w Bejtarze, 5.
23. Propes, "Hakdama," 4.
24. Remba, "Hakdama," 2.
25. Goldberg, Der beytarisher ken, 10–12.
26. Propes, "Command 5," April 10, 1929, in B33-4/2, JI.
27. Circular 64, October 28, 1935, JI/B33-4/2, JI.
28. See, for example, Moʾetset Ha-mifkadot ha-gliliyot.
29. See, for example, Propes, Eynike onvayzungen, 21; and Schelles, Praca kulturalno wychowacza w Bejtarze, 17–20.
30. Ajzik Remba, "Ha-tsaʾad ha-rishon," Madrikh Betar, November 1932, 22.
31. Epsztajn, Horaʾot le-hachshara ha-tarbutit ba-kenim, 6–15.
32. Ibid.
33. See, for example, ʿAvodatenu [month unknown] 1932, 1–3, in PR-251, JI; and Biuletin brit trumpeldor, mifkedet galil baranowicze, December 22, 1934, B33-3/2, JI.
34. Y. Kaplanski, Biuletin 2: Misrad ha-hinukh veha-tarbut December 22, 1934, B33-3/2, JI.
35. Remba, "Ha-tsaʾad ha-rishon," 21.
36. Y. Krelman, "Kultur fun togteglekhn lebn in betar," Ha-medina, March 30, 1934, 7.
37. "Lezn," ʿAvodatenu [month unknown] 1932, 10, in PR-251, JI.
38. Epsztajn, Horaʾot la-hakhshara ha-tarbutit ba-kenim, 24, 47.
39. Ibid., 51–56.
40. Sh. Yamueli-Milkowski, "Skira ve-hotsaʾot," Madrikh Betar, November 1932, 38–39.
41. Propes, "Hozer #52 (Vegn uniform), Netsivut betar be-Polanyah (1933)," in B33-4/2, JI.
42. Margri, "Mir un unzere ʿfraynt,'" Tel Hai, December 1929, 7–8.
43. See, for example, circular 17 (1931), in G33-1/10, JI; and Propes to Grossman, February 8, 1931, in G2-5/47, JI.
44. A. Remba, "Le-melitse ha-yosher ha-mashtinim!," Tel Hai, June–July 1931, 11.
45. Yona, "Nihyeh kulanu halutsim," 241.
46. Oppenheim, "Hahakhshara ha-kibutsit," 295.
47. Yona, "Nihyeh kulanu halutsim," 72–110.
48. Yosef Khrust, "Al ha-hakhshara ve-haʾaliyah," in Moʾetset Ha-mifkadot ha-gliliyot, 11. See also Khrust, "Le-sheʾelat ha-hakhsharah ha-miktsoʾit," Madrikh Betar, October 1933, 11–13; and Chrust, "Hovat hakhsharah," Madrikh Betar, December 1933, 41–43.

49. "Divre ha-natsiv Aharon Propes," in *Mo'etset Ha-mifkadot ha-gliliyot*, 13.

50. On the formation of similar battalions in Mandate Palestine, see Shtain-Ashkenazi, *Betar be-erets Yisra'el*, 93–112.

51. "Hakhsharah," *'Avodatenu*, May 1933, 17–20.

52. Bornsztejn, "Di revizionistishe organizatsye," 199; and Levinson, "Tenuat ha-noar Betar be-Podvolochiskah," 64.

53. Yosef Pa'amoni, "Toldot hayav shel Y. Halperin," 64–72, in P77-8/10, JI.

54. "Yedi'ot," *'Avodatenu*, December 1932, 5; and Remba, *Shnatayim*, 11–13.

55. Ben-Yerucham, *Sefer Betar*, 2:553–55; Kaplan, *Jewish Radical Right*, 155–58; and Yirmiyahu Halperin, "Toldot ha-Yamaut ha-Ivrit," in H1-19, JI.

56. Remba, *Shnatayim*, 3.

57. See, for example, Berkowitz, *Zionist Culture and West European Jewry*, 99–118; and Pinsker, "Imagining the Beloved," 105–27.

58. Gershon Bacon, "Agudat Israel: Interwar Poland," *Jewish Women: A Comprehensive Historical Encyclopedia*, March 1, 2009, Jewish Women's Archive, http://jwa.org/encyclopedia/article/agudat-israel-interwar-poland.

59. See, for example, N. Zayidin, "Hahaverah bi-tnuot hano'ar hatsiyoniyot"; Bacon: "Woman? Youth? Jew?," 3–28; Kaniel, "Gender, Zionism and Orthodoxy," 346–67; Jacobs, *Bundist Counterculture in Interwar Poland*, 82–97; and Mickute, "Modern, Jewish, and Female," 31–76, 125–85.

60. Y. Krelman, "Betaryah (ma'amar sheni)," *Madrikh Betar*, December 1933, 47.

61. See also Josef Blatt, "Ha-isha be-betar," *Madrikh Betar*, May 1933, 18.

62. Ibid., 48.

63. Libertal, "Ne'um li-vnot betar," *Madrikh Betar*, October 1933, 17.

64. Blatt, "Ha-isha be-betar," 18.

65. Krelman, "Betaryah (ma'amar sheni)," 48.

66. See, for example, Abengózar, "Shaping Women," 75–92; Koonz, *Mothers in the Fatherland*; Maarten, "Gender, the Extreme Right," 265–84; and Clark, "Die Damen der Legion," 193–216.

67. "Vegn instruktors kurs," *'Avodatenu*, July 1932, 6.

68. For an example of inspector evaluation forms, see B33-4/3, JI.

69. "Hora'ot le-pe'ulat ha-ve'idah ha-merkazit li-bhinat 'ole betar," *'Avodatenu*, December 1932, 3–4.

70. Epsztajn, *Hora'ot la-hakhsharah ha-tarbutit ba-kenim*, 17.

71. "Pkudah," *'Avodatenu*, May 1933, 23.

72. Goldberg, *Der beytarisher ken*, 15–16; and "Muster fun a raport ishi," *'Avodatenu*, May 1933, 21–22.

73. "Circular 4/9, mifkedet galil Baranowicze," July 2, 1934, B33-3/2, JI.

74. "Pkudah 51," *'Avodatenu*, April 1933, 3.

75. "Osowa Wyszka," 31–32; Aron Toll interview by Adrienne Berger, September 4, 1998, interview 44696, Visual History Archive, USC Shoah Foundation (hereafter VHA).

76. "Sufferer 1001," folder 3511, RG 4, YIVO, reprinted in Novershtern, *Alilot ne'urim*, 497.

77. Ibid., 498.

78. Ibid., 496.

79. "Sufferer 1001," folder 3511, RG 4, YIVO, in Novershtern, *Alilot ne'urim*, 493; and folders 3676 and 3587, RG 4, YIVO.

80. "F. J.," folder 3514, RG 4, YIVO.

81. "K.S.V.," folder 3644, p. 40, RG 4, YIVO.

82. See folder 3774, RG 4, YIVO, reprinted in Novershtern, *Alilot ne'urim*, 714, 718; and folder 3652, pp. 22–23, RG 4, YIVO.

83. "K. S.," folder 3814, pp. 27–34, RG 4, YIVO.

84. Folder 3571, p. 13, RG 4, YIVO.

85. Folder 3687, p. 25, RG 4, YIVO.

86. "Modestus," folder 3822, p. 53, RG 4, YIVO.

87. Ibid., 34.

88. Ibid., 61.

89. "K.S.V.," p. 46, YIVO.

90. Ibid., 47.

91. Ibid., 45.

92. Folder 3687, p. 27, RG 4, YIVO.

93. "Sufferer 1001," YIVO, reprinted in Novershtern, *Alilot ne'urim*, 498.

94. *Yalkut volin* 1, no. 2 (June 1945): 24.

95. Remba, *Shnatayim*, 6.

96. Revisionist Regional Executive in Lwów to London Revisionist Executive, September 29, 1931, JI/G2/5/40.

97. London Revisionist Executive to Revisionist Regional Executive in Lwów, November 15, 1931, JI/G2/5/40.

98. Remba, *Shnatayim*, 9–10.

99. Shechter, "Yeme Ne'urim," 10, 31.

100. *Mo'etset Ha-mifkadot ha-gliliyot*, 7–8.

101. "Pkudah la-madrikhim," *Biuletin shel betar be-Polin: 'Avodatenu*, May 1933, 2.

102. Yosef Khrust to Avraham Axelrod, March 29, 1932, P14-3, JI.

103. Aharon Propes to Avraham Axelrod, September 19, 1931, P14-3, JI.

104. Netsivut Betar to Axelrod, October 31, 1932, P14-3, JI.

105. *Yoman ha-pkudot: hahozrim veha-hora'ot shel netsivut betar be-Polanyah*, 2, Thomas Fisher Rare Book Library, University of Toronto.

106. Ibid., 3.

107. On Zionist efforts to spread the use of Hebrew in linguistically diverse Mandate Palestine, see Halperin, *Babel in Zion*.

108. Y. Krelman, "Der beytarisher lokal," *Ha-medina*, January 9, 1936.

109. Command from Netsivut Betar in Poland, May 10, 1932, B33-4/2, JI.

110. Ha-shomer Ha-tsa'ir Branch, Mołczadź, to Ha-shomer Headquarters in Warsaw, 1937, archive code (6).41.1–2, location 1477, Yad Ya'ari Archives, Ha-shomer Ha-tsa'ir Archives, Giv'at Haviva, Israel (hereafter YY).

111. See, for example, Jabotinsky, "'Al ha-nashim ha-feministiot veha-sufragistiot," 178–81.

112. "'Almah be-ken betar," *Ha-medina*, March 19, 1933, 3.

113. See Mickute, "Making of the Zionist Woman," 149–55.

114. M. Shaked, "Di betariyah," *Ha-medina*, April 2, 1933, 4.

115. Batya Kremer, "Di bahura oyf hachshara," *Ha-medina*, March 30, 1935.

116. Tova Kaplan, "Davar la-betariyot," *Ha-medina*, May 31, 1934, 5; and Genia Steiner, "Dziewczęta w Bejtarze," *Trybuna Narodowa*, April 19, 1935.

117. "Ha-betariyah," *Ha-medina*, April 10, 1933, 4.

118. Lola Freundówna, "Kwestia wychowania dziewcząt w Betarze," *Trybuna Narodowa*, June 22, 1934, 5.

119. See, for example, "Sarah Aharonson," *Ha-medina*, October 5, 1934, 15; and "Dvora Ha-nevi'a," *Igron ha-betariyah*, March 4, 1937, 5–6.

120. See, for example, "Vegn instruktors kurs," 6–7; and "Vegn der rosh betar aktsye," *'Avodatenu*, January 1932, 14.

121. Propes, "Pkudah," *'Avodatenu*, May 1933, 3.

122. "Hora'ot la-avoda," *'Avodatenu*, February 1932, 18.

123. "Circular 4/9, mifkedet galil Baranowicze," July 2, 1934, in B33-3/2, JI.

124. To Avraham Axelrod, November 6, 1931; and Isaac Remba to Avraham Axelrod, October 6, 1932, both in P14-3, JI.

125. Tuvi, *Milhama bli gvulot*, 71–94; "Hakhrazah 'al vitur al zekhuyot be-'shediyul,'" October 27, 1933, reprinted in Ben-Yerucham, *Sefer Betar*, 2:184.

126. "Pkudah 60," October 27, 1933, reprinted in Ben-Yerucham, *Sefer Betar*, 2:187; and undated letter from the netsivut in Poland to regional commanders (1934), in B33-4/2, JI.

127. The decision of the Zionist Organization's Department of Immigration (*makhlakat ha-'aliya*) to forbid the Land of Israel offices from distributing immigration certificates to Betar members was made on January 7, 1934. It stipulated that the Zionist Organization would distribute certificates to Betar members only once its leaders called off their protest and put an end to their attempts to find alternative ways for their members to immigrate to Palestine. The Revisionist movement's leaders refused to comply with the Zionist Organization's demands. See Tuvi, *Milhama bli gvulot*, 91.

128. "Pkudah: 'Inyan 'aliyah," 1934, B33-4/2, JI.

129. Netsivut to Regional Commanders, 1934, B33-4/2, JI.

130. See Tuvi, *Milhama bli gvulot*. Tuvi estimates that between 1934 and 1940, the Revisionist movement organized eighteen ships to bring approximately 10,000 Jewish immigrants from Europe, mostly from Poland, illegally to Palestine. He also estimates that an additional 7,200 illegal immigrants arrived in Palestine with the help of Zionists indirectly associated with the Revisionist movement. Shavit places the number of illegal immigrants aided by the Revisionist movement at 15,000. Shavit, *Jabotinsky and the Revisionist Movement*, 376.

131. Kijek, "Świadomość i socjalizacja polityczna," 629–47.

132. Pa'amoni, "Toldot hayav shel Y. Halperin," 62.

133. Halperin to Axelrod, February 24, 1932, P14-3, JI.

Chapter 6: Terror

1. Testimony of Arie Alotin in "Depositions, Minutes of the Court, July 27, 1933–January 24, 1934," in H8-11/1, JI.

2. Y. Khrust, "Tsvey telegramen," *Ha-medina*, June 15, 1934, 4.

3. On the escalating economic competition between the Zionist Left and Right in Mandate Palestine, see Shapira, *Ha-ma'avak ha-nihzav*, 193–213; and Shtain-Ashkenazi, *Betar*

be-erets Yisra'el, 67–93. On the Baranowicze incident, see Yona, "Nihyeh kulanu halutsim," 256–66.

4. Poster issued by the General Federation of Workers in the Land of Israel, October 18, 1932, translated by Eran Kaplan, in Kaplan and Penslar, *Origins of Israel*, 150.

5. Jabotinsky to Betar in the Land of Israel, May 1, 1933, in A1-2, JI.

6. "Ven vet kumen a sof tsum roytn teror in erts-yisroel?," *Di Velt*, April 28, 1933, 11; and "Un unzere haveyrim in 'hazit ha'am' shraybn," *Di Velt*, May 12, 1933, 6.

7. B. Lubotzky, "Mifletset ha-demagogyah be-Yisrael," *Ha-medina*, June 23, 1933.

8. Y. Halperin, "Konsekventsiyot!," *Ha-medina*, May 14, 1933.

9. Uri Zvi Grinberg, "Arlosorov's hitleryade," *Di Velt*, June 9, 1933, 3.

10. Ibid.

11. David Ben-Gurion, *Yedi'ot He-haluts*, June 25, 1933.

12. Teveth, *Ben-Gurion*, 414–15.

13. Jabotinsky, "A filozofishe nakht," *Der Moment*, May 19, 1933.

14. Abba Achimeir, "Histadrut ha-tsionit ha-shlishi," *Hazit Ha'am*, March 28, 1933. For a discussion of the movement's early assessments of Nazism, see Heller, *Stern Gang*, 20–22.

15. Jabotinsky to Hans Bloch, May 5, 1933, in A1-2, JI.

16. Jabotinsky to the editors of *Hazit Ha'am*, May 17, 1933, in A1-2, JI.

17. See, for example, Jabotinsky to Yirmiyahu Halperin, April 5, 1929; and Jabotinsky to Y. H. Yeivin, August 9, 1932, both in A1-2, JI.

18. Jabotinsky, "A filozofishe nakht."

19. "Impozante troyer-akademiye in 'Nowości' tsum ondenk fun Dr. Haim Arlosoroff," *Haynt*, June 19, 1933; and Y. Grinboym, "Haim Arlosoroff," *Haynt*, June 28, 1933.

20. "Ver iz der merder?," *Haynt*, June 21, 1933. See also "Der fardekhtiker in dermordn Dr. Arlosoroff iz a revisionist fun poyln," *Naye Folktsaytung*, June 21, 1933; and "Vegn bashuldiktn in mord fun arlozorov," *Naye Folktsaytung*, June 26, 1933.

21. A. Goldberg, "Ruhig!," *Haynt*, June 21, 1933.

22. M. Nayman, "Dos vort," *Haynt*, June 24, 1933.

23. Ben Shlomo, "Jabotinsky ferbreytet zayn operatsions baze," *Haynt*, July 17, 1933.

24. Bezalel Katz, "An ofener briv tsu h.Vl.Jabotinsky," *Haynt*, July 2, 1933.

25. B. Yeushson [Moshe Yustman], "Mashiah ben meser," *Haynt*, July 9, 1933.

26. B. Yeushson, "Betar," *Haynt*, December 19, 1933.

27. M. Kleynman, "Koydem kol—erlekh zayn!," *Haynt*, July 17, 1933.

28. Katz, "An ofener briv tsu h.Vl.Jabotinsky."

29. Jabotinsky, "Yo, brekhn!," *Haynt*, November 4, 1932.

30. Jabotinsky, "A gut yor," *Der Moment*, October 27, 1933.

31. "Jabotinskys ruf tsu terror," *Haynt*, June 30, 1933.

32. See, for example, "Ershiterende dokumentn," *Haynt*, July 29, 1933; and "Der vayterdiger fehrer vegn dem 'brit ha-biryonim,'" *Haynt*, September 15, 1933.

33. Jabotinsky, "Kalt un fest," *Der Moment*, June 22, 1933.

34. Ibid.; "Über Dr. Arlosoroff und das an ihm verübte Verbrechen," *Der Judenstaat*, June 23, 1933, 1; and "Nisht a farteydikung, nor a bashuldikung," in *Di naye beylisade*, 4.

35. "Nisht a farteydikung," 4.

36. Sh. Y. Stupnicki, "Der korbn tomid," *Der Moment*, June 22, 1933.

37. "Dos land fun libe," *Der Moment*, July 1, 1934.

38. On the role of the Balkans in the European political imagination, see Todorova, *Imagining the Balkans*.

39. "Men shrayt 'bitsh zhiduv' un men befalt—revizionistn," *Der Moment*, June 23, 1933.

40. Jabotinsky, "Sholem Bayis," *Der Moment*, July 13, 1933.

41. "Di miuse hetse fun 'haynt' un ire rezultatn: shtimen fun lezer," *Der Moment*, July 17, 1933.

42. "Dos yudishe yugnt entgeht in blut!," *Der Moment*, July 18, 1933.

43. Y. Grinboym, "Tsu di khaveyrim tsionistn!," *Haynt*, July 23, 1933; "Oyfgerisn di valn in kielcer voyevud," *Der Moment*, July 24, 1933; and "Vahl teror in Polenits," *Der Moment*, July 25, 1933.

44. Ezriel Carlbach, "'Klasn Kampf' un heyliger lign," *Haynt*, September 3, 1933.

45. Carlbach, "A shlakht?—A skandal!," *Haynt*, August 28, 1933.

46. "Onfal fun di 'linke' oyf Jabotinskin," *Der Moment*, August 25, 1933.

47. Ibid.

48. See, for example, A. S. Lirik, "Stavsky als korbn," *Haynt*, July 20, 1934; B. Yehoashson, "Genug!," *Haynt*, July 24, 1934; and Tsvi Prilutski, "Di shtim fun doyres," *Der Moment*, July 21, 1934.

49. "Ha-milhamah ba-reviziyonizem: Maskanot she-nitkablu be-merkaz mifleget po'alei erets-Yisra'el ve-ushru ba-mo'atsah," reprinted in *Davar*, March 26, 1934. See also Yona, "Nihyeh kulanu halutsim," 264.

50. Jabotinsky, "A perek emes fun erts-yisroel," *Der Moment*, January 26, 1934.

51. See, for example, Jabotinsky to Joseph Klausner, April 22, 1934, in A1-2, JI; and "A brif fun dem arlosorof protses," *Haynt*, May 8, 1934.

52. "Ha-hakhsharah Ha'haganatit be-betar," *Ha-medina*, April 10, 1933; "Ha-militarizatsya shel ha-atletikah ha-kalah," *Ha-medina*, April 30, 1933; "Targile mishtar mefuzar," *Madrikh Betar*, May 1933; and Halperin, *She'elat ha-bitahon ha-'ivri*.

53. Zelig Lerner, "Kana'ut," *Madrikh Betar*, December 1933, 15.

54. Ibid.

55. See, for example, Jabotinsky to Pinhas Rutenberg, October 17, 1934, in A1-2, JI. On the negotiations, see Sarid, *La-shilton behartanu*, 385–514.

56. Jabotinsky to David Ben-Gurion, October 29, 1934, in A1-2, JI.

57. Ibid.

58. Jabotinsky to the National Branches of the Union of Revisionist Zionists, November 2, 1934, in A1-2, JI.

59. "Prese shtimen," *Ha-medina*, December 2, 1934.

60. Jabotinsky to Shlomo Jacobi, November 15, 1934, in A1-2, JI.

61. Jabotinsky to Pinhas Rutenberg, December 12, 1934, in A1-2, JI.

62. "Fayerlekhe erefnung fun der 6-ter konferentz fun alveltlekhn 'brit ha-tzohar,'" *Konferentz tsaytung*, January 9, 1935, 7.

63. "Der 2-ter alveltlekher kinus betar," *Konferentz tsaytung*, January 9, 1935, 2.

64. "Di val fun rosh Betar," *Konferentz tsaytung*, January 9, 1935, 3.

65. Ibid. Emphasis mine.

66. "Di general debate," *Konferentz tsaytung*, January 11, 1935, 1.

67. See, for example, "Listy z kraju," *Trybuna Narodowa*, March 2, 1934.

68. Menachem Begin, "A nayer transparent," *Di Velt*, December 1, 1933; Begin, *Betar un zayn vort tsu di idishe eltern*; Begin, "A vikhtiger etap," *Ha-medina*, February 16, 1933; and Begin, "Unzer matone," *Ha-medina*, October 25, 1934.

69. "Der parad fun di katsinim," *Ha-medina*, February 28, 1934.

70. Shindler, *Rise of the Israeli Right*, 126.

71. See, for example, Begin, "A nayer transparent"; Begin, *Betar un zayn vort tsu di idishe eltern*; and Begin, "Unzer matone."

72. Begin, "A vikhtiger etap."

73. Begin, *Betar un zayn vort tsu di idishe eltern*, 6.

74. "General debate: hemshekh," *Konferentz tsaytung*, January 13, 1934, 2–3.

75. Jabotinsky, "Vegn maximalizm," *Der Moment*, February 1, 1935.

76. Ibid.

77. Jabotinsky to Jonah Freulich, January 7, 1935; Jabotinsky to Tamar Jabotinsky-Kop, January 7, 1935; and Jabotinsky to Rutenberg, February 25, 1935, all in A1-2, JI.

78. Jabotinsky to Jabotinsky-Kop, January 17, 1935, in A1-2, JI.

79. Jabotinsky to Aharon Zvi Propes, February 11, 1935, in A1-2, JI.

80. Jabotinsky to Shlomo Jacobi, February 18, 1935, in A1-2, JI.

81. Jabotinsky to Jabotinsky-Kop, January 17, 1935.

82. Jabotinsky to Shlomo Zaltsman, March 19, 1935, in A1-2, JI.

83. Completed in 1935, Jabotinsky's autobiography first appeared in Jabotinsky, *Ktavim nivharim*. It was serialized in Poland's main Yiddish Revisionist paper in 1939; "Di geshikhte fun mayn lebn," *Unzer Velt*, March 3, 1939–July 14, 1939. See Natkovich, *Ben 'ananei zohar*, 267–73; and Horowitz, introduction to *Vladimir Jabotinsky's Story*, 1–31.

84. Jabotinsky, *Piatero*.

85. Jabotinsky to David Ben-Gurion, March 30, 1935, in A1-2, JI.

86. Jabotinsky, "Ayzn," *Der Moment*, March 11, 1934.

87. Felicjan Sławoj-Składkowski, quoted in Rudnicki, "Anti-Jewish Legislation in Interwar Poland," 159.

88. Estimates vary of Jews wounded and killed as a result of antisemitic violence in Poland in the late 1930s. Citing a list prepared by Ya'akov Leszczynski, historian Ezra Mendelsohn estimated that in 1935–1936, 1,289 Jews were wounded in antisemitic attacks, and that, in Leszczynski's words, "hundreds were killed." Jolanta Żyndul has called attention to the difficulty in assessing the number of casualties, citing significant discrepancies in numbers provided by Palestine's Jewish press, Polish government reports, and a representative of the Joint Distribution Committee. Mendelsohn, *Jews of East Central Europe*, 74; and Żyndul, *Zajścia antyżydowskie w Polsce*, 52–55.

89. Shapira, *Land and Power*, 221–38.

90. Halperin, *Ha-hakhshara ha'haganatit*.

91. Halperin, "Hagana be-hatkafa," *Ha-medina*, March 12, 1933, 3.

92. Ibid.

93. Halperin, *She'elat ha-bitahon ha-'ivri*, 41–77, 101; and Shtain-Ashkenazi, *Betar be-erets Yisra'el*, 149–57.

94. Jabotinsky to Halperin, May 3, 1934, and September 29, 1934, in A1-2, JI.

95. Halperin, *She'elat ha-bitahon ha-'ivri*, 39–40, 57–60, 101.

96. Yosef Klarman, "Fun vokh tsu vokh," *Unzer Velt*, March 13, 1936.

97. Klarman, "Fun vokh tsu vokh," *Unzer Velt*, March 20, 1936.

98. Jabotinsky elaborated upon this distinction in *Jewish War Front*, 55–66. On Jabotinsky's evolving conceptions of antisemitism, see Amir Goldshtain, *Derekh rabat panim*.

99. Weinbaum, *Marriage of Convenience*, 9–13, 100–122; Tzur, "Yehasim mesukanim," 390–402; and Robinson, *Se'arah mesaya'at*, 175–214.

100. Weinbaum, *Marriage of Convenience*, 100–211.

101. Ibid.

102. Snyder, *Black Earth*, 58–76.

103. See, for example, "Pilsudski ha'emtan," *Metsudah*, June 10, 1938. See also "Z pism Józefa Piłsudskiego: Polityka walki czynnej," *Jerozolima Wyzwolona*, September 11, 1938, 12–13; and "Yosef Pilsuski: Zayn leben un verk," *Ha-medina*, May 12, 1939.

104. Seweryn Liwa, "Dwie Ojczyzny," *Chad-Ness*, May 1939, 12–13.

105. For cases of retaliatory attacks staged by Revisionist youth against Catholic Polish rioters across central and eastern Poland, see Fefer, "Tenuat ha-tsohar"; Zahavi-Zlotnicki, "Pra'ot 1936," 77; Shohat, "Ben shetey milhamot haolam," 231; Feldman, "Di onshteyung fun betar in praga," 105; and Ben Ami, *Years of Wrath, Days of Glory*, 134.

106. Markowicz, "Brit Trumpeldor," 275–77.

107. Ya'akov Hetman, "Betar be-Luboml," 220.

108. Ibid., 219–21.

109. Historians need to exercise great caution when using memorial anthologies (*yizker bikher*) published by Holocaust survivors to commemorate Jewish communities in towns and cities across Poland. Many of them were published decades after the historical events they describe. The accounts of the past provided by yizker bikher contributors frequently bear the imprint of the trauma of the Holocaust, nostalgia for a "vanished world," as well as the authors' political and religious commitments. See Horowitz, *Memorial Books of Eastern European Jewry*.

110. Tabacznik [Ben Yosef] letters, p. 14, K16-1/3, JI.

111. Tuvi, *Milhama bli gvulot*, 371; and Robinson, *Se'arah mesaya'at*, 215–84.

112. Shalom Tabacznik to Rahel Tabacznik, June 28, 1938, item 18, in K16-1/3, JI.

113. Shindler, *Triumph of Military Zionism*, 203.

114. Tabacznik [Ben Yosef] letters, p. 25, in K16-1/3, JI.

115. See "A nay sefer vert itst tsugeshribn tsum tanakh," *Di Tat*, December 6, 1938; and "Ze'ev Jabotinsky tsum folk vegn 'irgun,'" *Di Tat*, May 16, 1939.

116. Stern, "Florence," June 20, 1934, in his *Be-damai la-'ad tihyi*, 40.

117. Maiman, *Pieśni Betaru*, 9.

118. Natan Yellin-Mor [Friedman-Yellin], *Shenot be-terem*, 11–20.

119. Ibid., 19.

120. Natan Yellin-Mor, interview with Baruch Avnon-Boch, March 24, 1976, in collection T-32/271, DRC.

121. Yellin-Mor, interview with Krulitski, June 23, 1976, in collection T-32/271, DRC.

122. "Notitsn," *Der Moment*, June 26, 1936.

123. Jabotinsky to Refa'el Rozov, April 25, 1936, in A1-2, JI.

124. *Ha-kinus ha-'olami ha-shlishi le-betar*, 58–63. Emphasis mine.

125. Eliav, *Zikhronot min ha-yamin*, 122.

126. Shindler, *Triumph of Military Zionism*, 206–12; and Shapira, Land and Power, 244.

127. *Ha-kinus ha-'olami ha-shlishi le-betar*, 72.

128. Ibid., 74.

129. See Propes, "Mit shturm un protest," *Ha-medina*, March 3, 1939; Yellin-Mor, interview with Avnon-Boch; Natan Yellin-Mor, interview with Natan Ban Halter, March 30, 1976, in collection T-32/271, DRC.

130. See Aharon Propes to Shimshon Yunitchman, December 16, 1938, and January 18, 1939, in P106-3/8, JI.

131. On Jabotinsky's attendance at an Irgun training course, see Natan Yellin-Mor, interview with Ya'akov Nashri, April 9, 1976, in collection T-32/271, DRC. On his plan to lead an armed insurrection in Palestine, see Halkin, *Jabotinsky: A Life*, 216.

132. Joseph Schechtman's account relies heavily on his own memories of Jabotinsky during this period and is supplemented by interviews with Menachem Begin, Shimshon Yunitchman, and Yaakov Meridor, among others. See *Fighter and Prophet*, 448–84.

133. In a letter to Begin in 1940, Propes recalled the tensions between them: "[Y]ou didn't work together with me in recent years and you are not obligated to believe or acknowledge me." See Propes to Begin, February 12, 1940, in P-183-4/5. Decades later, Yochanan Bader and Israel Eldad suggested that Jabotinsky had tried to delay Begin's appointment as *natsiv* of Betar in Poland. No documentation from the era has been found to support these claims. Shilon, *Begin: A Life*, 20–21, 456.

134. See, for example, Jabotinsky to the New Zionist Organization Executive, May 16, 1939; June 19, 1939; and August 7, 1939, in A1-2, JI.

135. Jabotinsky to Aharon Heichman, February 9, 1939; Jabotinsky to Shimshon Yunitchman, March 14, 1939; Jabotinsky to Shlomo Jacobi, March 16, 1939; Jabotinsky to David Raziel, April 19, 1939; and Jabotinsky to the New Zionist Organization Executive, May 8, 1939; June 2, 1939; and August 12, 1939, all in A1-2, JI.

136. Jabotinsky to Raziel, March 16, 1939, and May 24, 1939, in A1-2, JI.

137. Jabotinsky to Raziel, June 24, 1939, in A1-2, JI.

138. Jabotinsky to the New Zionist Organization Executive, June 24, 1939, in A1-2, JI.

139. Jabotinsky, "Ha'almoni," *Ha-medina*, June 28, 1939.

140. Shapira, Land and Power, 250–57.

Epilogue

1. Jabotinsky to Ignacy Mościcki, September 2, 1939, in A1-2, JI.
2. M. Y. Sheves, "Betar Sosnovits," in K7a-3/86/2, JI.
3. Ya'akov Alster et al., "Tenu'at ha-tsohar u-betar be-Sanok," 187.
4. Cohen, "Betar u-pe'ulotah," 76.
5. Yavin, *Sambatyon*, 64.
6. Frailikh, *'Ahim be-mivhan*, 52.
7. Perlis, *Tenu'ot ha-no'ar ha-halutsiyot*, 47.
8. Peleg, "Metsada o Modi'in," 289.
9. Frailikh, *'Ahim be-mivhan*, 56.
10. Propes to Begin, undated letter, in P183-4/5, JI.

11. Propes to Begin, February 12, 1940, in P183-4/5, JI.
12. Shilon, *Begin: A Life*, 27.
13. Frailikh, *'Ahim be-mivhan*, 54–56.
14. Propes to Begin, February 12, 1940.
15. For biographies of Lehi members from Poland and elsewhere, see "Lohamim ve-lohamot," *Ha-'amutah le-hantsahat moreshet Lohamei Herut Yisra'el (leh"i) u-halalehem*, accessed October 25, 2015, http://lehi.org.il/?page_id=125.
16. For a comprehensive overview of Lehi's ideology and activities, see Heller, *Stern Gang*.
17. Frailikh, *'Ahim be-mivhan*, 58.
18. Glazman and Begin to Jabotinsky, June 6, 1940, in A1-3/28/2, JI.
19. Jabotinsky to Arieh Altman, July 28, 1940, in A1-2, JI. Propes wrote Begin and assured him that they would pass their request on to the American Joint Distribution Committee. Frailikh, *'Ahim be-mivhan*, 60.
20. For Begin's well-known account of his interrogation and imprisonment, see Begin, *White Nights*. For a fascinating analysis of the NKVD file recounting Begin's arrest and interrogation, see Weiner and Rahi-Tamm, "Getting to Know You," 11–14.
21. See, for example, "Plitim mesaprim," *Ha-mashkif*, March 19, 1940; "Hurban ha-kehilah ha-yehudit be-Lodz," *Ha-mashkif*, March 27, 1940; "Be-shurot oyev hadashot me-hagolah ha-yehudit," *Ha-mashkif*, May 7, 1942; "Hanora'ot ba-geto ha-yehudi be-varsha," *Ha-mashkif*, May 28, 1942; and "17 yamim ba-gehenom shel Polin," *Ha-mashkif*, May 29, 1942.
22. "Ketsad hayim yehude Brisk," *Ha-mashkif*, October 22, 1942.
23. For a detailed study of the Yishuv leadership's attitudes toward the Holocaust, see Dina Porat's classic study, *The Blue and the Yellow Stars of David*. Porat's study has been followed by numerous works by Israeli historians on the Yishuv and the Holocaust. These works have generated numerous debates concerning what the Yishuv's leaders knew, when they knew it, and what they did with this information. On these debates, see Weitz, "Dialectical Versus Unequivocal," 278–98. In the wake of November 1942, Revisionists writing in Ha-mashkif criticized the Yishuv leadership's response to the news that European Jews were being exterminated. See Weitz, "Revisionist Criticism of the Yishuv Leadership During the Holocaust."
24. Begin, "Ken-efshar le-hatsil!" *Herut—iton hofshi*, February 1, 1943.
25. Peleg, "Metsada o Modi'in," 291–94. On the Irgun's activity between 1944 and 1948, see Hoffman, *Anonymous Soldiers*.
26. For a detailed study of the Yishuv leadership's attitudes toward the Holocaust, see Dina Porat's classic study, *The Blue and the Yellow Stars of David*. Porat's study has been followed by numerous works by Israeli historians on the Yishuv and the Holocaust. On these works and the historical debates they have generated, see Weitz, "Dialectical Versus Unequivocal," 278–98.
27. Peleg, "Metsada o Modi'in," 294–99.
28. For a painstakingly researched account of the ŻZW's activities in the Warsaw ghetto, see Libionka and Weinbaum, *Bohaterowie, hochsztaplerzy, opisywacze*, 229–576.
29. Libionka and Weinbaum, "Deconstructing Memory and History," 87–104.
30. Peleg, "Metsada o Modi'in," 295. Emphasis mine.
31. See Michaeli et al., *Rishonim La-mered*, 1–299; and Frailikh, *'Ahim be-mivhan*, 101–7.
32. Testimony of Emanuel Verman, Museum of Fighters and Partisans, K7a-3/31, JI.

33. See, for example, testimony of Avigdor Leizerovicz, K7a-3/51, JI; and testimony of Shamai Kizelstein, K7a-3/106, JI. Cooperation between Białystok's various youth movements only occurred once news arrived of the Warsaw Ghetto Uprising. Beforehand, the city's political parties had divided into two blocs, one of socialists and communists, and the other primarily consisting of General Zionists, religious Zionists, and Revisionists. See Bender, *Jews of Białystok*, 160–69, 204–11, 224–33, 252–64.

34. "She'elonim 'im pratim shel lohamim be-milhemet ha-'olam ha-shniyah," K7a-11/4, JI. See also Weichselfisch, *Elef Lohame Betar*.

35. Testimony of Yosef Foksman, Museum of Fighters and Partisans, K7a-3/61, JI; and testimony of Avraham Keren Paz, Museum of Fighters and Partisans, K7a-3/77, JI. For a detailed account of the participation of Revisionist supporters in the Vilna ghetto's resistance activity, as well as the various divisions among them, see Frailikh, *'Ahim be-mivhan*, 74–92. The head of the Jewish Police was Jacob Gens, a veteran captain in the Lithuanian army and former administrative director of Vilna's Jewish Hospital. He appointed former Betar members to prominent posts in the police. In contrast, much of Vilna's Judenrat was under Bundist influence. The clash between Gens and the FPO began in the spring of 1943. See Arad, *Ghetto in Flames*, 124–28, 377–428.

36. Libionka and Weinbaum, *Bohaterowie, hochsztaplerzy, opisywacze*, 1–229.

37. See, for example, "Bezdany—parashat ha-gvurah shel Pilsduski," *Ha-mashkif*, May 13, 1942; "Le-ma'an herutenu u-herutkhem Za naszą i waszą wolność," *Ha-mashkif*, June 5, 1942; "'Im tsva Polin ha-mitkonen li-plishah," *Ha-mashkif*, July 4, 1943; and "Ve-shuv—Ha-brigadah ha-rishonah," *Ha-mashkif*, July 16, 1943.

38. Engel, "Frustrated Alliance."

39. Yirmiyahu Halperin, quoted in ibid., 34.

40. Engel, "Frustrated Alliance," 25–27, 35.

41. For accounts from Betar members who participated in Beriha activity, see Lazar, *Betar bi-she'erit ha-plitah*; and Lazar-Litai, *Pirke berihah*.

42. *Kol tsion ha-lohemet*, July 10, 1946.

43. Engel, "Frustrated Alliance," 35.

44. On Lehi's shift toward the Soviet Union, see Heller, *Stern Gang*, 117–21, 126–29, 132–34, 145–47, 170–73, 185–92, 207–20, 231–34.

45. On links between Lehi, the Soviet Union, and the Hulanicki assassination, see Ginor and Remez, "A Cold War Casualty in Jerusalem," 135–56.

46. The estimates are based on a memorial book for Irgun and Lehi fighters during the final years of the British Mandate and the 1948 war, as well as on a memorial website for Lehi members. See Hetman, *Zikhram netsah*; and "Lohamim ve-lohamot."

47. See, for example, Rolinek, "Clandestine Operators," 47–68.

48. Morris, "Historiography of Deir Yassin," 85–88.

49. Begin, *The Revolt*, 163–65. See also ibid., 80–85.

50. Begin, *The Revolt*, 164.

51. Morris, "Historiography of Deir Yassin," 83.

52. Eldad, *The First Tithe*, 49. Emphasis mine.

53. Menachem Begin to Anya Jabotinsky, March 9, 1943, in Begin, *Mori, Ze'ev Z'abotinski*, 36–37.

54. "Kruz etse"l el ha-'am (1944)," in Begin, *Mori, Ze'ev Z'abotinski*, 49.
55. "Kruz etse"l el ha-'am (1945)," in ibid., 55–56.
56. "Avi ha-mered ha'ivri (1949)," in ibid., 80–88.
57. For a detailed account of the internal conflicts that nearly paralyzed the Herut Party, see Weitz, *Ha-tsa'ad ha-rishon le-khes ha-shilton*.
58. Ibid., 63.
59. On their activity, see Baumel, *Bergson Boys*.
60. Shilon, *Begin: A Life*, 155.
61. For a useful overview of Begin's rise to power, see Shindler, *Rise of the Israeli Right*, 250–311.
62. Vladimir Jabotinsky, "Tsurik tsum tsharter," *Di tribune*, October 15, 1915, cited in Shindler, *Rise of the Israeli Right*, 353.
63. See, for example, Yisrael Medad, "Quoting the Wrong Quotations," *My Right Word* (blog), November 2, 2004, http://myrightword.blogspot.ca/2004/11/quoting-wrong-quotations.html.
64. For an example of Rivlin invoking Jabotinsky to justify the expansion of Jewish settlements in the West Bank, see Maayan Miskin, "Rivlin: Settlements Guarantee our Existence," *Aruts Sheva*, July 18, 2012, http://www.israelnationalnews.com/News/News.aspx/157986.
65. Shindler, *Rise of the Israeli Right*, 10.
66. Jabotinsky, *Jewish War Front*, 221–23.
67. Ishaan Tharoor, "Israeli Foreign Minister Says Disloyal Arabs Should Be Beheaded," *Washington Post*, March 10, 2015, https://www.washingtonpost.com/news/worldviews/wp/2015/03/10/israeli-foreign-minister-says-disloyal-arabs-should-be-beheaded.
68. "Israel's Foreign Minister Avigdor Lieberman: Disloyal Arabs Should be Beheaded," *NBC News*, March 10, 2015, http://www.nbcnews.com/storyline/isis-terror/israels-lieberman-disloyal-arabs-should-be-beheaded-n320501.
69. See, for example, Ravit Hecht, "Rubi rivlin hu ha-opozitsiya," *Haaretz*, June 17, 2006, http://www.haaretz.co.il/opinions/.premium-1.2978076.
70. Reuven (Ben-Shem) Feldschuh, "Oyf Der Vokh," *Der Emes*, September 28, 1928, 3.
71. On the history of Holocaust commemoration in Israel, and the role of the Holocaust in Israeli public discourse, see, for example, Young, *Texture of Memory*, 209–282; and Stauber, *Holocaust in Israeli Public Debate*.
72. "Referat in varshe (in teater 'Nowości')," *Unzer Velt*, August 12, 1938.
73. Shavit and Steir-Livny, "Mi kara ze'ev?," 345–69.
74. Netanyahu, *A Place Among the Nations*, 359.
75. Ibid., 363–64. Emphasis mine.
76. Ibid., 66.

BIBLIOGRAPHY

Archives and Libraries

AAN	Archiwum Akt Nowych (Archive of Modern Records), Warsaw
ANK	Archiwum Narodowe w Krakowie (National Archives of Kraków)
APL	Archiwum Państwowe w Lublinie (National Archives in Lublin)
APW	Archiwum Państwowe w Warszawie (National Archives of Warsaw)
APK	Archiwum Państwowe w Kielcach (National Archives in Kielce)
CAHJP	Central Archives for the History of the Jewish People, Jerusalem
CAW	Centralne Archiwum Wojskowe (Central Military Archives), Warsaw
CZA	Central Zionist Archives, Jerusalem
DRC	Goldstein-Goren Diaspora Research Center Archive, Tel Aviv
JI	Archives of the Jabotinsky Institute, Tel Aviv
NL-I	National Library of Israel, Jerusalem
NL-W	National Library, Warsaw
TFL	Thomas Fisher Rare Book Library, University of Toronto, Ontario
VHA	Visual History Archive, USC Shoah Foundation, Los Angeles, California
YIVO	YIVO Institute for Jewish Research, New York
YY	Yad Ya'ari Archives, Ha-shomer Ha-tsa'ir Archives, Giv'at Haviva

Newspapers and Journals

'Avodatenu
Ba-derekh
Bafrayung Arbeter Shtime
Baranovitsher Vokh
Biuletin shel betar be-Polin: 'avodatenu
Biuletyn Ekonomiczno-Statystyczny: Materiały i cyfry z życia ludności żydowskiej w Polsce
Chad-Ness
Chwila
Cyjon
Davar
Degalenu
Der Emes
Der Judenstaat
Derekh Ha-shomer Ha-le'umi
Der Moment
Der Nayer Veg
Di Tat
Di Velt
Doar Hayom
Dziennik Warszawski
Ha'aretz
Ha-mashkif
Ha-medinah
Haneszer
Ha-yarden
Haynt
Hazit Ha'am
Igron ha-betariyah
Igrot
Igrot Livne Betar
Jardenu
Jerozolima Wyzwolona
Jewish Telegraphic Agency
London Times
Ma'ariv la-no'ar

Madrikh Betar	*Naye Folktsaytung*	*Tsiyonistishe Bleter*
Massuot	*Nowy Dziennik*	*Unzer Frayhayt*
Menorah	*Rassvet*	*Unzer Velt*
Mishmar Hayarden	*Sprawy Narodowościowe*	*Unzer Vort*
Morgn Zhurnal	*Tel Hai*	*Yedi'ot He-haluts*
Nasz Przegląd	*Trybuna Narodowa*	*The Zionist*

Pamphlets, Articles, Books

Abengózar, Mercedes Carbayo. "Shaping Women: National Identity Through the Use of Language in Franco's Spain." *Nations and Nationalism* 7, no. 1 (January 2001): 75–92.

Abrams, Philip. "Rites de Passage: The Conflict of Generations in Industrial Society." *Journal of Contemporary History* 5, no. 1 (1970): 175–90.

Abramson, Henry. *A Prayer for the Government: Ukrainians and Jews in Revolutionary Times, 1917–1920*. Cambridge, MA: Harvard University Press, 1999.

Alaimo, Kathleen. "Review Essay: Childhood and Adolescence in Modern European History." *Journal of Social History* 24, no. 3 (1991): 591–601.

———. "Shaping Adolescence in the Popular Milieu: Social Policy, Reformers, and French Youth, 1870–1920." *Journal of Family History* 17, no. 4 (1992): 419–38.

Aleksiun, Natalia. "Regards from My Shtetl: Polish Jews Write to Piłsudski, 1933–1935." *Polish Review* 56 (2011): 57–71.

Alster, Ya'akov, Yitzhak Hal-or, Binyamin Lazar, and Eliyahu Leshner. "Tenu'at ha-tsohar u-betar be-Sanok." In *Sanok: Sefer zikaron li-kehilat Sanok veha-svivah*, edited by Elazar Sharvit, 181–87. Tel Aviv: Irgun yotse Sanok veha-svivah be-Yisra'el, 1969.

Apelboim, Y., D. Milshtain, A. Rimon, and N. Shtainman. "Tenuat hatsohar u-betar." In *Entsiklopedya shel galuyot*, vol. 5, *Lublin*, edited by Nahman Blumental and Meir Koz'an, 425–45. Jerusalem: Hevrat Entsiklopedya shel galuyot, 1957.

Arad, Yitzhak. *Ghetto in Flames: The Struggle and Destruction of the Jews in Vilna in the Holocaust*. Jerusalem: Ahva, 1980.

Ariès, Philippe. *Centuries of Childhood: A Social History of Family Life*. New York: Knopf, 1962.

Aschheim, Steven. *Brothers and Strangers: The East European Jew in German and German-Jewish Consciousness, 1800–1923*. Madison: University of Wisconsin Press, 1982.

'*Avodatenu: Din ve-heshbon shel mifkedet ha-galil le-betar le-Polanyah ha-ktana ha-mizrahit belevov*. Lwów: n.p., 1935.

Bacon, Gershon. "Agudat Israel: Poland." In *Jewish Women: A Comprehensive Historical Encyclopedia*, accessed March 2, 2009, https://jwa.org/encyclopedia/article/agudat-israel-interwar-Poland.

———. "National Revival, Ongoing Acculturation: Jewish Education in Interwar Poland." *Simon Dubnow Institute Yearbook* 1, no. 1 (2002): 71–92.

———. *The Politics of Tradition: The Agudat Yisrael in Poland, 1916–1939*. Jerusalem: Magnes Press, 1996.

———. "The Poznanski Affair of 1921. Kehillah Politics and the Internal Political Realignment of Polish Jewry." *Studies in Contemporary Jewry* 4 (1988): 135–43.

———. "Warsaw-Radom-Vilna: Three Disputes over Rabbinical Posts in Interwar Poland and Their Implications for the Change in Jewish Public Discourse." *Jewish History* 13, no. 1 (1999): 103–26.

———. "Woman? Youth? Jew? The Search for Identity of Young Jewish Women in Interwar Poland." In *Gender, Place, and Memory in the Modern Jewish Experience: Re-placing Ourselves*, edited by Judith Baumel and Tova Cohen, 3–28. London: Valentine Mitchell, 2003.

Baden-Powell, Robert. *Scouting for Boys*. London: H. Cox, 1908.

Bader, Ya'akov. *Darki le-tsiyon, 1901–1948: Otobiyografya*. Jerusalem: Mekhon Z'abotinski be-Yisrae'l, 1998.

Bartal, Israel. "Imagined Geography: The Shtetl, Myth and Reality." In *The Shtetl: New Evaluations*, edited by Steven Katz, 179–92. New York: New York University Press, 2007.

Bartal, Israel, and Magdalena Opalski. *Poles and Jews: A Failed Brotherhood*. Hanover, NH: University Press of New England/Brandeis University Press, 1992.

Bassok, Ido. "Mavo." In *Alilot ne'urim: Otobiyografyot shel bene no'ar yehudim me-polin ben shete milhamot ha-olam*, edited by Avraham Novershtern, 7–25. Tel Aviv: Institute for the History of Polish Jewry, 2011.

———. "Tenu'ot ha-no'ar ha-yehudiyot be-polin ben shete milhamot ha-olam." In *Alilot ne'urim: Otobiyografyot shel bene no'ar yehudim me-polin ben shete milhamot ha-olam*, edited by Avraham Novershtern, 769–92. Tel Aviv: Institute for the History of Polish Jewry, 2011.

Bassok, Ido, and Avraham Novershtern. "Ma'arakhot ha-hinukh li-yehudei polin ben shete milhamot ha-olam." In *Alilot ne'urim: Otobiyografyot shel bene no'ar yehudim me-polin ben shete milhamot ha-olam*, edited by Avraham Novershtern, 736–51. Tel Aviv: Institute for the History of Polish Jewry, 2011.

Baumel, Judith Taylor. *The Bergson Boys and the Origins of Contemporary Zionist Militancy*. Translated by Dena Ordan. Syracuse, NY: Syracuse University Press, 2005.

Begin, Menachem. *Der Betar un zayn vort tsu di idishe eltern*. Warsaw: Kairo, 1934.

———. *Mori, Ze'ev Z'abotinski*. Edited by Efraim Even. Jerusalem: Merkaz Moreshet Menachem Begin, 2001.

———. *The Revolt*. New York: Nash, 1977.

———. "Sheloshah devarim." In *Entsiklopedya shel galuyot*, vol. 2, edited by Eliezer Steinman, 249–51. Jerusalem: Hevrat Entsiklopedya shel galuyot, 1958.

———. *White Nights: The Story of a Prisoner in Russia*. Translated by Katie Kaplan. London: MacDonald, 1957.

Ben Ami, Yitzhak. *Years of Wrath, Days of Glory: Memoirs from the Irgun*. New York: R. Speller, 1982.

Ben Baruch, Shalom. *Z'abotinski, lohem ha-umah*. Jerusalem: Shalom Shvarts, 1943.

Ben-Eliezer, Uri. *The Making of Israeli Militarism*. Bloomington: Indiana University Press, 1998.

Ben-Shem (Feldshuh), Reuven. *Betar be-Polanyah: Igrot ha-mifkadah ha-rashit mispar alef: Tarshim tokhnit ha-avodah (arbayts-plan)*. Warsaw: Renoma, 1928.

———. *Yugend tsionizm: Ha-shomer ha-le'umi*. Warsaw: Rekord, 1929.

Ben-Yerucham, Chen. *Sefer Betar: Korot u-mekorot*. Vols. 1–3. Tel Aviv: Ha-Merkaz, 1969–1973.

Bender, Sara. *The Jews of Białystok during World War II and the Holocaust*. Translated by Yaffa Murciano. Hanover, NH: University Press of New England/Brandeis University Press, 2008.

Benecke, Werner. *Die Ostgebiete der Zweiten Polnischen Republik. Staatsmacht und öffentliche Ordnung in einer Minderheitenregion 1918–1939*. Cologne: Bohlau, 1999.

Berkowitz, Michael. *Zionist Culture and West European Jewry before the First World War*. New York: Cambridge University Press, 1993.

Bessel, Richard. "The 'Front Generation' and the Politics of Weimar Germany." In *Generations in Conflict: Youth Revolt and Generation Formation in Germany, 1770–1968*, edited by Mark Roseman, 121–36. Cambridge: Cambridge University Press, 1995.

Białowąs, M. *Pan Jezus wśród ludzi, Podręcznik do nauki religii rzymskokatolickiej dla VI klasy szkół powszechnych trzeciego stopnia*. Lwów: K. S. Jakubowski właść. J. Jakubowski i Ska, 1939.

Bilski Ben-Hur, Raphaella. *Kol yachid hu melekh: Ha-mahshavah ha-hevratit ve-ha-medinit shel Ze'ev Z'abotinski*. Tel Aviv: Devir, 1988.

Biskupski, Mieczysław. *Independence Day: Myth, Symbol, and the Creation of Modern Poland*. Oxford: Oxford University Press, 2012.

Bjork, Jim. *Neither German nor Pole: Catholicism and National Indifference in a Central European Borderland*. Ann Arbor: University of Michigan Press, 2008.

Blobaum, Robert, ed. *Antisemitism and Its Opponents in Modern Poland*. Ithaca, NY: Cornell University Press, 2005.

Bornsztejn, Yaakov. "Di revizionistishe organizatsye." In *Sefer Biala Podlaska*, edited by M. Y. Feigenboim, 199. Tel Aviv: Ahdut, 1961.

Brenner, Lenni. *The Iron Wall: Zionist Revisionism from Jabotinsky to Shamir*. London: Zed Books, 1984.

Brit Trumpeldor: Hartsa'ot, vikuhim, hahlatot. Paris: Betar Command, 1931.

Brumberg, Abraham. "The Bund and the Polish Socialist Party in the Late 1930s." In *The Jews of Poland between Two World Wars*, edited by Yisrael Gutman, Ezra Mendelsohn, Samuel D. Kassow, Jehuda Reinharz, and Chone Shmeruk, 75–97. Hanover, NH: University Press of New England/Brandeis University Press, 1989.

Brykczynski, Paul. *Primed for Violence: Murder, Antisemitism, and Democratic Politics in Interwar Poland*. Madison: University of Wisconsin Press, 2016.

Bucur, Maria. *Eugenics and Modernization in Interwar Romania*. Pittsburgh, PA: University of Pittsburgh Press, 2002.

Cała, Alina, ed. *Ostatnie pokolenie: Autobiografie polskiej młodzieży żydowskiej okresu międzywojennego: ze zbiorów YIVO Institute for Jewish Research w Nowym Jorku*. Warsaw: Wydawnictwo Sic!, 2003.

———. "Wstęp." In *Ostatnie pokolenie: Autobiografie polskiej młodzieży żydowskiej okresu międzywojennego*, edited by Alina Cała, 18–50. Warsaw: Wydawnictwo Sic!, 2003.

Canning, Kathleen. "Culture of Politics—Politics of Culture: New Perspectives on the Weimar Republic." *Central European History* 43 (2010): 576–80.

Capkova, Katerina. "Piłsudski or Masaryk? Zionist Revisionism in Czechoslovakia, 1925–1940." *Judaica Bohemiae* 35 (1999): 210–39.

Ciancia, Kathryn Ward. "Poland's Wild East: Imagined Landscapes and Everyday Life in the Volhynian Borderlands, 1918–1939." PhD diss., Stanford University, 2011.

Clark, Roland. "Die Damen der Legion: Frauen in rumäischen faschistischen Gruppierungen." In *Inszenierte Gegenmacht von rechts: Die "Legion Erzengel Michael" in Rumänien*, edited by Armin Heinen and Oliver Jens Schmitt, 193–216. Munich: Oldenberg Verlag, 2013.

Cohen, Gary B. *The Politics of Ethnic Survival: Germans in Prague, 1861–1914*. Princeton, NJ: Princeton University Press, 1981.

Cohen, Hillel. *Year Zero of the Arab-Israeli Conflict: 1929*. Translated by Haim Watzman. Waltham, MA: Brandeis University Press, 2015.

Cohen, Munia. "Betar u-pe'ulotah." In *Sefer Burshtin*, edited by Sh. Kants, 71–76. Jerusalem: Hotsa'at Entsiklopedyah shel galuyot, 1960.

Corni, Gustavo. "State and Society: Italy and Germany Compared." In *The Oxford Handbook of Fascism*, edited by R.J.B. Bosworth, 279–95. New York: Oxford University Press, 2009.

Corrsin, Stephen D. *Warsaw before the First World War: Poles and Jews in the Third City of the Russian Empire, 1880–1914.* Boulder, CO: East European Monographs, 1989.

Dabrowski, Patrice. *Commemorations and the Shaping of Modern Poland.* Bloomington: Indiana University Press, 2004.

De Felice, Renzo. *Interpretations of Fascism.* Translated by Brenda Huff Everett. Cambridge, MA: Harvard University Press, 1977.

De Grand, Alexander. *Italian Fascism: Its Origins and Development.* 3rd ed. Lincoln: University of Nebraska Press, 2000.

Diggins, John. "Flirtation with Fascism: American Pragmatic Liberals and Mussolini's Italy." *American Historical Review* 71, no. 2 (January 1966): 487–506.

Di naye beylisade: Di stavski afere. Warsaw: Provizorishn sekretariat fun velt-union fun tsionistn-revizionistn, 1933.

Donson, Andrew. *Youth in a Fatherless Land: War Pedagogy, Nationalism, and Authority in Germany, 1914–1918.* Cambridge, MA: Harvard University Press, 2010.

Dowe, Dieter, ed. *Jugendprotest und Generationenkonflikt in Europa im 20. Jahrhundert.* Bonn: Verlag Neue Gesellschaft, 1986.

Eatwell, Roger. *Fascism: A History.* London: Chatto and Windus, 1995.

Edwards, G. "The Foreign Office and Fascism, 1924–1929." *Journal of Contemporary History* 5, no. 2 (1970): 53–161.

Efron, John. *Defenders of the Race: Jewish Doctors and Race Science in Fin-de-Siècle Europe.* New Haven, CT: Yale University Press, 1994.

Elam, Yigal. *Ha-Gedudim ha-'ivriyim be-milhemet ha-'olam ha-rishonah.* Tel Aviv: Ma'arakhot, 1973.

Eldad, Israel. *The First Tithe.* Translated by Zev Golan. Tel Aviv: Jabotinsky Institute, 2012.

Eliav, Binyamin. *Zikhronot min ha-yamin.* Tel Aviv: Hotsa'at am oved, 1990.

Elkar, Rainer. "The Battle for the Young: Mobilizing Young People in Wilhemine Germany." In *Generations in Conflict: Youth Revolt and Generation Formation in Germany, 1770–1968*, edited by Mark Roseman, 92–104. Cambridge: Cambridge University Press, 1995.

Engel, David. "The Frustrated Alliance: The Revisionist Movement and the Polish Government in Exile, 1939–1945." *Studies in Zionism* 7 no. 13 (1986): 11–36.

———. "Ha-she'ela ha-polanit ve-ha-tenu'ah ha-tsiyonit: Ha-vikuakh al ha-shilton ha-'atsmi be-'are Polin ha-kongresa'it, 1910–1911." *Gal-Ed* 13 (1993): 59–82.

———. "Poland from 1795 to 1939." In *The YIVO Encyclopedia of Jews in Eastern Europe*, vol. 2, edited by Gershon Hundert, 1381–1411. New Haven, CT: Yale University Press, 2008.

Epsztajn, Israel, ed. *Hora'ot la-hakhshara ha-tarbutit ba-kenim.* Warsaw: Futura, 1935.

Esden-Tempska, Carla. "National and Civic Education in Polish Elementary School Textbooks in the Interwar Period." PhD diss., Indiana University, 1991.

Esler, Anthony ed., *The Youth Revolution: The Conflict of Generations in Modern History.* Lexington: Heath, 1974.

Fefer, Yehuda. "Tenuat ha-tsohar." In *Pinkas Bendin*, edited by A. Sh. Shtain, 271–73. Tel Aviv: n.p., 1959.

Feldman, Joseph. "Di onshteyung fun betar in praga." In *Sefer Praga*, edited by Gabriel Vaysman, 103–6. Tel Aviv: Orli, 1974.

Fishman, David. *The Rise of Modern Yiddish Culture*. Pittsburgh, PA: University of Pittsburgh Press, 2005.

Frailikh, Miri. *'Ahim be-mivhan: Ha-ma'avak ha-ideologi veha-irguni 'al demutah shel tenu'at Betar be-Eropah, 1939–1946*. Ramat Gan: Yad Tabenkin, 2010.

Frankel, Jonathan. "The Yizkor Book of 1911." In *Religion, Ideology, and Nationalism in Europe and America: Essays in Honor of Yehoshua Arieli*, edited by H. Ben Israel, 355–84. Jerusalem: Zalman Shazar Center for Jewish History, 1986.

Friedländer, Saul. *The Years of Extermination, 1939–1945*. Vol. 2 of *Nazi Germany and the Jews*. New York: Harper Perennial, 2007.

Fritzsche, Peter. *Rehearsals for Fascism: Populism and Political Mobilization in Weimar Germany*. Oxford: Oxford University Press, 1990.

Gajówna, D. *Krajoznawstwo: Dla 4-go oddziału szkoły powszechnej i 1-ej klasy gimnazjum*. Warsaw: Nasza Księg, 1931.

Garbowska, Wanda. *Szkolnictwo powszechne w Polsce w latach 1932–1939*. Wrocław: Zakład Narodowy im. Ossolinskich, 1976.

Gelber, Yo'av. "Hitpathut kokho ha-tsva'i shel ha-Yishuv." *Toldot ha-Yishuv ha-yehudi be-erets Yisra'el*, edited by Moshe Lissak and Zohar Shavit, 625–32. Jerusalem: Mossad Bialik, 1998.

Gervasi, Frank. *The Life and Times of Menachem Begin: Rebel to Statesman*. New York: Putnam, 1979.

Gillis, John. "The Evolution of Juvenile Delinquency in England, 1890–1914." *Past and Present* 67 (1975): 96–126.

———. *Youth and History: Tradition and Change in European Age Relations, 1770–Present*. New York: Academic Press, 1974.

Ginor, Isabella, and Gideon Remez. "A Cold War Casualty in Jerusalem, 1948: The Assassination of Witold Hulanicki." *Israel Journal of Foreign Affairs* 4, no. 3 (2010): 135–56.

Gitelman, Zvi. *A Century of Ambivalence: The Jews of Russia and the Soviet Union, 1881 to the Present*. New York: Schocken Books, 1988.

Glerter, Menachem. "Kehillat Stanislawow bi-shenot 1918–1939." In *Arim ve-imahot be-Yisra'el: Matsevat kodesh le-kehilot Yisra'el she-nehrevu bi-yede 'aritsim u-teme'im*, edited by Y. L. Ha-Cohen Maimon, 189–382. Jerusalem: Mossad ha-Rav Kuk, 1946.

Goldberg, Moshe. *Der beytarisher ken: instruktsyes un onvayzungen*. Warsaw: Styldruk, 1934.

Goldshtain, Amir. *Derekh rabat panim: Tsiyonuto shel Ze'ev Z'abotinsky le-nokhah ha- antishemiyut*. Jerusalem: Mekhon Z'abotinski, Universitat Ben Gurion, mekhon Ben Gurion le-heker Yisra'el, 2015.

Goldshtain, Yosef. *Ben tsiyonut medinit le-tsiyonut ma'asit: Ha-tenu'ah ha-tsiyonit be-rusyah be-reshitah*. Jerusalem: Magnes Press, 1991.

Goldstein, Jacob N. *From Fighters to Soldiers: How the Israeli Defense Forces Began*. Portland, OR: Sussex Academic Press, 1998.

Gordon, Robert S. C. "Race." In *The Oxford Handbook of Fascism*, edited by R.J.B. Bosworth, 296–316. New York: Oxford University Press, 2009.

Goren, Ya'acov. *Ha-imut ha-kove'a: Bein tenu'at ha-avodah la'tenu'a ha-Revisionistit*. Tel Aviv: Hotsa'at ha-kibutz ha'me'uchad, 1986.

Gorenberg, Gershom. *The Accidental Empire: Israel and the Birth of the Settlements, 1967–1977*. New York: Times Books, 2006.

Gothelf, Yehuda, and Avraham Kohen, eds. *Sefer ha-Shomrim: Antologyah la-yovel ha-20 shel ha-Shomer ha-Tsa'ir, 1913–1933*. Warsaw: ha-Hanhagah ha-ʿelyonah le-hist. ha-Shomer ha-Tsa'ir, 1934.

Gourevitch, Adolf. "Jabotinsky and the Hebrew Language." In *The Life and Times of Vladimir Jabotinsky: Fighter and Prophet*, by Joseph Schechtman, 577–99. Silver Spring, MD: Eshel Books, 1986.

Grant, Mariel. *Propaganda and the Role of the State in Interwar Britain*. New York: Oxford University Press, 1994.

Gra'ur, Minah. *Kitve Ze'ev Z'abotinski: Bibliyografyah, 1897–1940*. Tel Aviv: Mekhon Z'abotinski be-Yisra'el, 2007.

Griffin, Roger, ed. *International Fascism: Theories, Causes, and the New Consensus*. London: Oxford University Press, 1998.

———. *The Nature of Fascism*. London: Routledge, 1993.

Grinboym, Y. "Yalduti." In *Entsiklopedya shel galuyot*, vol. 12, edited by H. Barlas, A. Tartakower, and D. Sadan, 45–64. Jerusalem: Hevrat Entsiklopedya shel galuyot, 1973.

Grozbard, Ofer. *Menahem Begin, deyokano shel manhig-biyografyah*. Tel Aviv: Resling, 2006.

Guż, Jerzy. "Realizacja programu przysposobienia wojskowego w Związku Harcerstwa Polskiego w latach 1918–1927." In *W służbie Ojczyznie: z działalności Związku Harcerstwa Polskiego w okresie międzywojennym*, edited by Monika Kała, 33–49. Wrocław: GAJT, 1998.

Ha-kinus ha-ʿolami ha-shlishi le-betar. Bucharest: Hotsa'at Shilton Betar, 1940.

Halkin, Hillel. *Jabotinsky: A Life*. New Haven, CT: Yale University Press, 2014.

Halperin, Liora. *Babel in Zion: Jews, Language, and National Diversity in Mandate Palestine*. New Haven, CT: Yale University Press, 2015.

Halperin, Yirmiyahu. *Ha-hakhsharah ha'haganatit*. Paris: Imprimerie Pascal, 1931.

———. *She'elat ha-bitahon ha-ʿivri: 'Ekronei ha-strategyah ve-ha-taktikah shel ha-haganah ha-'ivrit*. Warsaw: Remona, 1934.

Hanebrink, Paul. *In Defense of Christian Hungary: Religion, Nationalism, and Antisemitism, 1890–1944*. Ithaca, NY: Cornell University Press, 2006.

"Hashanim ha-rishonim be-Galitsyah." In *Sefer ha-Shomrim: Antologyah la-yovel ha-20 shel ha-Shomer ha-Tsa'ir, 1913–1933*, edited by Yehuda Gothelf and Avraham Kohen, 6. Warsaw: Ha-Hanhagah ha-ʿelyonah le-hist. ha-Shomer ha-Tsa'ir, 1934.

Hart, Mitchell. "Jews and Race: An Introductory Essay." In *Jews and Race: Writings on Identity and Difference, 1880–1940*, edited by Mitchell Hart, xiii–xxxix. Waltham, MA: Brandeis University Press, 2011.

———, ed. *Jews and Race: Writings on Identity and Difference, 1880–1940*. Waltham, MA: Brandeis University Press, 2011.

———. *Social Science and the Politics of Modern Jewish Identity*. Stanford, CA: Stanford University Press, 2000.

Haumann, Heiko. "Adam Mickiewicz und der jüdisch-polnischen Messianusmus." In *Fenster zur Geschichte, 20 Quellen, 20 Interpretationen*, edited by Bernhard Degen, 247–59. Basel: a. M., 1992.

Hein, Heidi. *Der Piłsudski-Kult und seine Bedeutung für den polnischen Staat, 1926–1939*. Marburg: Verlag Herder Institut, 2002.

Heller, Celia. *On the Edge of Destruction: Jews of Poland between the Two World Wars.* New York: Columbia University Press, 1977.

Heller, Joseph. "Ha-monizm shel ha-matara o ha-monizm shel ha-emtsa'im? Ha-mahloket ha-ra'ayonit ve-ha-politit ben Ze'ev Z'abotinski leven aba ahimeir, 1928–1933." *Tsion* 52, no. 3 (1987): 315–69.

———. "Jabotinsky's Use of National Myths in Political Struggles." *Studies in Contemporary Jewry* 12 (1996): 185–201.

———. *The Stern Gang: Ideology, Politics, and Terror, 1940–1949.* London: Frank Cass, 1995.

———. "Ze'ev Jabotinsky and the Revisionist Revolt against Materialism—In Search of a World View." *Jewish History* 12, no. 2 (1998): 51–67.

Henschel, Christhardt, and Stephan Stach. "Nationalisierung und Pragmatismus: Staatliche Institutionen und Minderheiten in Polen 1918–1939." *Zeitschrift für Ostmitteleuropa-Forschung* 62, no. 2 (2013): 165–86.

Hertz, Jacob. *Di geshikhte fun a yugnt: Der kleyner bund tsukufnt in poyln.* New York: Unzer Tsayt, 1946.

Hetman, Ya'akov. "Betar be-Luboml." In *Sefer Yizkor lekehilat Luboml*, edited by Berl Cohen and Ya'akov Hetman, 218–21. Tel Aviv: Mofet, 1974.

———. *Zikhram netsah: sefer yizkor le-gibore ha-Irgun ha-Tseva'i ha-Le'umi.* Tel Aviv: Shelah, 1959.

Hirschler, Gertrude, and Lester S. Eckman. *Menachem Begin: From Freedom Fighter to Statesman.* New York: Shengold, 1979.

Hoffman, Bruce. *Anonymous Soldiers: The Struggle for Israel, 1917–1947.* New York: Knopf, 2015.

Holman, Valerie, and Debra Kelly, eds. *France at War in the Twentieth Century: Myth, Metaphor, and Propaganda.* New York: Berghahn Books, 2000.

Horowitz, Brian. Introduction to *Vladimir Jabotinsky's Story of My Life*, edited by Brian Horowitz and Leonid Katsis, 1–32. Detroit, MI: Wayne State University Press, 2016.

Horowitz, Rosemary, ed. *Memorial Books of Eastern European Jewry: Essays on the History and Meanings of Yizker Volumes.* Jefferson, NC: McFarland, 2011.

Ignatowicz, Aneta. *Przygotowanie obronne społeczeństwa w Polsce (1921–1939).* Warsaw: Wydawnictwo Neriton, 2010.

Jabotinsky, Eri. *Avi, Ze'ev Z'abotinski.* Jerusalem: Hotsa'at steimatzki, 1980.

———, ed. *Ketavim.* 18 vols. Jerusalem: Hotsa'at Sefarim/Hotsa'at 'Amihai, 1947–1959.

Jabotinsky, Vladimir. "'Al ha-nashim ha-feministiot veha-sufragistiot." In *Dmut ha-ishah be-'ene Z'abotinski*, edited by Yosef Nedava, 178–81. Tel Aviv: Hamerkaz, 1963.

———. "Anahnu ha-burganim." In *Ha-Reviziyonizem ha-Tsiyoni be-hitgabshuto: Kovets ma'amarim be-"Razsvyet" la-shanim 1925–1929*, edited by Yosef Nedava, 211–17. Tel Aviv: Mekhon Z'abotinski be-Yisra'el, 1985. Originally published in *Rassvet*, April 17, 1927, 5–7.

———. "Otobiografyah." In *Ketavim nivharim*, 11–189. Vol. 1. Jerusalem: Amihai, 1947.

———. "Ha-Hashmona'i ha-riga'i." In *Ketavim*, vol. 16, edited by Eri Jabotinsky, 191. Tel Aviv: Hotsa'at 'Amihai, 1958.

———. "Hefker." In *Ha-derekh el ha-revizyonizm ha-tsiyoni: Kovets ma'amarim be-"Rassvet" la-shanim 1923–1924*, 103. Translated and edited by Yosef Nedava. Tel Aviv: Mekhon Jabotinsky be-Yisra'el, 1984. Originally published in *Rassvet* 19, nos. 40–41 (October 28, 1923): 5–6.

———. *The Jewish War Front.* London: George, Allen and Unwin, 1940.

———. *Ketavim.* Vol. 5. Tel Aviv: Hotsa'at 'Eri Jabotinski, Hotsa'at sefarim, 1957–1958.

———. *Ktavim nivharim: Golah ve-hitbolelut*. Edited by Shlomo Zaltsman. Tel Aviv: n.p., 1936.
———. *Ma rotsim tsionim reviziyonistim?* Jerusalem: Hotsa'at Ha-va'ad ha-merkazi shel histadrut ha-tsiyonim ha-reviziyonistim be-erets Yisra'el, 1925.
———. "On the Iron Wall (1923)." Translated from the Russian by Denis Kozlov. In *The Origins of Israel: A Documentary History*, edited by Eran Kaplan and Derek Penslar, 257–63. Madison: University of Wisconsin Press, 2011. Originally published in Russian under the title "O zheleznoi stene," *Rassvet* 19, nos. 42–43 (November 4, 1923): 2–4.
———. *Piatero*. Paris: ARS, 1936.
———. *Ra'ayon betar: An umrum fun beytarisher veltanshoyung*. Lwów: Netsivut betar be-Polanyah, 1934.
———. *Samson the Nazarite*. Translated by Cyrus Brooks. London: M. Secker, 1930.
———. *The Story of the Jewish Legion*. Translated by Shmuel Katz. New York: B. Ackerman, 1945. Originally published in weekly installments in *Haynt* and *Morgn Zhurnal* between November 1926 and December 1927.
———. "Trumpeldor's yortsayt." In *Dos lebn fun yosef trumpeldor*, by Aharon Propes, i–v. Warsaw: n.p., 1930.
———. *Zamelbukh far betarisher yugend*. Warsaw: Renoma, 1933.
Jacobs, Jack. *Bundist Counterculture in Interwar Poland*. Syracuse, NY: Syracuse University Press, 2009.
Judson, Pieter M. *Guardians of the Nation: Activists on the Language Frontiers of Imperial Austria*. Cambridge, MA: Harvard University Press, 2006.
Judson, Pieter, and Marsha Rozenblit. "Introduction: Constructing Nationalities in East Central Europe." In *Constructing Nationalities in East Central Europe*. Edited by Pieter Judson and Marsha Rozenblit, 1–18. New York: Berghahn Books, 2005.
Juśko, Edmund. *Szkolnictwo powszechne w powiecie tarnowskim w latach 1918–1939*. Lublin: Towarzystwo Naukowe Katolickiego Uniwersytetu Lubelskiego, 2008.
Kała, Monika, ed. *W służbie Ojczyznie: z działalności Związku Harcerstwa Polskiego w okresie międzywojennym*. Wrocław: GAJT, 1998.
Kaniel, Asaf. "Ben hilonim, mesoratiyim ve-ortodoksim: Shemirat mitsvot bere'i ha-hitmodedut im gezerat ha-kashrut: 1937–1939." *Gal-Ed* 22 (2010): 75–106.
———. "Beys Yankev." *The YIVO Encyclopedia of Jews in Eastern Europe*, accessed July 26, 2010, http://www.yivoencyclopedia.org/article.aspx/Beys_Yankev.
———. "Gender, Zionism, and Orthodoxy: The Women of the Mizrahi Movement in Poland, 1916–1939." *Polin* 22 (2009): 346–67.
———. *Yomrah u-ma'as: Ha-Mizrahi be-Polin ben shete milhamot ha-olam*. Ramat Gan: Hotsa'at Universitat Bar Ilan, 2011.
Kaplan, Eran. *The Jewish Radical Right: Revisionist Zionism and Its Ideological Legacy*. Madison: University of Wisconsin Press, 2005.
Kaplan, Eran, and Derek Penslar, eds. *The Origins of Israel: A Documentary History*. Madison: University of Wisconsin Press, 2011.
Kassow, Samuel D. "Communal and Social Change in the Polish Shtetl: 1900–1939." In *Jewish Settlement and Community in the Modern Western World*, edited by Ronald Dotterer, Deborah Dash Moore, and Steven M. Cohen, 39–55. London: Associated University Presses, 1991.

———. "Community and Identity in the Interwar Shtetl." In *The Jews of Poland between Two World Wars*, edited by Yisrael Gutman, Ezra Mendelsohn, Samuel D. Kassow, Jehuda Reinharz, and Chone Shmeruk, 198–220. Hanover, NH: University Press of New England/Brandeis University Press, 1989.

———. "Polish Jews and the Landkentenish Movement in the 1920s and 1930s." In *Jewish Topographies: Visions of Space, Traditions of Place*, edited by Julia Brauch, Anna Lipphardt, and Alexandra Nocke, 241–64. Hampshire: Ashgate, 2008.

———. "The Shtetl in Interwar Poland." In *The Shtetl: New Evaluations*, edited by Steven Katz, 121–39. New York: New York University, 2007.

Katz, Shmuel. *Lone Wolf: A Biography of Vladimir (Ze'ev) Jabotinsky*. 2 vols. New York: Barricade Books, 1996.

———, ed. *The Shtetl: New Evaluations*. New York: New York University Press, 2007.

———. *Z'abo: Biografiya shel Ze'ev Z'abotinski*. 2 vols. Tel Aviv: Devir, 1993.

Keren, Michael, and Shlomit Keren. *We Are Coming, Unafraid: The Jewish Legions and the Promised Land in the First World War*. Lanham, MD: Rowman and Littlefield, 2010.

Kęsik, Jan. *Naród pod bronią: Społeczeństwo w programie polskiej polityki wojskowej, 1918–1939*. Wrocław: Wydawnictwo Uniwersytetu Wrocławskiego, 1998.

Khrust, Yosef. "Al ha-hakhshara ve-ha'aliyah." In *Mo'etset ha-mifkadot ha-gliliyot shel Brit Trumpeldor be-Polanyah*, 11. Warsaw: Renoma, 1933.

Kijek, Kamil. "Max Weinreich, Assimilation, and the Social Politics of Jewish Nation-Building." *East European Jewish Affairs* 41, nos. 1–2 (April–August 2011): 25–55.

———. "Świadomość i socjalizacja polityczna ostatniego pokolenia Żydów Polskich w II Rzeczypospolitej." PhD diss., Polska Akademia Nauk Instytut Historii im. Tadeusza Maneuffla, 2013.

———. "Was It Possible to Avoid 'Hebrew Assimilation'? Hebraism, Polonization, and Tarbut Schools in the Last Decade of Interwar Poland." *Jewish Social Studies* 21, no. 2 (2016): 105–41.

King, Jeremy. *Budweisers into Czechs and Germans: A Local History of Bohemian Politics, 1848–1948*. Princeton, NJ: Princeton University Press, 2003.

Kirshenblatt-Gimblett, Barbara. "Coming of Age in the Thirties: Max Weinreich, Edward Sapir, and Jewish Social Sciences." *YIVO Annual* 26 (1996): 1–104.

Kirshenblatt-Gimblett, Barbara, Marcus Moseley, and Michael Stanislawski. Introduction to *Awakening Lives: Autobiographies of Jewish Youth in Interwar Poland*. Edited by Jeffrey Shandler, xi–xlii. New Haven, CT: Yale University Press, 2002.

Klein, Shira. "A Persistent Past: Italian Jews from Emancipation to Post World War II." PhD diss., New York University, 2012.

Kleiner, Israel. *From Nationalism to Universalism: Vladimir (Ze'ev) Jabotinsky and the Ukrainian Question*. Edmonton: Canadian Institute of Ukrainian Studies Press, 2000.

Klein-Pejšová, Rebekah. *Mapping Jewish Loyalties in Interwar Slovakia*. Bloomington: Indiana University Press, 2015.

Kligsberg, Moshe. "Di yidishe yugnt-bavegung in poyln tsvishn beyde velt milkhomes." In *Shtudies vegn yidn in poyln 1919–1939*, edited by Joshua Fishman, 137–228. New York: YIVO Institute for Jewish Research, 1974.

Koestler, Arthur. *Arrow in the Blue: An Autobiography*. New York: MacMillan, 1952.

Koonz, Claudia. *Mothers in the Fatherland: Women, the Family, and Nazi Politics*. London: Jonathan Cape, 1987.

Krzywiec, Grzegorz. "Czy państwo w Polsce pomajowej było czynnikiem antyżydowskim (1926–1939)? Stan badań i perspektywy badawcze." *Metamorfozy społeczne* 8 (2014): 369–88.
Kunicki, Mikołaj Stanisław. *Between the Brown and the Red: Nationalism, Catholicism, and Communism in Twentieth-Century Poland*. Athens: Ohio State University Press, 2012.
Kuznitz, Cecile Esther. *YIVO and the Making of Modern Jewish Culture: Scholarship for the Yiddish Nation*. New York: Cambridge University Press, 2014.
Landau-Czajka, Anna. "Koledzy czy wrogowie: Obraz mniejszości żydowskiej w podręcznikach szkolnych okresu międzywojennego." In *Biuletyn Żydowskiego Instytutu Historycznego* 3–4 (1997): 3–12.
———. *Polska—to nie oni: Polska i Polacy w polskojęzycznej prasie żydowskiej II Rzeczypospolitej*. Warsaw: Żydowski Instytut Historyczny, 2015.
———. *Syn będzie Lech . . . Asymilacja Żydów w Polsce międzywojennej*. Warsaw: Neriton, 2006.
Laqueur, Thomas M. "Memory and Naming in the Great War." In *The Politics of Commemoration*, edited by John Gillis, 150–67. Princeton, NJ: Princeton University Press, 1994.
Laqueur, Walter. *Fascism: Past, Present, Future*. New York: Oxford University Press, 1996.
———. *A History of Zionism*. New York: Random House, 1972.
———. *Young Germany: A History of the German Youth Movement*. New York: Basic Books, 1962.
Lazar, Hayim. *Betar bi-she'erit ha-plitah: 1945–1948*. Tel Aviv: Muze'on ha-lohamim veha-partizanim, mekhon Z'abotinski be-Yisra'el, 1997.
Lazar-Litai, Hayim. *Pirke berihah*. Tel Aviv: Muze'on ha-lohamim veha-partizanim, 1986.
Le Bon, Gustave. *Psychologie des foules*. Paris: Félix Alcan, 1895.
Lerner, Zelig. *Mahanot kayitz/Zumer Lagern*. Warsaw: Grafja, 1932.
Levinson, Zunio. "Tenuat ha-noar Betar be-Podvolochiskah." In *Sefer Podvolochiskah ve-hasviva*, edited by Zunio Levinson and Dov Brayer, 64–67. Haifa: Dfus gestlit, 1988.
Lewakowski, Jerzy. *Terenoznawstwo i kartografia wojskowa: podręcznik dla organizacji wojskowych i drużyn skautowych*. Warszawa: Związek Polskich Gimnast. Towarzystw Sokolich, 1916.
Libertal, Hanna. *Sefer ha-nesharim: Sefer-ezer le-rashei ha-darga alef shel brit-trumpeldor, helek alef*. Warsaw: Hotsa'at Ha-shilton ve-netsivut betar be-polanya, 1934.
Libionka, Dariusz, and Laurence Weinbaum. *Bohaterowie, hochsztaplerzy, opisywacze: Wokół Żydowskiego Związku Wojskowego*. Warszawa: Stowarzyszenie Centrum Badań nad Zagładą Żydów, 2011.
———. "Deconstructing Memory and History: The Jewish Military Union (ŻZW) and the Warsaw Ghetto Uprising." *Jewish Political Studies Review* 18, nos. 1–2 (Spring 2006): 87–104.
Lichtenstein, Tatjana. *Zionism in Interwar Czechoslovakia: Minority Nationalism and the Politics of Belonging*. Bloomington: Indiana University Press, 2016.
Linton, Derek. *Who Has the Youth, Has the Future: The Campaign to Save Young Workers in Imperial Germany*. Cambridge: Cambridge University Press, 1991.
Linz, Juan L. *Totalitarian and Authoritarian Regimes*. Boulder, CO: Lynne Rienner, 2000.
Lipman, A. *Revizionistishe grund-problemen fun revizionistishe teoretiker*. Warsaw: 1931.
Livezeanu, Irina. *Cultural Politics in Greater Romania: Regionalism, Nation Building and Ethnic Struggle, 1918–1930*. Ithaca, NY: Cornell University Press, 1995.
Lyttelton, Adrian. *The Seizure of Power: Fascism in Italy, 1919–1929*. 3rd ed. Princeton, NJ: Princeton University Press, 2004.
Maarten, V. G. "Gender, the Extreme Right, and Flemish Nationalist Women's Organizations in Interwar Belgium." *Nations and Nationalism* 11, no. 2 (April 2005): 265–84.

Maiman, M. *Pieśni Betaru*. Lwów: Chad Ness, 1939.
Małkowski, Andrzej. *Scouting jako system wychowania młodżiezy: Na podstawie dzieła generała Baden-Powella*. Lwów: Nakładem Związku polskich gimn. tow. Sokolich, 1911.
Mann, Michael. *Fascists*. New York: Cambridge University Press, 2004.
Mannheim, Karl. "The Problem of Generations." In *Karl Mannheim: Essays*, edited by Paul Kecskemeti, 276–322. New York: Routledge, 1952.
Marcus, Joseph. *Social and Political History of the Jews in Poland, 1919–1939*. New York: Mouton Publishers, 1983.
Markowicz, Leon. "Brit Trumpeldor." In *Sefer zikaron le-kehilat Tomashov-mazovyetski*, edited by Moshe Visberg, 275–77. Tel Aviv: Orli, 1969.
Margalit, Elkana. "Social and Intellectual Origins of Hashomer Hatzair." *Journal of Contemporary History* 4, no. 2 (1969): 25–46.
Martin, Sean. *Jewish Life in Cracow, 1918–1939*. London: Vallentine Mitchell, 2004.
Mauersberg, Stanisław. *Szkolnictwo powszechne dla mniejszości narodowych w Polsce w latach 1918–1939*. Warsaw: Ossolineum, 1968.
Maynes, Mary Jo. *Schooling in Western Europe: A Social History*. Albany: State University of New York, 1985.
Mazower, Mark. *Dark Continent: Europe's Twentieth Century*. New York: Penguin, 1998.
Mędrzecki, Włodzimierz. *Województwo wołyńskie 1921–1939: Elementy przemian cywilizacyjnych, społecznych i politycznych*. Wrocław: Zakład Narodowy im. Ossolińskich, 1988.
Melzer, Emanuel. *No Way Out: The Politics of Polish Jewry, 1935–1939*. Cincinnati, OH: Hebrew Union College Press, 1997.
Mendelsohn, Ezra. "From Assimilation to Zionism in Lvov: The Case of Alfred Nossig." *Slavonic and East European Review* 49 (1971): 521–34.
———. "Jewish Politics in Interwar Poland: An Overview." In *The Jews of Poland between the Two World Wars*, Yisrael Gutman, Ezra Mendelsohn, Samuel D. Kassow, Jehuda Reinharz, and Chone Shmeruk, 1–19. Hanover, NH: New England University Press/ Brandeis University Press, 1989.
———. *The Jews of East Central Europe Between the World Wars*. Bloomington: Indiana University Press, 1983.
———. *On Modern Jewish Politics*. New York: Oxford University Press, 1993.
———. *Zionism in Poland: The Formative Years, 1915–1926*. New Haven, CT: Yale University Press, 1981.
Merchavia, Hen Melekh. *Likrat Ha-medinah: Le-she'elot he-halutsiyut veha-binyan*. Białystok: M. Prużanski, 1930.
Michaeli, Haim, Y. Lichtsheyn, Y. Moravchik, and H. Sklar, eds. *Rishonim La-mered: Lahva*. Jerusalem: Entsiklopedya shel galuyot, 1957.
Michlic, Joanna Beata. *Poland's Threatening Other: The Image of the Jew from 1880 to the Present*. Lincoln: University of Nebraska Press, 2006.
Mickute, Jolanta. "Making of the Zionist Woman: Zionist Discourse on the Jewish Woman's Body and Selfhood in Interwar Poland." *East European Politics and Societies* 28, no. 1 (February 2014): 137–62.
———. "Modern, Jewish, and Female: The Politics of Culture, Ethnicity, and Sexuality in Interwar Poland, 1918–1939." PhD diss., Indiana University, 2011.

Mikulski, Antoni Jan, and Juliusz Saloni. *W Lipkach: Czytanki dla II klasy szkół powszechnych*. 2nd ed. Lwów: Ossolineum, 1933.

Ministerstwo Wyznań Religijnych i Oświecenia Publicznego (MWRiOP). *Program nauki w publicznych szkołach powszechnych drugiego stopnia z polskim językiem nauczania, Historja*. Warsaw: Państwowe Wydawnictwo Książek Szkolnych, 1935.

Mintz, Matityahu. *Havle ne'urim: ha-tenu'ah ha-Shomrit 1911–1921*. Jerusalem: Publishing House of the World Zionist Organization, 1995.

Miron, Dan. *The Image of the Shtetl and Other Studies of Modern Jewish Literary Imagination*. Syracuse, NY: Syracuse University Press, 2000.

———. *A Traveler Disguised: A Study in the Rise of Modern Yiddish Fiction in the Nineteenth Century*. New York: Schocken Books, 1973.

Mironowicz, Eugeniuz. *Białorusini i Ukraińcy w polityce obozu piłsudczykowskiego*. Białystok: Wydawn. Uniwesyteckie Trans Humana, 2007.

Mo'etset Ha-mifkadot ha-gliliyot shel Brit Trumpeldor be-Polanyah. Warsaw: Renoma, 1933.

Morgan, Philip. *Italian Fascism, 1919–1945*. Basingstoke: Macmillan, 1995.

Morris, Benny. "The Historiography of Deir Yassin." *Journal of Israeli History* 24, no. 1 (March 2005): 79–107.

Moseley, Marcus. "Life, Literature: Autobiographies of Jewish Youth in Interwar Poland." *Jewish Social Studies* 7, no. 3 (2001): 1–51.

Moss, Kenneth. "Negotiating Jewish Nationalism in Interwar Warsaw." In *Warsaw: The Jewish Metropolis: Essays in Honor of the 75th Birthday of Professor Antony Polonsky*, edited by Glenn Dynner and François Guesnet, 390–436. Leiden: Brill, 2015.

———. "Not the *Dybbuk* but *Don Quixote*: Translation, Deparochialization, and Nationalism in Jewish Culture." In *Culture Front: Representing Jews in Eastern Europe*, edited by Benjamin Nathans and Gabriella Safran, 196–240. Philadelphia: University of Pennsylvania Press, 2008.

———. "Thinking with Restriction: Immigration Restriction and Polish Jewish Accounts of the Post-Liberal State, Empire, Race, and Political Reason, 1929–1939." *East European Jewish Affairs* 44, nos. 2–3 (2014): 205–24.

Mosse, George. "Introduction: The Genesis of Fascism." *Journal of Contemporary History* 1 (1966): 14–26.

Mussolini, Benito. *The Doctrine of Fascism*. Translated by Jane Soames. New York: Howard Fertig, 1968.

Myers, David. *Reinventing the Jewish Past: European Intellectuals and the Zionist Return to History*. New York: Oxford University Press, 1995.

Naor, Arye. "Jabotinsky's New Jew: Concepts and Models." *Journal of Israeli History* 30, no. 2 (September 2011): 144–48.

Natkovich, Svetlana. *Ben 'ananei zohar: Yetsirato shel Vladimir (Ze'ev) Z'abotinski ba-heksher ha-hevrati*. Jerusalem: Magnes Press, 2015.

Nedava, Yosef, ed. *Demut ha-ishah be-'ene Z'abotinski*. Tel Aviv: Hamerkaz, 1963.

———, trans and ed. *Ha-derekh 'el ha-revizyonizem ha-tsiyoni: Kovets ma'amarim be-"Rassvyet" la-shanim 1923–1924*. Tel-Aviv: Makhon Z'abotinski be-Yisra'el, 1984.

———. *Ha-revizyonizem ha-tsiyoni be-hitgabshuto: Kovets ma'amarim be-"Razsvyet" la-shanim 1925–1929*. Tel Aviv: Makhon Jabotinsky, 1985.

———. *Z'abotinski be-hazon ha-dor*. Tel Aviv: Shelah, 1950.
Netanyahu, Benjamin. *A Place Among the Nations: Israel and the World*. New York: Bantam, 1993.
Neumann, Matthias. *The Communist Youth League and the Transformation of the Soviet Union, 1917–1932*. New York: Routledge, 2011.
Nietzsche, Friedrich. *Beyond Good and Evil: Prelude to a Philosophy of the Future*. Translated and edited by Rolf-Peter Horstmann and Judith Norman. New York: Cambridge University Press, 2002.
Nolte, Claire E. *The Sokol in the Czech Lands to 1914: Training for the Nation*. New York: Palgrave Macmillan, 1993.
Nowogrodzki, Emanuel. *The Jewish Labor Bund in Poland, 1915–1939: From Its Emergence as an Independent Political Party until the Beginning of World War II*. Rockville, MD: Shengold, 2001.
Nur, Ofer. *Eros and Tragedy: Jewish Male Fantasies and the Masculine Revolution of Zionism*. Brighton, MA: Academic Studies Press, 2014.
———. "The Relevance of Countercultures and Visions for the Future: Examining the Historical Example of Hashomer Hatzair." In *Revisiting Youth Political Participation: Challenges for Research and Democratic Practice in Europe*, edited by Joerg Forbrig, 37. Strasbourg: Council of Europe, 2005.
Nye, Robert. *The Origins of Crowd Psychology: Gustave Le Bon and the Crisis of Mass Democracy in the Third Republic*. London: Sage Publications, 1975.
Odziemkowski, Janusz. *Armia i społeczeństwo II Rzeczypospolitej*. Warsaw: Wydawnictwo Bellona, 1996.
Oppenheim, Israel. "Hahakhshara ha-kibutsit shel betar be-Polin bi-shnot ha-30 (1930–1936)." *Divre ha-kongres ha-ʾolami le-madaʾe ha-yahadut* 2 (1973): 295–305.
———. *Tenuat he-haluts be-Polin, 1929–1939*. Jerusalem: Magnes Press, 1982.
"Osowa Wyszka." In *Pinkas ha-kehilot: Entsiklopedyah shel ha-Yishuvim ha-Yehudiyim le-min hivasdam ve-ʾad le-ahar shoʾat milhemet ha-ʿolam ha-shniyah*, vol. 5, edited by D. Dąbrowska, Abraham Wein, and Aharon Vais, 31–32. Jerusalem: Yad Vashem, 1990.
Paruch, Waldemar. *Od konsolidacji państwowej do konsolidacji narodowej: Mniejszości narodowe w myśli politycznej obozu piłsudskiego, 1926–1939*. Lublin: Wydawnictwo Uniwersytetu Marii Curie-Skłodowskiej, 1997.
Passmore, Kevin. *Fascism: A Very Short Introduction*. New York: Oxford University Press, 2002.
Paxton, Robert. *The Anatomy of Fascism*. New York: Vintage Books, 2005.
———. "The Five Stages of Fascism." *Journal of Modern History* 70, no. 1 (March 1998): 1–23.
Payne, Stanley. *Fascism: Comparison and Definition*. Madison: University of Wisconsin Press, 1980.
———. *A History of Fascism, 1914–1945*. Madison: University of Wisconsin Press, 1995.
Peleg, Amir. "Metsada o Modiʾin: Menachem Begin ve-yahaso le-mered geto varsha." *ʿIyunim bi-tkumat Yisraʾel* 19 (2009): 283–305.
Perelman, Jakub [Jakób]. *Moje przeżycia, spostrzeżenia*. Haifa: PEN, 1977.
———. *Rewizjonizm w Polsce, 1922–1936r*. Warsaw: Wydawnictwo Europa, 1937.
Perlis, Rivka. *Tenuʾot ha-noʾar ha-halutsiyot be-Polin ha-kvushah*. Tel Aviv: ha-kibuts ha-meʾuhad, 1987.
Perlmutter, Amos. *The Life and Times of Menachem Begin*. Garden City, NY: Doubleday, 1987.
Petrovski-Shtern, Yochanan. *Golden-Age Shtetl: A New History of Jewish Life in Eastern Europe*. Princeton, NJ: Princeton University Press, 2014.

Peukert, Detlev. *Grenzen der Sozialdisziplinierung: Aufstieg und Krise der deutschen Jugendfürsorge 1878 bis 1932*. Cologne: Bund, 1986.

Pinchuk, Ben-Cion. "The Shtetl: An Ethnic Town in the Russian Empire." *Cahiers du Monde Russe* 41, no. 4 (October–December 2000): 495–504.

Pinsker, Shahar. "Imagining the Beloved: Gender and Nation-Building in Early Twentieth-Century Literature." *Gender and History* 20, no. 1 (2008): 105–27.

Pinto, Vincenzo. "Between *imago* and *res*: The Revisionist-Zionist Movement's Relationship with Fascist Italy, 1922–1938." *Israel Affairs* 10, no. 3 (2004): 90–109.

Plach, Ewa. *The Clash of Moral Nations: Cultural Politics in Piłsudski's Poland, 1926–1935*. Athens: University of Ohio Press, 2006.

Polonsky, Antony. *History of the Jews in Russia and Poland*. Vol. 2. London: Littman Library of Civilization, 2010.

———. *Little Dictators: The History of Europe Since 1918*. Boston: Routledge / London: K. Paul, 1975.

———. *Politics in Independent Poland, 1921–1939: The Crisis of Constitutional Government*. Oxford: Clarendon Press, 1972.

———. "'Why did they hate Tuwim and Boy so much?' Jews and 'Artificial Jews' in the Literary Polemics of the Second Polish Republic." In *Antisemitism and Its Opponents in Modern Poland*, edited by Robert Blobaum, 189–209. Ithaca, NY: Cornell University Press, 2005.

Polonsky, Antony, and Joanna Michlic, eds. *The Neighbors Respond: The Controversy over the Jedwabne Massacre in Poland*. Princeton, NJ: Princeton University Press, 2004.

Pomfret, David M. "Lionized and Toothless: Young People and Urban Politics in Britain and France, 1918–1940." In *European Cities, Youth, and the Public Sphere in the Twentieth Century*, edited by Axel Schildt and Detlef Siegfried, 27–42. Hampshire: Ashgate, 2005.

———. "Youth Movements in Europe." In *Encyclopedia of the Modern World*, vol. 8, edited by Peter N. Stearns, 139–42. New York: Oxford University Press, 2008.

Porat, Dina. *The Blue and the Yellow Stars of David: The Zionist Leadership in Palestine and the Holocaust, 1939–1945*. Cambridge, MA: Harvard University Press, 1990.

Porter, Brian. *When Nationalism Began to Hate: Imagining Modern Politics in Nineteenth-Century Poland*. New York: Oxford University Press, 2000.

Porter-Szűcs, Brian. *Faith and Fatherland: Catholicism, Modernity, Poland*. New York: Oxford University Press, 2011.

———. *Poland in the Modern World: Beyond Martyrdom*. West Sussex: Wiley Blackwell, 2014.

Prokop-Janiec, Eugenia. *Polish-Jewish Literature in the Interwar Years*. Translated by Abe Shenitzer. Syracuse, NY: Syracuse University Press, 2003.

Propes, Aharon. *Dos lebn fun yosef trumpeldor*. Warsaw: n.p., 1930.

———. *Eynike onvayzungen*. Warsaw: Sława, 1929.

———. "Hakdama." In *Hora'ot la-hakhsharah ha-tarbutit ba-kenim*, edited by Israel Epsztajn, 4. Warsaw: Futura, 1935.

Radliński, Tadeusz. *Krajoznawstwo: podręcznik dla klasy pierwszej szkół średnich i miejskich*. Warsaw: M. Arct, 1919.

Reinharz, Jehuda. *Chaim Weizmann: The Making of a Statesman*. New York: Oxford University Press, 1993.

Remba, Isaac. "Hakdama." In *Der beytarisher ken: instruktsyes un onvayzungen*, by Moshe Goldberg, 2. Warsaw: Styldruk, 1934.

———, ed. *Shnatayim: Din ve-heshbon shel netsivut Betar be-Polanyah*. Warsaw: Futura, 1934.
Report of the Commission on the Palestine Disturbances of August 1929. London: HMSO, 1930.
Rezmer, Waldemar. "Służba wojskowa Żydów w siłach zbrojnych Drugiej Rzeczypospolitej." In *Mniejszości narodowe i wyznaniowe w siłach zbrojonych Drugiej Rzeczypospolitej, 1918–1939*, edited by Zbigniew Karpusa and Waldemara Rezmera, 97–110. Toruń: Wydawnictwo Uniwersytetu Mikołaja Kopernika, 2001.
Riley, Dylan. *The Civic Foundations of Fascism in Europe: Italy, Spain, and Romania, 1870–1945*. Baltimore, MD: Johns Hopkins University Press, 2010.
Robinson, Rinat-ya Gorodenchik. *Seʻarah mesayaʻat: Ha-tnuʻah ha-revizyonistit ba-shanim 1925–1940*. Jerusalem: Yad Yitshak Ben Tsvi, Machon Z'abotinski, 2010.
Rodogno, Davide. *Fascism's European Empire: Italian Occupation during the Second World War*. New York: Cambridge University Press, 2006.
Rogger, Hans. "Afterthoughts." In *The European Right: A Historical Profile*, edited by Hans Rogger and Eugen Weber, 575–89. Berkeley: University of California Press, 1966.
Rolinek, Susanne. "Clandestine Operators: The *Bricha* and *Betar* Network in the Salzburg Area, 1945–1948." In *Escape through Austria: Jewish Refugees and the Austrian Route to Palestine*, edited by Thomas Albrich and Ronald W. Zweig, 47–68. London: Frank Cass, 2002.
Rosenthal, Michael. *The Character Factory: Baden-Powell and The Origins of the Boy Scout Movement*. London: Collins, 1986.
Roskies, David. *The Jewish Search for a Usable Past*. Bloomington: Indiana University Press, 1999.
Ross, Corey. "Mass Politics and the Techniques of Leadership: The Promise and Perils of Propaganda in Weimar Germany." *Modern German History* 24, no. 2 (2006): 184–211.
Rossol, Nadine. "Performing the Nation: Sports, Spectacles, and Aesthetics in Germany, 1926–1936." *Central European History* 43 (2010): 616–38.
Rothschild, Joseph. *East Central Europe between the Two World Wars*. Seattle: University of Washington Press, 1974.
———. *Piłsudski's Coup d'Etat*. New York: Columbia University Press, 1966.
Rozwadowski, Piotr. *Państwowy Urząd Wychowania Fizycznego i Przysposobienia Wojskowego, 1927–1939*. Warsaw: Wydawnictwo Bellona, 2008.
Rudnicki, Szymon. "Anti-Jewish Legislation in Interwar Poland." In *Antisemitism and Its Opponents in Modern Poland*, edited by Robert Blobaum, 148–70. Ithaca, NY: Cornell University Press, 2005.
———. *Obóz Narodowo Radykalny: Geneza i działalność*. Warsaw: Czytelnik, 1985.
———. *Równi, ale niezupełnie*. Warsaw: Stowarzyszenie "Midrasz," 2008.
———. *Żydzi w parlamencie II Rzeczypospolitej*. Warsaw: Wydawnictwo Sejmowe, 2004.
Sarid, Menachem. *La-shilton behartanu: Ha-maʼavak al ha-hegemoniya be-yishuv u-ve-tsiyonut, 1930–1935*. Hertseliyah: Hotsaʼat "Oren," 2004.
Schatz, Jaff. "Jews and the Communist Movement in Interwar Poland." In *Studies in Contemporary Jewry*, vol. 20, *Dark Times, Dire Decisions: Jews and Communism*, edited by Jonathan Frankel, 13–37. New York: Published for the Avraham Harman Institute of Contemporary Jewry by Oxford University Press, 2004.
Shechter, Yaʼakov. "Yeme Neʼurim." In *Josef Klarman*, 10-11. Jerusalem: 1987.
Schechtman, Joseph. *Fighter and Prophet: The Last Years*. New York: A. S. Barnes, 1961.
———. *Rebel and Statesman: The Vladimir Jabotinsky Story*. New York: T. Yoseloff, 1955.

Schechtman, Joseph, and Yehuda Benari. *History of the Revisionist Movement*. Tel Aviv: Hadar, 1970.

Schelles, József. *Praca kulturalno wychowacza w Bejtarze*. Lwów: Wydawnictwo Komendy Okręgowej Bejtaru, 1934.

Schenke, Cornelia. *Nationalstaat und nationale Frage: Polen und die Ukrainer 1921–1939*. Hamburg: Dölling und Galitz, 2004.

Schreiber, Mieczysław, and Eugeniusz Piasecki. *Harce Młodzieży Polskiej*. Lwów: Książn. Polska Tow. Naucz. Szk. Wyższ, 1917.

Sefer Radom. Tel Aviv: Irgun yots'e Radom be-Yisra'el, 1961.

Shamir, Yitzhak. *Summing Up: An Autobiography*. London: Weidenfeld and Nicolson, 1994.

Shandler, Jeffrey, ed. *Awakening Lives: Autobiographies of Jewish Youth in Poland before the Holocaust*. New Haven, CT: Yale University Press, 2002.

——— . *Shtetl: A Vernacular Intellectual History*. New Brunswick, NJ: Rutgers University Press, 2014.

Shanes, Joshua. *Diaspora Nationalism and Jewish Identity in Habsburg Galicia*. New York: Cambridge University Press, 2012.

Shapira, Anita. *Ben-Gurion: Father of Modern Israel*. New Haven, CT: Yale University Press, 2014.

——— . "'Black Night–White Snow': Attitudes of the Palestinian Labor Movement to the Russian Revolution, 1917–1929." *Studies in Contemporary Jewry* 4 (1988): 144–71.

——— . *Ha ma'avak ha-nihzav: Avoda ivrit, 1929–1939*. Tel Aviv: Tel Aviv University, 1977.

——— . *Land and Power: The Zionist Resort to Force, 1881–1948*. Translated by William Templer. New York: Oxford University Press, 1992. Reprint, Stanford, CA: Stanford University Press, 1999. Citations are to the Stanford edition.

——— . "The Religious Motifs of the Labor Movement." In *Zionism and Religion*, edited by Shmuel Almog, Jehuda Reinharz, and Anita Shapira, 251–272. Jerusalem: Zalman Shazar Center, 1994.

Shapiro, Jonathan. *The Road to Power: Herut Party in Israel*. Translated by Ralph Mandel. Albany: State University of New York, 1991.

Shavit, Ya'akov. *Jabotinsky and the Revisionist Movement, 1925–1948*. London: Frank Cass, 1988.

——— . *Me-rov li-medinah: Ha-tnu'ah ha-revizyonistit, ha-tokhnit ha-hityashvut veha-ra'ayon ha-hevrati, 1925–1935*. Tel Aviv: Yariv, 1978.

——— . "Politics and Messianism: The Zionist Revisionist Movement and Polish Political Culture." *Studies in Zionism* 6, no. 2 (1985): 229–46.

Shavit, Ya'akov, and Liat Shtayer-Livny. "Mi kara ze'ev? Ekh hevin Ze'ev Z'abotinski et tivah shel Germaniyah hanatsit ve-et kavanoteha?" In *Ish ba-sa'ar: Masot u-mehkarim 'al Ze'ev Z'abotinski*, edited by Avi Bar'eli and Pinhas Ginosar, 345–69. Sedeh-Boker: Ben Gurion University Press, 2004.

Shilon, Avi. *Menachem Begin: A Life*. Translated by Danielle Zilberberg and Noam Sharett. New Haven, CT: Yale University Press, 2012.

Shindler, Colin. *A History of Modern Israel*. New York: Cambridge University Press, 2013.

——— . *The Rise of the Israeli Right: From Odessa to Hebron*. New York: Cambridge University Press, 2015.

——— . *The Triumph of Military Zionism: Nationalism and the Origins of the Israeli Right*. London: IB Taurus, 2009.

Shneer, David. *Yiddish and the Creation of Soviet Jewish Culture, 1918–1930*. New York: Cambridge University Press, 2004.

Shohat, Azriel. "Ben shetey milhamot haolam." In *Pinsk: Sefer Edut ve-zikaron le-kehilat Pinsk-karlin*, vol. 1, edited by Wolf Ze've Rabinovitsh, 5–293. Tel Aviv: Dfus ha-merkaz, 1966.

Shorrock, William I. "France and the Rise of Fascism in Italy, 1919–1923." *Journal of Contemporary History* 10, no. 4 (October 1975): 591–610.

Shtain-Ashkenazi, Esther. *Betar be-erets Yisra'el, 1925–1947*. Jerusalem: Mekhon Z'abotinski, 1997.

Shternshis, Anna. *Soviet and Kosher: Jewish Popular Culture in the Soviet Union, 1923–1939*. Bloomington: Indiana University Press, 2006.

Shukman, Harold. *War or Revolution: Russian Jews and Conscription in Britain, 1917*. London: Valentine Mitchell, 2006.

Sienkiewicz, Witold, ed. *Atlas Historii Żydów Polskich*. Warsaw: Demart, 2010.

Sikorski, Eugeniusz. *Szkice z dziejów harcerstwa polskiego w latach 1911–1939*. Warsaw: Wydawnictwo Interpress, 1989.

Silber, Marcos. *Le'umiut shonah, ezrahut shavah! Ha-ma'amats le-hasagat otonomyah li-Yehude Polin be-milhemet ha-olam ha-rishonah*. Tel Aviv: Universitat Tel Aviv, 2014.

Sliwinski, Walerjan Jeremi. *Sygnalizacja: podręcznik dla harcerzy*. Warsaw: Nakład księgarni SW Wojciecha, 1921.

Snyder, Timothy. *Black Earth*. New York: Tim Duggan Books, 2015.

Springhall, John. *Youth, Empire, and Society: A Social History of British Youth Movements, 1883–1940*. Hamden, CT: Archon Books, 1977.

Stach, Stephan. "Minderheitenpolitik der Zweiten Polnischen Republik, 1918–1939." *Zeitschrift für Ostmitteleuropa-Forschung* 59, no. 3 (2010): 394–412.

Stanislawski, Michael. *Zionism and the Fin de Siècle: Cosmopolitanism and Nationalism from Nordau to Jabotinsky*. Berkeley: University of California Press, 2001.

Stauber, Roni. *The Holocaust in Israeli Public Debate in the 1950s*. Translated by Elizabeth Yuval. London: Valentine Mitchell, 2007.

Stauter-Halstead, Keely. "Jews as Middleman Minorities in Rural Poland." In *Antisemitism and Its Opponents in Modern Poland*, edited by Robert Blobaum, 39–59. Ithaca, NY: Cornell University Press, 2005.

———. *The Nation in the Village: The Genesis of Peasant National Identity in Austrian Poland, 1848–1914*. Ithaca: Cornell University Press, 2001.

Steffen, Katrin. "Das eigene Durch das Andere: Zur Konstruktion *jüdischer Polonität*." *Jahrbuch des Simon-Dubnows Institut* 3 (2004): 89–111.

———. *Jüdische Polonität: Ethnizität und Nation im Spiegel der polnischsprachigen jüdischen Presse, 1918–1939*. Göttingen: Vandenhoeck and Ruprecht, 2004.

Steinlauf, Michael. "Jewish Politics and Youth Culture in Interwar Poland: Preliminary Evidence from the YIVO Autobiographies." In *The Emergence of Modern Jewish Politics: Bundism and Zionism in Eastern Europe*, edited by Zvi Gitelman, 91–104. Pittsburgh, PA: University of Pittsburgh Press, 2003.

Stern, Avraham. *Be-damai la-'ad tihyi: Shirim*. Jerusalem: Hotsa'at Ya'ir al shem Avraham Shtern, 1976.

Sternhell, Ze'ev, Mario Sznajder, and Maia Asheri. *The Birth of Fascist Ideology: From Cultural Rebellion to Political Revolution*. Princeton, NJ: Princeton University Press, 1994.

Tahor, Ze'ev. "The Histadrut: From Marginal Organization to State-in-the-Making." In *Essential Papers on Zionism*, edited by Anita Shapira and Jehuda Reinharz, 473–508. New York: New York University Press, 1996.

Teveth, Shabtai. *Ben Gurion: The Burning Ground, 1886–1948*. Boston: Houghton Mifflin, 1987.

Todorova, Maria. *Imagining the Balkans*. New York: Oxford University Press, 1997.

Tomaszewski, Jerzy. "The Role of Jews in Polish Commerce, 1918–1939." In *The Jews of Poland between the Two World Wars*, edited by Yisrael Gutman, Ezra Mendelsohn, Samuel D. Kassow, Jehuda Reinharz, and Chone Shmeruk, 141–57. Hanover, NH: University Press of New England/ Brandeis University Press, 1989.

Trzebiatowski, Klemens. *Szkolnictwo powszechne w Polsce w latach 1918–1932*. Warsaw: Wydawnictwo Polskiej Akademii Nauk, 1970.

Tuvi, Ya'akov. *Milhama bli gvulot: Ha-tnu'ah ha-tsionit ha-reviziyonistit ve-sugiyat ha-ʻaliyah le-erets Yisra'el ba-shanim 1930–1940*. Jerusalem: Haifa University and Jabotinsky Institute, 2011.

Tzur, Eli. *Lifnei bo ha-afelah: Ha-shomer ha-tsa'ir be-polin u-ve galitsiya, 1930–1940*. Kiryat Sde Boker: Machon Ben Gurion, 2006.

———. "Yechasim mesukanim: Ze'ev Z'abotinski u-misrad ha-huts shel Polin." In *Ish ba-sa'ar: Masot u-mehkarim al Ze'ev Z'abotinski*, edited by Avi Bar'eli, Eli Tzur, and Pinhas Ginosar, 390–402. Sede Boker: Universitat Ben-Gurion ba-Negev, 2004.

Ury, Scott. *Barricades and Banners: The Revolution of 1905 and the Transformation of Warsaw Jewry*. Stanford, CA: Stanford University Press, 2012.

Veidlinger, Jeffrey. *Jewish Public Culture in the Late Russian Empire*. Bloomington: Indiana University Press, 2009.

Verhey, Jeffrey. "Some Lessons of the War: The Discourse on Propaganda and Public Opinion in Germany in the 1920s." In *War, Violence, and the Modern Condition*, edited by Bernd Hueppauf, 99–118. Berlin: Walter de Gruyter, 1997.

Walasek, Stefania. *Szkolnictwo powszechne na ziemiach północno-wschodnich II Rzeczypospolitej, 1915–1939*. Kraków: Oficyna Wydawnicza Impuls, 2006.

Walicki, Jacek. *Ruch syjonistyczny w Polsce w latach, 1926–1930*. Łódź: Ibidem, 2005.

Ward, James. *Priest, Politician, Collaborator: Jozef Tiso and the Making of Fascist Slovakia*. Ithaca, NY: Cornell University Press, 2013.

Weeks, Theodore. *From Assimilation to Antisemitism: The "Jewish Question" in Poland, 1850–1914*. Dekalb: Northern Illinois University Press, 2006.

Weichselfisch, Efraim. *Elef Lohame Betar*. Tel Aviv: Muze'on ha-lohamim veha-partizanim, 1989.

Weinbaum, Laurence. *A Marriage of Convenience: The New Zionist Organization and the Polish Government, 1936–1939*. Boulder, CO: East European Monographs, 1993.

———. "'Shaking the Dust Off': The Story of the Warsaw Ghetto's Forgotten Chronicler, Ruben Feldschu (Ben Shem)." *Jewish Political Studies Review* 22, nos. 3–4 (Fall 2010): 7–44.

Weiner, Amir, and Aigi Rahi-Tamm. "Getting to Know You: The Soviet Surveillance System 1939–1957." *Kritika* 13, 4 (Winter 2012): 5–45.

Weinreich, Max. *Der veg tsu unzer yugnt: Yesoydes, metodn, problemen fun yidishn yugnt forshung*. Wilno: Drukarnia D. Krejensa, 1935.

Weiser, Kalman. *Jewish People, Yiddish Nation: Noah Prylucki and the Folkists in Poland*. Toronto: University of Toronto Press, 2011.

Weitz, Yechiam. *Ha-tsa'ad ha-rishon le-khes ha-shilton: Tenu'at ha-herut, 1949–1955*. Yerushalayim: Yad Yitshak Ben Tzvi, Mosad Hertsel, Universitat Haifa, 2007.

———. "Revisionist Criticism of the Yishuv Leadership During the Holocaust." *Yad Vashem Studies*, no. 23 (1993): 369–95.

———. "The Revisionist Movement and Democracy." *Modern Jewish Studies* 10, no. 2 (2011): 185–204.

Weizmann, Chaim. *Trial and Error: The Autobiography of Chaim Weizmann*. New York: Harper, 1949.

Whitney, Susan B. *Mobilizing Youth: Communists and Catholics in Interwar France*. Durham, NC: Duke University Press, 2009.

Williams, Robert Chadwell. *Culture in Exile: Russian Emigres in Germany, 1881–1941*. Ithaca, NY: Cornell University Press, 1972.

Wohl, Robert. *The Generation of 1914*. Cambridge, MA: Harvard University Press, 1979.

Wojtas, Dorota. *Learning to Become Polish: Education, National Identity, and Citizenship in Interwar Poland, 1918–1939*. Leipzig: Lambert Academic Publishing, 2009.

Wróbel, Piotr. "The Rise and Fall of Parliamentary Democracy in Interwar Poland." In *The Origins of Modern Polish Democracy*, edited by M.B.B. Biskupski, James Pula, and Piotr Wróbel, 110–64. Athens: Ohio University Press, 2010.

Wyrobek, Zygmunt. *Harcerz w polu: Ćwiczenia w terenie*. Lwów: Zakład Narodowy im. Ossolińskich, 1926.

———. *Yoman ha-pkudot: Ha-hozrim ve-ha-hora'ot shel netsivut betar be-Polanyah*. Warsaw: Druk. Renoma, 1935.

Yellin-Mor, Natan. *Shenot be-terem*. Tel Aviv: Kineret, 1990.

Yevin, Ada Amichal. *Sambatyon: Ide'ologyah be-mihan tamid*. Bet-El: Sifriyat Bet-El, 1995.

Yona, Rona. "Nihyeh kulanu halutsim: Halutsiut ve-le'umiut 'amamit bi-tn'uat he-haluts be-Polin ben milhamot ha-'olam." PhD diss., Tel Aviv University, 2013.

Young, James E. *The Texture of Memory: Holocaust Memorials and Meaning*. New Haven, CT: Yale University Press, 1993.

Z'abotinski, Eri. *Avi, Ze'ev Z'abotinski*. Jerusalem: Hotsa'at steimatzki, 1980.

Zahavi-Zlotnicki, M. "Pra'ot 1936." In *Sefer kehilat Suvalk u-bnoteha*, edited by Yehuda Alroey and Yosef Khrust, 76–77. Tel Aviv: 1989.

Zahra, Tara. *Kidnapped Souls: National Indifference and the Battle for Children in the Bohemian Lands, 1900–1948*. Ithaca, NY: Cornell University Press, 2008.

Zait, David. *Ha-utopia ha-shomrit: Ha-shomer ha-tsa'ir be-Polin, 1921–1931*. Givat Haviva: Ha-Merkaz le-moreshet Ben Gurion, 2002.

Zayidin, N. "Hahaverah bi-tnuot hano'ar hatsiyoniyot be-Polin ben shete milhamot ha'olam." PhD diss.: Ben Gurion University, 2000.

Żblikowski, Andrzej. "Poles and Jews in the *Kresy Wschodnie*—Interethnic Relations in the Borderlands, 1918–1939." *Jahrbuch des Simon-Dubnows Institut* 1 (2002): 41–53.

Zerubavel, Yael. *Recovered Roots: Collective Memory and the Making of Israeli National Tradition*. Chicago: University of Chicago Press, 1995.

Zimmerman, Joshua, ed. *Jews in Italy under Fascist and Nazi Rule, 1922–1945*. New York: Cambridge University Press, 2005.

Zloch, Stephanie. *Polnischer Nationalismus: Politik und Gesellschaft zwischen den beiden Weltkriegen*. Cologne: Böhlau Verlag, 2010.

Zouplna, Jan. "Beyond a One-Man Show: The Prelude of Revisionist Zionism, 1922–1925." *Israel Affairs* 19, no. 3 (2013): 401–32.

———. "Vladimir Jabotinsky and the Split within the Revisionist Union: From the Boulogne Agreement to the Katowice Putsch." *Journal of Israeli History* 24 (January 2005): 35–63.

Żydnul, Jolanta. *Zajścia antyżydowskie w Polsce w latach 1935–1937*. Warsaw: Fundacja im. Kelles-Krauza, 1994.

INDEX

Achimeir, Abba, 79–80, 109–11, 121, 181, 201, 205, 214, 218–19
Action française, 6
agriculture, 3, 36–37, 60, 88, 150, 179–80, 185, 193
Agudat Yisrael (Union of Israel), 5, 22, 144, 182, 223, 273n10
Ahad Ha'am, 190
al-Aqsa Mosque, 83
Al-Hamishmar (On Guard), 60
Alliance Israélite Universelle, 29
Alotin, Arie, 201
Altalena (ship), 248–50
Altman, Arieh, 61
Anders army, 240, 244–45
"Anonymous Soldiers" (Stern), 230–31
anthems, 2, 4, 104, 112, 128, 134, 230–31
antisemitism: Anders army and, 245; Begin and, 245–46; Catholics and, 19, 244–45; Endecja and, 14; European Right and, 6–8, 13; fascism and, 76, 81; Polish nationalism and, 134, 138–44, 164–66; rebellion and, 112; state discrimination and, 14–15; terror and, 222–28; youth movements and, 42–45
Arab Revolt, 27, 224, 231, 248
Arabs: Ben Yosef and, 229–30; Islam and, 32, 77, 83, 119; Revisionists and, 158–59; terror and, 229–36
Archive of Modern Records, Warsaw, 1
Arlosoroff, Haim, 201, 203–14, 249
Arlosoroff, Sima, 201
assassinations, 8, 156, 203, 207, 210, 239, 246, 289n45

Auschwitz-Birkenau, 240, 253
Auster, Maks, 42
Austro-Hungarian Empire, 7, 16, 21, 35, 43–44, 46, 94, 225
authoritarianism: Betar and, 50–58, 65, 88–92, 97–99, 122–28; democracy and, 252; European Right and, 6–11; fascism and, 70, 72, 74, 80, 89, 91, 101–2, 257n33; Jabotinsky and the public case for, 66, 118–23; Polish Jews and, 7–8, 55–58; Piłsudksi and, 124–25; Revisionists and, 25, 102–3, 106–18; Sanacja and, 2, 13–14, 18–19, 30, 55–58, 62, 67, 80, 125, 134, 136–40, 143–47, 155, 160, 162, 165, 207, 252; youth movements and, 30, 51, 54, 56, 66
Autobiographies (YIVO Contest), 23–24, 135–44, 166, 185–93
Axelrod, Avraham, 194–95, 198, 200, 281n103

Baden-Powell, Robert, 43
Bader, Jan, 45
Balfour, Arthur James, 32, 38
Balilla movement, 21, 76
Balkans, 210, 284n38
Bartel, Kazimierz, 56
Beck, Józef, 227
Begin, Aliza, 238, 249
Begin, Menachem, 132f; Achimeir and, 218–19; Altalena and, 248–49; arrest of, 240; background of, 217–18; Ben-Gurion and, 219, 248; Betar and, 218–22, 232–43; birth of son, 249; childhood, 217–18; Deir Yassin massacre and, 247–48; fight against British and, 241–42; German

Begin, Menachem (*continued*)
occupation and, 237–43; Herut Party and, 249–50; Histadrut and, 219; Holocaust and, 242–43; Irgun and, 242, 245, 247–50; Jabotinsky and, 218–19, 232–33, 238–40, 249–50; Kielce pogrom and, 245–46; murder of family, 241; as prime minister, 1; Propes and, 234, 238–39, 241–42, 287n133, 288n19; solidarity with Poland and, 1–2, 237–38

Belarusians, 1, 8, 16, 56, 137, 139, 151, 161–62, 171, 243, 255n1

Ben-Gurion, David, 82, 206, 214–15, 219–21, 248

Ben Yosef, Shlomo, 229–33, 235

Bergson Boys, 250

Beriha (Escape), 245–46

Betar: anonymous report on, 167–68; anthems and, 2, 4, 104, 112, 128, 134, 230–31; autobiographers and, 186–93; authoritarianism and, 104–28; Begin and, 239–43; Beriha (Escape) and, 245–46; Bibring and, 42–47, 50–51, 55, 63–65; clubrooms of, 174–75, 178; Brit Ha-Biryonim and, 106–13, 204–5; clashes with Labor Zionists, 81–82, 201–5; Command 51 and, 185; communism and, 244, 246; Diaspora and, 174, 178, 195, 228, 238; education and, 47, 75, 99, 114–15; establishment of in Poland, 30, 34–35, 41–42, 44, 46–47, 50–51, 62–67; European Right and, 9–13, 68–77, 86–92, 127–28; exponential growth of, 106; fascism and, 2, 10, 26, 68–102, 104; Feldschuh and, 47–55, 62, 64, 74–78, 252; field reports and, 193–200; first national conference of, 64–65; First World Conference of, 67–68; flight of leaders from Warsaw, 237–38; founding of, 4; Friedman-Yellin and, 231; Gentlemen's Agreement and, 114–18; German occupation and, 237–44; *Ha-medina* newspaper and, 126, 168, 171, 196, 203, 218, 225, 233–34; Hannukah revolt and, 99–100; Hebrew and, 2–3, 17, 34, 46–47, 64, 66, 68, 81, 91, 97, 105, 110, 115, 149–50, 153, 163, 171–78, 184, 195, 225–26, 244, 249; Holocaust and, 240–44; ideal Polish patriot and, 144–59; illegal immigration and, 245; Irgun and, 222–36, 248; Jewish Legion and, 4, 47, 50, 77, 87, 89, 146, 150–51, 155, 166, 174, 179; Jewish Military Union and, 242; as Joseph Trumpeldor League, 2; leadership of, 71–77, 90–92; legends and, 12, 75, 86, 96, 99, 145, 151, 154, 157, 177, 219, 244; Lehi and, 239, 244, 246–48; Lorberbojm and, 73–74, 78; militarism and, 2–4, 13, 47, 50, 70, 76–78, 87, 90, 106, 113, 115, 135, 144, 149, 153, 159–63, 180–83, 197, 224–26, 228–29, 231, 238, 246; Mussolini and, 69, 80; myths and, 26, 34, 70, 101, 138, 145, 147, 150, 177; National Agency for Physical Education and Military Preparation (PW) and, 159–63; Nazis and, 240, 243; Netanyahu and, 253; netsivut and, 172–85, 191–200, 238; newspapers and, 11, 13, 20, 68–69, 106–8, 111, 124, 126, 133, 142, 146, 152–53, 165, 182, 185–86, 190, 194, 196–97, 203, 205, 212, 214, 218, 225, 230, 241; Palestinian Arabs and, 92–5, 100–103, 158–59, 191–93, 222–24, 229–36, 246–48; parades and, 2, 13, 22, 68, 106, 130*f*, 134–35, 142–44, 146, 154–55, 224, 229; passport fees and, 173, 185; Piłsudski and, 8–9, 13, 19, 30, 80, 124, 134, 141–42, 145–47, 155–59, 164–66, 222, 228; pins of, 189–91; pledges of obedience and, 2, 13, 47, 107–8, 134, 138, 144, 155, 162, 214–15, 218–19, 237; police and, 19–20; opposition to socialists, 47–50, 81–82, 91–92, 97–98, 201–12; Polish nationalism and, 1–2, 12–20, 41–47, 50–58, 133–66, 222–29; Propes and, 34, 37, 62–63, 67, 85–86, 90–93, 99–101, 107, 110, 114, 123–26, 129*f*, 148, 156–57, 167, 171, 173–74, 179–81, 184, 189, 193–95, 198–200, 220, 233–34, 238–39, 241; as refugees, 238, 244–45; regional commands and, 173, 175, 180, 193–94, 198, 218; religion and, 23, 68–70, 95–100, 156–57; Revisionists and, 5, 105–28, 240–44,

246, 250; Sanacja and, 18–20, 55–58, 62, 133–66; scouting and, 17, 44, 46–47, 51, 76, 143–44, 149–50, 154, 162–63; Second Polish Republic and, 27, 154, 244; shatnez and, 97; shtetl life and, 27, 167–200; *sihot* and, 176–77; socialism and, 8, 210, 243–44; solidarity with Poland and, 2, 5–6, 237–38; *Tel Hai* and, 86–95; terror and, 201–36; Trumpeldor and, 4; United Partisans Organization and, 244; violence and, 25, 76–77, 82–86, 92–95, 99–100, 201–36; visas and, 184–85; Warsaw and, 2, 23–27, 41, 50–51, 64–65, 67–74, 77–78, 85, 91–92, 102, 110, 124, 140–42, 153–57, 160, 162, 166–68, 171, 173–99, 204, 206, 210, 217–18, 225–26, 230–33, 237–44, 248, 253; Western Wall demonstration and, 83–84; women and, 132f, 149, 181–84

Betar Authority (Shilton Betar), 172–73, 199

Betar Leader, The (Madrikh Betar) bulletin, 175

Bialik, Hayim, 75

Białystok, 28, 48, 90, 148, 170, 181, 197, 230, 243

Bible, 31, 48–49, 63–64, 96–99, 120, 145, 178, 225

Bibring, Adalbert, 42–47, 50–51, 55, 63–65

Bitanya, 48

Boiko, David, 124–26

Bolsheviks, 38, 43, 79

bombs, 223, 230, 237, 242, 247

bourgeoisie, 40, 60–61, 210

boycotts, 14, 127, 204, 222

Boy Scouts, 21, 76, 259n85. *See also* scouting

Bregman, Zvi, 198

Brisk, 201, 206, 241

Brit Ha-Biryonim (the Alliance of Hooligans): Arlosoroff trial and, 214; Begin and, 218–19; founding of, 109; netsivut and, 200; rejection of political patience by, 200; radicalism of, 200, 202; Revisionists and, 106, 109–13, 118, 120, 123, 127, 200–205, 214–25, 238, 250–51; Talmud and, 109–10; von Weisl and, 204

Brit Ha-amlanim, 61

British: Arabs and, 3–4, 13, 39, 83–85, 87; Army of, 3, 31, 43, 83, 239–40; Balfour and, 32, 38; Boy Scouts and, 21, 43; colonialism of, 3, 13, 31, 234–35; Hashemite rule and, 37–38; Irgun and, 247; Jabotinsky and, 31–32, 82–86, 118–19, 234–36; Jerusalem and, 32; Jewish Legion and, 31–32, 39, 150; King David Hotel bombing and, 247; Mandate Palestine and, 4 (*see also* Mandate Palestine); Ottoman Palestine and, 3; rebellion and, 107–12, 118–19; Revisionists and, 4, 13, 37–39, 83–84, 87, 107–12, 118–19, 150, 199, 219, 226, 231–32, 235, 242–45; underground movements against, 249; Zionists and, 3–4, 13, 31–32, 37–38, 43, 83–87, 107–8, 112, 119, 150, 199, 202, 214, 219, 223, 231–36, 239, 244–45, 249

British Intelligence Service and Document Bureau, 244

Bund, 5, 22, 51, 55, 68–69, 99, 143–44, 192, 242

Cahan, Ya'akov, 54–55, 58–59, 62

Carlbach, Ezriel, 212

Catholics: democracy and, 256n28; Diaspora and, 19; Endecja and, 8, 14, 20, 24, 57, 62, 117, 207; ethnic issues and, 8, 19–20; German occupation and, 244; Holocaust and, 244; loyalty and, 154; minorities and, 7; pogroms and, 245–46; Poland and, 1, 7–8, 14–16, 19–21, 42–43, 46, 56, 62, 76, 134–44, 150–51, 154, 157, 162–63, 165, 169, 190, 224, 226–28, 237, 244–45; political power of, 14; Revisionists and, 244; scouting and, 163; self-defense unit of, 237; shtetl life and, 169

Cecil, Robert, 85

censorship, 17, 101

Chajes, Zwi Perez, 48

Chamberlain, Houston Stewart, 143

choirs, 22

Chrust, Yosef, 180

citizenship, 70, 72, 173, 222, 251

civil war, 13, 24, 56, 246–47, 249

clubrooms, 174–75, 178
colonialism, 3, 13, 31, 234–35
communism: Betar and, 75, 77, 79, 82, 101 244, 246; European Right and, 7–8; fascism and, 71–72; Polish Communist Party and, 25; politics of nationality and, 19–20; shtetl life and, 189, 193; United Partisans Organization and, 244; violence and, 61; youth movements and, 30, 43, 48–50, 57, 61, 242
conflict of generations, 24, 26, 113, 121, 127, 209, 211–12, 271n36
conservatives, 7, 9
Constitution Day, 141
corruption, 7–9, 55–58, 107, 127, 207, 209
Cossacks, 137
Crimean War, 150–51
Czechs, 1, 21, 94, 220, 255n1, 256n16

Darwin, Charles, 76
De Amicis, Edmondo, 177
death camps, 240–41
Decline of the West, the (Spengler), 79
"Defense through Attack" (Halperin), 225
Defoe, Daniel, 177
Deir Yassin massacre, 247–48
democracy: antisemitism and, 256n28; authoritarianism and, 252; Catholics and, 256n28; European Right and, 6–8, 10–11; fascism and, 69–70, 72–73, 79–80, 95, 102; Jewish future and, 4; Mussolini and, 72–73; parliamentary rule and, 69, 72, 121; rebellion and, 26, 105–6, 115, 121–22, 125, 127–28; terror and, 206, 211; youth movements and, 38, 56
dictatorships: fascism and, 71–72, 79–80; politics of belonging and, 146–47; rebellion and, 106, 110–11, 114–15, 118, 121, 124–26, 128; youth movements and, 65
Dmowski, Roman, 8
Doar Hayom newspaper, 40, 80–81, 83–84
drama clubs, 22, 192, 196
Drymmer, Tomir, 227
Dworzec Wiedeński, 28

education: Agudat Yisrael and, 273n10; Betar and, 47, 75, 99, 114–15; book lists and, 177–78; bulletins and, 175–78, 182–85; cultural programming and, 69, 75, 174, 176; Feldschuh and, 75–76; financial issues and, 138; first aid training and, 137; geography and, 15; gymnasiums and, 16, 43, 45, 48, 136, 174, 179, 218; *hachshara* and, 175–76, 179–81, 193–94, 197–98, 203; Halperin and, 181, 184, 194, 200; heroic figures and, 176–77; hygiene and, 178–79; identity and, 135–44; language and, 15; Mickiewicz and, 137–38; Ministry of Education and, 161–62; moral, 54; National Agency for Physical Education and Military Preparation (PW) and, 159–63; netsivut exams and, 184–85; pedagogy techniques and, 170–71, 175–76; physical culture and, 54, 178–79; politics of nationality and, 14–15, 19, 135–42; public schools and, 15–16, 18, 44, 135–46, 150–51, 160, 163, 166, 186, 188, 222, 273n10, 274n13; Sanacja and, 136–40, 143–50; scouting and, 17, 21–22, 35, 42–55, 76, 137, 143–44, 149–50, 154, 159, 162–63; shtetl life and, 170–71, 175–79, 182–83, 185, 195–96; Sienkiewicz and, 137–38; *sihot* and, 176–77; summer camps and, 5, 276n67; synagogues and, 52, 68–69, 71, 96, 140, 154, 156–57, 169, 268n96; Tarbut school network and, 17, 34, 141, 170, 174, 176, 178, 239, 275n39; violence and, 139; vocational, 3, 179; women and, 137, 183–84, 198
Egypt, 32, 98, 120, 248
"El Maleh Rachamim" (medieval prayer), 96, 157
Emes, Der (The Truth) journal, 71, 74, 77
engineers, 173, 230
European Right: authoritarianism and, 6–11; Betar and, 9–13, 68–77, 86–92, 127–28; communism and, 7–8; democracy and, 6–8, 10–11; Feldschuh and, 50; Germans and, 6–9; identity and, 11; Jabotinsky and, 10–11; Mandate Palestine

and, 8; Mussolini and, 7–9; nationalism and, 6, 9, 244; Nazis and, 6–7, 9, 240–44; Trumpeldor and, 12, 89–90; useful comparisons of, 67

Evacuation Plan, 227

Evreiskaia zhizn' newspaper, 38

fascism: authoritarianism and, 70, 72, 74, 80, 89, 91, 101–2, 257n33; Balilla movement and, 21, 76; Betar and, 2, 10, 26, 68–102, 104, 266n8; communism and, 71–72, 75, 77, 79, 82, 101; definition of, 71–77, 256n32; democracy and, 69–70, 72–73, 79–80, 95, 102; dictatorships and, 71–72, 79–80; ethnic issues and, 81; Feldschuh and, 74–78; Germans and, 68, 94; immigration and, 82, 84, 87; Italy and, 7, 9, 21, 24, 26, 69–73, 75–76, 79–80, 89, 98, 101, 112, 239; Jabotinsky and, 70–71, 77–86; journalists and, 68–69, 73, 75, 94; Lejzerowicz and, 65–66, 74–75, 95, 101, 118; liberalism and, 70–72, 94; Lorberbojm and, 73–74, 78; Mandate Palestine and, 79, 82–83, 85, 89–90, 99; Mussolini and, 7, 9, 13, 24, 26, 69, 71–73, 76, 79–80, 112, 146; nationalism and, 72, 76, 81, 93–95, 98, 101; newspapers and, 68–69, 79, 83; parades and, 68–69; Piłsudski and, 80; Propes and, 85–86, 90–93, 99–101; radical right and, 70, 86, 88, 95–102; rebellion and, 70; religion and, 10, 69, 75, 79, 83, 86, 95–98; Revisionists and, 69–90, 101–3; rhetoric and, 72, 74, 79, 89, 97, 102; Russians and, 79, 87, 94, 103; Sanacja and, 80; socialism and, 68–77, 80, 82, 88–94, 97–99, 101; state of flux of, 10; Trumpeldor and, 86–100; violence and, 70, 74, 76, 78, 83–85, 93, 96, 99–100; Weizmann and, 69, 79, 107–9; Zionists and, 68–103

Feldschuh, Reuven: altered spellings of, 263n70; as Ben-Shem, 48; Betar and, 47–55, 62, 64, 74–78, 252; education and, 75–76; fascism and, 74–78

folklore, 75, 151, 171

France, 6–7, 21, 31, 44, 68, 248

Franz Joseph II, 44

Frayhayt, 22

Freud, Sigmund, 76

Friedman-Yellin, Natan, 230–31, 239

Galicia: Bibring and, 42–47, Betar leadership and, 124–26, 173–74, 193–94; Feldschuh and, 47–50; eastern, 41, 43–44, 46–47, 73, 114, 117, 124, 126, 159, 167, 169, 174, 193–94, 197; ethnic conflict and, 44; Habsburg Empire and, 16, 42–43, 154; politics of nationality and, 16–18; shtetl life and, 167, 169, 172–74, 193–94, 197; Stanisławów, 41–47; Stryj, 73; western, 47–50; youth movements and, 28, 41–49, 59, 63; Zionism and, 15–16, 117–18

Galilee, 4, 48, 86–87, 229

Galili, Yisraeli, 248

Garibaldi, Giuseppe, 94–95, 147

gas chambers, 240–41

Gaza, 251

Gazeta Warszawska Poranna (newspaper), 62

Gegenwartsarbeit, 258n70

General Union of Jewish Workers (Bund), 5, 22, 51, 55, 68–69, 99, 143–44, 192, 242

Gentlemen's Agreement, 114–18

George, David Lloyd, 31

Germans: European Right and, 6–9; fascism and, 68, 94; Histadrut and, 82, 203–4, 206, 208, 211, 215, 219, 221; killing centers of, 240–41; Luftwaffe and, 237; march on Warsaw, 237; Nazis and, 9 (*see also* Nazis); occupation of Poland by, 6, 51, 237–44; Operation Barbarossa and, 237; Third Reich and, 6–7, 9, 212, 237, 239, 241, 253; Vilnius and, 240; Wandervogel movement and, 21, 45; Yiddish and, 3; youth movements and, 21, 34–35, 40–41, 44–46, 48, 51, 56

ghettos, 33, 224, 241–44, 289n35

Glazman, Yosef, 243–44

Goldanski, B., 168–69, 171

Goldberg, Avrom, 206–7
Goldberg, Moshe, 174–75
Gordonia, 22, 88, 189–91
Gourevitch, Adolf, 104–5, 128
Great Synagogue, 68–69, 71
Grinberg, Uri Zvi, 109–10, 123, 203–4, 208
Grinboym, Yitzhak, 17, 60–61, 133–34, 161
Grodno, 11, 51, 186, 230
Grossman, Meir, 39, 80, 107, 115–17, 123–26, 272n60
gymnasiums, 16, 21, 43–45, 48, 136, 159, 174, 179, 218

Habsburg Empire, 14, 43–44, 94, 154, 193–94
hachshara (preparation), 175–76, 179–81, 193–94, 197–98, 203
hadar (honor), 66, 104–5, 149, 177
Haganah, 3, 32, 223–24, 246–48
Haganah Bet. *See* Irgun
Haggadah, 98
Hall, Stanley, 176
Haller, Józef, 44
Halperin, Yirmayahu: background of, 181; "Defense through Attack" and, 225; education and, 181, 184, 194, 200; ethical codes and, 224; guidebook of, 225–26, 228; Histadrut and, 203; idolization of, 200; Irgun and, 224, 250; Jabotinsky and, 226; militarism and, 200, 225–26, 245; violence and, 224–25
Ha-mashkif (the Observer) newspaper, 241, 244
Ha-medina newspaper, 126, 168, 171, 196, 203, 218, 225, 233–34
Hannukah, 99–101
Hapoel Hatzair, 61
Haram esh-Sharif (the Noble Sanctuary), 83
Harce Młodzieży Polskiej (Scouting Guide for Polish Youth), 149
Ha-shachar (the Dawn), 51–55, 58, 73
Hashemite dynasty, 37–38
Ha-shomer Ha-tahor/Ha-le'umi (the Pure/National Guard), 47, 49–50, 75

Ha-shomer Ha-tsa'ir (the Young Guard), 17, 22, 45, 48–49, 75, 88, 143–44, 167, 187, 196, 212, 218
Ha-shomer (the Guardsman), 45
haskalah (Jewish enlightenment), 169–70
havlaga (self restraint), 223–24, 233, 235
Haynt newspaper, 52, 55, 61, 65, 78, 98, 107, 120–21, 186, 206–11
Hazit Ha'am (the Nation's Frontline) journal, 110, 205
Hebrew: Betar and, 2–3, 17, 34, 46–47, 64, 66, 68, 81, 91, 97, 105, 110, 115, 149–50, 153, 163, 171–78, 184, 195, 225–26, 244, 249; biblical, 97; Diaspora and, 195; education and, 3, 17, 34–36, 49, 81, 91, 178, 195; military guidebooks and, 225–26; netsivut and, 172–85, 191–200, 238; newspapers and, 40, 80, 110; translations into and, 150, youth movements and, 34–36, 40, 46–49, 54, 64, 66, 68
Hebrew Resistance Movement (Tenuat Ha-meri Ha-ivri), 247
He-Halutz (the Pioneer), 22, 87–90, 180, 203
Herut (Liberation) Party, 250
Herzl, Theodor, 45, 48, 96, 141, 143, 174, 182
Hetman, Ya'akov, 160–61, 228
Histadrut (General Federation of Laborers in the Land of Israel), 82, 203–4, 206, 208, 211, 215, 219, 221, 267n48, 283n4
Hitler, Adolf: Aryanism and, 207, 243; Jabotinsky as, 204; Mussolini and, 9; Piłsudski and, 146
Holitscher, 75
Holocaust: Auschwitz and, 240, 253; Begin's use of, 242; Betar and, 240–44; conditions on eve of, 1; Diaspora and, 242, 252; identity and, 252; memorial anthologies and, 286n109; Netanyahu and, 253; Porat on, 288n23, 288n26
Holy Temple, 97, 100, 187
Hulanicki, Witold, 227, 246
Hungarians, 7, 9, 16, 21, 44, 76, 225
hygiene, 178, 179

identity cards, 173, 185
Igrot Livne Betar (Letters to Betar Members) magazine, 73
immigration: Balkans and, 210, 284n38; Begin and, 250; Beriha (Escape) and, 245–46; Betar and, 245; British white paper and, 239; Evacuation Plan and, 227; fascism and, 82, 84, 87; *hachshara* and, 175–76, 179–81, 193–94, 197–98, 203; Histadrut and, 82, 203–4, 206, 208, 211, 215, 219, 221; illegal, 13, 120, 199–200, 229, 231, 245; Irgun and, 248; Jabotinsky and, 199–200; Mandate Palestine and, 239–41, 245 (*see also* Mandate Palestine); preparation for, 179–80, 184, 198–99; restriction of, 239; Russians and, 29, 31, 35; Yishuv and, 3, 5, 38, 40, 82–84, 90, 150, 152, 158, 200–204, 213, 223, 226, 235, 238, 241; youth movements and, 31–32, 37–38, 40, 50, 60; Zionist Organization Department of Immigration and, 198–99, 282n127
Iran, 240
Iraq, 4, 240, 248
Irgun: Agudat Yisrael and, 223; *Altalena* and, 248–50; Arabs and, 246; Begin and, 242, 245, 247–50; Beriha (Escape) and, 245–46; Betar and, 248; British and, 239, 247; Deir Yassin massacre and, 247–48; Evacuation Plan and, 227; Friedman-Yellin and, 231; General Zionists and, 223; Haganah Bet and, 223; Halperin and, 224, 250; Hulanicki and, 246; Israel Defense Forces (IDF) and, 248–49; Jerusalem and, 247–48; Jewish State Party and, 224; Jeziernicki and, 239; King David Hotel bombing and, 247; Lehi and, 246–47; military training and, 13, 223, 227; Mizrahi and, 223; Paris Agreement and, 233–34; Polish government and, 227–29, 231; Revisionists and, 245; Stern and, 231, 239; supervisory committee of, 223–24; terror and, 223–24, 227–35
Israel Defense Forces (IDF), 248–49

Italy: Balilla movement and, 21, 76; fascism and, 7, 9, 21, 24, 26, 69–73, 75–76, 79–80, 89, 98, 101, 112, 239; Jabotinsky and, 3, 79, 81, 94; Mussolini and, 7 (*see also* Mussolini, Benito); Revisionists and, 79

Jabotinsky, Anya, 28–29, 40–41, 58, 249
Jabotinsky, Eri, 104–5, 250
Jabotinsky, Vladimir (Ze'ev), 129f: arrest of, 32; arrival in Poland, 5; authoritarianism and, 2, 26, 118–23; background of, 3–4; Begin and, 218–19, 232–33, 238–40, 249–50; Ben-Gurion and, 220–21; Ben Yosef and, 232; Betar anthem and, 104–5 (*see also* Betar); Bible and, 97–98; British and, 31–32; as champion of economic interests, 60, 62, 180; description of, 3–4; *Doar Hayom* and, 40, 80–84; as duce, 29–30; eastern Galicia and, 41–47; eulogy for Piłsudski by, 146–47; European Right and, 10–11; Evacuation Plan of, 227; fascism and, 70–71, 77–86; frustration with Zionist Organization's leadership, 32–34, 107–09, 112, 221–22; Gentlemen's Agreement and, 114–18; glorification of, 71; *hadar* and, 177; Haganah and, 3; Halperin and, 181, 226; as Hitler, 204; ideal pioneer and, 89; ideal Polish patriot and, 145, 150–51; initial ambivalence of toward youth, 30–41; Israeli Right and, 250–54; Italy and, 3, 79, 81, 94; Jerusalem and, 3, 32, 40, 78, 80, 83, 181, 203, 227; Jewish Legion and, 3–4, 31–32, 39, 46–47, 52–55, 77, 87, 89, 146, 150–51; Jewish National Fund and, 32, 106; Latvian trip of, 34–36; legacy of, 250–54; liberalism and, 10–11, 94, 121–23, 221, 252; manifestos and, 61, 124–26, 196; mass immigration and, 199–200; militarism and, 3–4, 13, 34, 39, 47, 53, 77–78, 87, 106, 115, 149, 181, 224, 226, 229, 231; Mościcki telegram and, 237; as Mussolini, 13, 69; necessity of violence and, 4; Netanyahu and, 253–54; netsivut and, 199–200; newspaper writings of, 11–12,

Jabotinsky, Vladimir (Ze'ev) (*continued*)
33–37, 40, 52–53, 59–61, 63, 78–84, 107, 120–25, 150–51, 234–35, 252; "On Adventurism" and, 120–21; "On Militarism" and, 90; "On the Iron Wall" and, 34, 66, 84–85, 89, 145, 158, 226; oration talents of, 3; Palestinian Arabs and, 3–4, 13, 34, 39–40, 82–87, 93–95, 98–99, 109, 158, 191, 203, 224, 229–35, 251; parliamentary rule and, 122–23, 212; *Piatero* and, 221; Piłsudski and, 146; Polish government and, 62, 146–48, 157–58, 165, 226–28; Polish nationalism and, 62; political emotionalism and, 29–30; prediction of Holocaust myth and, 253; putsch of, 123–28, 217–18; *Rassvet* and, 33–37, 40, 53, 59–61, 63, 78–79; rebellion and, 104–32, 212–22, 229–36; Revisionists and, 3–4, 270n9 (*see also* Revisionists); rhetoric of, 3, 40, 89, 127–28, 202, 205, 209, 216–17; Rivlin and, 251, 290n64; Russians and, 11, 221; self-presentation by, 60–66; Sharon and, 251; Shavit and, 10; Slavinsky and, 33; socialism and, 97–98; State of Israel and, 250; Tabacznik and, 229; Taverne du Panthéon conference and, 37; terror and, 202–36; Trumpeldor and, 31, 87–89, 92–95; U.S. lecture tour of, 40; Weizmann and, 32; women and, 234–35, 251

Jacobi, Shlomo, 215–16

Jerusalem: Arabs and, 3, 27, 40, 246–48; Arlosoroff murder and, 201–3; British and, 32; Holy Temple and, 97, 100, 187; Irgun and, 247–48; Jabotinsky and, 3, 32, 40, 78, 80, 83, 181, 203, 227; Old City, 32; Poland's consul general in, 227, 246; Revisionists and, 78, 80, 203, 227, 246; riots of 1920 and, 3, 181; siege of, 247; riots of 1929 and, 82–86; Temple Mount and, 83; Western Wall and, 83–84; youth movements and, 32, 40; Zionists and, 3, 27, 32, 40, 82–83, 187, 201, 203, 227, 246

Jesus Christ, 14, 140

Jewish Combat Organization (Żydowska Organizacja Bojowa), 242–43

Jewish Institute for Scientific Research (Yidisher visnshaftlekher institut, YIVO), 23–24, 27, 138, 186–92, 273n10

Jewish Legion: Betar and, 4, 47, 50, 77, 87, 89, 146, 150–51, 155, 166, 174, 179; British and, 31–32, 39, 150; Egypt and, 32; founding of, 3–4, 31; Jabotinsky and, 3–4, 31–32, 39, 46–47, 52–55, 77, 87, 89, 146, 150–51; Revisionists and, 53–55; Zionists and, 3–4, 31–32, 39, 46, 50, 52–53, 77, 87, 89, 150–51, 166, 179

Jewish Military Union (Żydowski Związek Wojskowy, ŻZW), 242

Jewish National Fund, 32, 106, 199

Jewish Scout (Żydowski Skaut), 42–47, 50–51, 55, 63–65

Jewish State Party, 224

Jewish Telegraphic Agency, 39

"Jews and Militarism" (Jabotinsky), 34

Jeziernicki, Yitzhak, 239, 244

Jordanians, 248

Jordan River, 32, 37, 97, 240

Joseph Trumpeldor Hebrew Youth League. *See* Betar

Joseph Trumpeldor Zionist Activist Youth Organization, 35

Judaism, 26, 70, 96–100, 140, 182, 250

Judenrat, 243

Kaplan, Aharon, 50

Katz, Bezalel, 207–8

kehilot (community councils), 57, 182

Key, Ellen, 76

Kijek, Kamil, 15, 260n90

Kishinev pogrom, 54

Kleynman, M., 208

Kobryń, 1

Komsomol, 21, 24

Kook, Hillel, 250

Korczak, Janusz, 76

Krafft-Ebbing, Richard von, 76

krajoznawstwo (knowing the land), 151
Kraków, 13; Betar and, 151, 154, 157, 222; Feldschuh and, 50; Jabotinsky and, 28, 59; Jewish life in, 23, 60; Nazi occupation and, 241; Revisionists and, 45, 146–47, 153–54, 173, 216, 219; youth movements and, 41, 47–50
Krelman, Yosef, 177, 182–83, 195
Kremer, Batya, 197

Labor Zionists, 61, 79, 82, 84, 87–88, 91–94, 98, 102, 109, 180, 198, 201–13, 223, 235–36, 246, 249
Landkentenish programs, 151
Latvia, 34–36, 68, 77, 240, 243
lawyers, 45, 173, 178
League of Nations, 13, 38, 227
Lebanese, 248
Leibniz, Gottfried Wilhelm, 176
Lejzerowicz, Moshe, 65–66, 74–75, 95, 101, 118
Lenin, Vladimir, 190
Lerner, Zelig, 152–53, 214, 276n67
Leszczynski, Ya'akov, 285n88
liberalism: conservatism and, 7, 9; fascism and, 70–72, 94; Jabotinsky and, 10–11, 94, 121–23, 221, 252; Perelman and, 51; rebellion and, 121–23; socialism and, 9; universal suffrage and, 7
Libertal, Helena, 183
Libionka, Darisz, 244
Lieberman, Avigdor, 251
Lithuanians, 1, 23, 56, 137, 139, 148, 151, 171, 238, 255, 289n35
Łódź, 28, 49, 58, 63–64, 124–25, 138, 181, 188, 196, 211
Łódź Manifesto, 124
Lohamei Herut Israel (Lehi), 239, 244, 246–48, 289n46
London Times newspaper, 119, 234
Lorberbojm, Ze'ev, 73–74, 78
Lublin, 51, 134, 160–61, 181, 194, 241
Lubocki, Benjamin, 173
Luftwaffe, 237
Lurie, Moshe, 61

Lwów: Betar and, 92, 136, 160, 168, 238; Jabotinsky and, 28, 58, 80, 92; Jewish life in, 23, 42; Nazi occupation and, 241; Revisionists and, 117, 125, 173, 193–94; Rothmann and, 117; scouting and, 43, 45; violence in, 211, 241

Maccabees, 99–100, 153
Macedonians, 210
Malkowski, Andrzej, 44
Mandate Palestine, 1–2; agricultural settlements and, 3; Arab Revolt and, 27, 224, 231, 248; Begin and, 249–50; Beriha (Escape) and, 245–46; Betar and, 6, 244, 250, 252; British rule and, 4, 32, 202, 214, 231, 239, 245; democracy and, 252; demography of, 176; European Right and, 8; Evacuation Plan and, 227; fascism and, 79, 82–83, 85, 89–90, 99; geography of, 176; immigration to, 240–42; Lehi and, 239; militarism and, 25; moral revolution and, 8; rebellion and, 107, 111, 242–43; *sihot* and, 176–77; terror and, 201–5, 207, 210, 213, 222–27, 230–31, 234–35; youth movements and, 32–34, 37–40, 60–61, 66
Markowicz, Leon, 228
Marxism, 38, 53, 57, 148, 189–90
Masada, 179
Maximalists, 106, 110–11, 219–22, 238, 250–51
Mendelsohn, Ezra, 256n16, 285n88
Menorah, 46, 69, 100, 174, 189
Merchavia, Hen-Melekh, 90–92
Merlin, Shmuel, 250
Mickiewicz, Adam, 137–38, 150–51, 165
middle class, 16, 39, 45, 47, 60, 188, 210, 221
militarism, 130f, 131f; Auster and, 42; Betar and, 3–4, 13, 47, 50, 70, 76–78, 87, 90, 106, 113, 115, 135, 144, 149, 153, 159–63, 180–83, 197, 224–31, 238, 246; Halperin and, 200, 225–26, 245; Jabotinsky and, 3–4, 13, 34, 39, 47, 53, 77–78, 87, 106, 115, 149, 181, 224, 226, 229, 231; Mickiewicz and, 137–38, 150–51, 165; Irgun and, 13, 223, 227; Ministry of Military Affairs and, 149, 159,

militarism (*continued*)
161; *mishtar* and, 178; Mussolini and, 27; National Agency for Physical Education and Military Preparation (PW) and, 159–63; netsivut and, 172–85, 191–200, 238; Perelman and, 55; rebellion and, 110, 113; regional commands and, 173, 175, 180, 193–94, 198, 218; scouting and, 149; Talmud and, 110; Trumpeldor and, 91; underground movements and, 13, 42, 147, 189, 225, 228, 230–31, 233, 236, 238–39, 242–45, 249; Warsaw Ghetto Uprising and, 242–43; women and, 34, 183–84, 197–98

Minority Rights Treaty, 14

Mizrahi, 25, 223

Modestus, 190

Molotov cocktails, 242

Moment, Der (newspaper), 52, 165, 205, 209–12, 219, 222

Morgn Zhurnal newspaper, 40

Mościcki, Ignacy, 56, 237

Moses, 98–99, 120

Muslims, 32, 77, 83, 119

Mussolini, Benito: antisemitism and, 7; appointment as prime minister of Italy, 221; Betar and, 69, 80; blackshirts of, 72; democracy and, 72–73; as Duce, 76, 80; European Right and, 7–9; fascism and, 7, 9, 13, 24, 26, 69, 71–73, 76, 79–80, 112, 146; Hitler and, 9; Jabotinsky as, 13, 69; leadership cult of, 79–80; loyalty and, 72; militarism and, 27; one-party rule and, 76; Piłsudski and, 80, 146; political admirers of, 7; Revisionists and, 204; Sarfatti and, 7; squadristi and, 24; Weizmann and, 79

Narutowicz, Gabriel, 8, 207

National Agency for Physical Education and Military Preparation (PW), 159–63

National Democrats (Endecja), 8, 14, 20, 24, 57, 62, 117, 207

National Military Organization (Irgun tsva'i le'umi). *See* Irgun

National Minorities' Bloc, 8, 161, 278n116

Natkovich, Svetlana, 64

Nayman, Y. M., 207

Nazis: Auschwitz and, 240, 253; Betar and, 240; death camps of, 240–41; European Right and, 6–7, 9, 240–44; gas chambers and, 240–41; Hitler and, 9, 13, 27, 101, 122, 146, 155, 204–5, 207, 212, 241; ideology and, 207, 243; killing centers of, 240–41; Luftwaffe and, 237; rebellion and, 112; Schutzstaffel (SS) and, 240, 242; terror and, 9, 13, 27, 101, 122, 146, 155, 203–5, 207, 212, 222, 227, 241; Third Reich and, 6–7, 9, 212, 237, 239, 241, 253; Zionists and, 204–5

Nebi Musa, 32

Netanyahu, Binyamin, 253–54

netsivut: Betar and, 172–85, 191–200, 238; collective punishment and, 185; Command 51 and, 185; economic tensions and, 179; exams of, 184–85; field reports and, 193–200; Jabotinsky and, 199–200; mobilizing the shtetl and, 172–85; Propes and, 173–74, 179–81, 184, 193–95, 198–200, 238; Yiddish and, 195–96

newspapers: Betar and, 11, 13, 20, 58–59, 68–69, 106–8, 111, 124, 126, 133, 142, 146, 152–53, 165, 182, 185–86, 190, 194, 196–97, 203, 205, 212, 214, 218, 225, 230, 241; fascism and, 68–69, 79, 83; Hebrew and, 40, 80, 110; Jabotinsky and, 3, 33–37, 40, 52–53, 59–61, 63, 78–84, 252; Jewish, 11, 17, 39, 68, 83, 124, 126, 152, 182; Polish, 11, 39, 42, 62, 126, 165; Russian, 3; shtetl life and, 170, 182, 185–86, 190, 194, 196–97; Warsaw and, 39; Yiddish, 39–40, 51–52, 61, 73, 107, 110, 126, 133, 203, 205–6, 209–10, 230; youth movements and, 11–13, 17, 20–21, 33, 37–42, 51–53, 59–62; Zionists and, 5

Nicholas I, 185

Nietzscheanism, 45, 71

Niewiadomski, 207

Nowy Dziennik newspaper, 48

Nuremberg Race Laws, 222

October Revolution, 48

"On Adventurism" (Jabotinsky), 120–21

"On Militarism" (Jabotinsky), 90

"On the Iron Wall" (Jabotinsky), 34, 66, 84–85, 89, 145, 158, 226
Opera Nazionale Balilla, 76
Operation Barbarosa, 237
Ortega y Gasset, José, 70
Orthodox Jews, 5, 22, 51, 144
Ottomans, 31, 79, 150, 181
Our Work (ʾAvodatenu) bulletin, 175

pacification campaigns, 19, 159
Palestinian Arabs: Arab Revolt and, 223; Begin and, 238, 241; Betar and, 76–77, 92–95, 99–103; British and, 3–4, 13, 39, 83–85, 87; *Doar Hayom* and, 84; calling for expulsion of, 191–92; Irgun and, 229–36; Islam and, 32, 77, 83, 119; Jabotinsky and, 3–4, 13, 34, 39–40, 82–87, 93–95, 98–99, 109, 158, 191, 203, 224, 229–35, 251; Jerusalem and, 3, 27, 40, 246–48; Lehi and, 246; militias of, 4, 86–87, 247; 1929 riots and, 82–86; terror and, 203, 223–24, 229–36; Trumpeldor and, 4, 13, 86–88, 92–94, 191–92
Pan Tadeusz (Mickiewicz), 138
parades: Betar and, 2, 13, 22, 68, 106, 130*f*, 134–35, 142–44, 146, 154, 155, 224, 229; Constitution Day, 141; fascism and, 68–69; ideal Polish patriot and, 154–55; patriotic, 136–38, 141, 163, 229; Piłsudski and, 146; Polish gaze and, 155; Polish Independence Day and, 136, 148; Revisionists and, 144, 146, 148, 154
Paris Agreement, 233–34
parliamentary rule: corruption and, 55–58; democracy and, 69, 72, 121, 206; discrimination and, 14; eastern Europe and, 7; Grinboym and, 17; Habsburgs and, 16; Herut Party and, 250; Jabotinsky and, 122–23, 212; limited power of, 2; National Minorities' Bloc and, 161; old liberal values and, 122; Polish Jews' criticism of, 8–9, 122; radical right and, 10; rebellion and, 108–9, 112, 117, 121–23, 127; Revisionists and, 9, 109; Slawoj-Skladkowski and, 222; Zionists and, 5, 9, 108, 112, 206

Passover, 98
passports, 173, 185, 227
Paxton, Robert, 10, 70
Peel Commission Report, 223
Perelman, Jakub, 51–55, 58
Piatero (Jabotinsky), 221
Piłsudski, Józef: authoritarianism and, 124–25; Betar and, 8–9, 13, 19, 30, 80, 124, 134, 141–42, 145–47, 155–59, 164–66, 222, 228; call for unity by, 8; coup d'état of, 165; death of, 222; as dictator, 146; Dmowski and, 8; Endecja and, 8; fascism and, 80; ideal Polish patriot and, 155–59; Irgun and, 228; Jabotinsky's eulogy for, 146–47; legend of, 44; Mussolini and, 80; new constitution and, 164; parades for, 146; parliamentary rule and, 9; Polish Legions and, 8; Polish Socialist Party and, 8; politics of nationality and, 13–14, 19; Revisionists and, 164–66; Sanacja and, 13–14, 19, 30, 55–58, 80, 134, 136, 139, 145–47, 165; Soviet Union and, 8; violence and, 8, 56; youth movements and, 30, 44, 55–58
Piłsudski Square, 142
Plato, 176
Pod Wypoczynkiem (At Leisure) hotel, 123–24
Poland: authoritarianism and, 2; Białystok, 28, 48, 90, 148, 170, 181, 197, 230, 243; Catholicism and, 1, 7–8, 14–16, 19–21, 42–43, 46, 56, 62, 76, 134–44, 150–51, 154, 157, 162–63, 165, 169, 190, 224, 226–28, 237, 244–45; Congress and, 16, 173–74; economic stability and, 8; Endecja and, 8, 14, 20, 24, 57, 62, 117, 207; German occupation of, 6, 51, 237–44; Grodno, 11, 51, 186, 230; Kraków, 13, 23, 28, 41, 45–50, 59–60, 146–47, 151–54, 157, 173, 216, 219, 222, 241; Łódź, 28, 49, 58, 63–64, 124–25, 138, 181, 188, 196, 211; loyalty to, 1, 13, 18, 138, 144, 154–55, 161, 163, 237; Lublin, 51, 134, 160–61, 181, 194, 241; Lwów, 23, 28, 42–43, 45, 58, 80, 92, 117, 125, 136, 160, 168, 173, 193–94, 211, 238, 241; Ministry of Education and, 161–62; Ministry of Internal

Poland (*continued*)

Affairs and, 2, 46, 155, 162, 227; Ministry of Military Affairs and, 149, 159, 161; minority populations of, 1, 6–20, 41–47, 55–58, 135–44, 155–56, 161–63, 168–69, 171; newly formed state of, 5–6; parliamentary rule and, 2, 8–9 (*see also* parliamentary rule); population demographics of, 255n1; public school system of, 135–44 (*see also* education); Radom, 51, 133, 135–36, 148, 154, 160, 166; Sanacja and, 2, 13–14, 18–19, 30, 55–58, 62, 67, 80, 125, 134, 136–40, 143–47, 155, 160, 162, 165, 207, 252; Soviet occupation of, 237–41, 245–46; Sowiniec, 28; Suwalki, 51, 230; Warsaw and, 2 (*see also* Warsaw); Wilno, 23, 28, 51, 102, 168, 170, 194, 238–40; Włocławek, 28, 51, 64

police: Archive of Modern Records and, 1; Begin and, 242; Betar and, 19–20, 155–56; Bibring and, 42–43; British, 239, 247; Grinboym and, 133–34, 161; Hetman and, 160; Jewish, 244, 289n35; Ministry of Internal Affairs and, 155; Perelman and, 55; Polish, 1–2, 41–42, 55, 134, 196; reports of as source material, 1–2, 5, 19; secret (squadristi), 24, 76, 101; Stanslawów and, 41–43; Stern and, 239; terrorists and, 201, 223, 225, 229; Vilna ghetto and, 243–44; violence against, 120, 243; Warsaw Ghetto Uprising and, 242–43

Polish Christian Democratic Party, 139

Polish Communist Party, 25

Polish identity, 18–20, 135, 144, 148–49, 165

Polish Independence Day, 136

Polish Jews: Catholics and, 14; diversity among, 12–20, 169; economic stability and, 8; European Right and, 6–12; future of, 4–5; generational conflict and, 20–25, 112–13, 118–23; German language and, 15–16; Hebrew and, 2–3 (*see also* Hebrew); identity and, 4–5 (*see also* identity); large community of, 4; parliamentary rule and, 8–9, 122; politics of nationality and, 13–20; religious rituals and, 14; schooling and, 135–43; State of Israel and, 250–54; as subjects, not citizens, 16; Yiddish and, 15. *See also* Yiddish; youth movements

Polish Legions, 8, 44, 46, 57, 134, 147

Polish Scouting Association (Związek Harcerstwa Polskiego), 43–44, 47, 144, 148–49, 154–55 159, 161–63

Polish Socialist Party (PPS), 8, 262n59

Porat, Dina, 288n23, 288n26

Porter-Szűcs, Brian, 140

poverty, 61, 198

prayer, 42, 68, 83, 96–97, 138, 148, 157, 169, 186, 188

Propes, Aharon Zvi: anonymous report on, 167–68; Begin and, 234, 238–39, 241–42, 287n133, 288n19; Betar and, 34, 37, 62–63, 67, 85–86, 90–93, 99–101, 107, 110, 114, 123–26, 129f, 148, 156–57, 167, 171, 173–74, 179–81, 184, 189, 193–95, 198–200, 220, 233–34, 238–39, 241; fascism and, 85–86, 90–93, 99–101; Gentlemen's Agreement and, 114; German occupation and, 238–39, 241–42; Hannukah and, 99–101; Jabotinsky's putsch and, 123–26; netsivut and, 173–74, 179–81, 184, 193–95, 198–200, 238; politics of belonging and, 148, 156–57; rebellion and, 107, 110, 114, 123–26, 129f; shtetl life and, 167, 171, 173–74, 179–81, 184, 189, 193–95, 198–200; terror and, 220, 233–34; uniforms and, 179

putsch, 123–28, 202, 205, 217–18

rabbis, 29, 48–49, 52, 68–69, 75, 96, 145, 178, 186, 250

Raczyński, Edward Bernard, 227

Radom, 51, 133, 135–36, 148, 154, 160, 166

Rappel, Józef, 52

Rassvet newspaper, 33–37, 40, 53, 59–61, 63, 78–79

Ravnitzky, Yehoshua, 75

Raziel, David, 233

rebellion: Arabs and, 109, 111; authoritarianism and, 105–7, 111, 113–15, 117–18, 120,

122–28; Betar and, 104–8, 111–18, 124–32; British and, 107–12, 118–19; conflict of generations and, 24, 26, 113, 121, 127, 209, 211–12; democracy and, 26, 105–6, 115, 121–22, 125, 127–28; dictatorships and, 106, 110–11, 114–15, 118, 121, 124–26, 128; fascism and, 70; Galicia and, 114, 117, 124, 126; Gentlemen's Agreement and, 114–18; Germans and, 112; immigration and, 120; Jabotinsky and, 70–71, 77–99, 102–3; liberalism and, 121–23; Maccabees and, 99–100, 153; Mandate Palestine and, 107, 111, 242–43; manifestos and, 20, 61, 124–26, 196, 225; militarism and, 110, 113; Mussolini and, 112; nationalism and, 117; Nazis and, 112; newspapers and, 106–8, 111, 118, 124, 126; parliamentary rule and, 108–9, 112, 117, 121–23, 127; Propes and, 107, 110, 114, 123–26, 129f; putsch and, 123–28; Revisionists and, 26, 105–27, 245; Trumpeldor and, 125; violence and, 106, 109–12, 119, 121, 249; Warsaw Ghetto Uprising and, 242–43; women and, 122; Zionists and, 104–9, 112–19, 123–27

Red Army, 33, 43, 52, 79, 240

Red Cross, 241

refugees, 34, 36, 38, 45, 48, 238, 244

regional commands, 173, 175, 180, 193–94, 198, 218

religion: Betar and, 23; Bible and, 31, 48–49, 63–64, 96–99, 120, 145, 178, 225; Catholics and, 14 (*see also* Catholics); colonialism and, 31; fascism and, 10, 69, 75, 79, 83, 86, 95–98; Haggadah and, 98; Hannukah and, 99–101; *haskalah* and, 169–70; identity and, 5, 14, 18, 61, 67; Mizrahi and, 25, 223; Muslims and, 32, 77, 83, 119; Passover and, 98; politics and, 7, 20, 28, 31, 134–35, 138, 140, 145, 162; prayer and, 42, 68, 83, 96–97, 138, 148, 157, 169, 186, 188; radical right and, 95–100; shatnez and, 97; shtetl life and, 3, 16, 169, 173, 176, 187–89; terror and, 210; Trumpeldor's death and, 96–97; Zionists and, 25

Remba, Isaac, 174, 177

Revisionists: authoritarianism and, 25; Begin and, 250; Betar and, 5, 240–44, 246, 250; Brit Ha-Biryonim and, 106, 109–13, 118, 120, 123, 127, 200–205, 214–25, 238, 250–51; British and, 4, 13, 37–39, 83–84, 87, 107–12, 118–19, 150, 199, 219, 226, 231–32, 235, 242–45; chief demands of, 4, 37–38; corruption and, 9; Diaspora and, 110, 229; *Der Emes* and, 71, 74, 77; European Right and, 9–10; factionalism and, 9; fascism and, 69–90, 101–3; financial woes of, 28; founding of, 4, 34–41, 252; Gentlemen's Agreement and, 114–18; German occupation and, 240–44; Hashemite rule and, 37–38; Hebrew and, 105, 115; Hitler and, 155; Holocaust and, 244–45; ideal Polish patriot and, 144–48; Intelligence Service and Document Bureau and, 244; Irgun and, 242, 245; Italy and, 79; Jerusalem and, 78, 80, 203, 227, 246; Jewish Legion and, 53–55; legends and, 145; Lorberbojm and, 73–74; loyalty and, 53; Maximalist, 106, 110–11, 219–22, 238, 250–51; militarism and, 25, 30; movement leaders and, 29, 33–34, 37, 41, 50, 66, 78, 84, 107–15, 118, 121, 123–24, 126, 173; Mussolini and, 204; new constitution and, 164; parades and, 144, 146, 148, 154; parliamentary rule and, 9, 109; party platform for, 39; Piłsudski and, 164–66; pledges of obedience and, 13, 46, 54, 107–8, 155, 162, 214–15, 218–19; Polishness and, 148–49; politics of nationality and, 13, 18, 135, 144–49, 162–66; popularity of, 4; rebellion and, 26, 105–27, 245; regional differences and, 194, 279n20; rhetoric and, 109, 209; Second Conference of, 65; Second World Revisionist Conference and, 111; shtetl life and, 168, 171, 173–76, 179–84, 189–95, 198–99; *sihot* and, 176–77; Soviet Union and, 245; Taverne du Panthéon conference and, 37; terror and, 201–20, 223–32, 235; Tiomkin

Revisionists (*continued*)
and, 41; Trumpeldor and, 125; Union of Revisionist Zionists and, 5, 25, 28, 35, 59, 106–7; Warsaw and, 59, 61–63, 65, 67, 69, 71, 73, 78, 85, 110, 119, 124, 153–55, 162, 166, 168, 171, 173–76, 179–82, 184, 189, 192–95, 204, 206, 210, 218, 226, 231, 243–44; Warsaw Ghetto Uprising and, 243; youth movements and, 28–30, 35–41, 45–46, 50, 53–67

Reymont, Władysław, 150

rhetoric: Begin and, 218; Betar and, 102; conflict of generations and, 212; fascism and, 72, 74, 79, 89, 97, 102; Jabotinsky and, 40, 89, 127–28, 202, 205, 209, 216–17; Labor Zionists and, 209; Revisionists and, 109, 209; revolutionary, 79, 109, 217; rituals and, 97; Sanacja and, 58; slogans and, 11, 22, 29, 54, 70, 72, 81, 97, 110, 134, 158, 175, 207; Trumpeldor and, 89; violent, 74, 109, 133; Yeivin and, 109

Riflemans Association (Związek Strzelecki), 159

riots, 3, 8, 27, 32, 83–85, 107, 167, 181, 189, 224–28, 231

rituals: Betar and, 22, 26, 64, 96, 101; calendars for, 14; ideal Polish patriot and, 145–46; "El Maleh Rachamim" and, 96; military drills and, 64; myths and, 26, 70, 101, 145, 150; normalization and, 17; parades and, 22 (*see also* parades); patriotic, 13, 134; Polishness and, 148–49; politics behind, 21, 57; politics of belonging and, 134, 138, 140, 142, 145–46, 150, 154–55, 166; religious, 96–97, 100, 138; rhetoric and, 97; Sea Holiday ceremonies and, 155; shtetl life and, 169, 191; theatrics and, 21–22, 63, 153, 177–78, 226; urn of soil ceremony and, 157–58; youth movements and, 13; Zionists and, 13, 97

Rivlin, Reuven, 251, 290n64

Road to Our Youth, The (Weinreich), 24–25

Robinson Crusoe (Defoe), 177

Rochczyn, Yitzhak, 243

Romania, 6, 9, 40, 68, 76, 167, 217, 225
Rothmann, Jakób, 117
Russian Civil War, 24
Russian Empire, 3, 7, 16–17, 41, 60, 194
Russian Jews, 31, 35
Russian language, 3, 33, 38, 165
Russians, 1; Bolsheviks and, 38, 43, 79; fascism and, 79, 87, 94, 103; immigration and, 29; Jabotinsky and, 11, 221; Trumpeldor and, 4 (*see also* Trumpeldor, Yosef); youth movements and, 29, 31, 33–36, 38, 41, 43–44, 46, 51, 53, 60, 63
Rutenberg, Pinhas, 214

Sabbath, 140, 228
Samson, 63–64
Sanacja: Betar and, 18–20; education and, 136–40, 143–50; European Right and, 13–14, 18–19; fascism and, 80; identity and, 136–37; Jewish, 55–58; Piłsudski and, 13–14, 19, 30, 55–58, 80, 134, 136, 139, 145–47, 165; Polish authoritarianism and, 2, 13–14, 18–19, 30, 55–58, 62, 67, 80, 125, 134, 136–40, 143–47, 155, 160, 162, 165, 207, 252; politics of belonging and, 134, 136–40, 143–47, 155, 160, 162, 165; as Purification, 2; rebellion and, 125; rhetoric of, 58; terror and, 207; youth movements and, 30, 55–58, 62, 67
Sarfatti, Margherita, 7
Saudia Arabia, 4
Schechtman, Joseph, 82, 287n132
Scheib, Israel, 239
Schutzstaffel (SS), 240, 242
scouting: Betar and, 17, 44, 46–47, 51, 76, 143–44, 149–50, 154, 162–63; Bibring and, 42–47, 50–51, 55, 63–65; Catholics and, 163; militarism and, 149; National Agency for Physical Education and Military Preparation (PW) and, 159–63; Polish nationalism and, 41–47, 50–55, 142–44, 154, 159–63; purity and, 149; *Scouting Guide for the Polish Youth* and, 149; youth movements and, 17, 21–22, 35,

42–55, 76, 137, 143–44, 149–50, 154, 159, 162–63
Scouting for Boys (Baden-Powell), 43–44
Second Temple, 110
Seleucid Empire, 99–100
Shanes, Joshua, 262n59
Sharon, Ariel, 251
Shavit, Ya'akov, 10
Shem Tov, Ze'ev, 73
shrines, 83, 139
shtetl life: Betar and, 27, 167–200; book lists and, 177–78; British and, 199–202, 214, 219, 223, 226, 230–36; Catholics and, 169; communism and, 189, 193; education and, 170–71, 175–79, 182–83, 185, 195–96; fictional portrayal of, 169–70; field reports and, 193–200; folklore and, 75, 151, 171; Galicia and, 167, 169, 172–74, 193–94, 197; gender issues and, 181–84, 196–98; Germans and, 176; ghettos and, 33, 224, 241–44, 289n35; Goldanski on, 168–69, 171; *hachshara* and, 175–76, 179–81, 193–94, 197–98, 203; *haskalah* and, 169–70; Hebrew and, 170–78, 184, 195; imagining, 168–72; immigration and, 179–80, 184, 198–99; journalists and, 173, 182; *kehilot* and, 57, 182; kosher beliefs and, 102, 222; Mandate Palestine and, 175–80, 184–85, 198–99; mobilization and, 172–85; modernization of, 168, 170–72, 176, 183; nationalism and, 170–71, 177, 184, 190; newspapers and, 170, 182, 185–86, 190, 194, 196–97; patriotism and, 193; Propes and, 167, 171, 173–74, 179–81, 184, 189, 193–95, 198–200; religion and, 3, 16, 169, 173, 176, 187–89; Revisionists and, 168, 171, 173–76, 179–84, 189–95, 198–99; rituals and, 169, 191; *shtiblekh* and, 42, 97, 169, 188; *sihot* and, 176–77; socialism and, 170, 180, 183, 187, 189–93, 196; stereotypes and, 168, 170; superstitions and, 170; synagogues and, 52, 68–69, 71, 96, 140, 154, 156–57, 169, 268n96; Talmud and, 49, 100, 109–10; Trumpeldor and, 175, 182,

191; Ukrainians and, 169, 171; violence and, 194; Warsaw and, 167–99; Yiddish and, 169–73, 178, 186, 195; Zionists and, 167, 170–84, 187–90, 193–200
shtiblekh (houses of prayer), 42, 97, 169, 188
Sienkiewicz, Henryk, 137–38
sihot (discussions), 176–77
Slavinsky, Maxim, 33
Sławoj-Składkowski, Felicjan, 222
slogans, 11, 22, 29, 54, 70, 72, 81, 97, 110, 134, 158, 175, 207
snipers, 247
socialism: Betar and, 8, 210, 243–44; Bund and, 22, 51, 55, 68–69, 99, 143–44, 192, 242; conservatives and, 7, 9; European Right and, 7–9; fascism and, 68–77, 80, 82, 88–94, 97–99, 101; Jewish, 2–5, 50, 156, 203, 206; liberalism and, 9; Polish, 8, 210, 262n59; politics of nationality and, 17; shtetl life and, 170, 180, 183, 187, 189–93, 196; terror and, 203, 206, 210, 212, 215, 218; Trumpeldor and, 88; violence and, 61, 74; youth movements and, 2–3, 22, 25, 30, 38–39, 47–50, 53, 57, 60–61, 66; Zionists and, 17, 22, 38, 48, 60, 69, 82, 88, 94, 97, 99, 143, 162, 167, 173, 180, 187, 203, 212, 244
Sokół Gymnastics Society, 159
songs, 13, 35, 104, 134, 137, 153, 155, 157, 231
Soviet Union, 8; Arab-Jewish riots and, 189; Bolsheviks and, 38, 43, 79; Komsomol and, 21, 24; occupation of Poland by, 237–41, 245–46; October Revolution and, 48; pogroms of, 14; Revisionists and, 245; violence of, 48; youth movements and, 21, 24, 33, 38, 43, 48–49, 57, 61; Zionists and, 245
Sowiniec, 28, 158
Special Night Squads, 236
Spengler, Oswald, 79
squadristi, 24, 76, 101
Stabiecki, D., 71–74, 102
Stalin, Joseph, 146, 240
Stanislawski, Michael, 11
Star of David, 53

State of Israel, 246–50
Stavsky, Avraham, 201, 206, 208–9, 212–15, 217, 229, 249
stereotypes, 27, 140, 168, 170
Stern, Avraham, 230–31, 239
Stern, Herbert, 176
Stupnicki, Sh. Y., 210
Sufferer 1001, 186–87, 192–93
summer camps, 5, 22, 132f, 152–53, 191, 214, 240, 276n67
superstitions, 170
Suskin, 75
Suwałki, 51, 230
Swedes, 137
synagogues, 52, 68–69, 71, 96, 140, 154, 156–57, 169, 268n96
Syria, 87, 248

Tabacznik, Shalom, 229
Tal Hai journal, 95, 150
Talmud, 49, 100, 109–10
Tarbut school network, 17, 34, 141, 170, 174, 176, 178, 239, 275n39
Tat, Di (The Deed) newspaper, 230–31, 239, 248
Tehomi, Avraham, 223–24
Tel Aviv, 27, 39–41, 84, 157, 175, 181, 201, 205, 209, 231, 239–43, 248–49
Tel Hai, 4, 13, 86–95, 157–58, 174
Tel Hai (Betar journal), 86, 95
terror: Arlosoroff and, 201, 203–14, 249; assassinations and, 8, 156, 203, 207, 210, 239, 246, 289n45; authoritarianism and, 207; Ben Yosef and, 229–33, 235; Betar and, 201–36; bombs and, 223, 230, 242, 247; defense through attack and, 222–29; democracy and, 206, 211; Diaspora and, 235; executions and, 229–30, 232, 242; Germans and, 203–7, 211–12, 222, 225, 227; grenades and, 210, 223, 225, 230, 242, 247; guidebook for, 225–26; Halperin and, 203, 224–26, 228; *havlaga* and, 223–24, 233, 235; Histadrut and, 82, 203–4, 206, 208, 211, 215, 219, 221; Hitler and, 9, 13, 27, 101, 122, 146, 155, 204–5, 207, 212, 241; holy war and, 203; immigration and, 214, 216, 218, 223, 227, 229, 231; incendiary language and, 11, 145, 186, 211, 214; Irgun and, 223–24, 227–35; Jabotinsky on trial and, 212–22; journalists and, 206–13, 228; killing centers and, 240–41; Mandate Palestine and, 201–5, 207, 210, 213, 222–27, 230–31, 234–35; military training and, 223–31; murder and, 33, 48–49, 76, 93, 100–101, 120, 201–14, 241, 245, 249; nationalism and, 207, 222; Nazis and, 9, 13, 27, 101, 122, 146, 155, 203–5, 207, 212, 222, 227, 241; newspapers and, 203, 205, 209, 211–12, 214, 218, 225, 230; Palestinian Arabs and, 203, 223–24, 229–36; pogroms and, 1, 14, 33, 48, 54, 203, 245; police and, 201, 223, 225, 229; Propes and, 220, 233–34; radical right and, 202, 206; religion and, 210; Revisionists and, 201–32, 235; Sanacja and, 207; socialism and, 203, 206, 210, 212, 215, 218; Stavsky and, 201, 206, 208–9, 212–15, 217, 229, 249; Ukrainians and, 161; usefulness of, 203; violence and, 202–3, 207–10, 213, 215, 217–28, 232–33, 236; Warsaw and, 204–6, 210, 217–18, 225–26, 230–33; youth politics on trial and, 205–14; Zionists and, 201–26
Tetmajer, Kazimierz Przerwa, 150
theatrics, 21–22, 63, 153, 177–78, 226
Third Reich, 6–7, 9, 212, 237, 239, 241, 253
Thon, Ozjasz, 59
Timokin, Vladimir, 41
Tombs of the Unknown Soldier, 155
Towarzystwo Ochrony (TOZ), 170, 178
traitors, 52, 72, 110, 134, 167, 203
Transjordan, 240
Trotsky, Leon, 43, 189–90
Trumpeldor, Yosef: Betar and, 2, 4 (*see also* Betar); death of, 4, 13, 86, 269n116; Diaspora and, 93; European Right and, 12, 89–90; fascism and, 86–100; ideal pioneer and, 89; ideal Polish patriot and, 154, 157–58; Jabotinsky and, 4, 31, 87–89, 92–95; legend of, 86–95, 99; militarism

and, 91; Palestinian Arabs and, 4, 13, 86–88, 92–94, 191–92; politics of belonging and, 154, 157–58; as rebbe of youth, 97; rebellion and, 125; religion and, 96–97; Revisionists and, 125; rhetoric and, 89; right-wing values and, 86–95; shtetl life and, 175, 182, 191; socialism and, 88; Tel Hai and, 4, 13, 86–95, 157–58, 174; urn of soil ceremony and, 157–58; youth movements and, 31, 35, 46, 59, 62
Trybuna Narodowa newspaper, 146–47, 151, 163
Tsukunft (the Future), 22, 143, 192
Turkey, 80

Ukrainian Democratic Republic, 33
Ukrainian People's Republic, 43
Ukrainians: anti-Ukrainian sentiment and, 62; assassinations and, 156; Catholic Poles and, 237; as citizens, 56, 139; Galicia and, 42, 169; Lachwa and, 243; as largest minority, 4, 16, 255n1; Narutowicz and, 8; National Minorities Bloc and, 161; pacification campaigns and, 19; pogroms and, 15; Revisionist reservist organizations and, 162; terrorism and, 161
uniforms, 21, 44, 52, 68, 96, 163, 179, 185, 191, 204, 216, 240
Union of Revisionist Zionists. *See* Revisionists
United Nations, 246
United Partisans Organization, 243–44

Verne, Jules, 177
Vilne. *See* Wilno
Vilnius. *See* Wilno
violence: against civilians, 201–36; antisemitic ideology and, 14, 245; authoritarianism and, 6; Catholics and, 111, 245; communism and, 61; education and, 139; exaltation of, 9; executions and, 229–30, 232, 242; fascism and, 70, 74, 76, 78, 83–85, 93, 96, 99–100; glorification of, 70; guerillas and, 94, 210, 214; Halperin and, 224–25; incendiary language and, 11, 145, 186, 211, 214; Jewish-Arab, 40; murder and, 33, 48–49, 76, 93, 100–101, 120, 201–14, 241, 245, 249; Netanyahu and, 253–54; Piłsudski and, 8, 56; rebellion and, 106, 109–12, 119, 121, 249; revenge and, 119, 223, 248; revolutionary models and, 19, 25, 27; rhetoric and, 74, 109, 133; scouting and, 149; socialism and, 61, 74; Soviet rule and, 48; survival and, 4; targeting women and, 234–35; terror and, 202–3, 207–10, 213, 215, 217–28, 232–33, 236; Warsaw Ghetto Uprising and, 242–43
vocational training, 3, 170, 179
von Weisl, Wolfgang, 124, 204, 208

Wandervogel movement, 21, 45
Warsaw: Archive of Modern Records and, 1; Betar and, 2, 23–27, 41, 50–51, 64–65, 67–74, 77–78, 85, 91–92, 102, 110, 124, 140–42, 153–57, 160, 162, 166–68, 171, 173–99, 204, 206, 210, 217–18, 225–26, 230–33, 237–44, 248, 253; commercial hubs of, 60; Dworzec Wiedeński and, 28; Ha-shomer Ha-tas'ir and, 48–50; main thoroughfares of, 68; Ministry of Internal Affairs and, 2; newspapers and, 39; Perelman and, 51–55, 58; police and, 43; Red Army and, 52; Revisionists and, 59, 61–63, 69, 71, 73, 78, 85, 110, 119, 124, 153–55, 162, 166, 168, 171, 173–76, 179–82, 184, 189, 192–95, 204, 206, 210, 218, 226, 231, 243–44; riots in, 8; shtetl life and, 167–99; terror and, 204–6, 210, 217–18, 225–26, 230–33; youth movements and, 41, 43
Warsaw Ghetto Uprising, 242–43
Warsaw University, 51
Weinbaum, Laurance, 244
Weinreich, Max, 23–25
Weinshal, Abraham, 124
Weinstein, Baruch, 61
Weizmann, Chaim, 29, 31–32, 38, 69, 79, 107–9
West Bank, 251

Western Wall, 83–84
Wilno, 23, 28, 51, 102, 168, 170, 194, 238–40
Wingate, Charles Orde, 236
Witos, Wincenty, 56
Włocławek, 28, 51, 64
women: autobiographies and, 23; Betar and, 132f, 149, 181–84; civic status of, 251; education and, 137, 183–84, 198; fascism and, 10, 83; first aid training and, 137; Irgun attacks and, 234; Jabotinsky and, 196–97, 234–35, 251; Krelman on, 182–83; Libertal and, 183; masculine, 183; massacres of, 83; militarism and, 34, 183–84, 197–98; percentage of in youth movements, 181–82; political rights and, 182–83, 196–98; rebellion and, 122; Stavsky and, 206; suffrage and, 196–98; targeting of, 234–35
Worker's Party for the Land of Israel (Mapai), 108, 206, 213
Worker's Voice of Liberation, The (newspaper), 69
World War I era, 3, 7–8, 21, 31, 43–45, 77, 85, 94, 113, 134, 146–49, 154, 161, 170, 189
World War II era, 6, 23, 234, 236, 247, 250
World Zionist Congress, 83, 87, 133, 201

Yeivin, Yehoshua H., 109
Yiddish: Brisk and, 201; education and, 135, 149–50; *Haynt* newspaper and, 52, 55, 61, 65, 78, 98, 107, 120–21, 186, 206–11; identity and, 5, 135; as native tongue, 5, 15–16; netsivut and, 195–96; newspapers and, 39–40, 51–52, 61, 73, 107, 110, 126, 133, 203, 205–6, 209–10, 230; politics of nationality and, 133, 135, 149–50, 165; shtetl life and, 169–73, 178, 186, 195; Vilne and, 23, 28; Weinreich and, 23
Yishuv: Betar's vision for, 86–103, 151–54, 158, 198–200; forging of, 3; immigration to, 5, Labor Zionism and, 38, 81–82; 1920 riots and, 32, 1929 riots and, 82–86
Yoelson, Moshe, 172–73, 193, 265n143
Yona, Rona, 260n90

youth movements: authoritarianism and, 30, 51, 54, 56, 66; Begin and, 1–2, 218, 220, 232, 234; Bibring and, 42–47, 50–51, 55, 63–65; book lists and, 177–78; clubrooms of, 174–75, 178; communism and, 30, 43, 48–50, 57, 61, 242; conflict of generations and, 24, 26, 113, 121, 127, 209, 211–12; cultural programming and, 69, 174, 176; democracy and, 38, 56; dictatorships and, 65; education and, 47, 54–55, 57, 64; fascism and, 2 (*see also* fascism); field reports and, 167–68, 193–200; France and, 6–7, 21, 31, 44, 68, 248; Galicia and, 28, 41–49, 59, 63; Gentlemen's Agreement and, 114–18; Germans and, 21, 34–35, 40–41, 44–46, 48, 51, 56; Hebrew and, 2–3, 17, 34–36, 40, 46–49, 54, 64, 66, 68, 81, 91, 97, 105, 110, 115, 149–50, 153, 163, 171–78, 184, 195, 225–26, 244, 249; immigration and, 31–32, 37–38, 40, 50, 60; Jabotinsky's initial ambivalence and, 30–41; Jerusalem and, 32, 40; journalists and, 29, 39, 58–59, 61–63; Komsomol and, 21, 24; limits of modern Jewish politics and, 20–25; loyalty and, 30; Mandate Palestine and, 32–34, 37–40, 60–61, 66; manifestos and, 20, 61, 124–26, 196, 225; militarism and, 3–4, 13, 25, 27, 30, 34, 39, 47, 53, 55, 70, 77–78, 87, 90, 106, 110, 113, 115, 149, 181, 224, 226, 229, 231; nationalism and, 20, 25–26, 30–31, 38, 41, 43–46, 50–53, 62; netsivut and, 172–85, 191–200, 238; newspapers and, 11–13, 17, 20–21, 33, 37–42, 51–53, 59–62, 68–69, 106–8, 111, 124, 126, 133, 142, 146, 152–53, 165, 182, 185–86, 190, 194, 196–97, 203, 205, 212, 214, 218, 225, 230, 241; patriotism and, 21, 56; Piłsudski and, 30, 44, 55–58; Polish patriotism and, 2; political emotionalism and, 29–30; rituals and, 13 (*see also* rituals); Sanacja and, 30, 55–58, 62, 67; scouting and, 17, 21–22, 35, 42–55, 76, 137, 143–44, 149–50, 154, 159, 162–63; slogans and, 11, 22, 29, 54,

70, 72, 81, 97, 110, 134, 158, 175, 207; socialism and, 22, 25, 30, 38–39, 47–50, 53, 57, 60–61, 66; Soviet Union and, 21, 24, 33, 38, 43, 48–49, 57, 61; theatrics and, 21–22, 63, 153, 177–78, 226; Trumpeldor and, 31, 35, 46, 59, 62; Warsaw and, 41, 43. *See also* specific group

Yunitchman, Shimshon, 234

Yustman, Moshe, 207

zealots, 12, 24, 49–50, 90, 110

"Zealots" (Feldschuh), 49

Zionists: authoritarianism and, 30; Begin and, 242; Beriha (Escape) and, 245–46; British and, 3–4, 13, 31–32, 37–38, 43, 83–87, 107–8, 112, 119, 150, 199, 202, 214, 219, 223, 231–36, 239, 244–45, 249; Congress of, 5, 40, 58–59, 83, 87, 108–9, 114, 123, 125, 127, 133, 201, 206, 208, 211–12; corruption and, 9; cultural programming and, 69, 174, 176; *Doar Hayom* and, 84; fascism and, 68–103; field reports and, 193–200; Gentlemen's Agreement and, 114–18; German occupation and, 238–39, 242–44; Hannukah and, 99–101; Herzl and, 45, 48, 96, 141, 143, 174, 182; Histadrut and, 82, 203–4, 206, 208, 211, 215, 219, 221; identity and, 30; Jerusalem and, 3, 27, 32, 40, 82–83, 187, 201, 203, 227, 246; Jewish Legion and, 3–4, 31–32, 39, 46, 50, 52–53, 77, 87, 89, 150–51, 166, 179; Jewish National Fund and, 32, 106, 199; Judaism and, 26, 70, 96–100, 140, 182, 250; Land of Israel and, 18, 46–47, 50–52, 82, 85, 92, 97, 149, 152–53, 175, 199, 206, 210, 213, 226, 228–30, 235; loyalty and, 13, 17; Mandate Palestine and, 1–2 (*see also* Mandate Palestine); middle class and, 16; Nazis and, 204–5; newspapers and, 5; parliamentary rule and, 5, 9, 108, 112, 206, 211; peaceful means of, 4; Polish culture and, 16; Polish nationalism and, 12–20, 57–58, 62–63, 133–66; radical right and, 95–100; rallies for, 1; rebellion and, 104–9, 112–19, 123–27; regional differences of, 15–17; religion and, 25; Revisionists and, 3–5, 9, 18, 25, 28, 35, 58–59, 65, 67, 87, 106–7 (*see also* Revisionists); right-wing values and, 86–95; rituals and, 13, 97; shtetl life and, 167, 170–84, 187–90, 193–200; socialist, 17, 22, 38, 48, 60, 69, 82, 88, 94, 97, 99, 143, 162, 167, 173, 180, 187, 203, 212, 244; Soviet Union and, 245; Special Night Squads and, 236; State of Israel and, 250–54; terror and, 201–26; Tiomkin and, 41; Union of Revisionist Zionists and, 5, 25, 28, 35, 59, 106–7; United Partisans Organization and, 244; Warsaw Ghetto Uprising and, 242–43; Weizmann and, 29, 31–32, 38, 69, 79, 107–9; youth movements and, 2–3, 12–13, 17–18, 27, 36, 45, 47–48, 57, 63, 69, 75, 85–92, 96, 99, 134, 141, 143, 174–76, 182, 187, 189, 198, 210, 232, 242

Żyndul, Jolanta, 285n88

A NOTE ON THE TYPE

This book has been composed in Arno, an Old-style serif font in the classic Venetian tradition, designed by Robert Slimbach at Adobe.

GPSR Authorized Representative: Easy Access System Europe - Mustamäe tee 50, 10621 Tallinn, Estonia, gpsr.requests@easproject.com